# Tenshi Ja Nai!!

## I'm No Angel!

## Volume 8

## Story and Art by
# Takako Shigematsu

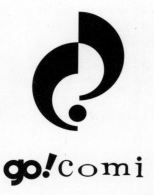

go!comi

# Concerning Honorifics

At Go! Comi, we do our best to ensure that our translations read seamlessly in English while respecting the original Japanese language and culture. To this end, the original honorifics (the suffixes found at the end of characters' names) remain intact. in Japan, where politeness and formality are more integrated into every aspect of the language, honorifics give a better understanding of character relationships. They can be used to indicate both respect and affection. Whether a person addresses someone by first name or last name also indicates how close their relationship is.

Here are some of the honorifics you might encounter in reading this book:

-san: This is the most common and neutral of honorifics. The polite way to address someone you're not on close terms with is to use "-san." it's kind of like Mr. or Ms., except you can use "-san" with first names as easily as family names.

-chan: Used for friendly familiarity, mostly applied towards young girls. "-chan" also carries a connotation of cuteness with it, so it is frequently used with nicknames towards both boys and girls (such as "Na-chan" for "Natsu").

-kun: Like "-chan," it's an informal suffix for friends and classmates, only "-kun" is usually associated with boys. it can also be used in a professional environment by someone addressing a subordinate.

-sama: indicates a great deal of respect or admiration.

Sempai: in school, "sempai" is used to refer to an upperclassman or club leader. it can also be used in the workplace by a new employee to address a mentor or staff member with seniority.

Sensei: Teachers, doctors, writers or any master of a trade are referred to as "sensei." When addressing a manga creator, the polite thing to do is attach "-sensei" to the manga-ka's name (as in Shigematsu-sensei).

Onii: This is the more casual term for an older brother. Usually you'll see it with an honorific attached, such as "onii-chan."

Onee: The casual term for older sister, it's used like "onii" with honorifics.

[blank]: Not using an honorific when addressing someone indicates that the speaker has permission to speak intimately with the other person. This relationship is usually reserved for close friends and family.

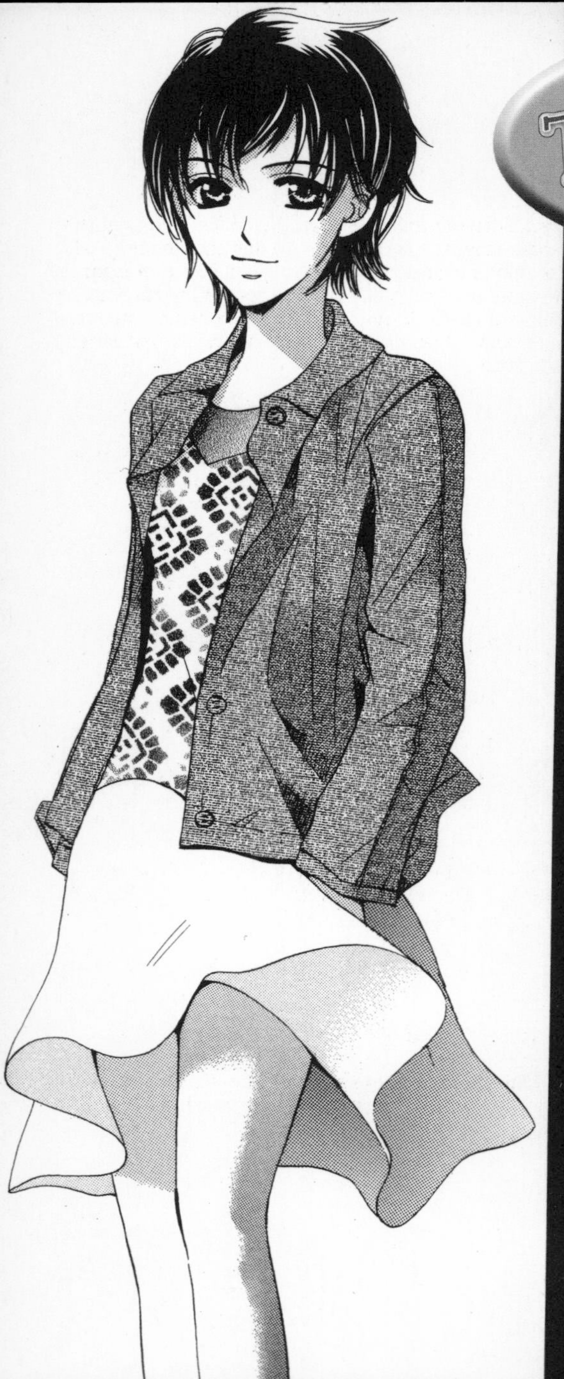

# TENSHI JA NAI!!

CONTENTS



VOL. 8

Tenshi Ja Nai!!
I'm No Angel!

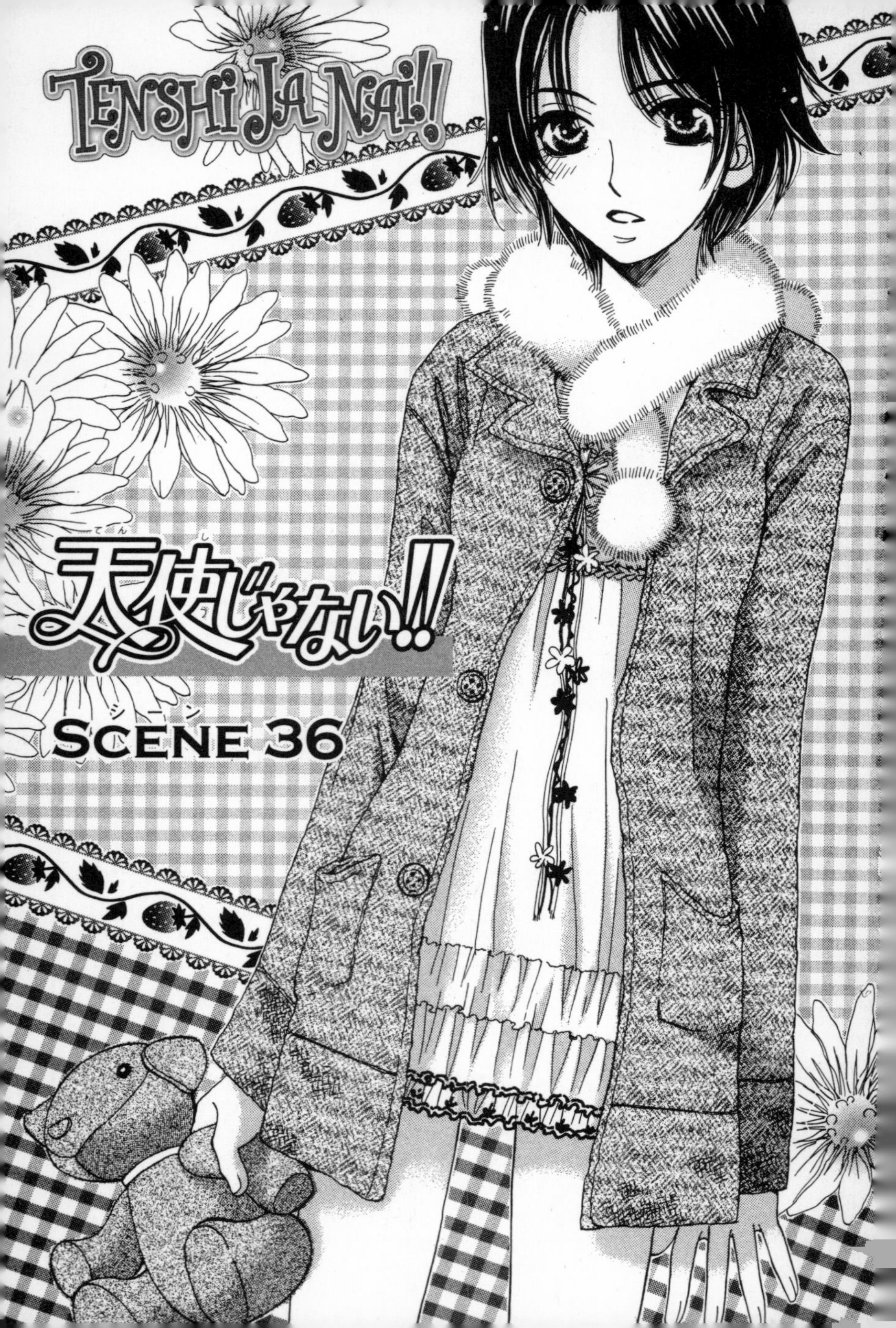
TENSHI JA NAI!!
天使じゃない!!
SCENE 36

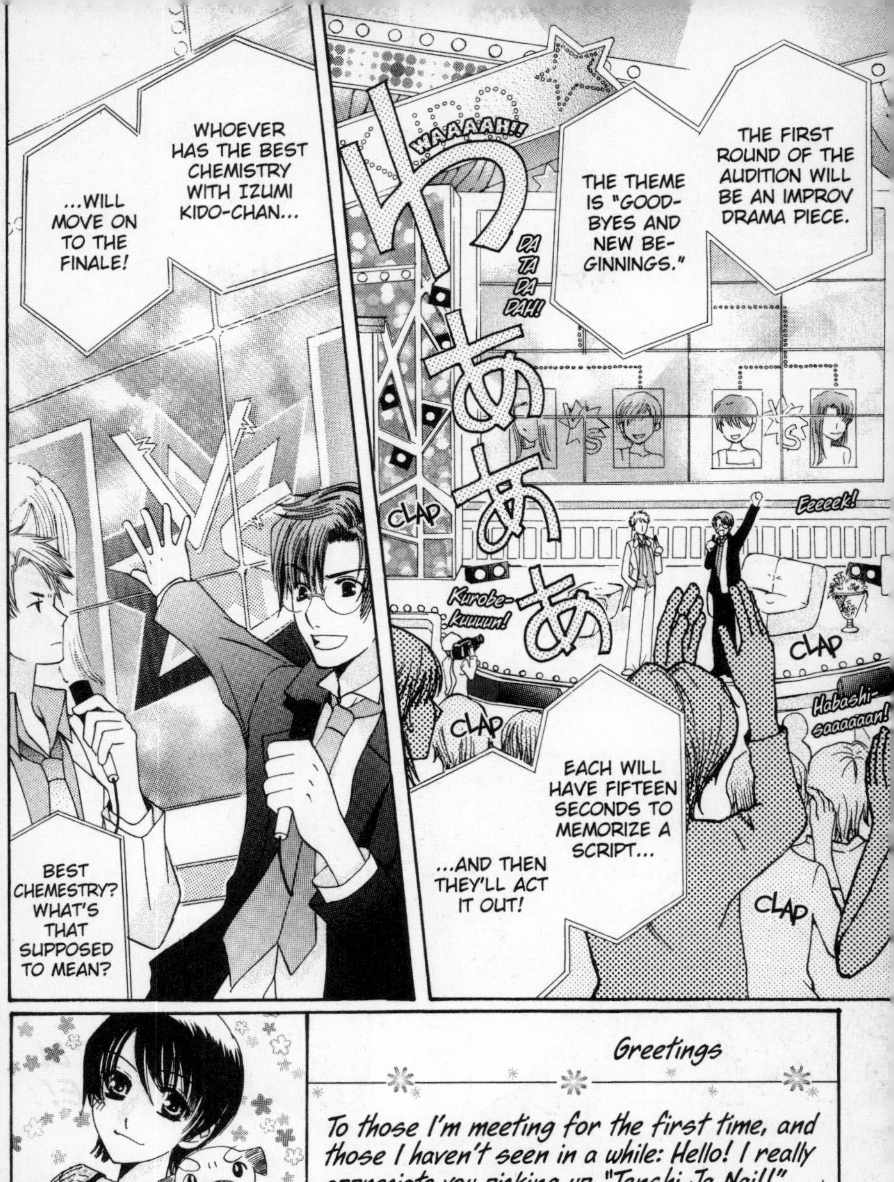
THE FIRST ROUND OF THE AUDITION WILL BE AN IMPROV DRAMA PIECE.
THE THEME IS "GOOD-BYES AND NEW BE-GINNINGS."
わあああ
WAAAAAH!!
DA TA DA DAH!
Eeeeek!
Kurobe-kuuuuun!
CLAP
CLAP
Habashi-saaaaaan!
EACH WILL HAVE FIFTEEN SECONDS TO MEMORIZE A SCRIPT...
...AND THEN THEY'LL ACT IT OUT!
CLAP
CLAP
WHOEVER HAS THE BEST CHEMISTRY WITH IZUMI KIDO-CHAN...
...WILL MOVE ON TO THE FINALE!
BEST CHEMESTRY? WHAT'S THAT SUPPOSED TO MEAN?

## Greetings

*To those I'm meeting for the first time, and those I haven't seen in a while: Hello! I really appreciate you picking up "Tenshi Ja Nai!!" volume 8! It's the last volume already... Please enjoy all the way up to the very last page!*

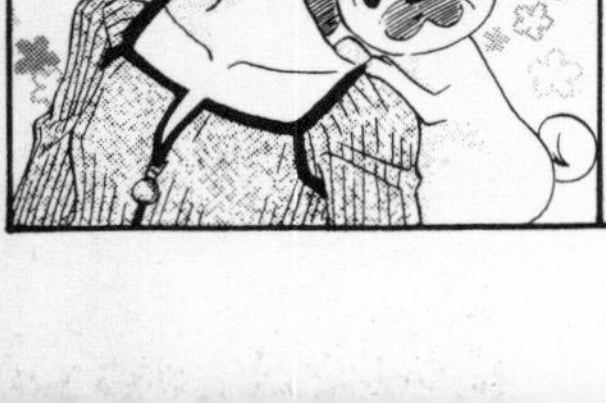

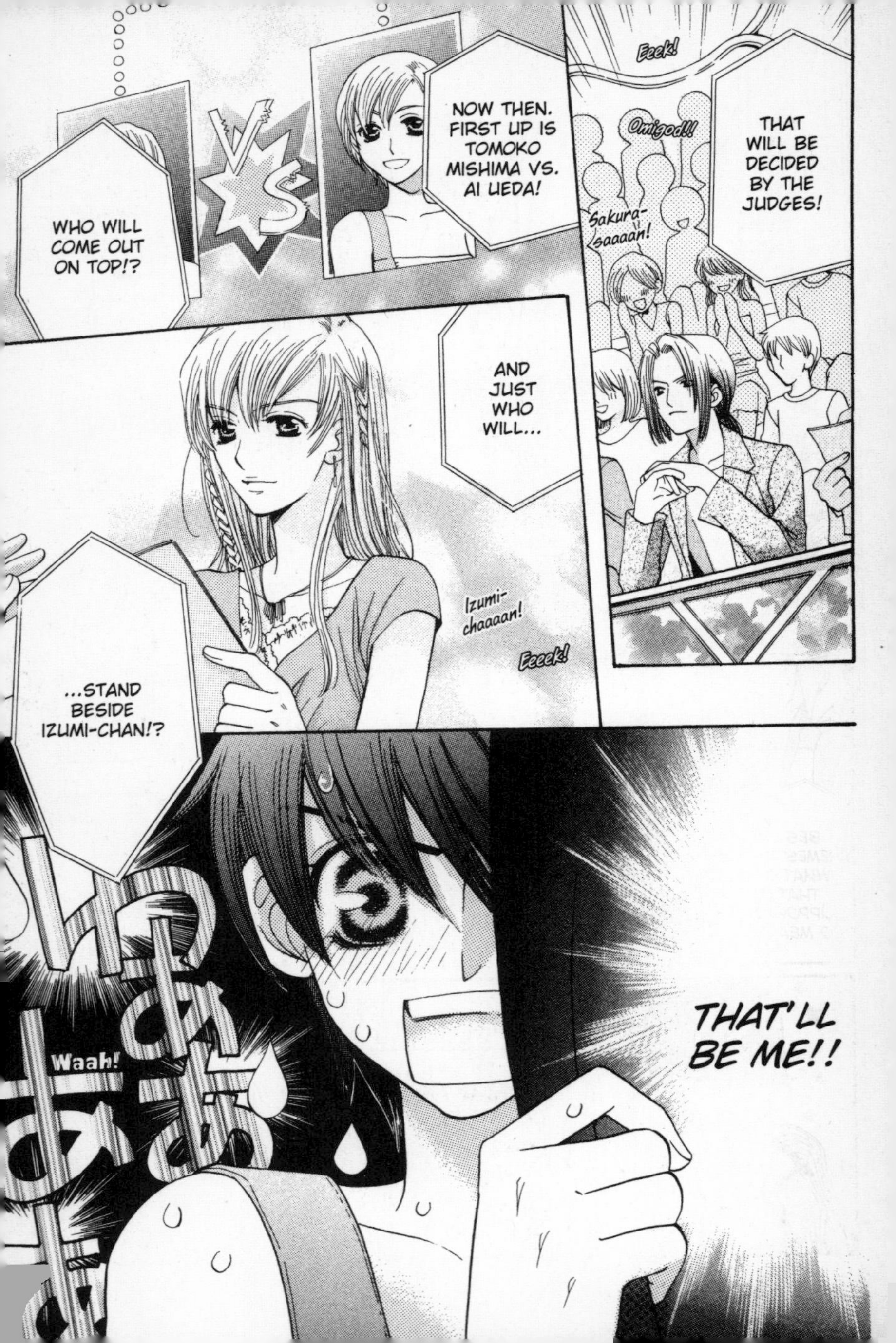
Eeek!
Omigod!!
THAT WILL BE DECIDED BY THE JUDGES!
Sakura-saaaan!
NOW THEN. FIRST UP IS TOMOKO MISHIMA VS. AI UEDA!
VS
WHO WILL COME OUT ON TOP!?
AND JUST WHO WILL...
Izumi-chaaaan!
Eeeek!
...STAND BESIDE IZUMI-CHAN!?
THAT'LL BE ME!!
Waah!

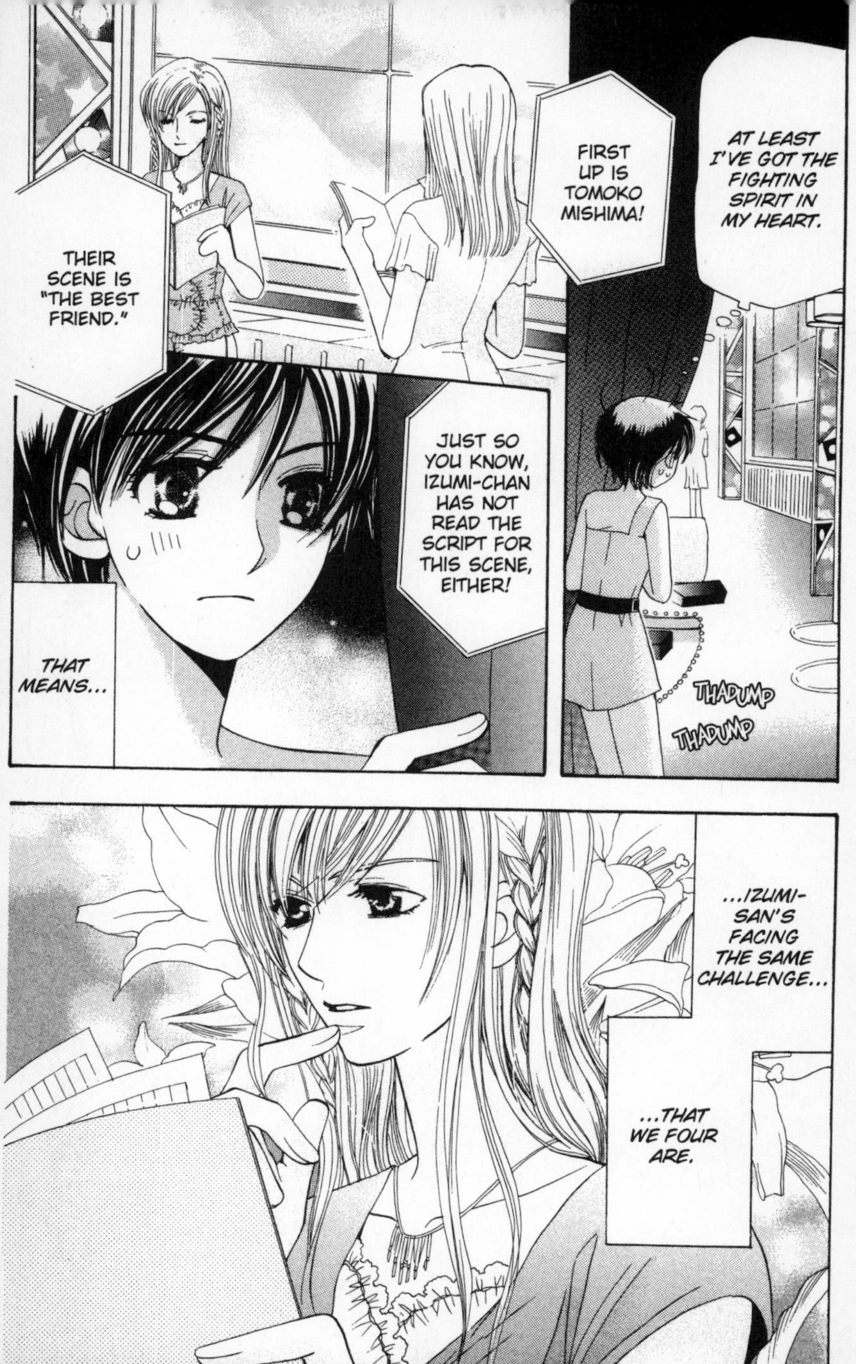
AT LEAST I'VE GOT THE FIGHTING SPIRIT IN MY HEART.
THADUMP
THADUMP
FIRST UP IS TOMOKO MISHIMA!
THEIR SCENE IS "THE BEST FRIEND."
JUST SO YOU KNOW, IZUMI-CHAN HAS NOT READ THE SCRIPT FOR THIS SCENE, EITHER!
THAT MEANS...
...IZUMI-SAN'S FACING THE SAME CHALLENGE...
...THAT WE FOUR ARE.

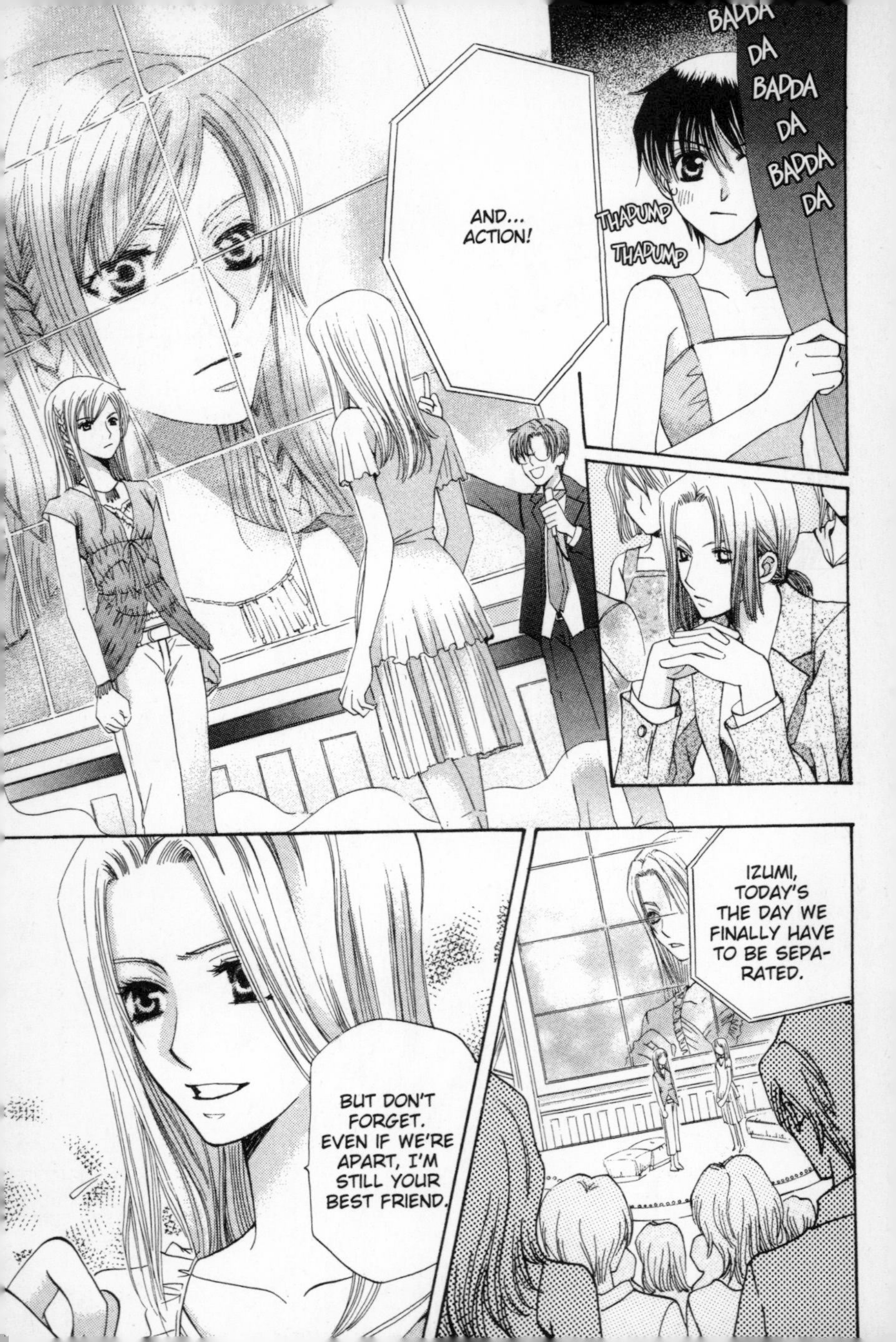
BADDA DA BADDA DA BADDA DA
THAPUMP THAPUMP
AND... ACTION!
IZUMI, TODAY'S THE DAY WE FINALLY HAVE TO BE SEPA-RATED.
BUT DON'T FORGET. EVEN IF WE'RE APART, I'M STILL YOUR BEST FRIEND.

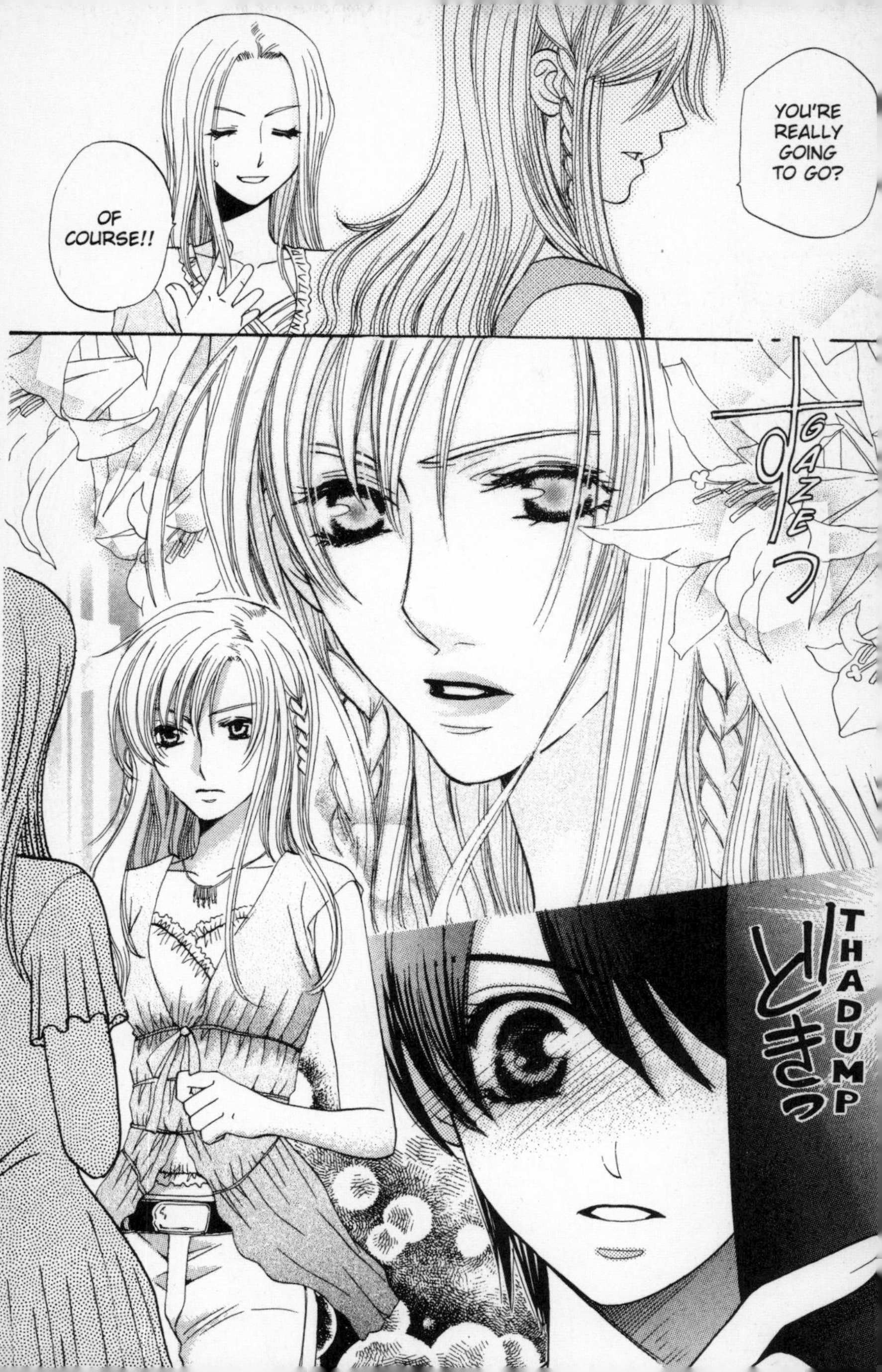

YOU'RE REALLY GOING TO GO?
OF COURSE!!
すっ GAZE
ときっ THADUMP

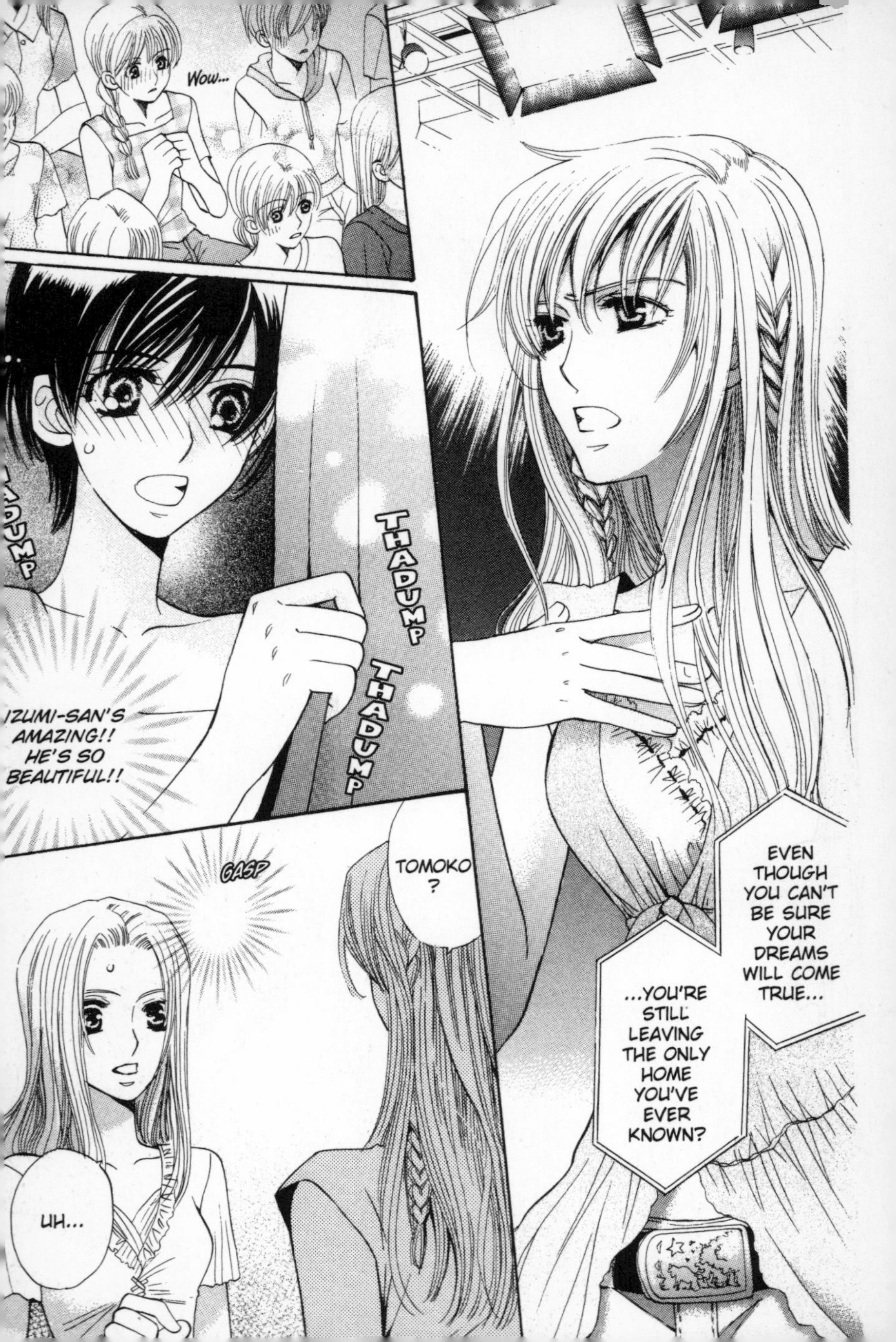
EVEN THOUGH YOU CAN'T BE SURE YOUR DREAMS WILL COME TRUE...
...YOU'RE STILL LEAVING THE ONLY HOME YOU'VE EVER KNOWN?
Wow...
THADUMP
THADUMP
THADUMP
IZUMI-SAN'S AMAZING!! HE'S SO BEAUTIFUL!!
TOMOKO?
GASP
UH...

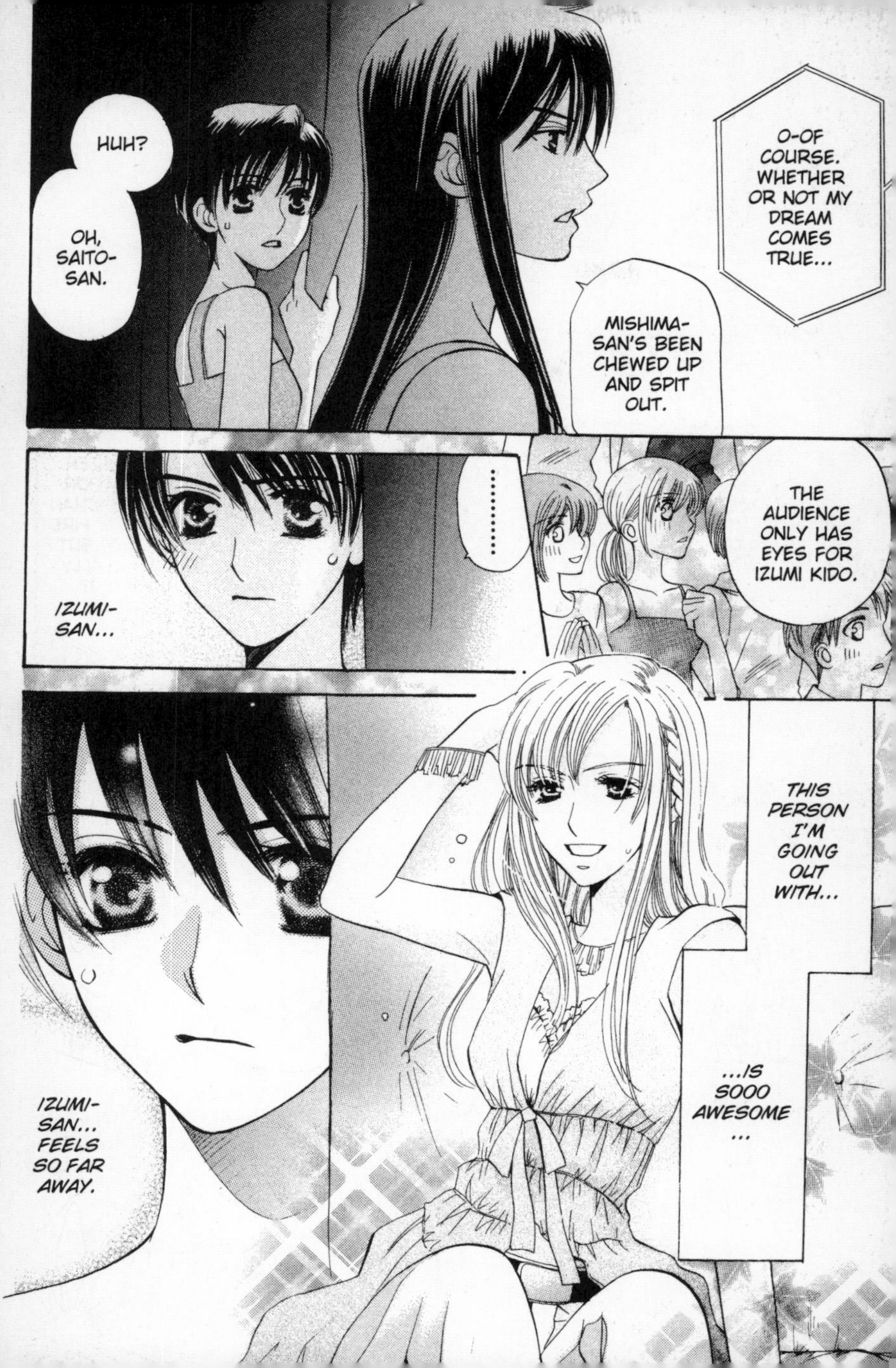
O-OF COURSE. WHETHER OR NOT MY DREAM COMES TRUE...
MISHIMA-SAN'S BEEN CHEWED UP AND SPIT OUT.
HUH?
OH, SAITO-SAN.
THE AUDIENCE ONLY HAS EYES FOR IZUMI KIDO.
......
IZUMI-SAN...
THIS PERSON I'M GOING OUT WITH...
...IS SOOO AWESOME ...
IZUMI-SAN... FEELS SO FAR AWAY.

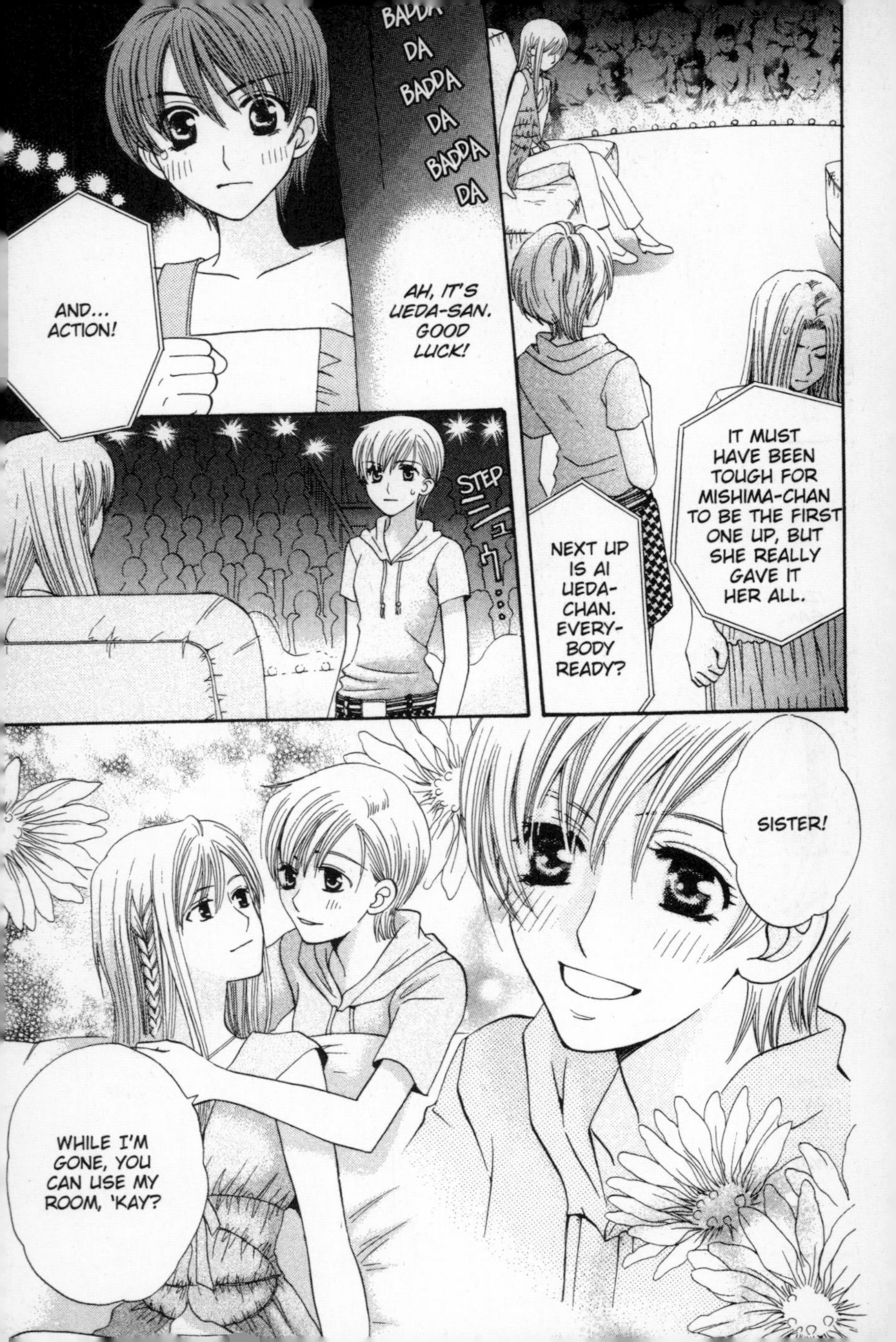
IT MUST HAVE BEEN TOUGH FOR MISHIMA-CHAN TO BE THE FIRST ONE UP, BUT SHE REALLY GAVE IT HER ALL.
NEXT UP IS AI UEDA-CHAN. EVERY-BODY READY?
BADDA DA BADDA DA BADDA DA
AH, IT'S UEDA-SAN. GOOD LUCK!
AND... ACTION!
STEP
SISTER!
WHILE I'M GONE, YOU CAN USE MY ROOM, 'KAY?

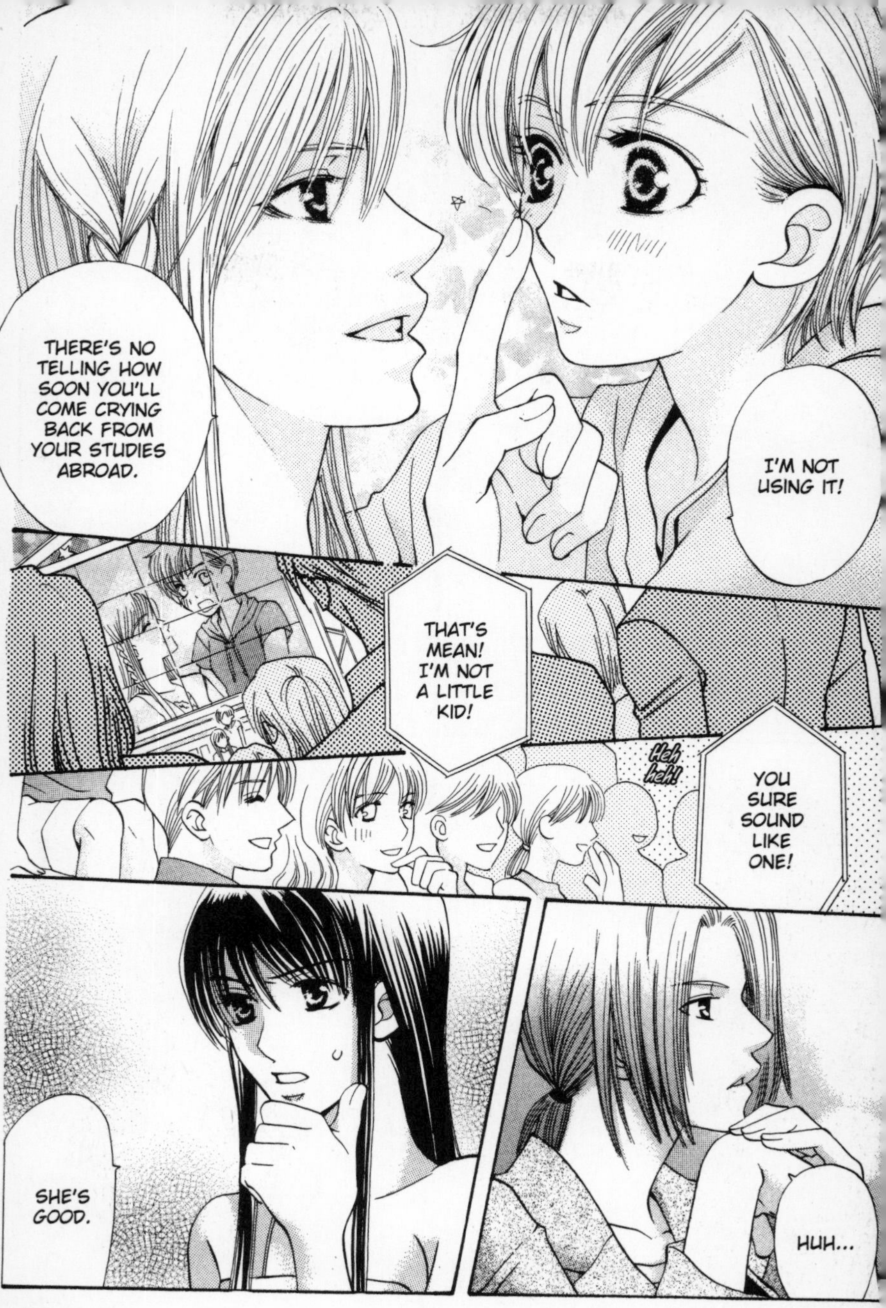
I'M NOT USING IT!
THERE'S NO TELLING HOW SOON YOU'LL COME CRYING BACK FROM YOUR STUDIES ABROAD.
THAT'S MEAN! I'M NOT A LITTLE KID!
YOU SURE SOUND LIKE ONE!
Heh heh!
HUH...
SHE'S GOOD.

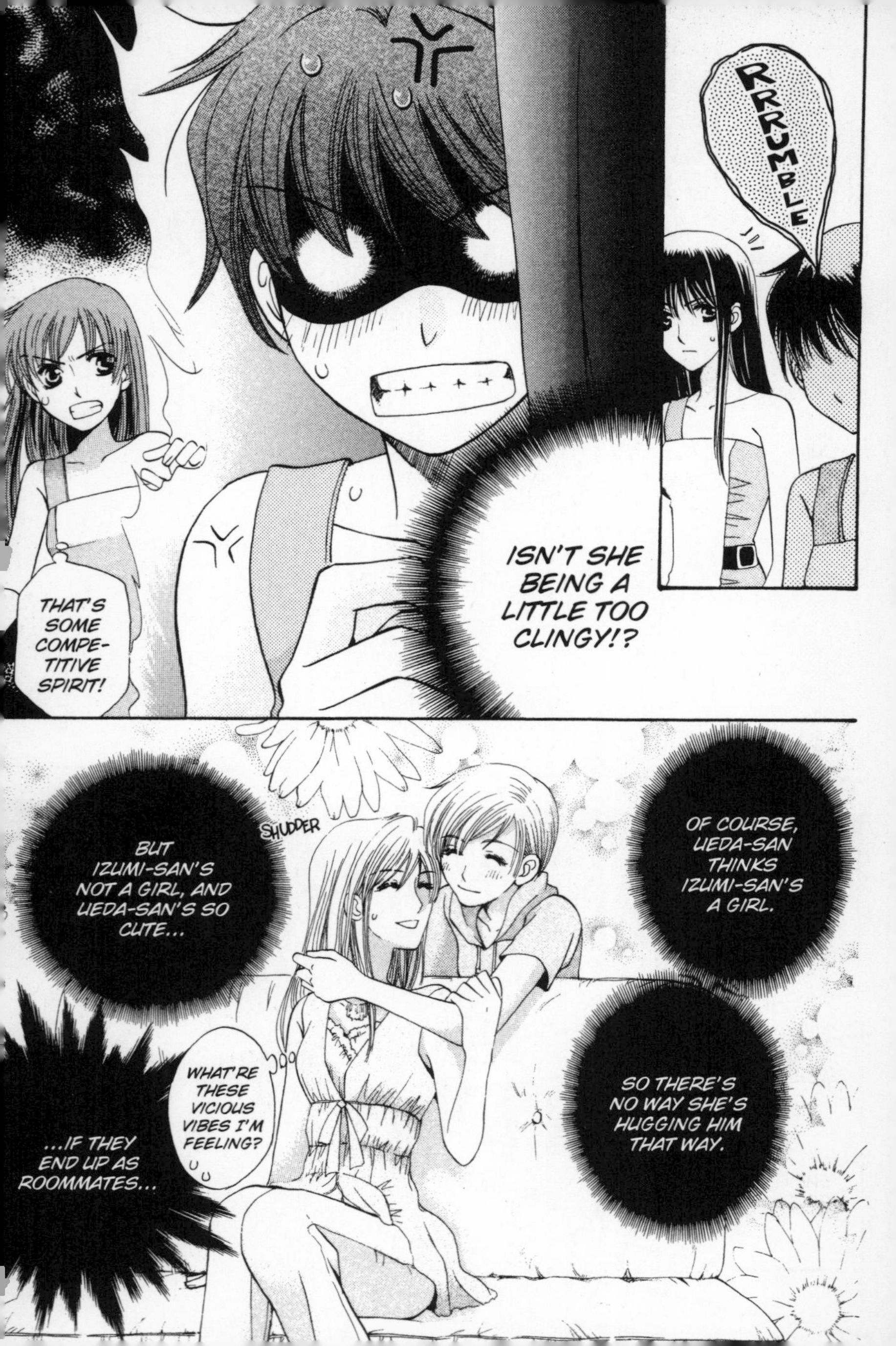
RRRUMBLE
ISN'T SHE BEING A LITTLE TOO CLINGY!?
THAT'S SOME COMPETITIVE SPIRIT!
OF COURSE, UEDA-SAN THINKS IZUMI-SAN'S A GIRL.
SO THERE'S NO WAY SHE'S HUGGING HIM THAT WAY.
BUT IZUMI-SAN'S NOT A GIRL, AND UEDA-SAN'S SO CUTE...
SHUDDER
WHAT'RE THESE VICIOUS VIBES I'M FEELING?
...IF THEY END UP AS ROOMMATES...

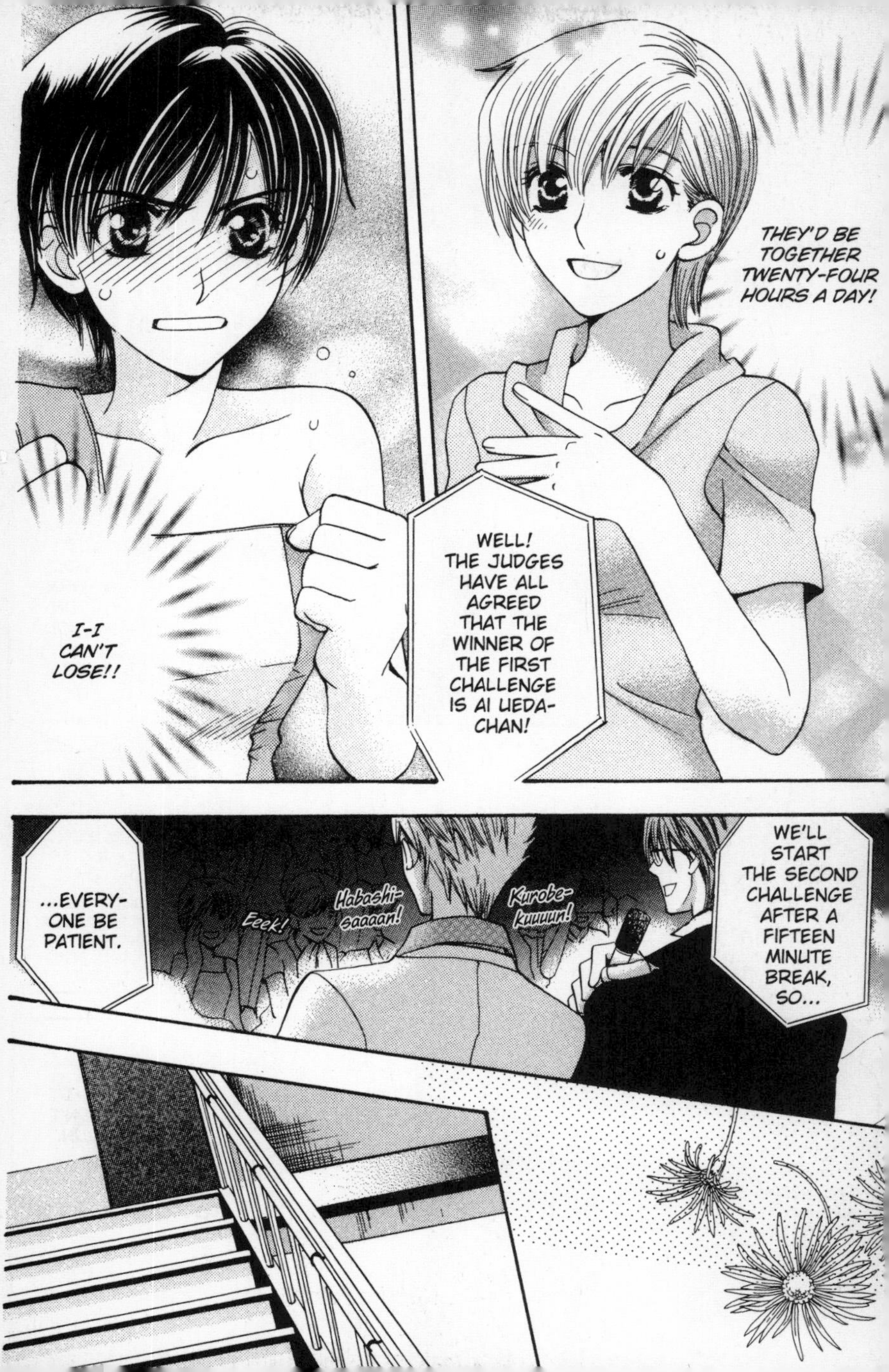
THEY'D BE TOGETHER TWENTY-FOUR HOURS A DAY!
WELL! THE JUDGES HAVE ALL AGREED THAT THE WINNER OF THE FIRST CHALLENGE IS AI UEDA-CHAN!
I-I CAN'T LOSE!!
WE'LL START THE SECOND CHALLENGE AFTER A FIFTEEN MINUTE BREAK, SO...
Kurobe-kuuuun!
Habashi-saaaan!
Eeek!
...EVERY-ONE BE PATIENT.

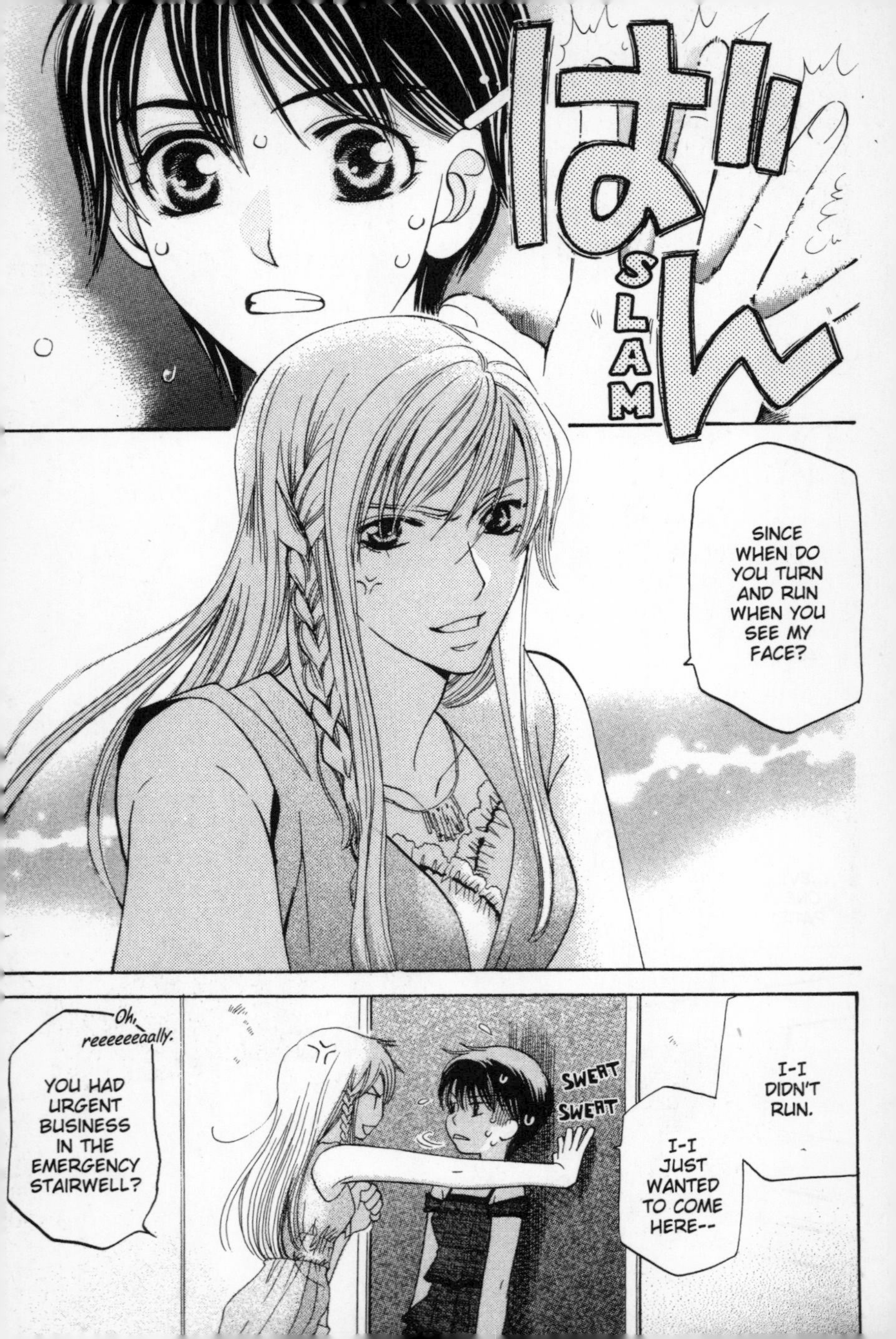
ばん
SLAM
SINCE WHEN DO YOU TURN AND RUN WHEN YOU SEE MY FACE?
I-I DIDN'T RUN.
I-I JUST WANTED TO COME HERE--
SWEAT
SWEAT
Oh, reeeeeeaally.
YOU HAD URGENT BUSINESS IN THE EMERGENCY STAIRWELL?

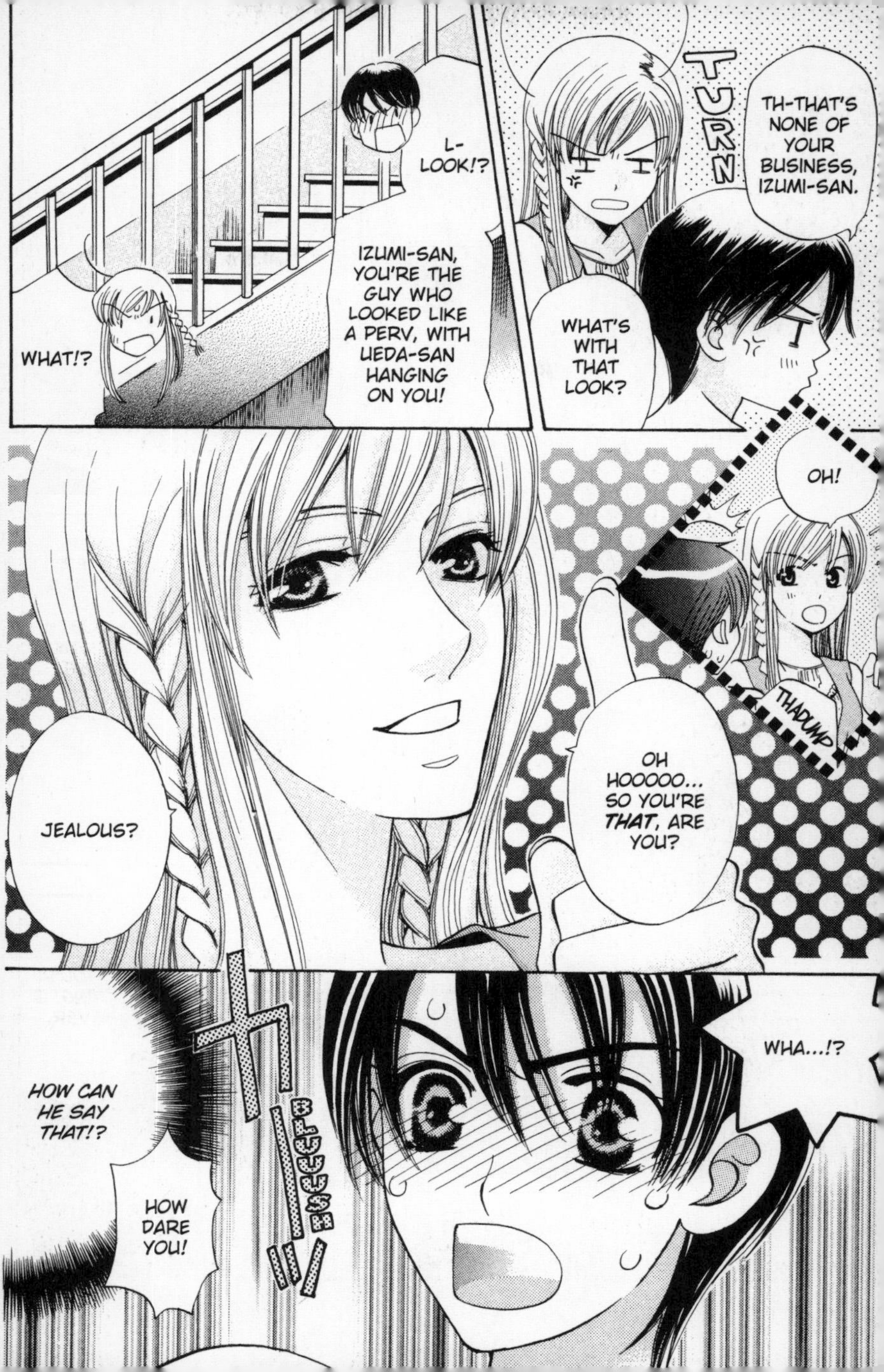
TURN
TH-THAT'S NONE OF YOUR BUSINESS, IZUMI-SAN.
WHAT'S WITH THAT LOOK?
L-LOOK!?
IZUMI-SAN, YOU'RE THE GUY WHO LOOKED LIKE A PERV, WITH UEDA-SAN HANGING ON YOU!
WHAT!?
OH!
THADUMP
OH HOOOOO... SO YOU'RE *THAT*, ARE YOU?
JEALOUS?
WHA...!?
BLUUSH
*HOW CAN HE SAY THAT!?*
HOW DARE YOU!

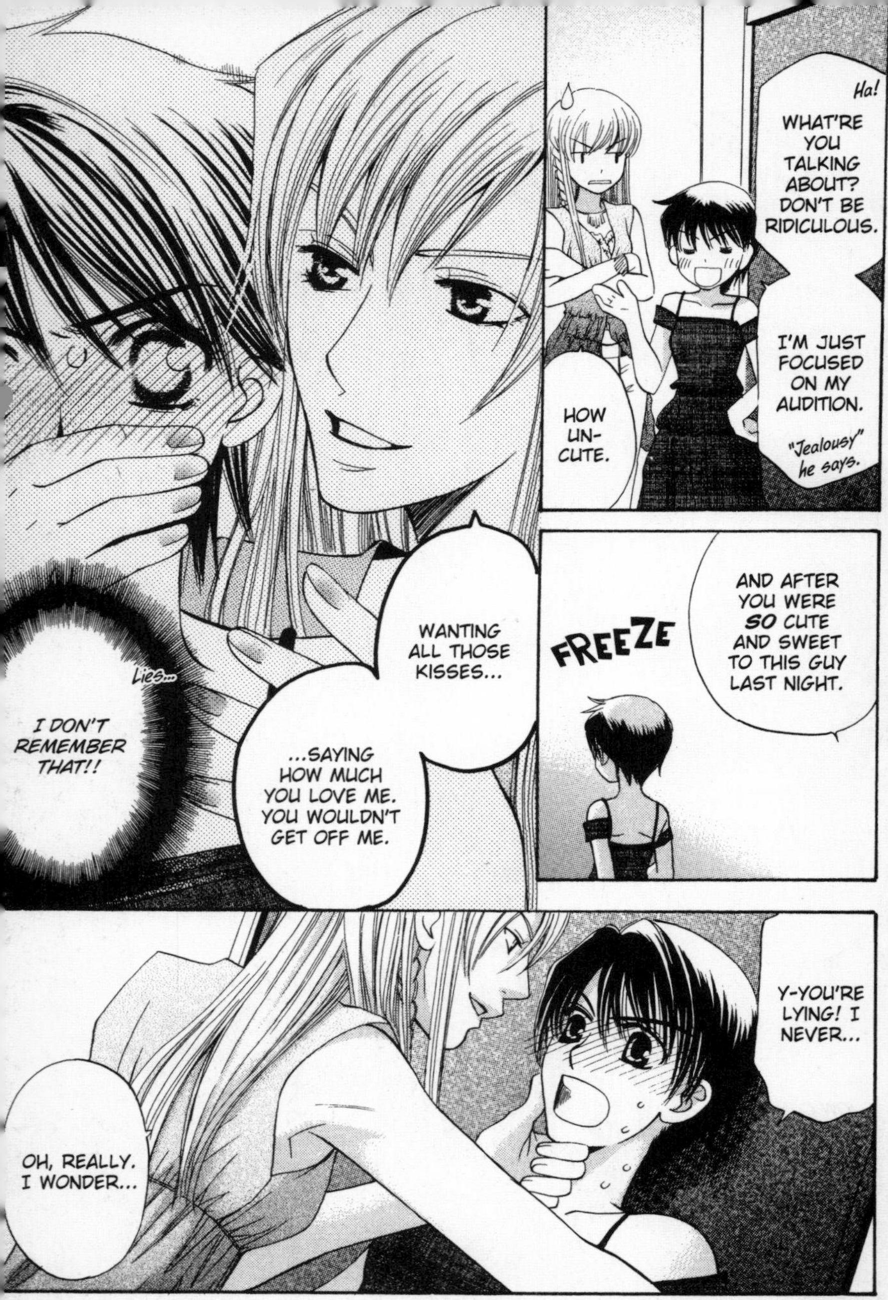
Ha!
WHAT'RE YOU TALKING ABOUT? DON'T BE RIDICULOUS.
I'M JUST FOCUSED ON MY AUDITION.
"Jealousy" he says.
HOW UN-CUTE.
AND AFTER YOU WERE SO CUTE AND SWEET TO THIS GUY LAST NIGHT.
FREEZE
WANTING ALL THOSE KISSES...
...SAYING HOW MUCH YOU LOVE ME. YOU WOULDN'T GET OFF ME.
Lies...
I DON'T REMEMBER THAT!!
Y-YOU'RE LYING! I NEVER...
OH, REALLY. I WONDER...

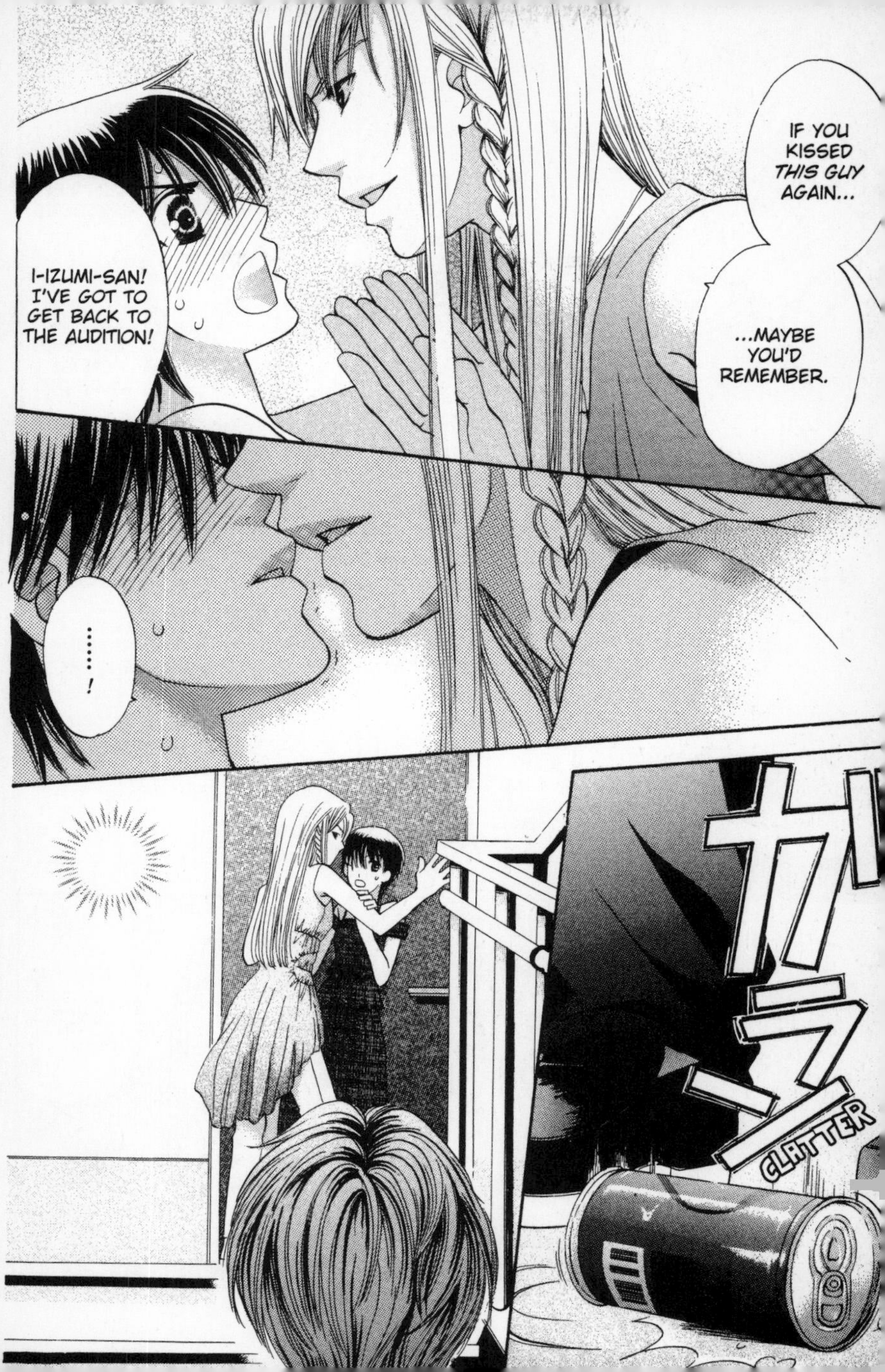
IF YOU KISSED THIS GUY AGAIN...
...MAYBE YOU'D REMEMBER.
I-IZUMI-SAN! I'VE GOT TO GET BACK TO THE AUDITION!
......!
ガラン
CLATTER

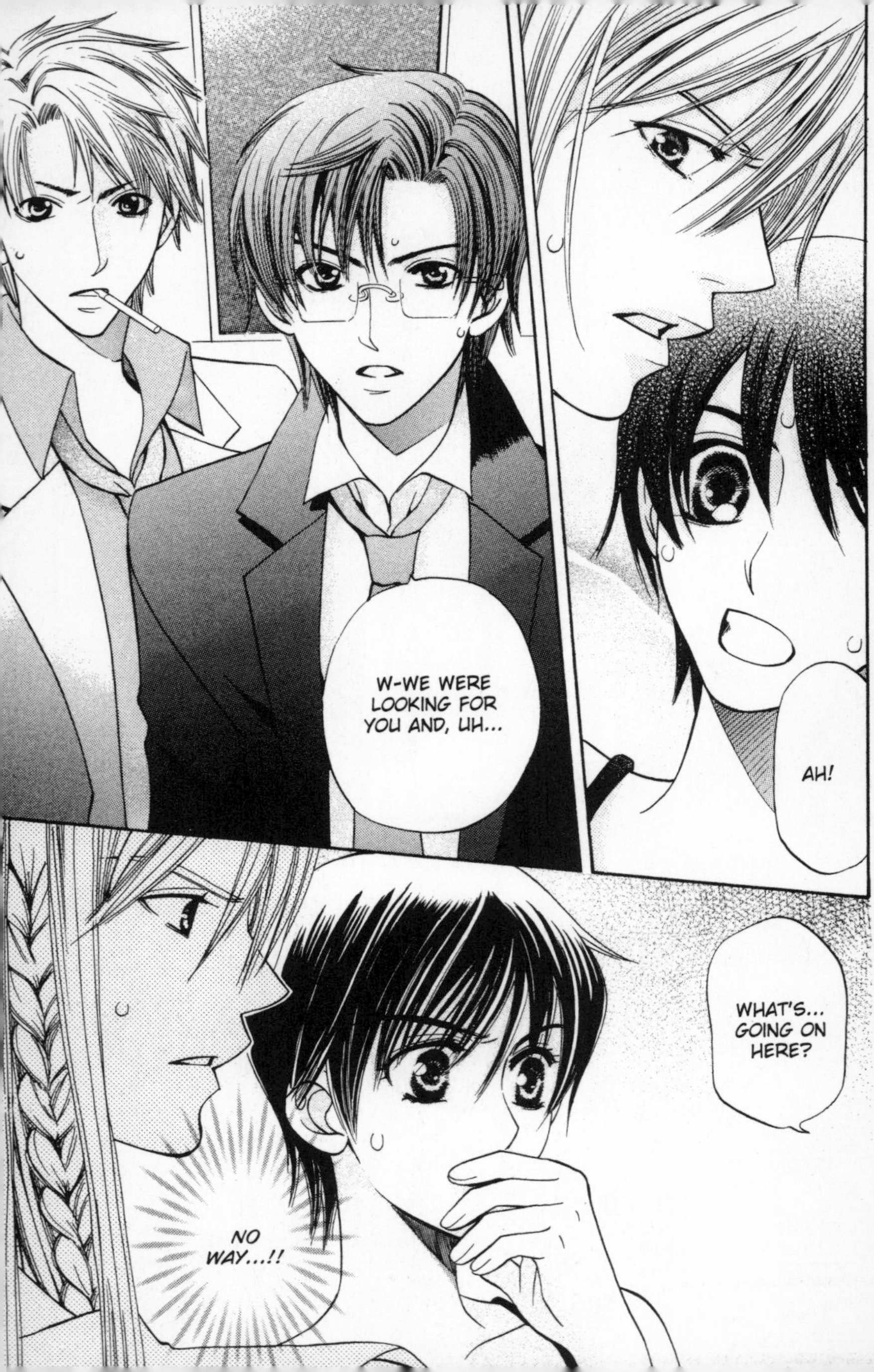
AH!
W-WE WERE LOOKING FOR YOU AND, UH...
WHAT'S... GOING ON HERE?
NO WAY...!!

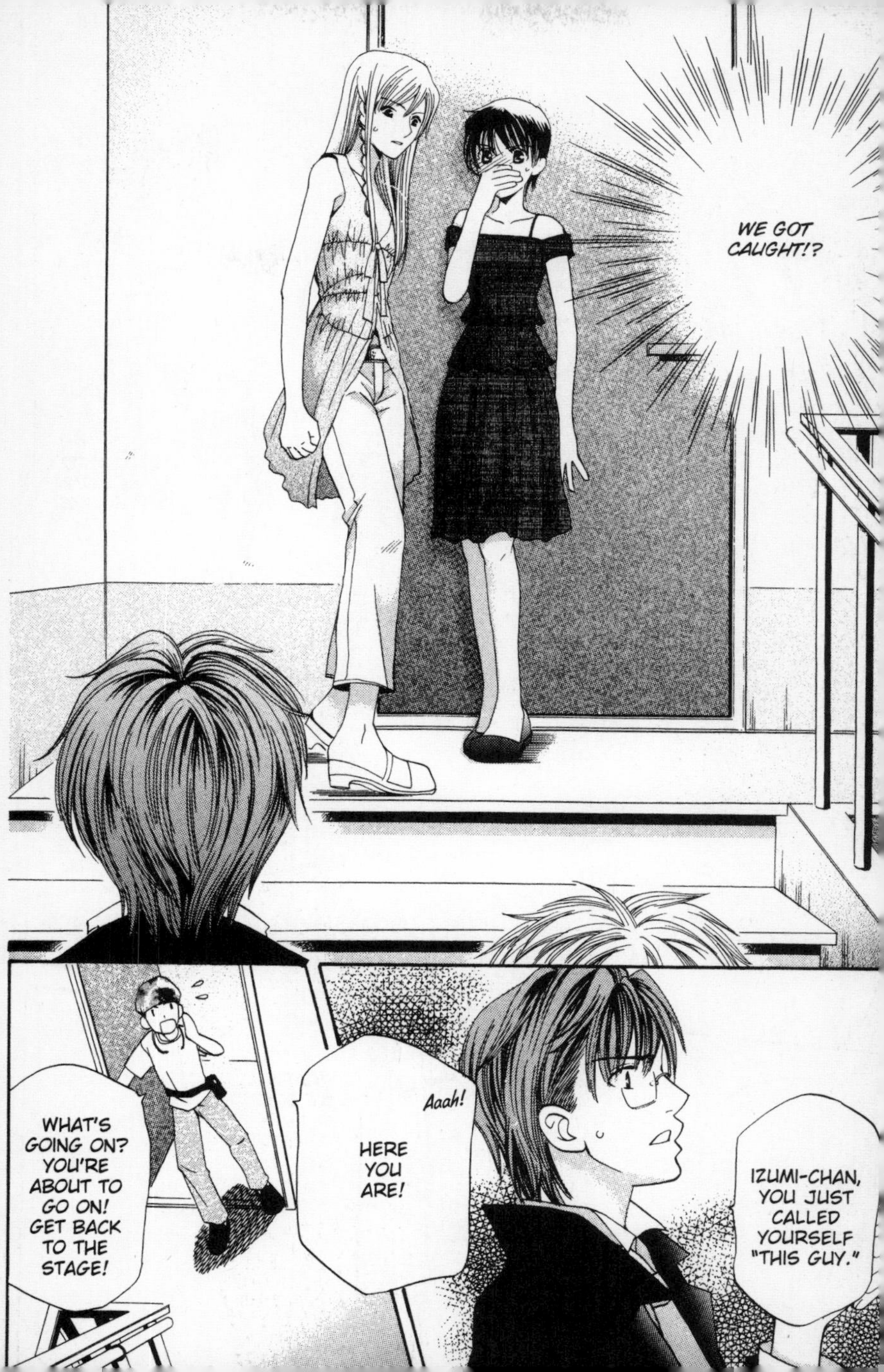
WE GOT CAUGHT!?
IZUMI-CHAN, YOU JUST CALLED YOURSELF "THIS GUY."
Aaah!
HERE YOU ARE!
WHAT'S GOING ON? YOU'RE ABOUT TO GO ON! GET BACK TO THE STAGE!

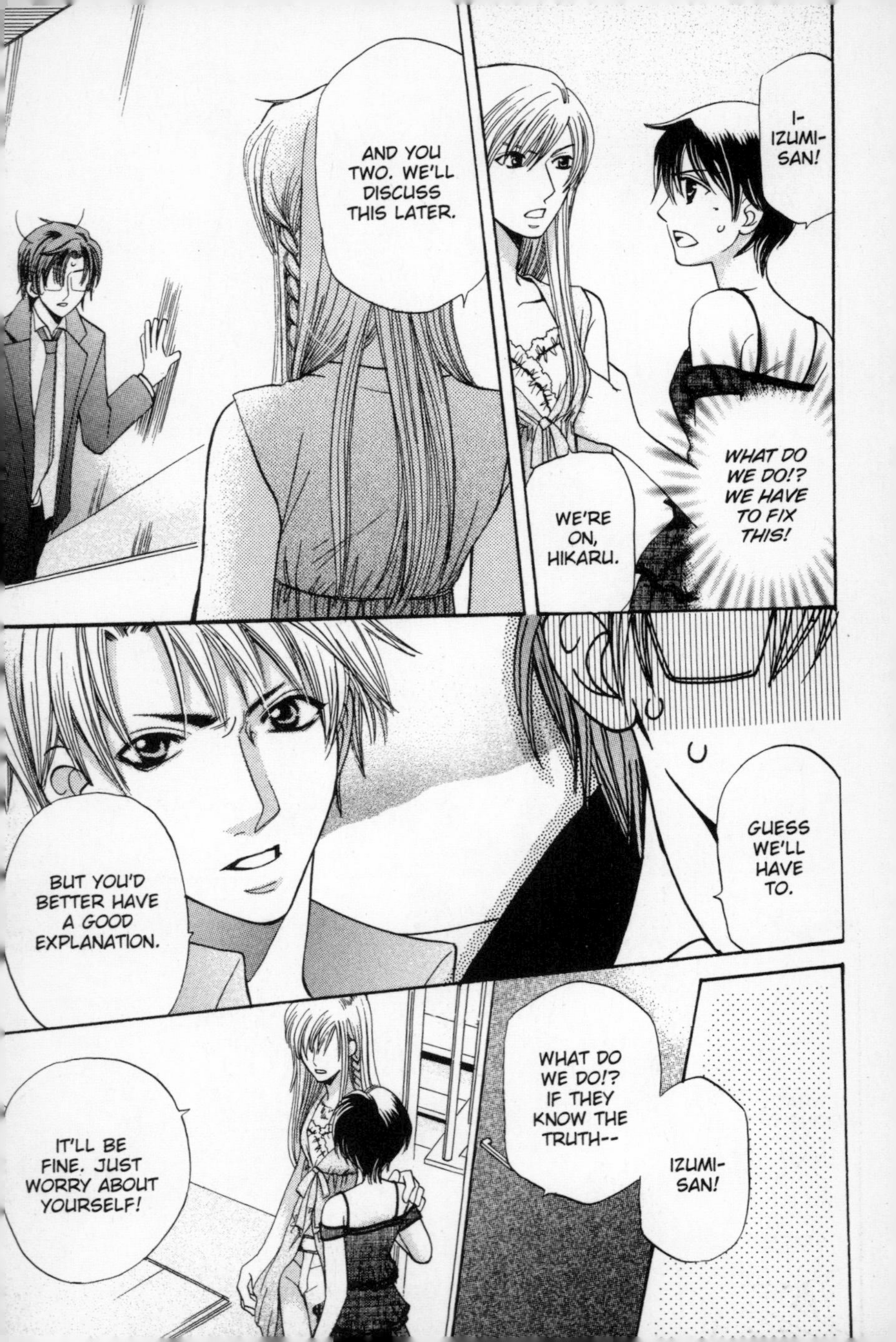
I- IZUMI-SAN!
WHAT DO WE DO!? WE HAVE TO FIX THIS!
WE'RE ON, HIKARU.
AND YOU TWO. WE'LL DISCUSS THIS LATER.
GUESS WE'LL HAVE TO.
BUT YOU'D BETTER HAVE A GOOD EXPLANATION.
WHAT DO WE DO!? IF THEY KNOW THE TRUTH--
IZUMI-SAN!
IT'LL BE FINE. JUST WORRY ABOUT YOURSELF!

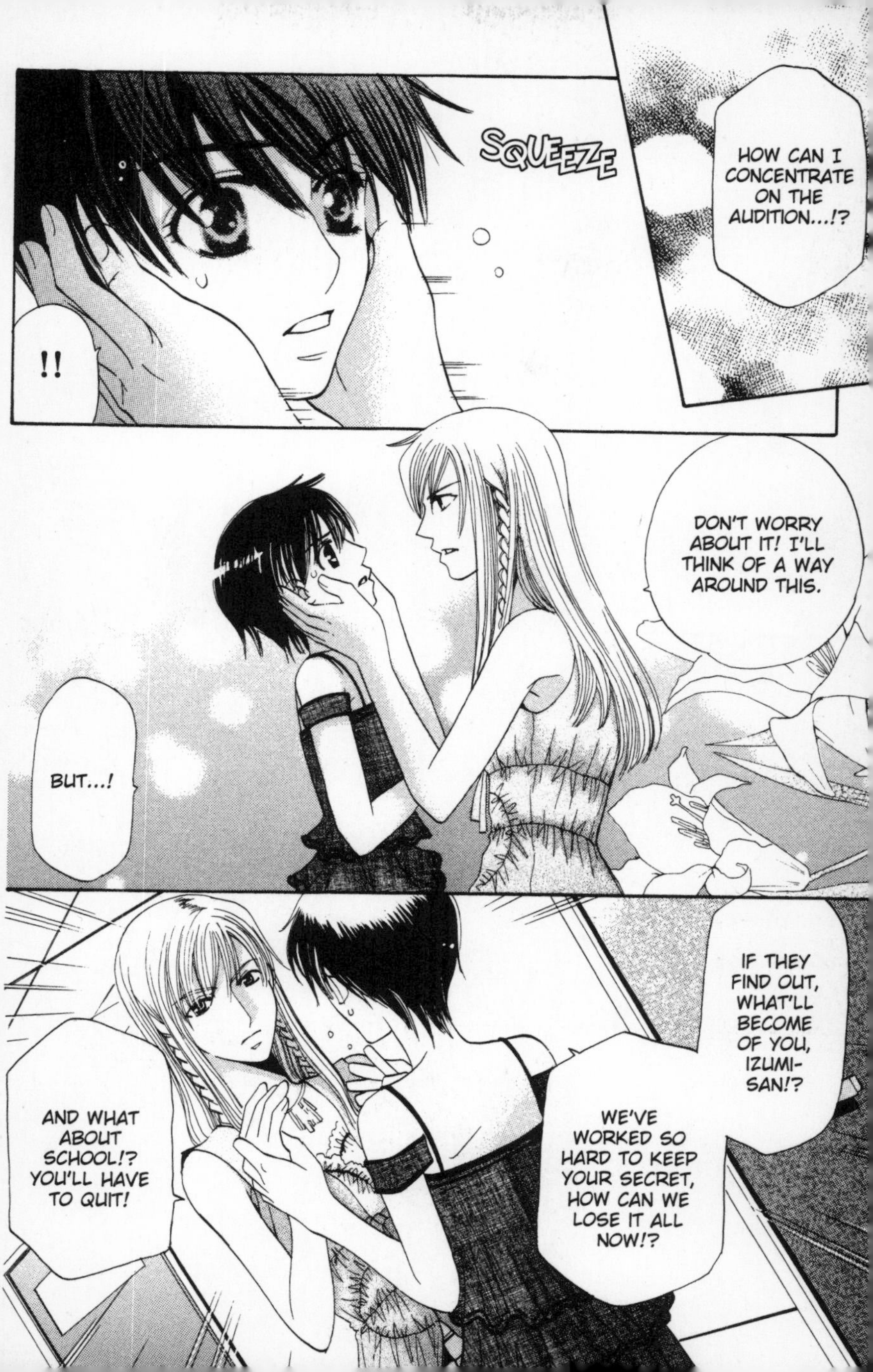
HOW CAN I CONCENTRATE ON THE AUDITION...!?
SQUEEZE
!!
DON'T WORRY ABOUT IT! I'LL THINK OF A WAY AROUND THIS.
BUT...!
IF THEY FIND OUT, WHAT'LL BECOME OF YOU, IZUMI-SAN!?
WE'VE WORKED SO HARD TO KEEP YOUR SECRET, HOW CAN WE LOSE IT ALL NOW!?
AND WHAT ABOUT SCHOOL!? YOU'LL HAVE TO QUIT!

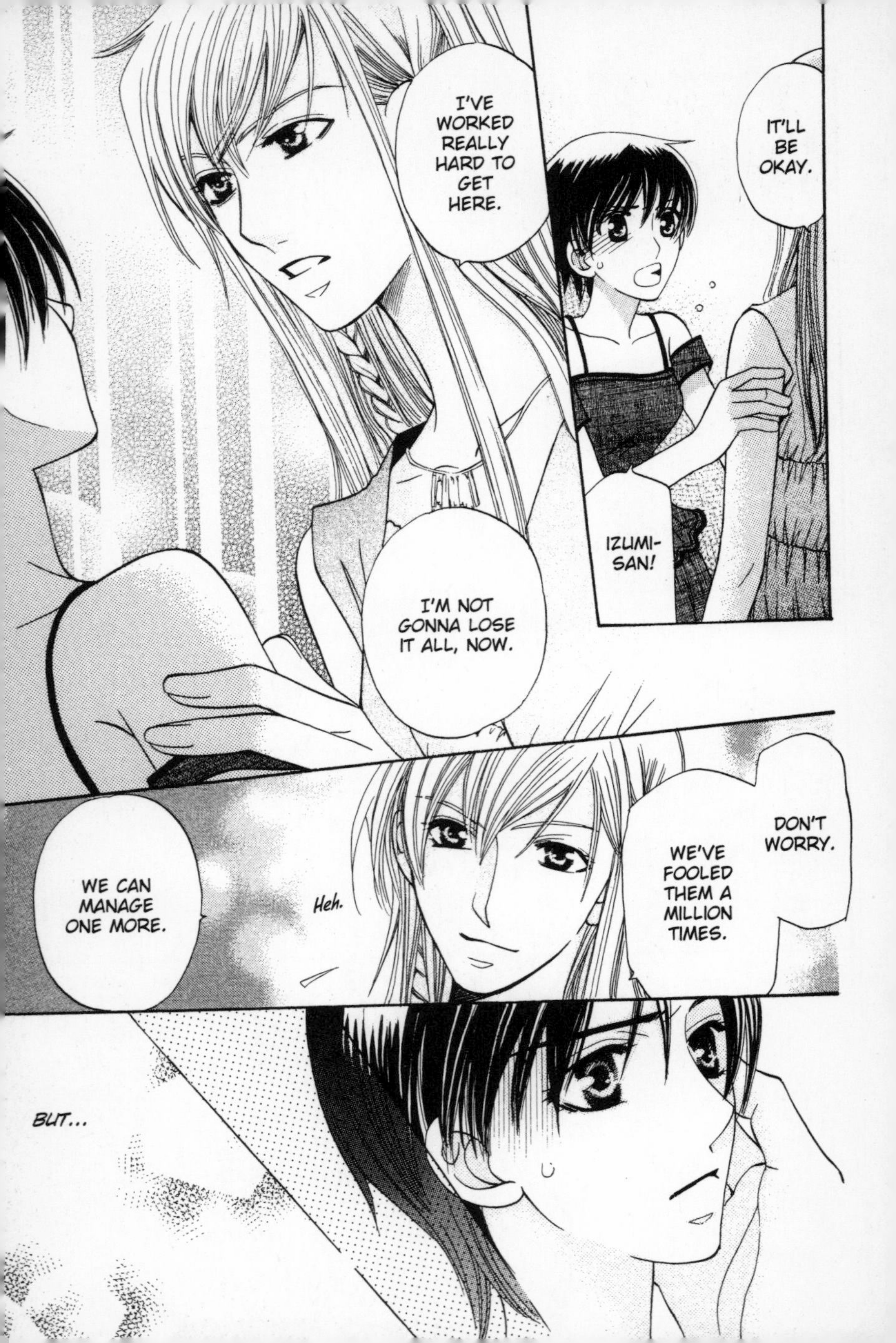
IT'LL BE OKAY.
IZUMI-SAN!
I'VE WORKED REALLY HARD TO GET HERE.
I'M NOT GONNA LOSE IT ALL, NOW.
DON'T WORRY.
WE'VE FOOLED THEM A MILLION TIMES.
Heh.
WE CAN MANAGE ONE MORE.
BUT...

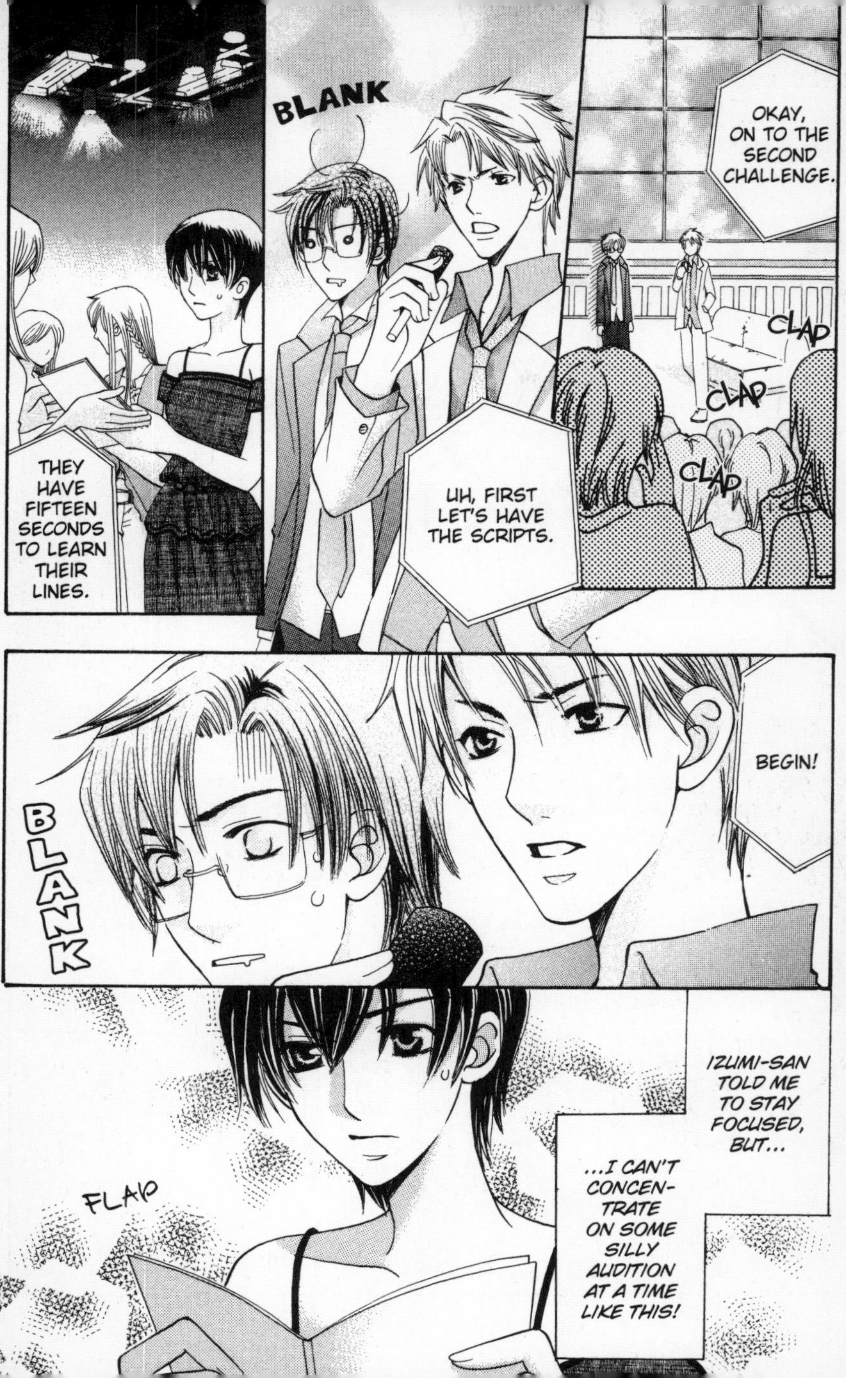
OKAY, ON TO THE SECOND CHALLENGE.
CLAP
CLAP
CLAP
BLANK
UH, FIRST LET'S HAVE THE SCRIPTS.
THEY HAVE FIFTEEN SECONDS TO LEARN THEIR LINES.
BEGIN!
BLANK
IZUMI-SAN TOLD ME TO STAY FOCUSED, BUT...
...I CAN'T CONCEN-TRATE ON SOME SILLY AUDITION AT A TIME LIKE THIS!
FLAP

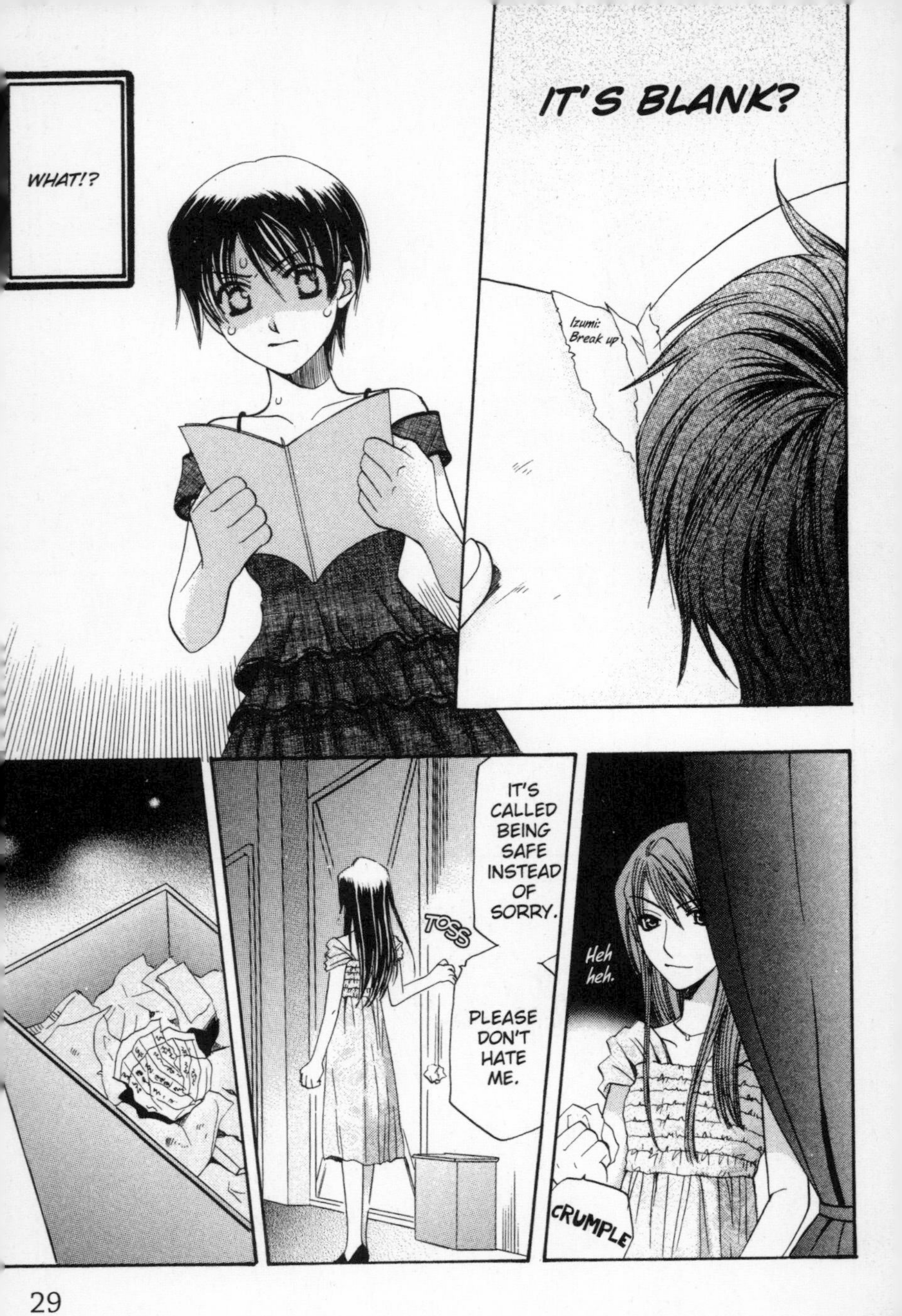
IT'S BLANK?
Izumi: Break up
WHAT!?
Heh heh.
CRUMPLE
IT'S CALLED BEING SAFE INSTEAD OF SORRY.
TOSS
PLEASE DON'T HATE ME.

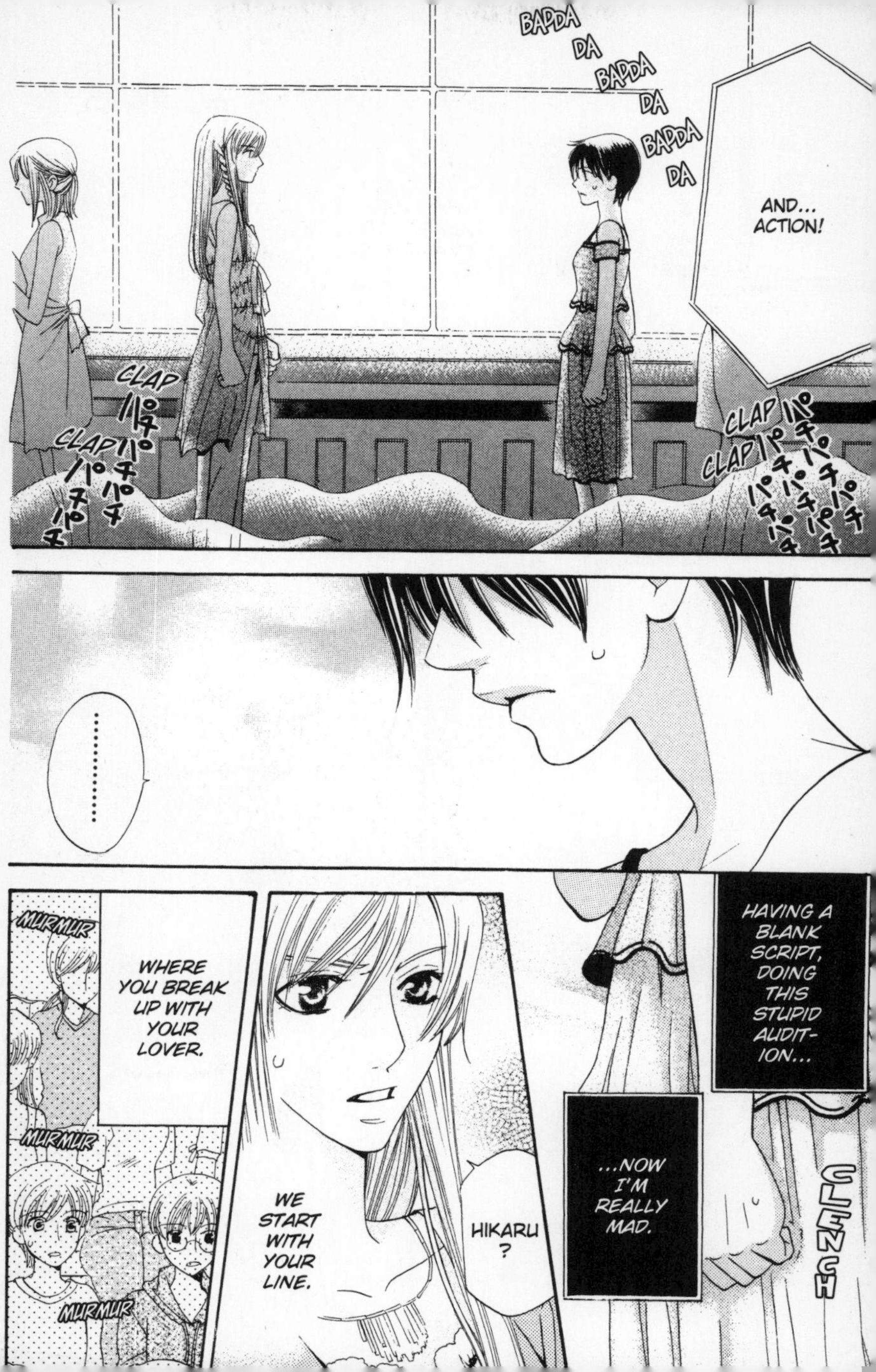

AND... ACTION!
BADDA DA BADDA DA BADDA DA
CLAP CLAP
パチパチ パチパチ
CLAP CLAP
パチパチ パチパチ
......
HAVING A BLANK SCRIPT, DOING THIS STUPID AUDITION...
...NOW I'M REALLY MAD.
CLENCH
HIKARU?
WE START WITH YOUR LINE.
WHERE YOU BREAK UP WITH YOUR LOVER.
MURMUR
MURMUR
MURMUR

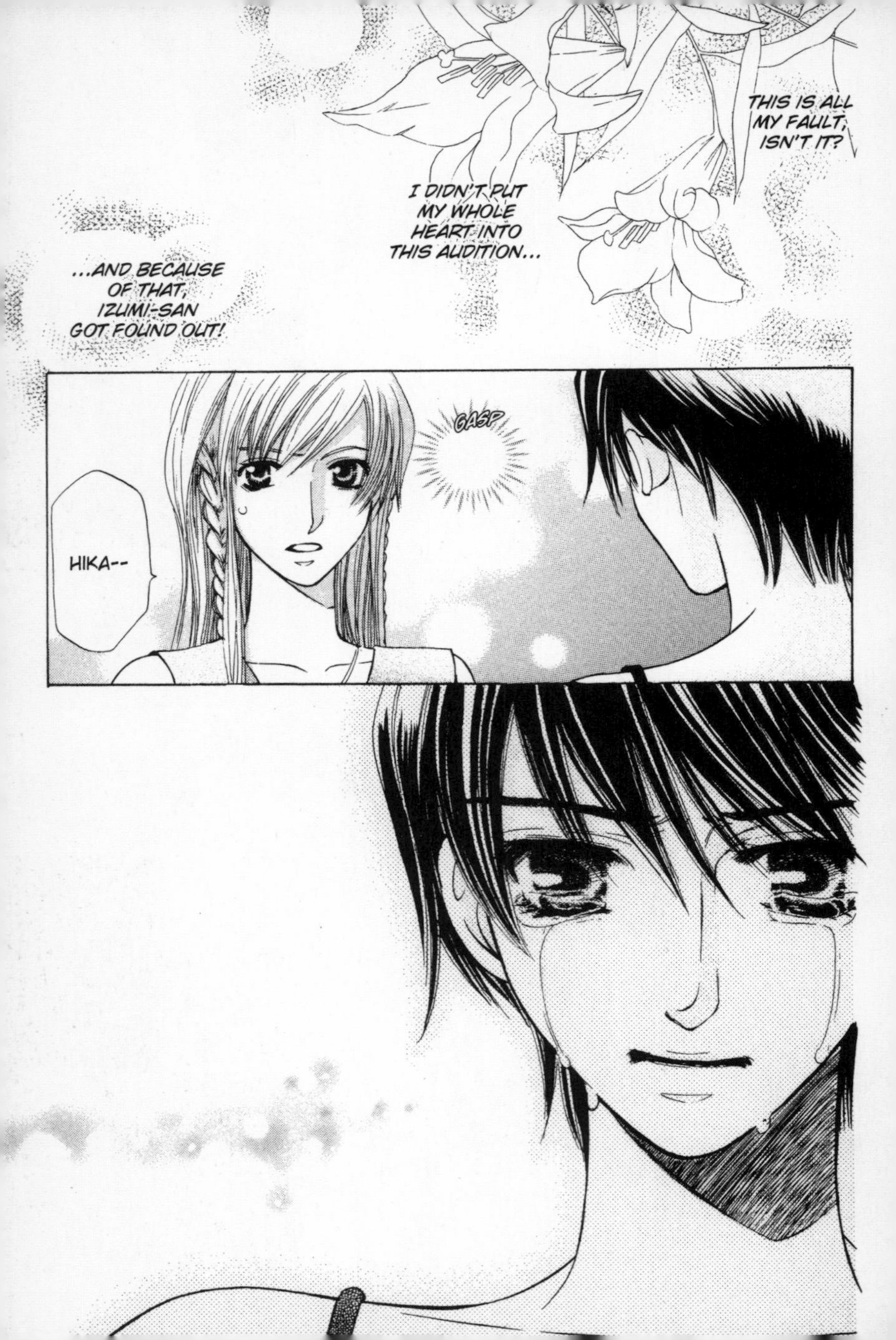
THIS IS ALL MY FAULT, ISN'T IT?
I DIDN'T PUT MY WHOLE HEART INTO THIS AUDITION...
...AND BECAUSE OF THAT, IZUMI-SAN GOT FOUND OUT!
GASP
HIKA--

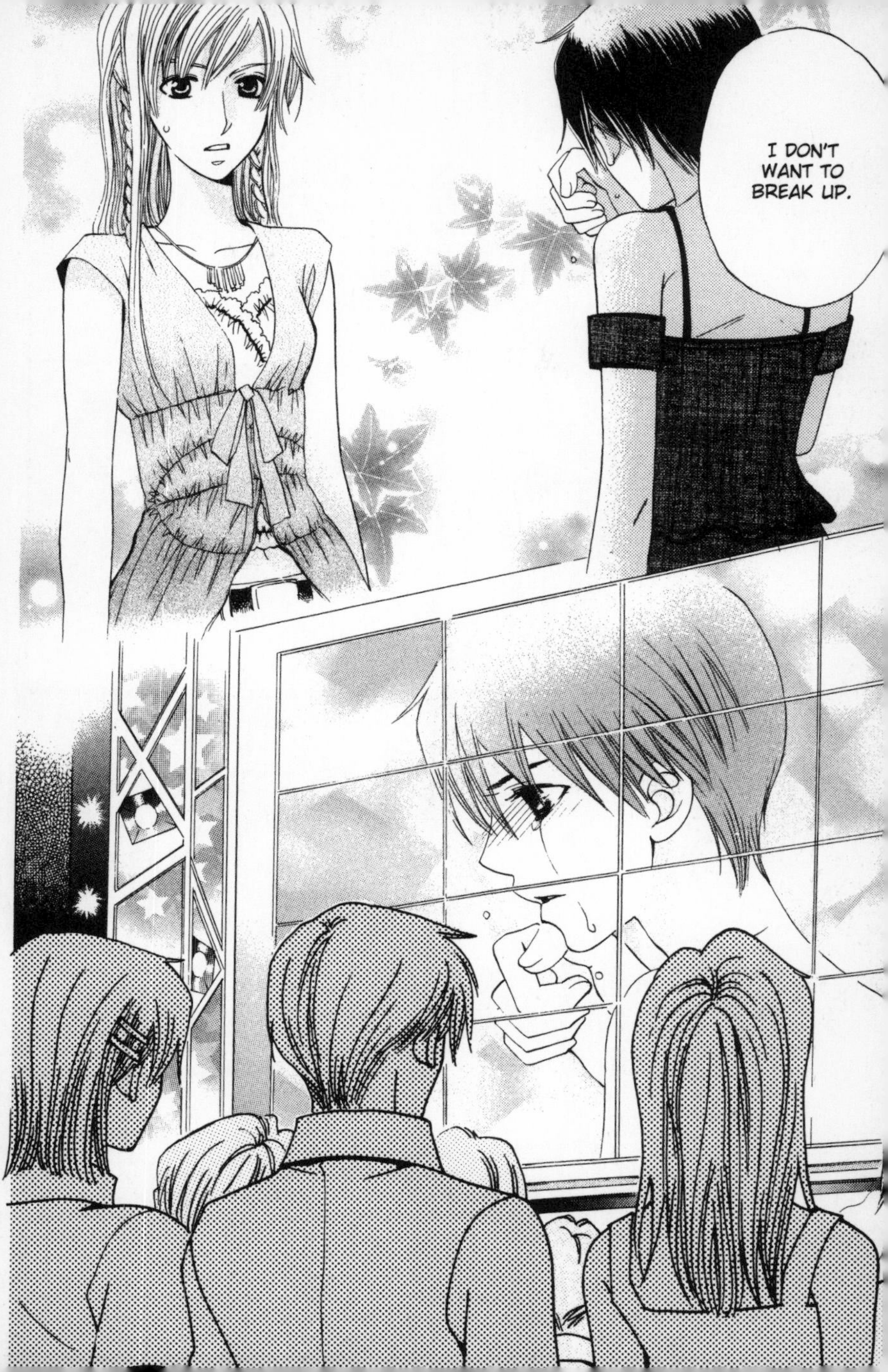
I DON'T WANT TO BREAK UP.

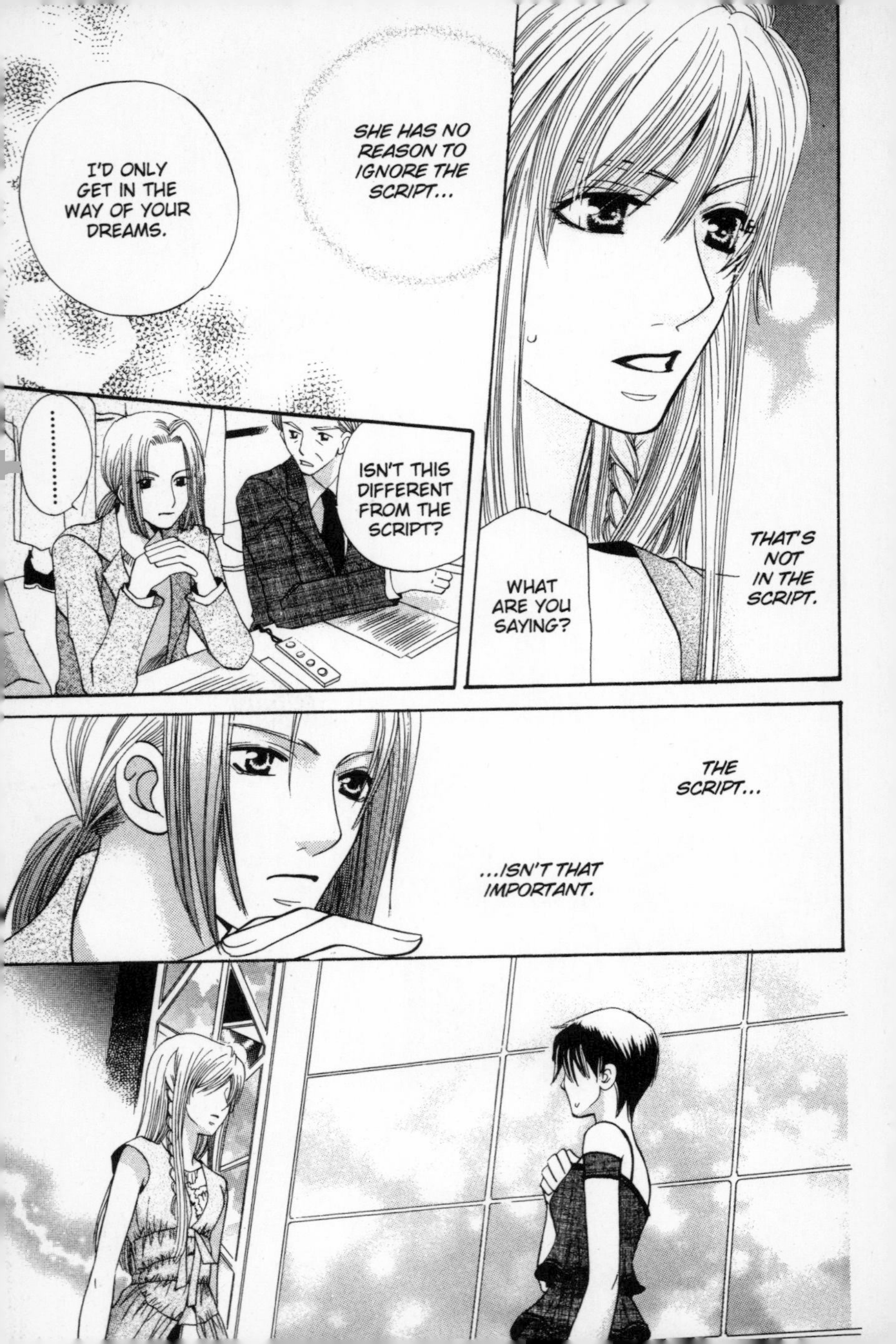

SHE HAS NO REASON TO IGNORE THE SCRIPT...
I'D ONLY GET IN THE WAY OF YOUR DREAMS.
THAT'S NOT IN THE SCRIPT.
WHAT ARE YOU SAYING?
ISN'T THIS DIFFERENT FROM THE SCRIPT?
......
THE SCRIPT...
...ISN'T THAT IMPORTANT.

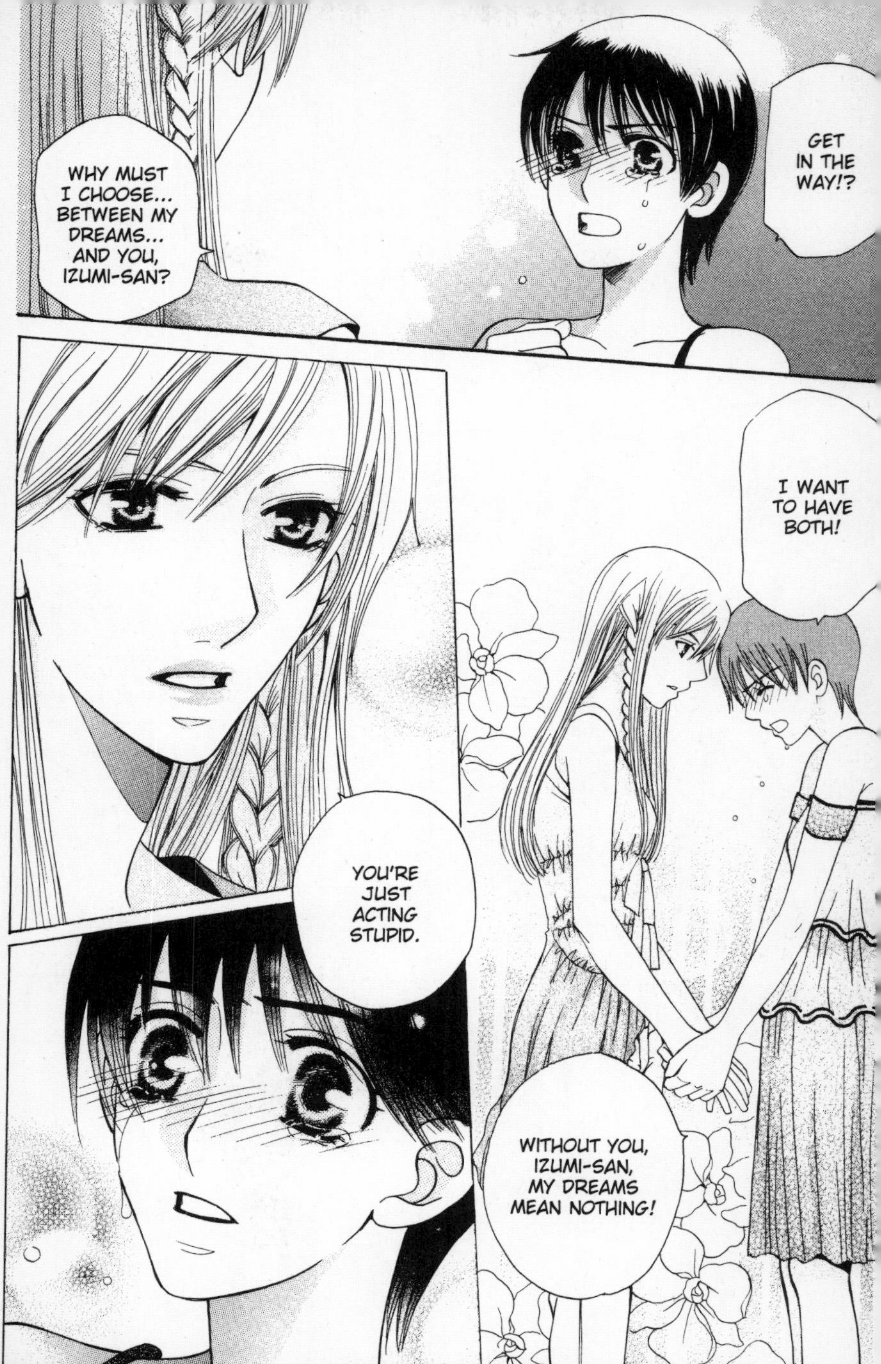
GET IN THE WAY!?
WHY MUST I CHOOSE... BETWEEN MY DREAMS... AND YOU, IZUMI-SAN?
I WANT TO HAVE BOTH!
WITHOUT YOU, IZUMI-SAN, MY DREAMS MEAN NOTHING!
YOU'RE JUST ACTING STUPID.

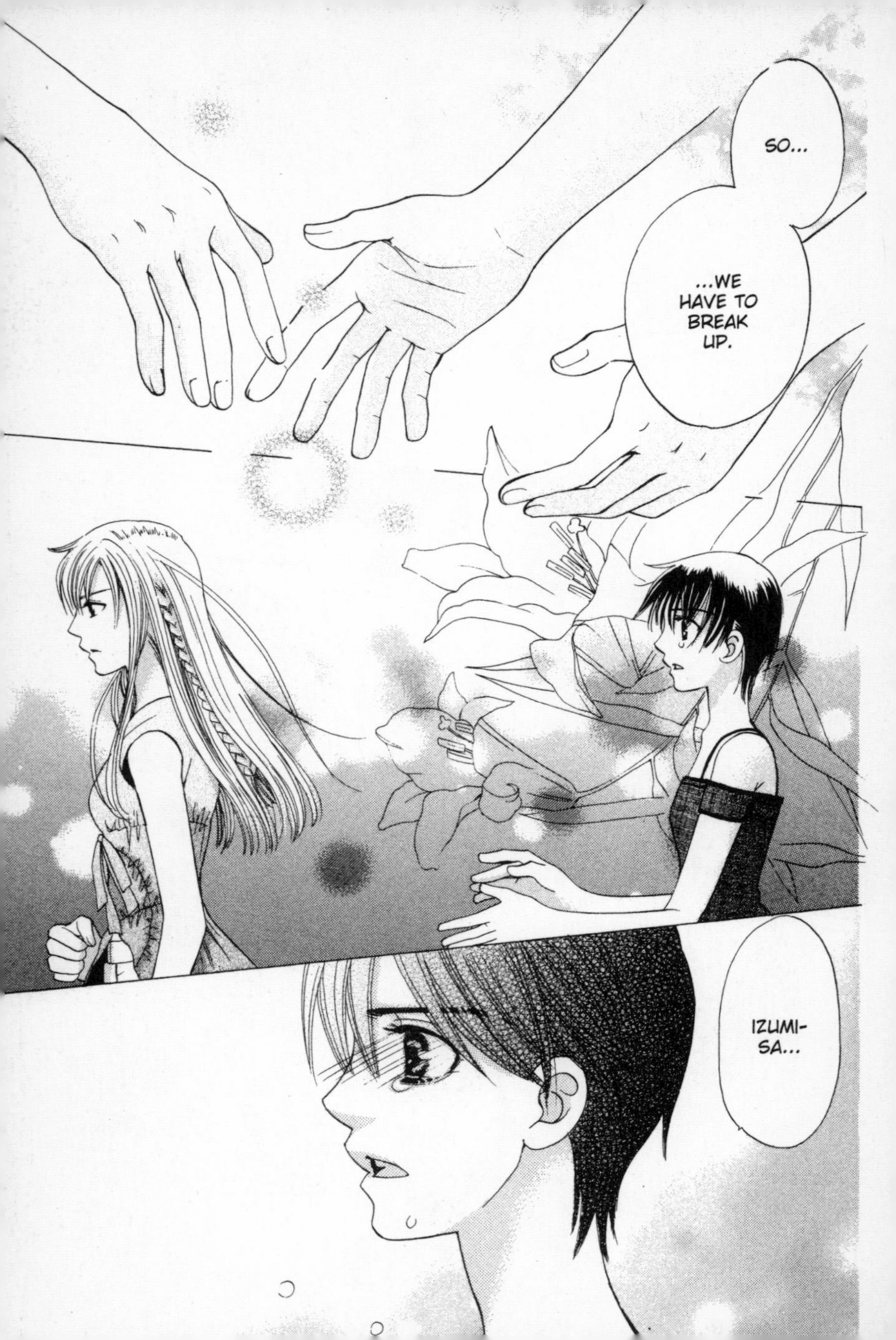
SO...
...WE HAVE TO BREAK UP.
IZUMI-SA...

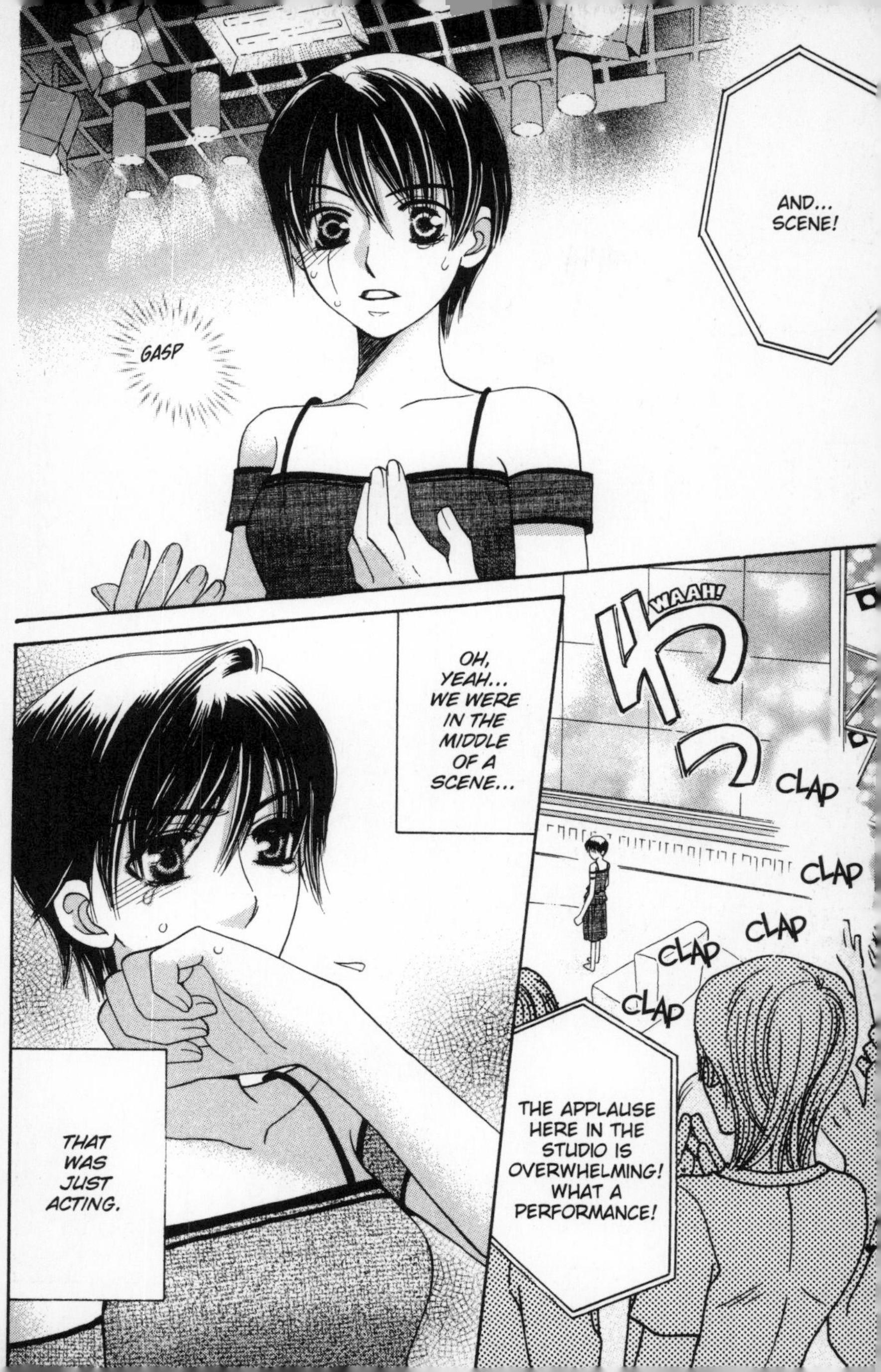
AND... SCENE!
GASP
WAAH!
CLAP
CLAP
CLAP
CLAP
CLAP
THE APPLAUSE HERE IN THE STUDIO IS OVERWHELMING! WHAT A PERFORMANCE!
OH, YEAH... WE WERE IN THE MIDDLE OF A SCENE...
THAT WAS JUST ACTING.

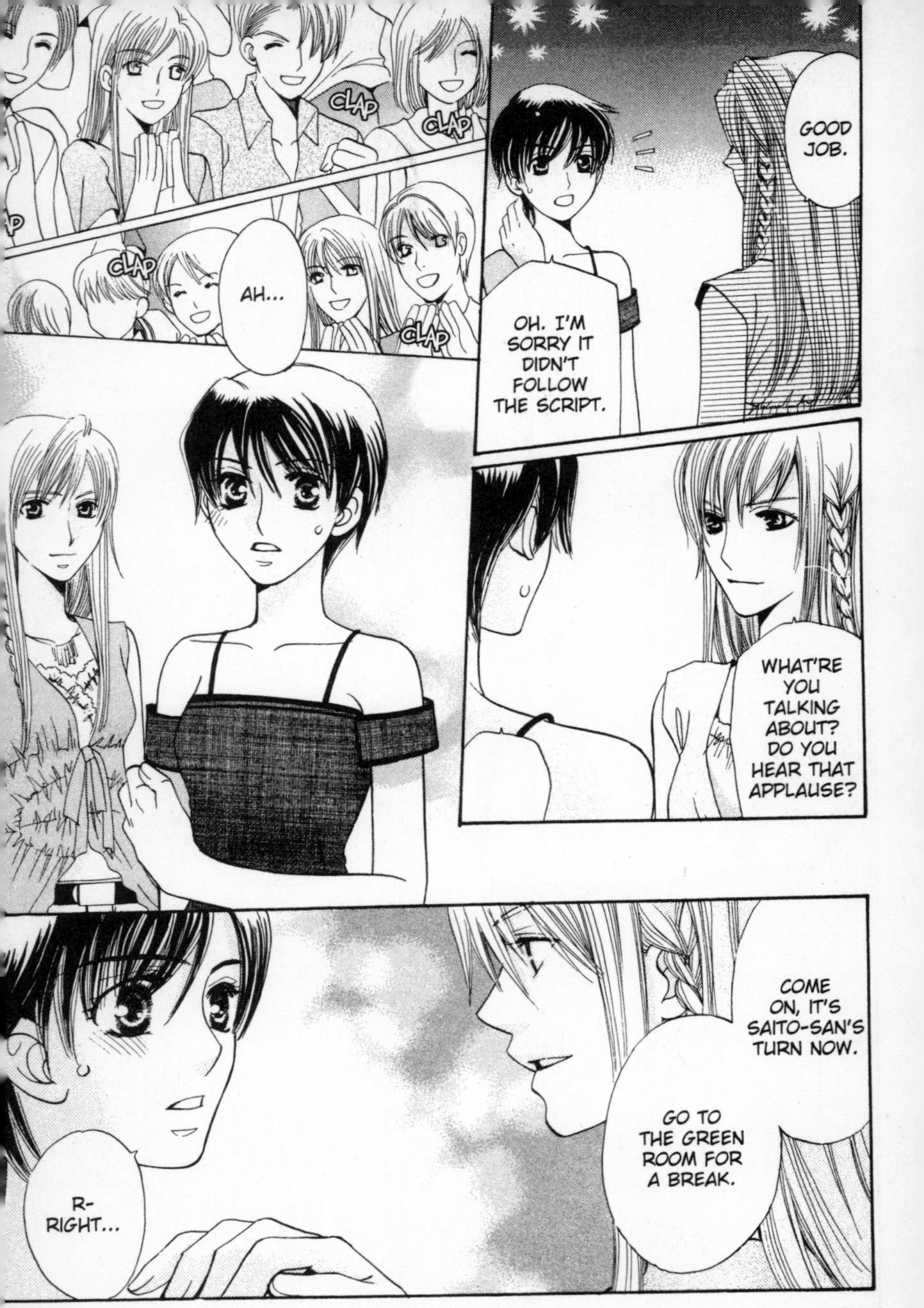

GOOD JOB.
OH. I'M SORRY IT DIDN'T FOLLOW THE SCRIPT.
CLAP
CLAP
CLAP
CLAP
AH...
WHAT'RE YOU TALKING ABOUT? DO YOU HEAR THAT APPLAUSE?
COME ON, IT'S SAITO-SAN'S TURN NOW.
GO TO THE GREEN ROOM FOR A BREAK.
R-RIGHT...

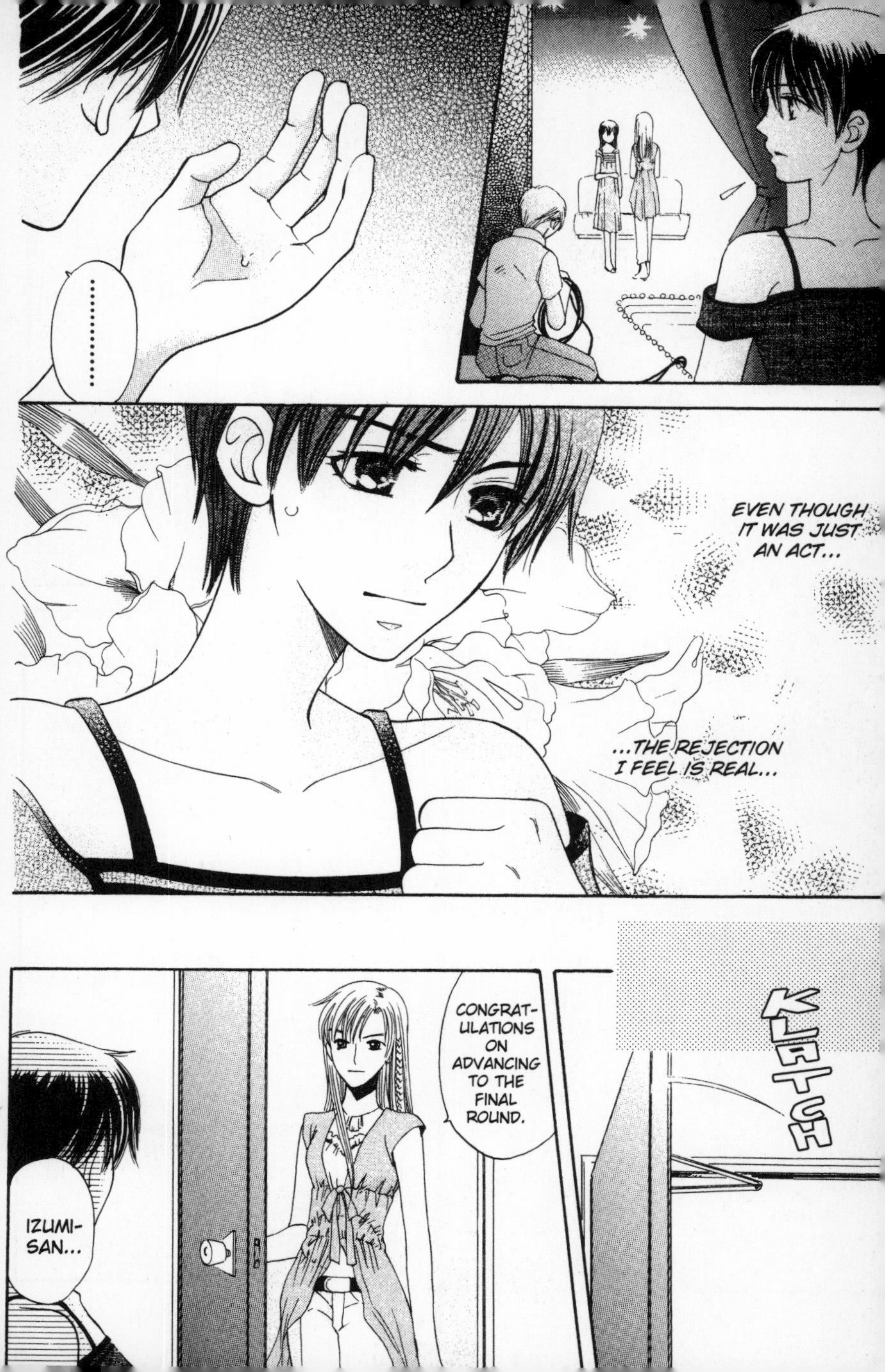
......
EVEN THOUGH IT WAS JUST AN ACT...
...THE REJECTION I FEEL IS REAL...
KLATCH
CONGRAT-ULATIONS ON ADVANCING TO THE FINAL ROUND.
IZUMI-SAN...

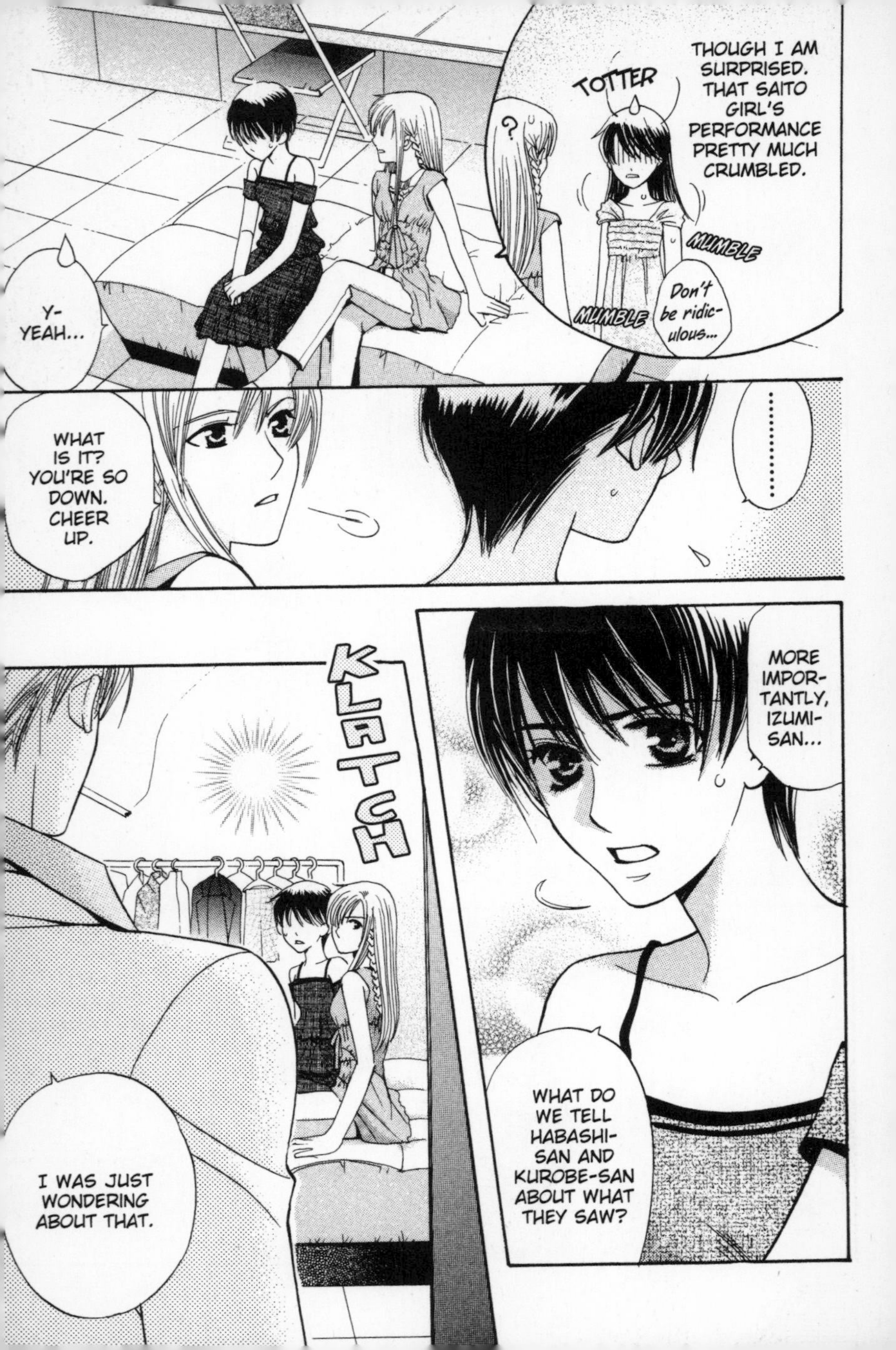
THOUGH I AM SURPRISED. THAT SAITO GIRL'S PERFORMANCE PRETTY MUCH CRUMBLED.
TOTTER
MUMBLE
Don't be ridiculous...
MUMBLE
?
Y-YEAH...
..........
WHAT IS IT? YOU'RE SO DOWN. CHEER UP.
MORE IMPORTANTLY, IZUMI-SAN...
WHAT DO WE TELL HABASHI-SAN AND KUROBE-SAN ABOUT WHAT THEY SAW?
KLATCH
I WAS JUST WONDERING ABOUT THAT.

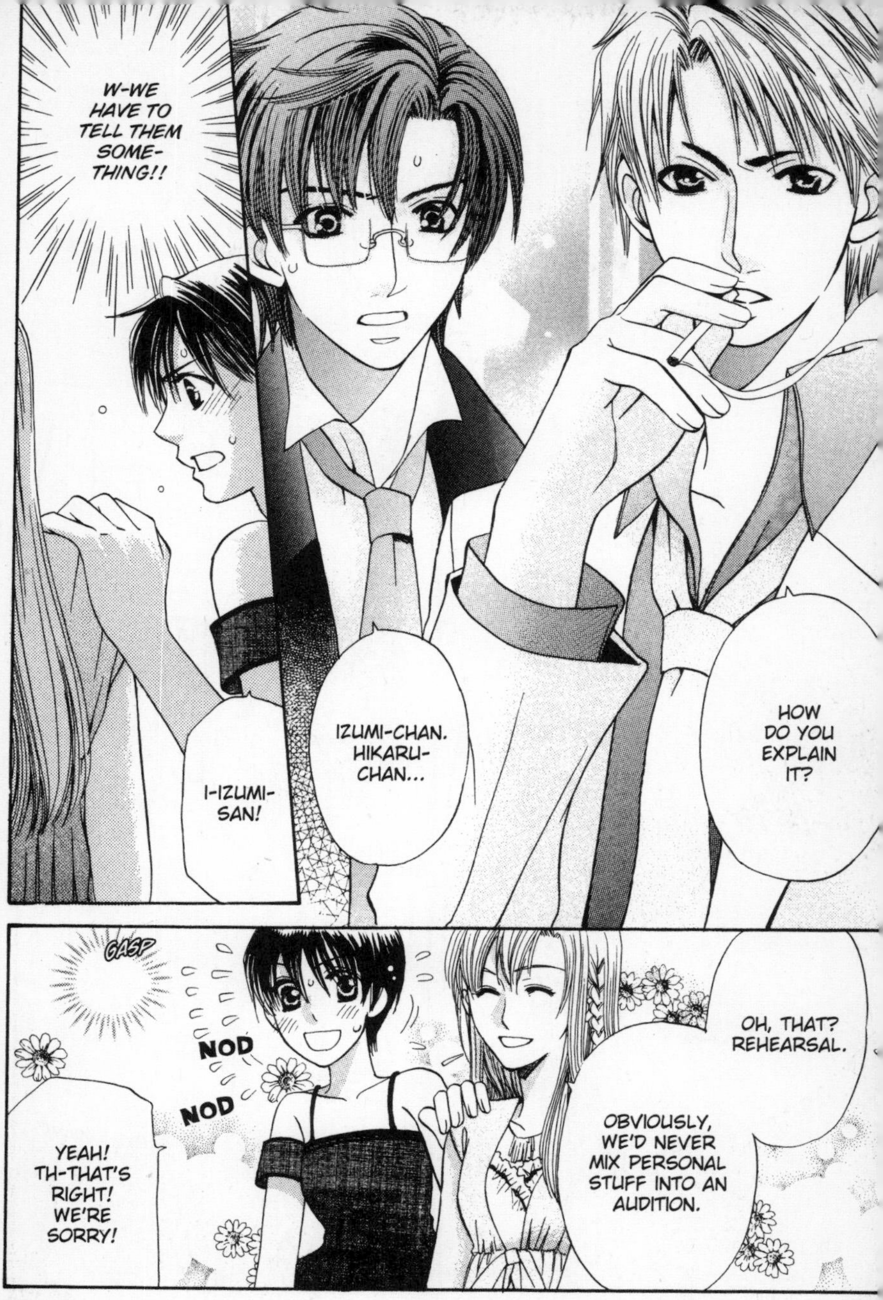
HOW DO YOU EXPLAIN IT?
IZUMI-CHAN. HIKARU-CHAN...
W-WE HAVE TO TELL THEM SOME-THING!!
I-IZUMI-SAN!
OH, THAT? REHEARSAL.
OBVIOUSLY, WE'D NEVER MIX PERSONAL STUFF INTO AN AUDITION.
NOD
NOD
GASP
YEAH! TH-THAT'S RIGHT! WE'RE SORRY!

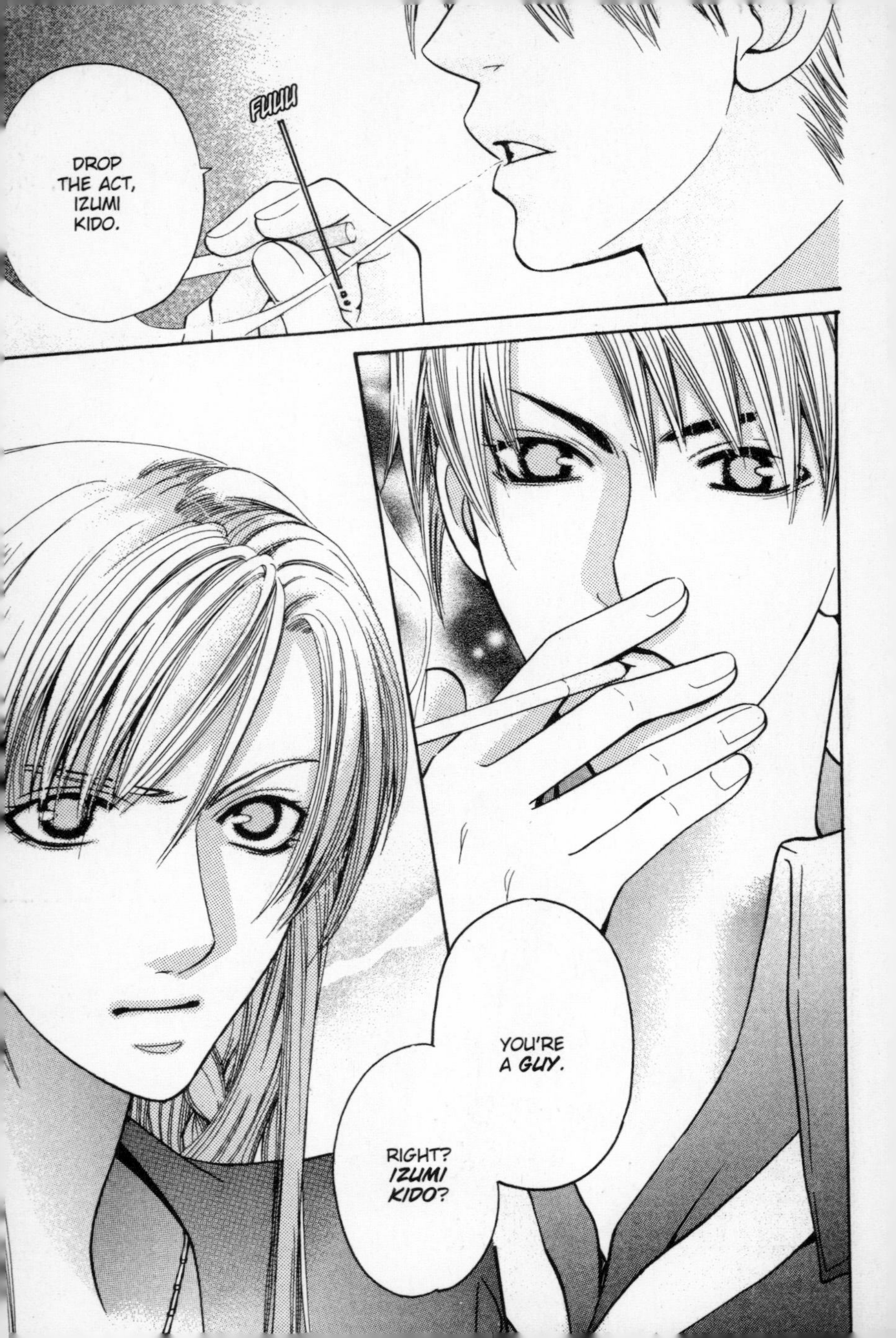
FUUU
DROP THE ACT, IZUMI KIDO.
YOU'RE A *GUY*.
RIGHT? *IZUMI KIDO?*

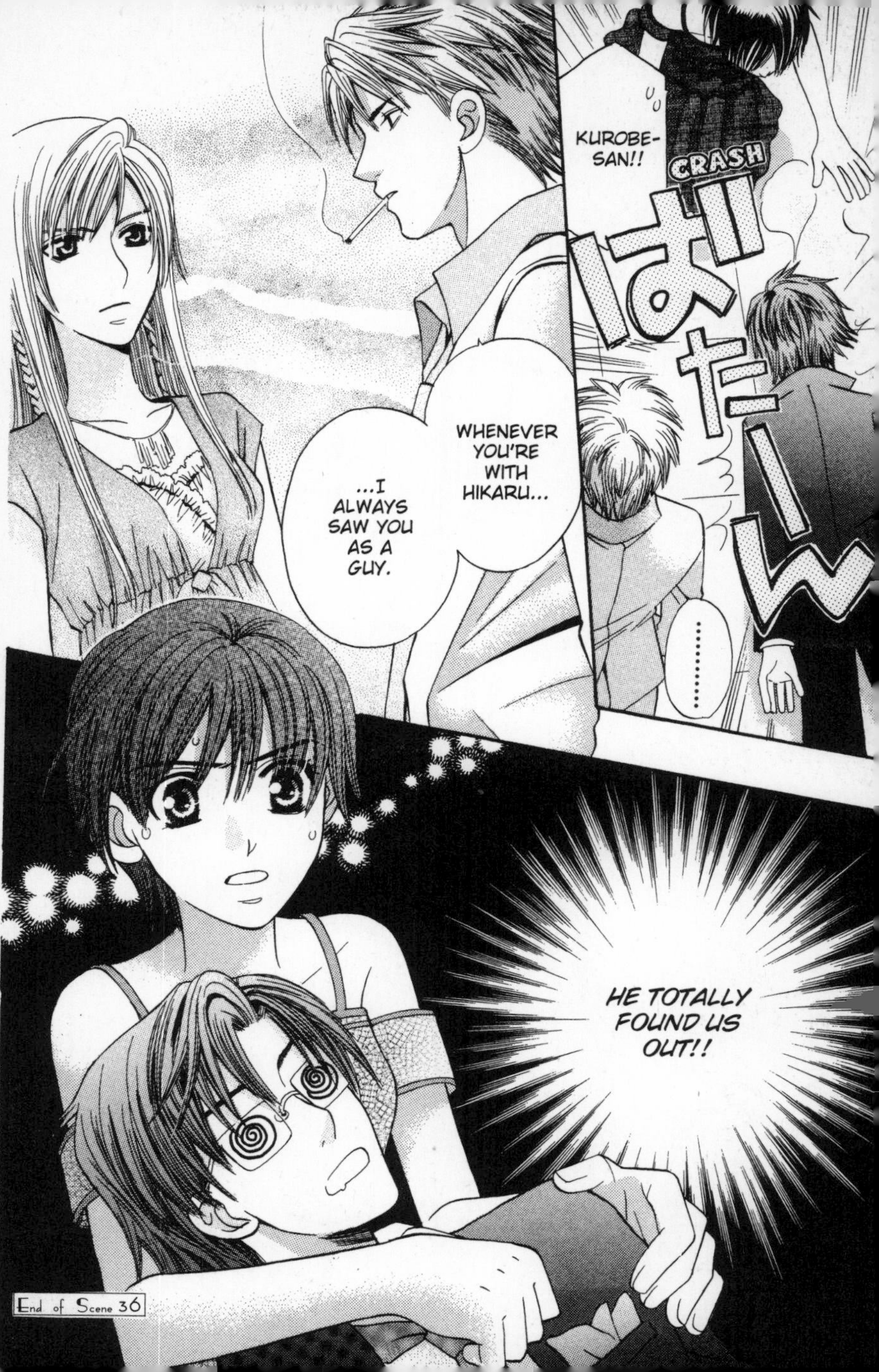
KUROBE-SAN!!
CRASH
ばたーん
......
WHENEVER YOU'RE WITH HIKARU...
...I ALWAYS SAW YOU AS A GUY.
HE TOTALLY FOUND US OUT!!

End of Scene 36

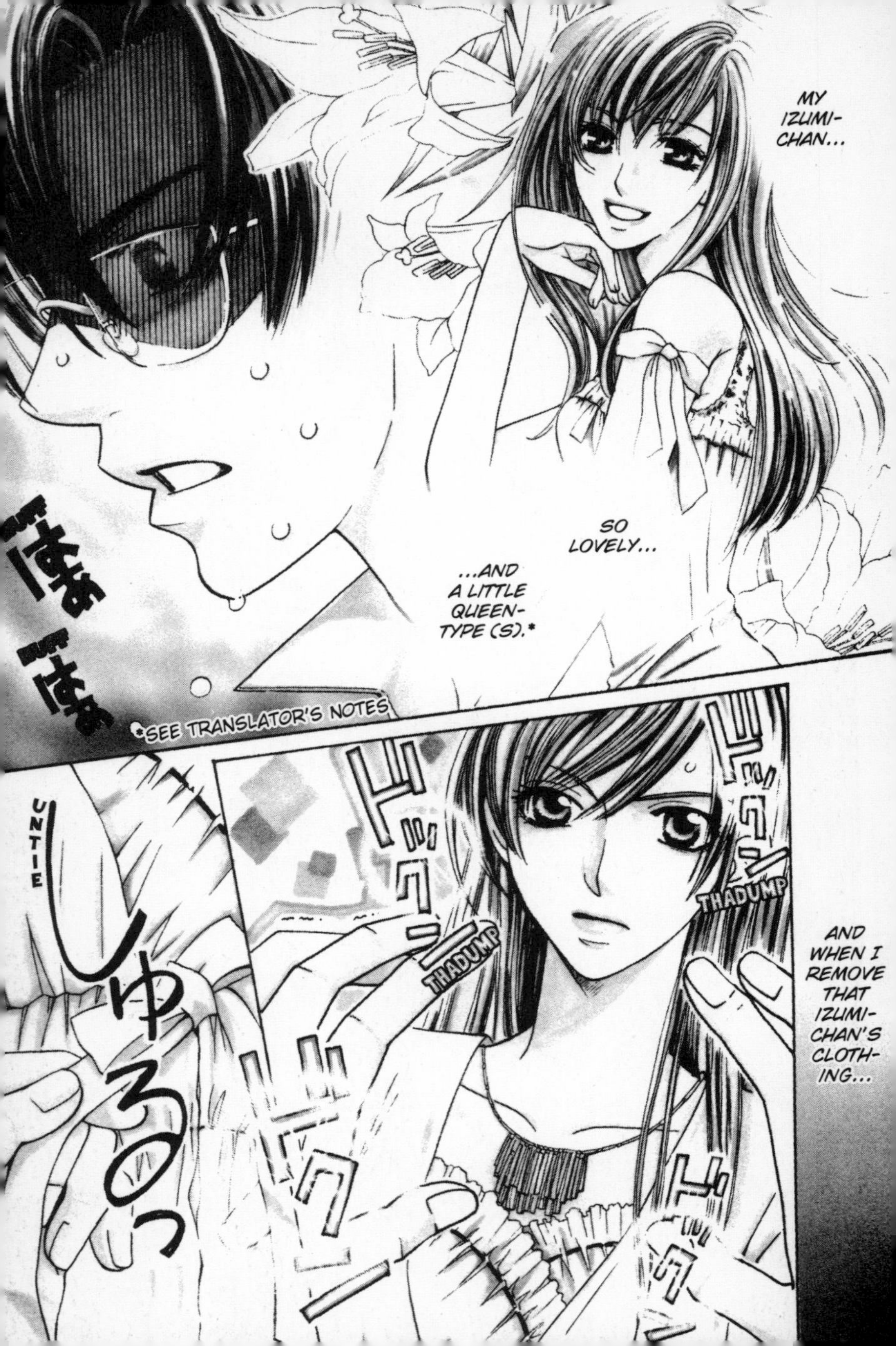
MY IZUMI-CHAN...
SO LOVELY...
...AND A LITTLE QUEEN-TYPE (S).*
はぁ
はぁ
*SEE TRANSLATOR'S NOTES
AND WHEN I REMOVE THAT IZUMI-CHAN'S CLOTHING...
THADUMP
THADUMP
UNTIE
しゅるっ

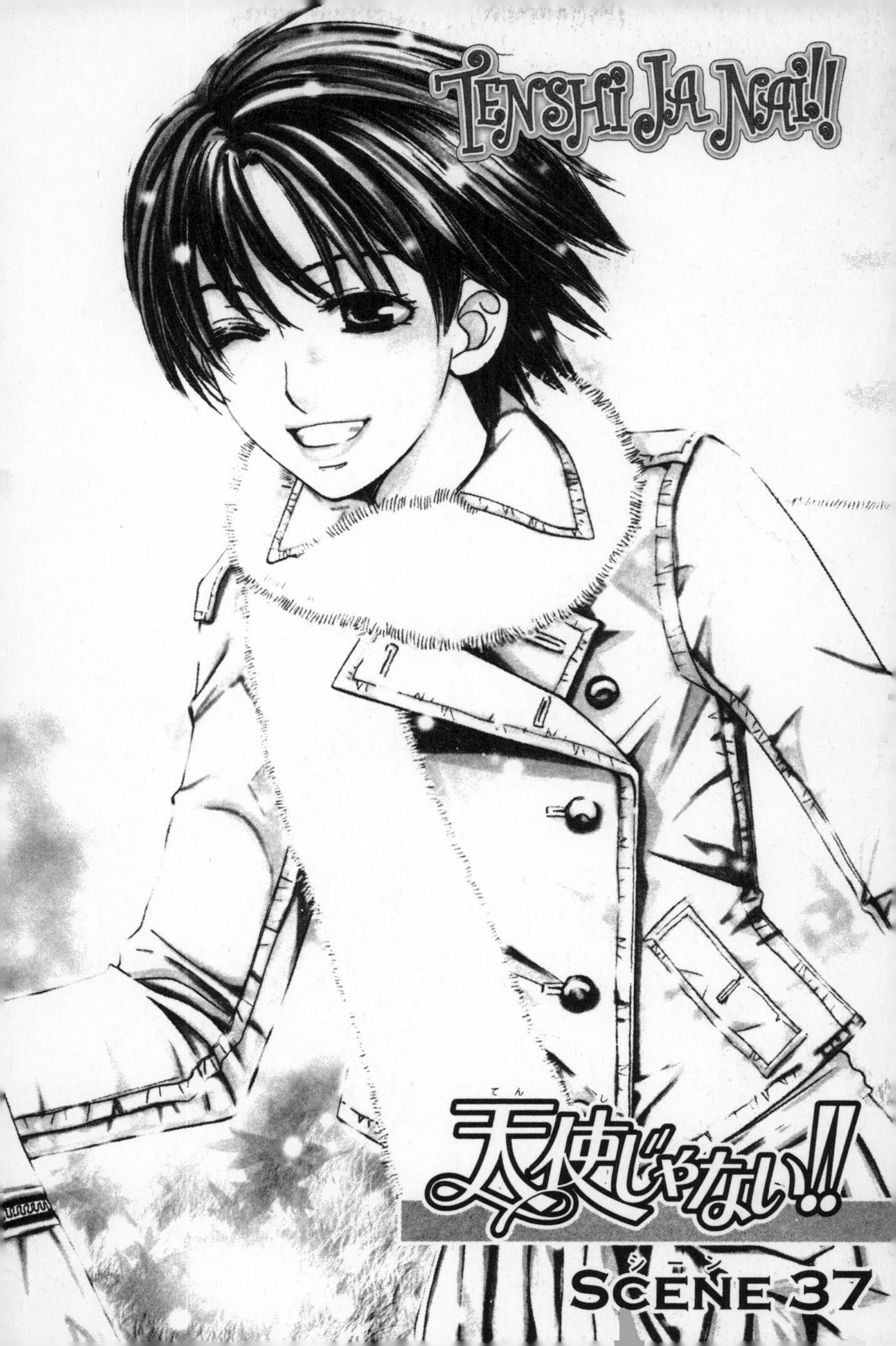
TENSHI JA NAI!!
天使じゃない!!
SCENE 37

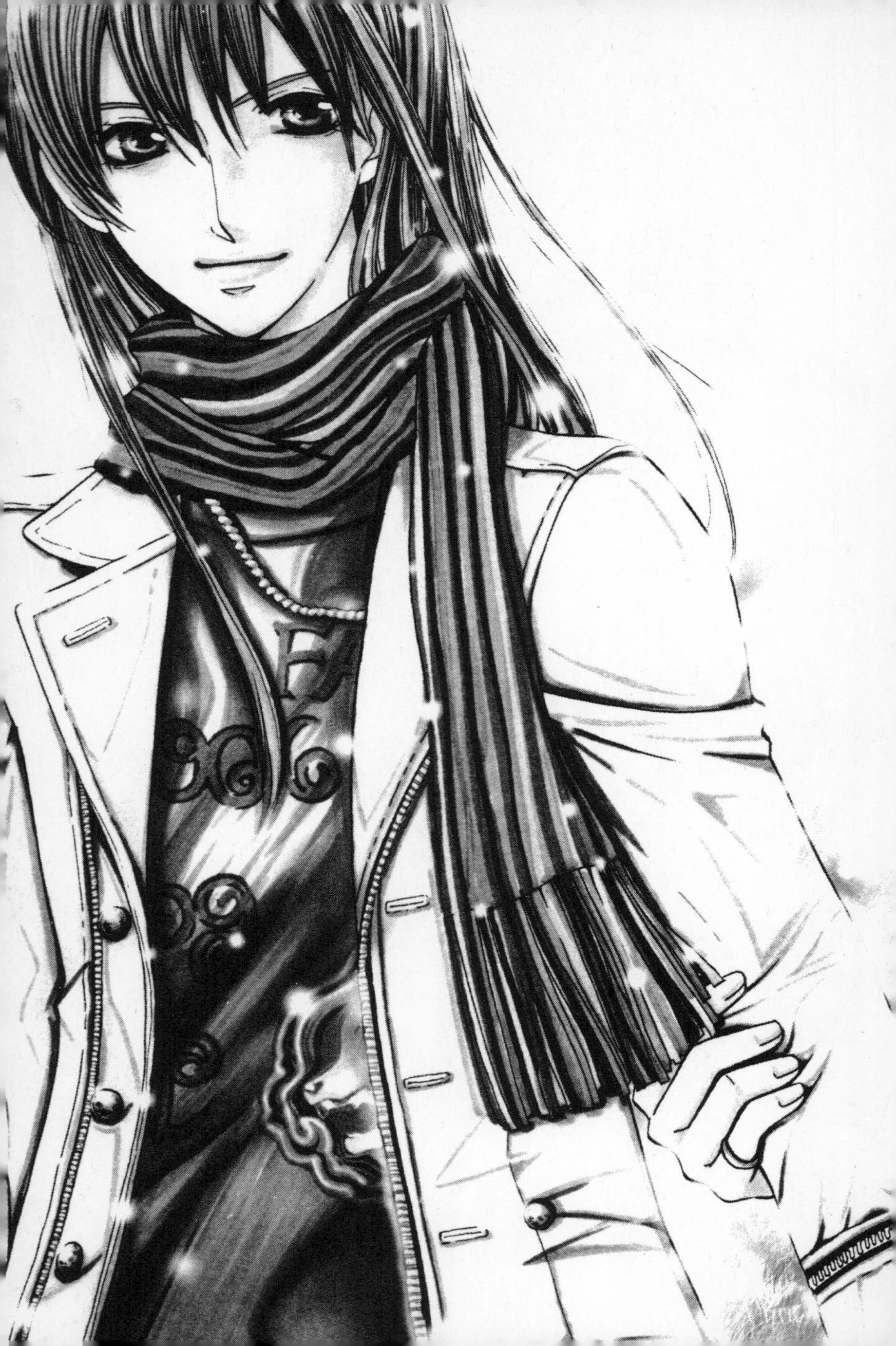

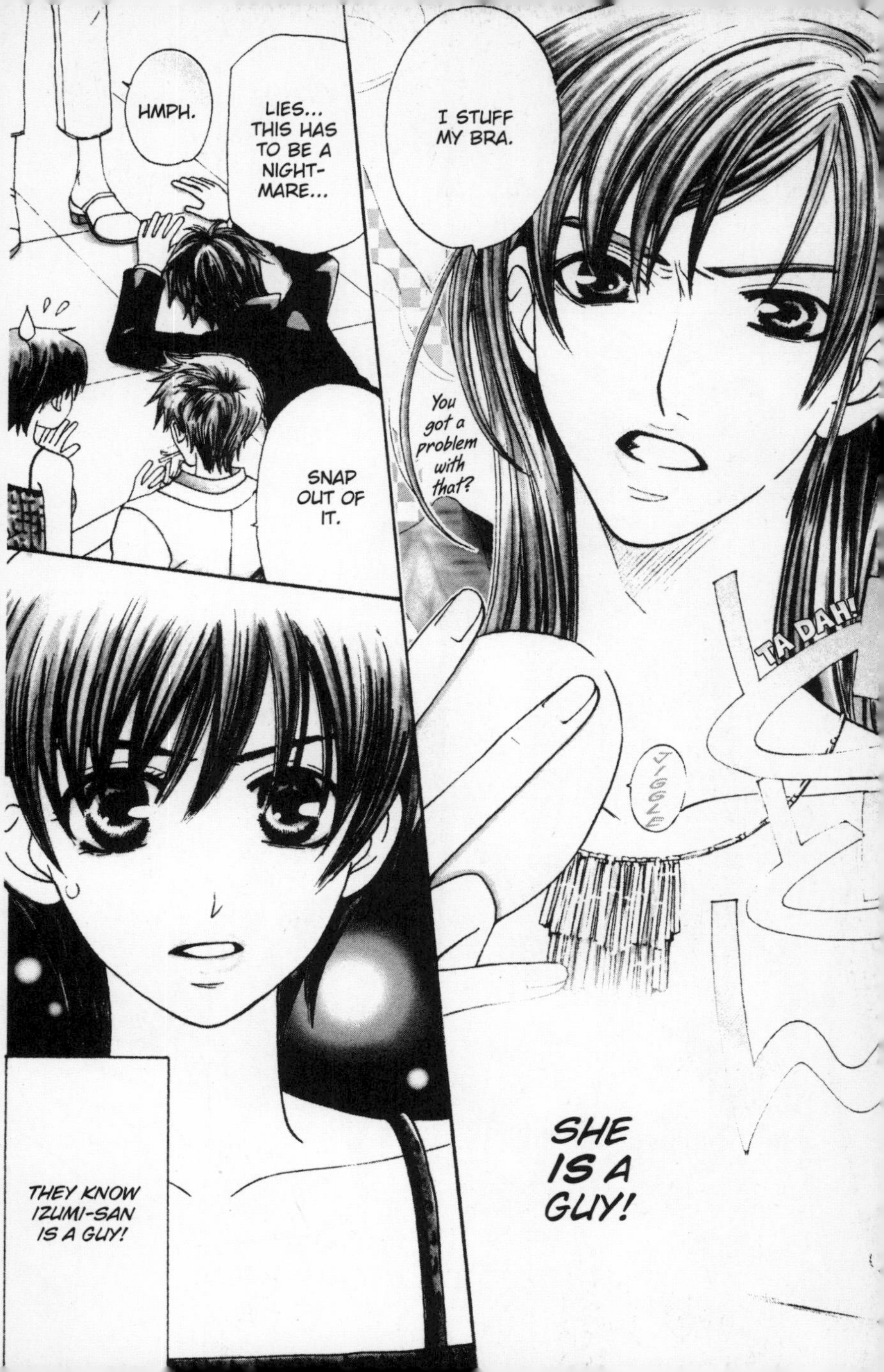
I STUFF MY BRA.
You got a problem with that?
TA DAH!
JIGGLE
SHE IS A GUY!
LIES... THIS HAS TO BE A NIGHT-MARE...
HMPH.
SNAP OUT OF IT.
THEY KNOW IZUMI-SAN IS A GUY!

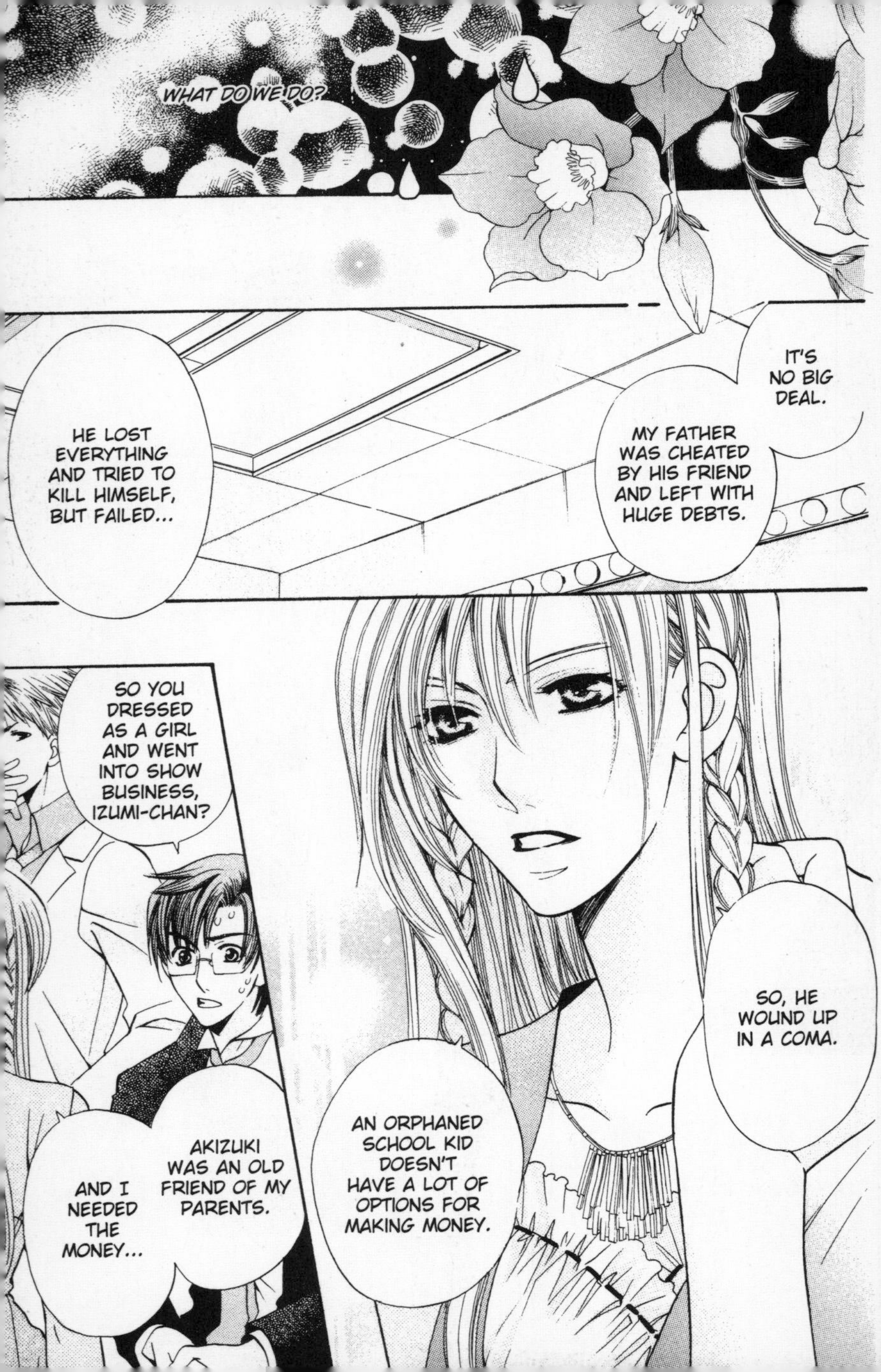
WHAT DO WE DO?
IT'S NO BIG DEAL.
MY FATHER WAS CHEATED BY HIS FRIEND AND LEFT WITH HUGE DEBTS.
HE LOST EVERYTHING AND TRIED TO KILL HIMSELF, BUT FAILED...
SO, HE WOUND UP IN A COMA.
AN ORPHANED SCHOOL KID DOESN'T HAVE A LOT OF OPTIONS FOR MAKING MONEY.
SO YOU DRESSED AS A GIRL AND WENT INTO SHOW BUSINESS, IZUMI-CHAN?
AKIZUKI WAS AN OLD FRIEND OF MY PARENTS.
AND I NEEDED THE MONEY...

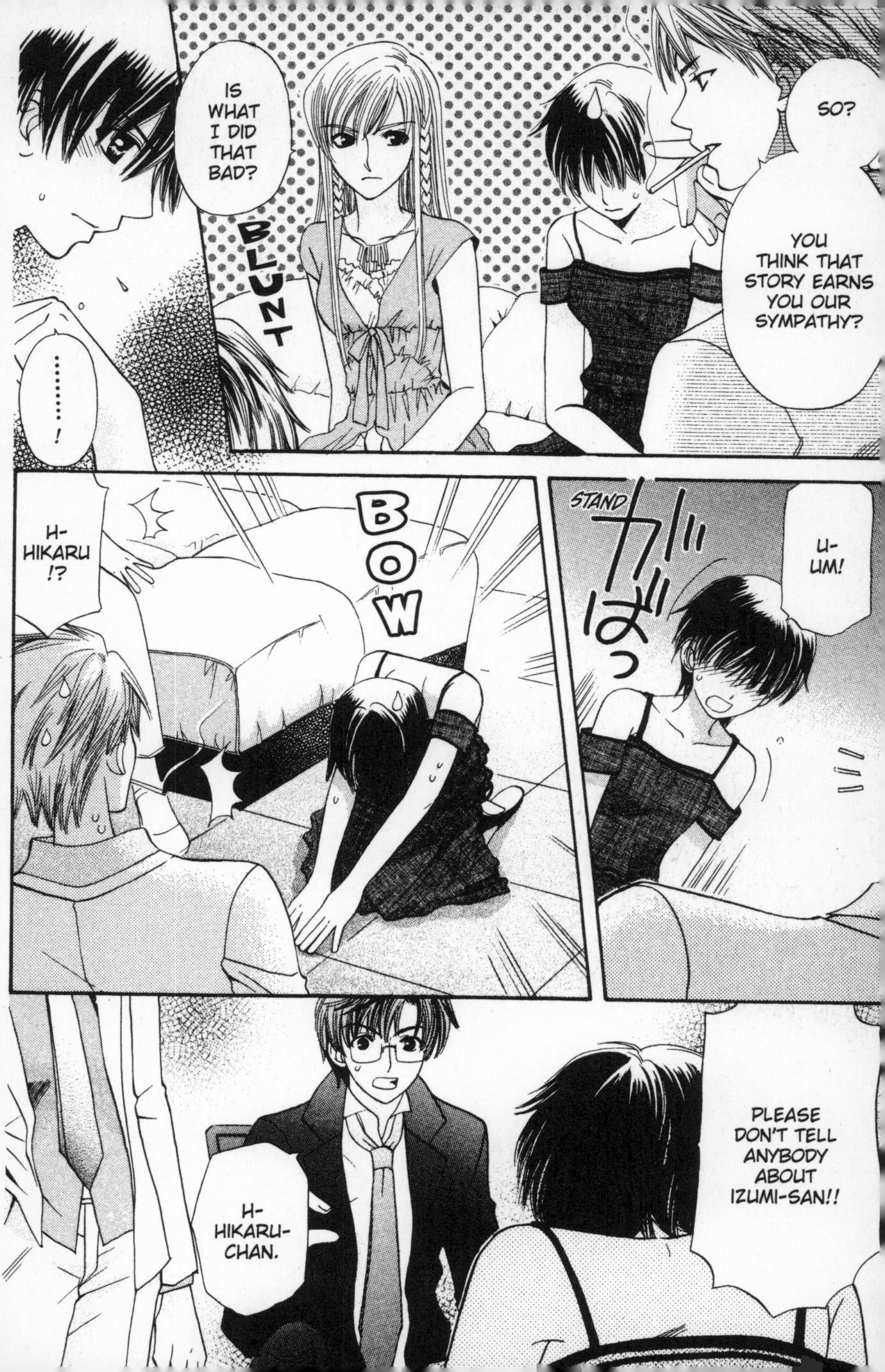
SO?
YOU THINK THAT STORY EARNS YOU OUR SYMPATHY?
IS WHAT I DID THAT BAD?
BLUNT
……!
STAND
がばっ
U-UM!
BOW
H-HIKARU!?
PLEASE DON'T TELL ANYBODY ABOUT IZUMI-SAN!!
H-HIKARU-CHAN.

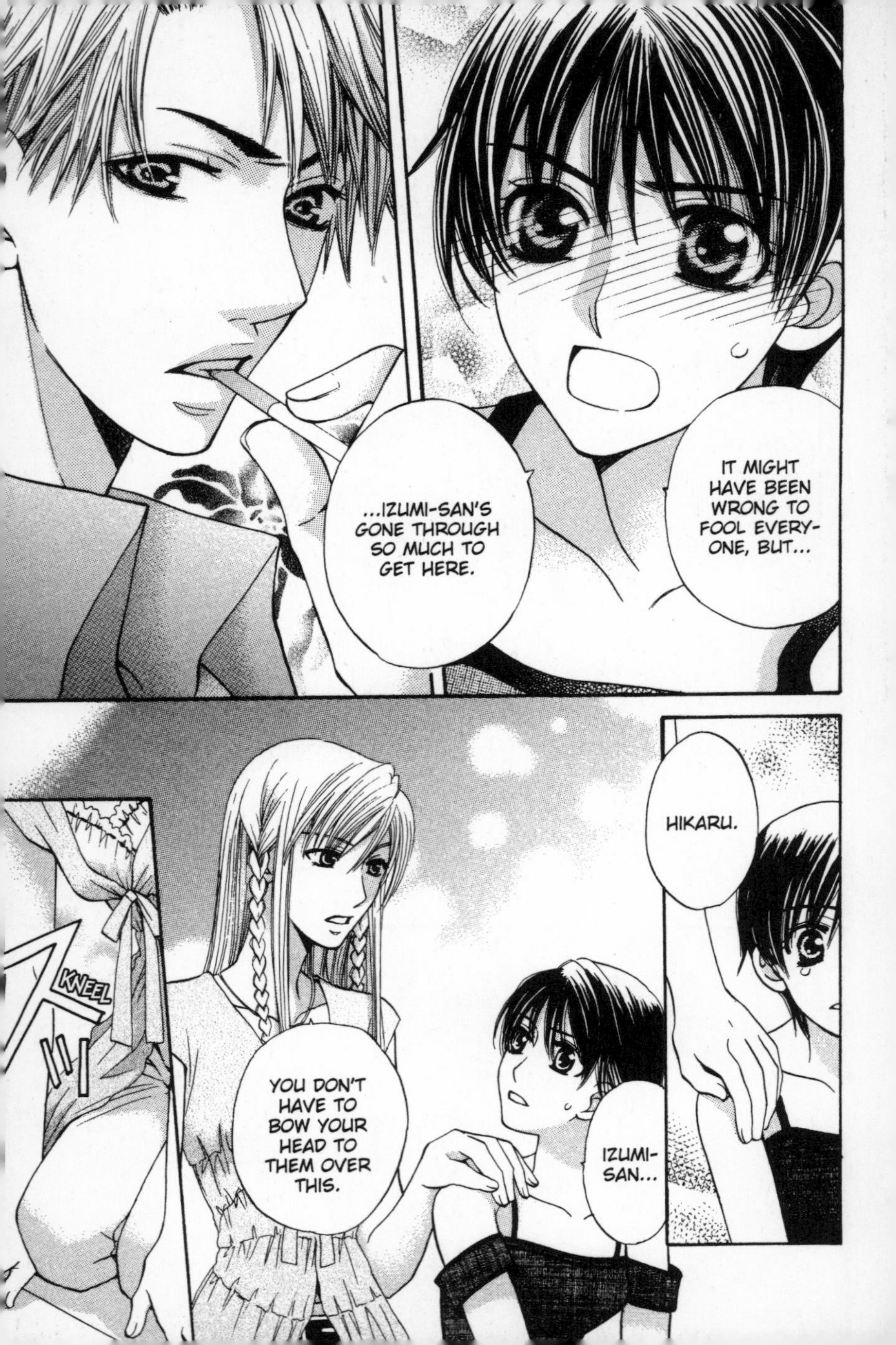
IT MIGHT HAVE BEEN WRONG TO FOOL EVERY-ONE, BUT...
...IZUMI-SAN'S GONE THROUGH SO MUCH TO GET HERE.
HIKARU.
IZUMI-SAN...
YOU DON'T HAVE TO BOW YOUR HEAD TO THEM OVER THIS.
KNEEL

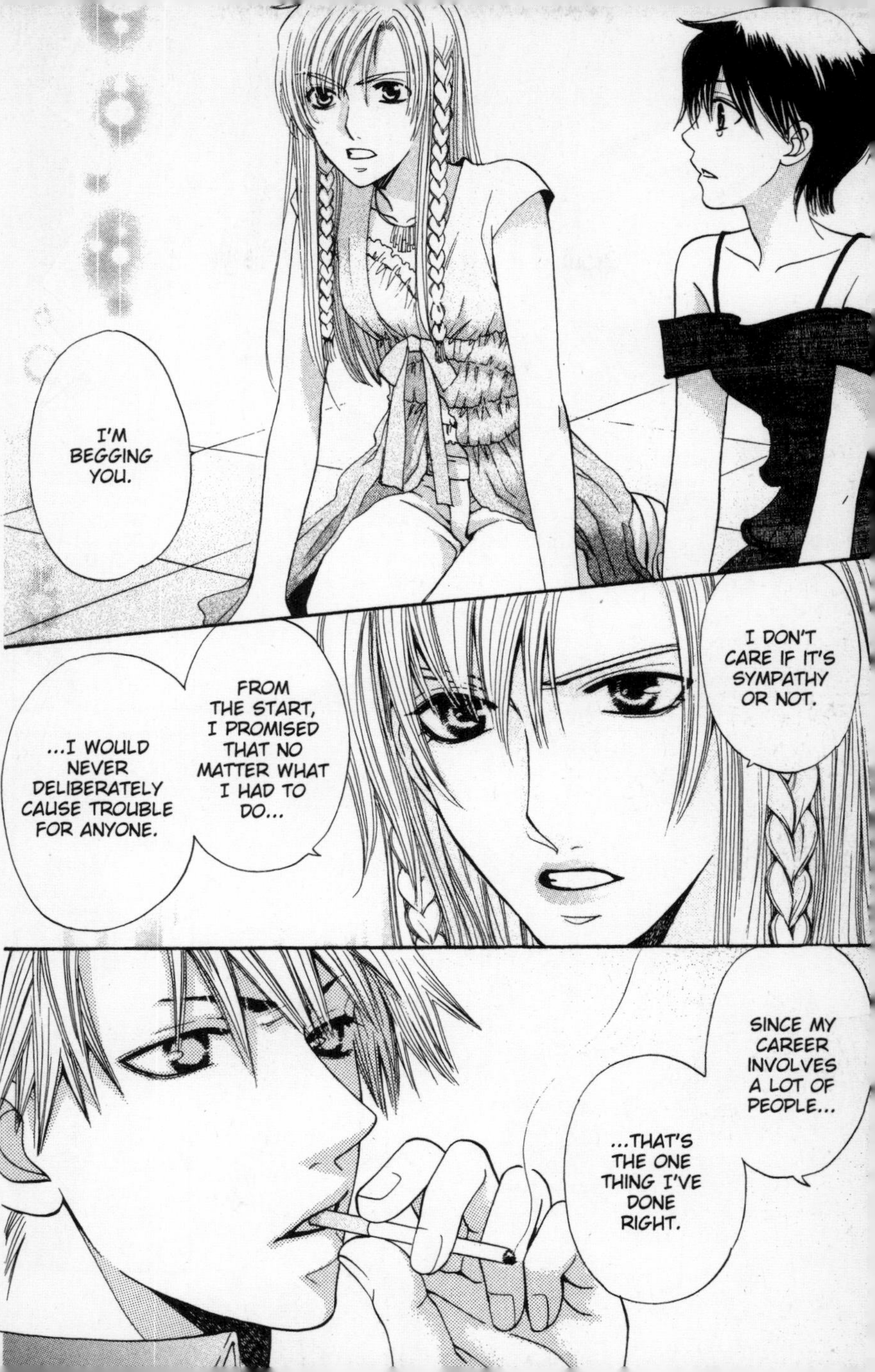
I'M BEGGING YOU.
I DON'T CARE IF IT'S SYMPATHY OR NOT.
FROM THE START, I PROMISED THAT NO MATTER WHAT I HAD TO DO...
...I WOULD NEVER DELIBERATELY CAUSE TROUBLE FOR ANYONE.
SINCE MY CAREER INVOLVES A LOT OF PEOPLE...
...THAT'S THE ONE THING I'VE DONE RIGHT.

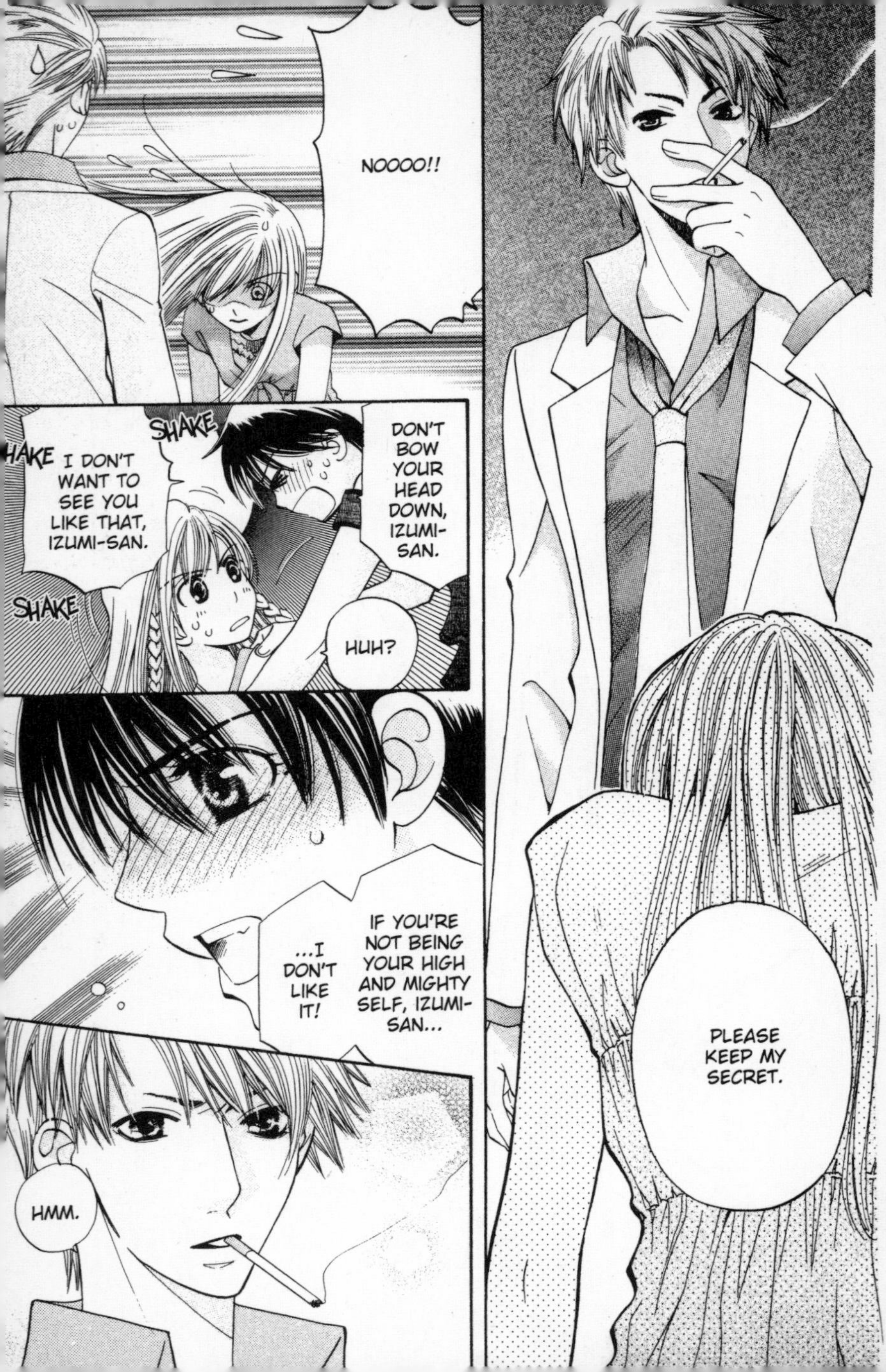
PLEASE KEEP MY SECRET.
NOOOO!!
DON'T BOW YOUR HEAD DOWN, IZUMI-SAN.
SHAKE
SHAKE
I DON'T WANT TO SEE YOU LIKE THAT, IZUMI-SAN.
SHAKE
HUH?
IF YOU'RE NOT BEING YOUR HIGH AND MIGHTY SELF, IZUMI-SAN...
...I DON'T LIKE IT!
HMM.

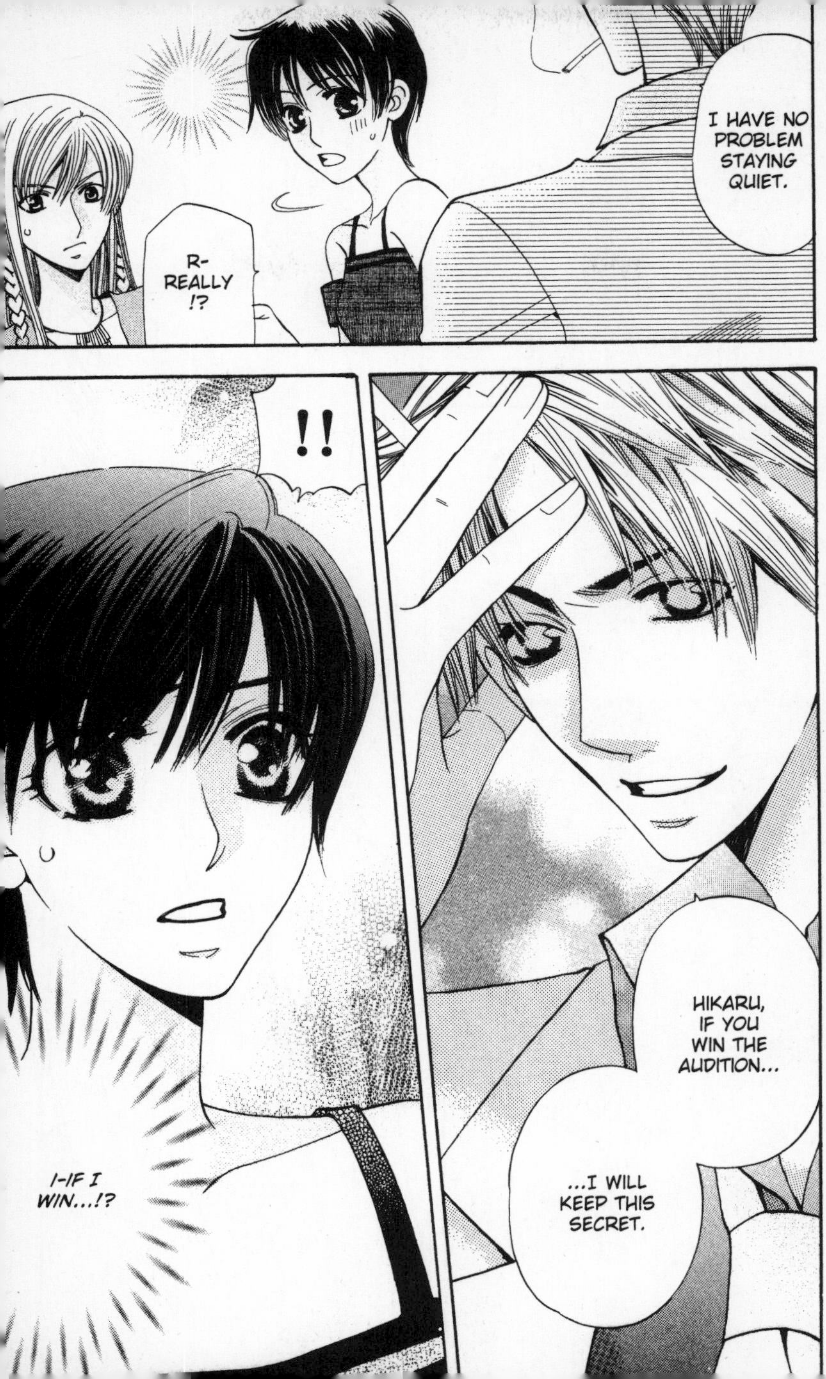
I HAVE NO PROBLEM STAYING QUIET.
R-REALLY!?
HIKARU, IF YOU WIN THE AUDITION...
...I WILL KEEP THIS SECRET.
!!
I-IF I WIN...!?

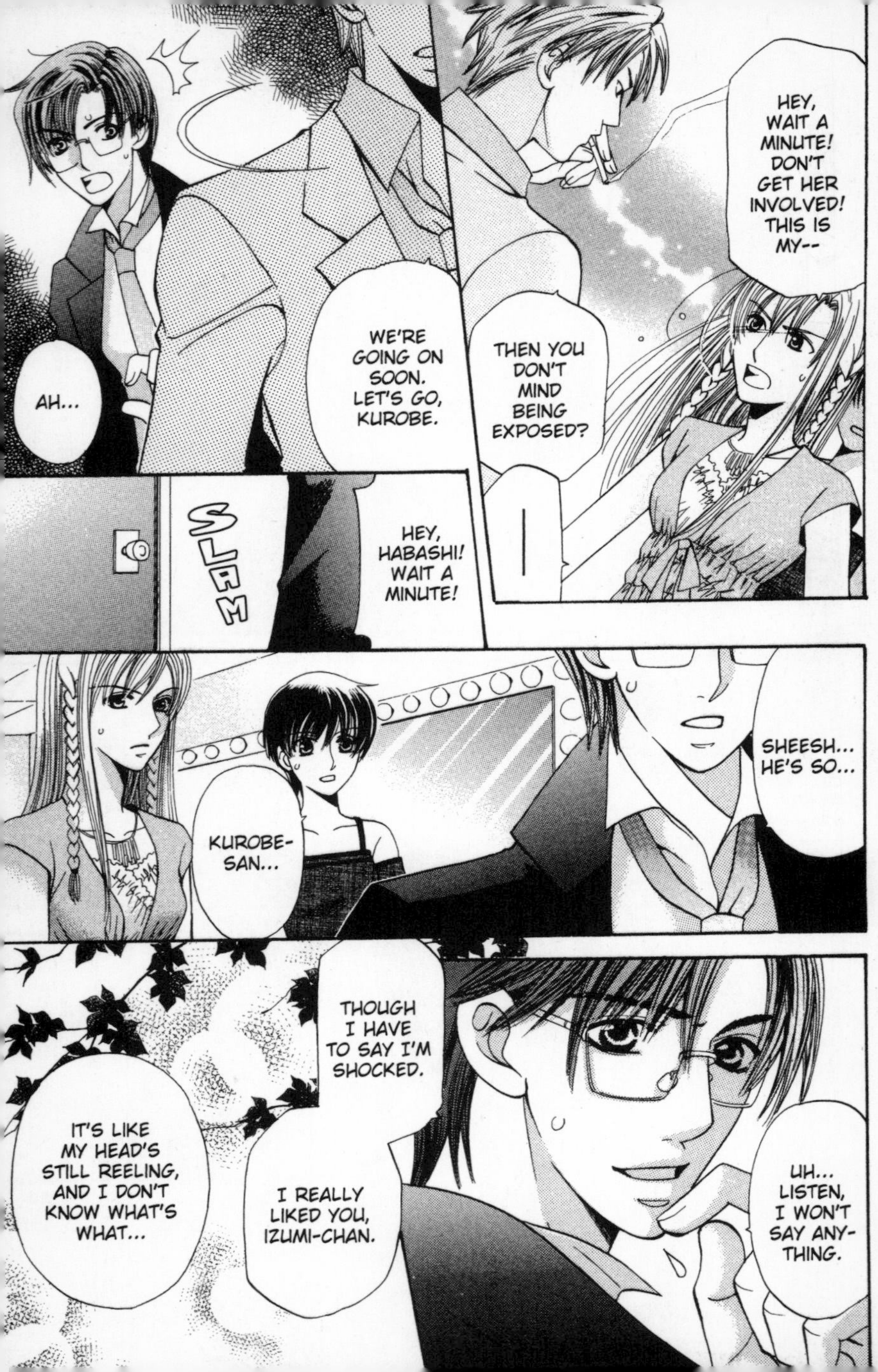
HEY, WAIT A MINUTE! DON'T GET HER INVOLVED! THIS IS MY--
THEN YOU DON'T MIND BEING EXPOSED?
WE'RE GOING ON SOON. LET'S GO, KUROBE.
AH...
HEY, HABASHI! WAIT A MINUTE!
SLAM
SHEESH... HE'S SO...
KUROBE-SAN...
UH... LISTEN, I WON'T SAY ANY-THING.
THOUGH I HAVE TO SAY I'M SHOCKED.
I REALLY LIKED YOU, IZUMI-CHAN.
IT'S LIKE MY HEAD'S STILL REELING, AND I DON'T KNOW WHAT'S WHAT...

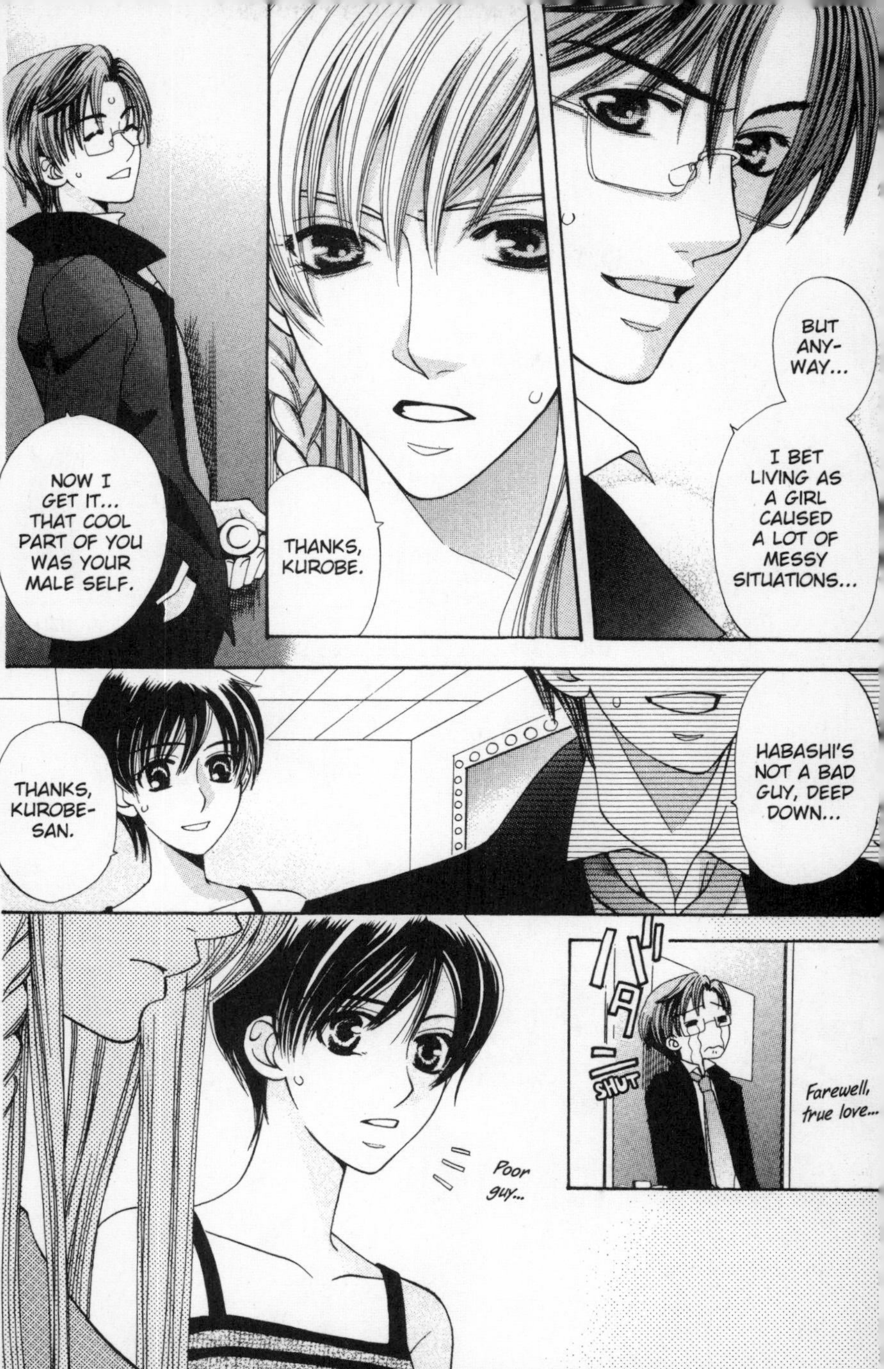
BUT ANY-WAY...
I BET LIVING AS A GIRL CAUSED A LOT OF MESSY SITUATIONS...
THANKS, KUROBE.
NOW I GET IT... THAT COOL PART OF YOU WAS YOUR MALE SELF.
HABASHI'S NOT A BAD GUY, DEEP DOWN...
THANKS, KUROBE-SAN.
SHUT
Farewell, true love...
Poor guy...

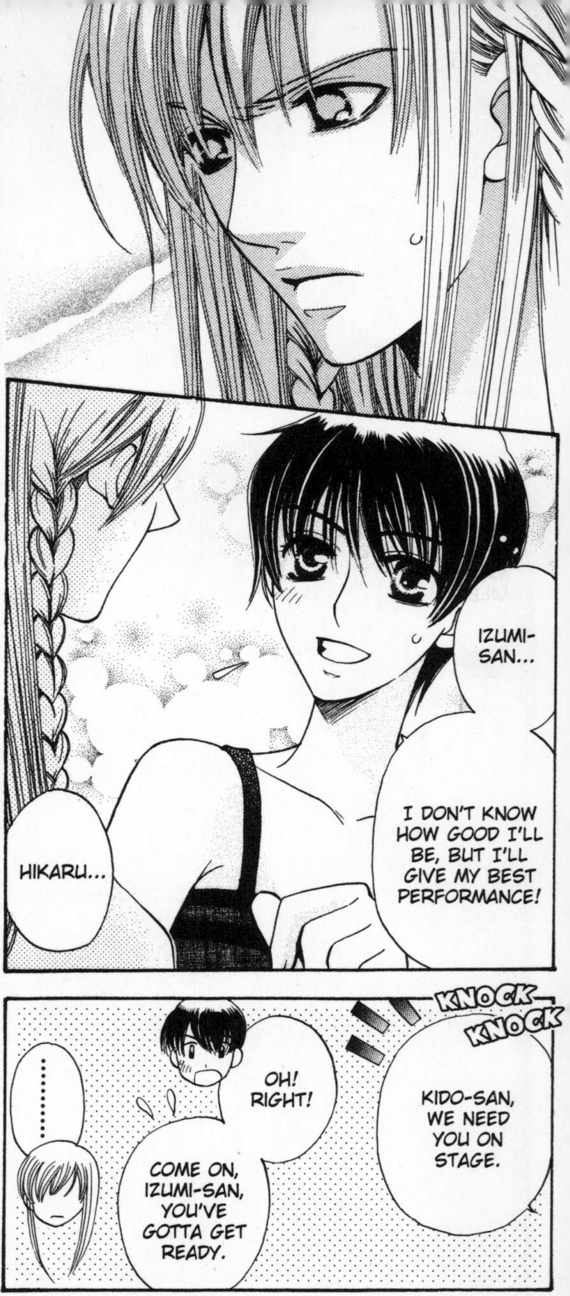
IZUMI-SAN...
I DON'T KNOW HOW GOOD I'LL BE, BUT I'LL GIVE MY BEST PERFORMANCE!
HIKARU...
KNOCK KNOCK
KIDO-SAN, WE NEED YOU ON STAGE.
OH! RIGHT!
COME ON, IZUMI-SAN, YOU'VE GOTTA GET READY.
......

*Let's Take a Relaxing Trip (1)*

*When I finished the last chapter of "Tenshi Ja Nai!!" my assistants and I went on a 2-day, 1-night trip. We met up at Tokyo Station at 6:00 am. Maybe it was too early, but on the Kinki Nippo Railway my assistant T-san, who'd joined us, was so quiet she was like a different person.*

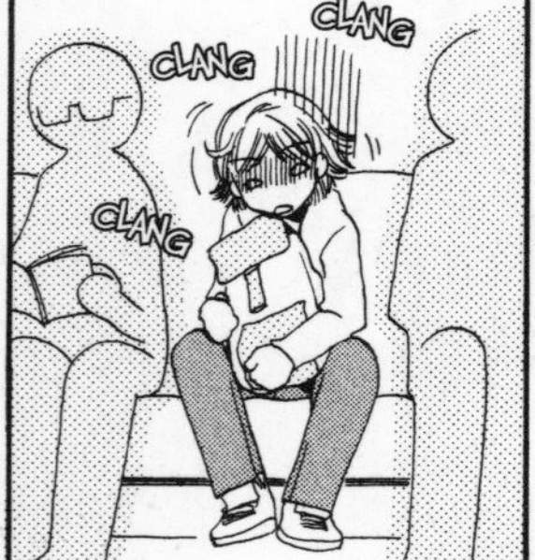
CLANG
CLANG
CLANG

*Anyway, we safely boarded the Shinkansen and arrived at a certain Mouse Kingdom. This long-winded report will continue later...*

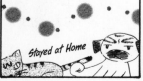

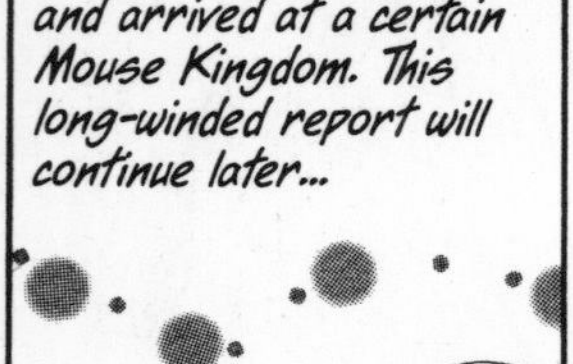
Stayed at Home

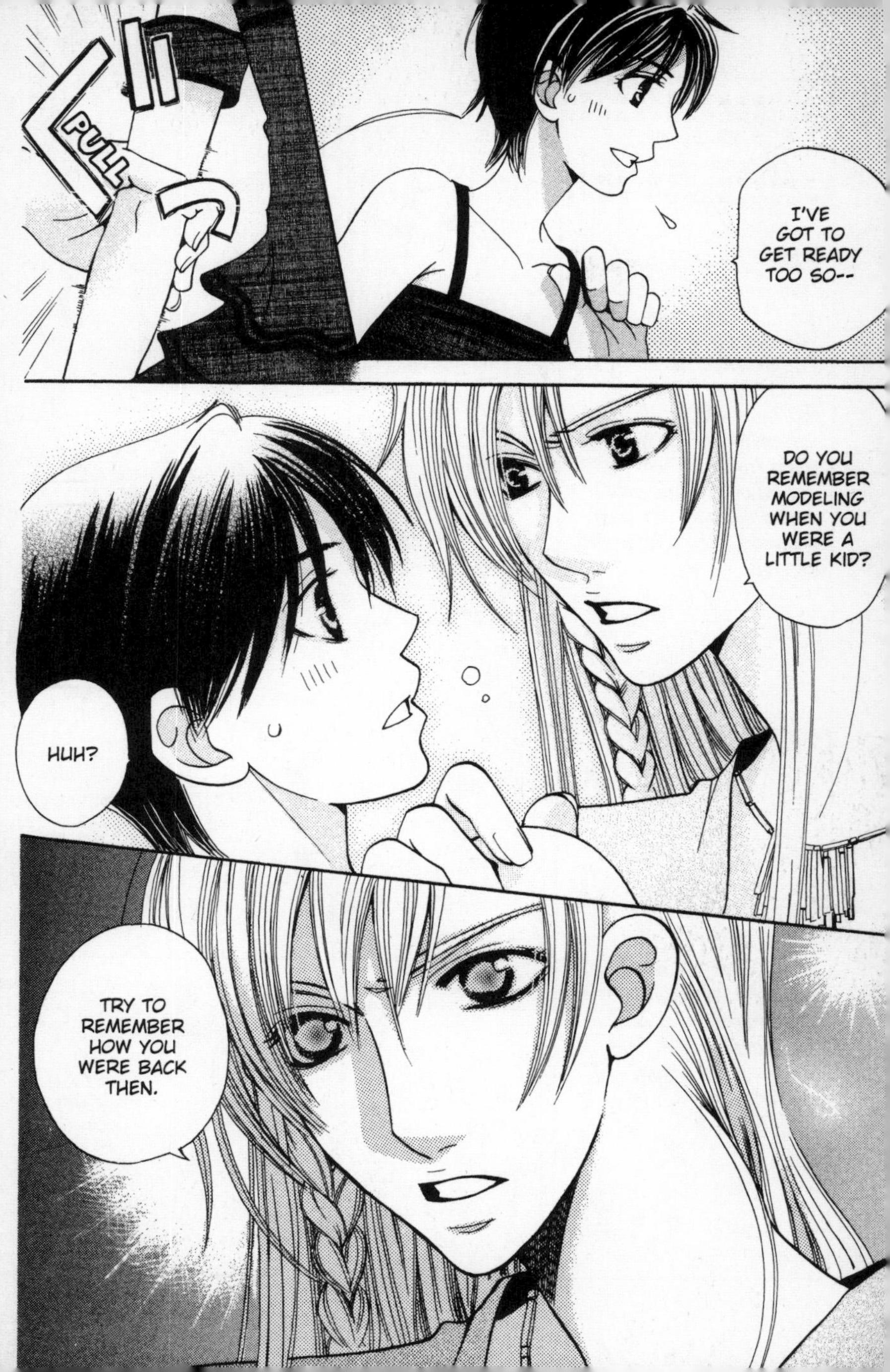
I'VE GOT TO GET READY TOO SO--
PULL
DO YOU REMEMBER MODELING WHEN YOU WERE A LITTLE KID?
HUH?
TRY TO REMEMBER HOW YOU WERE BACK THEN.

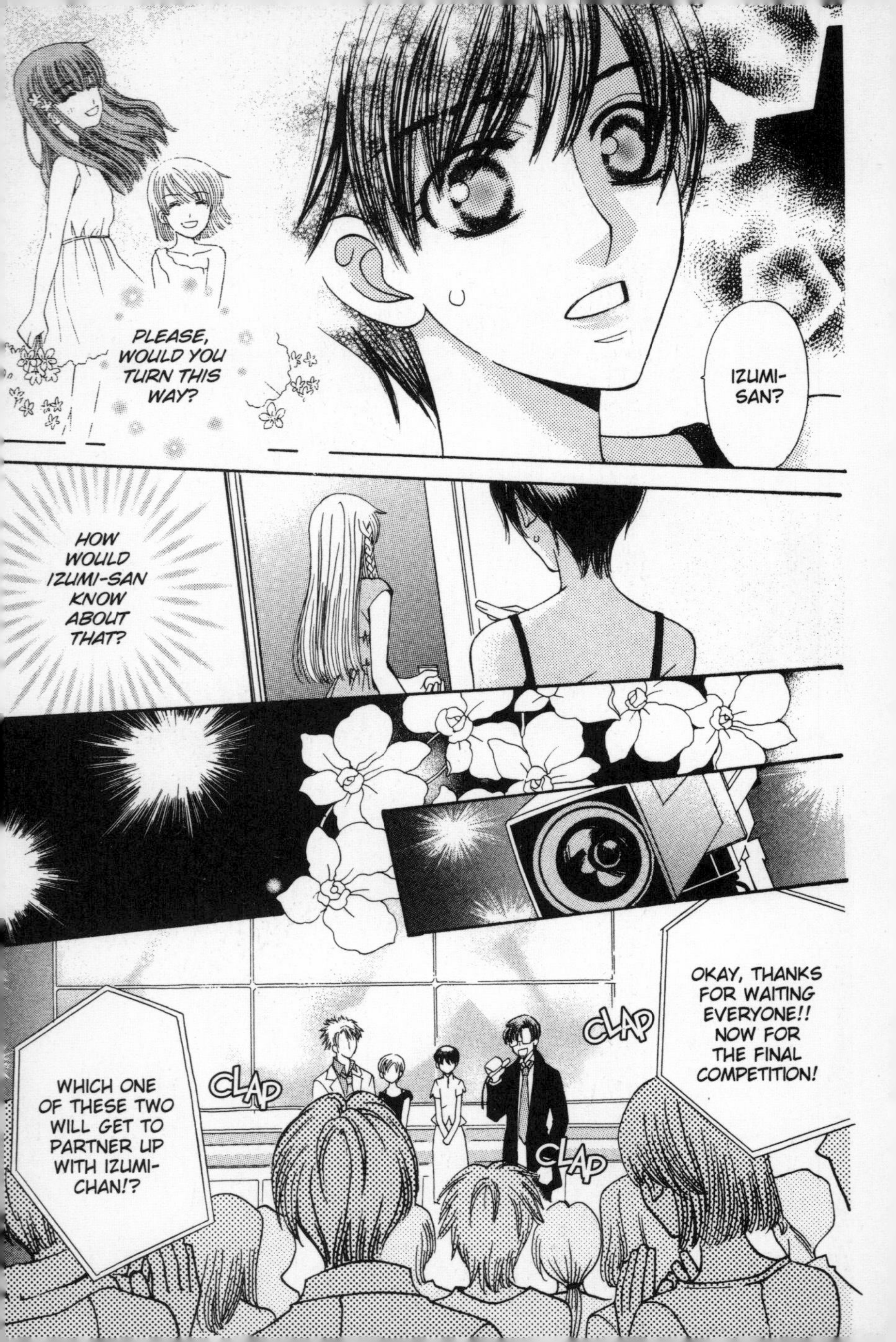

IZUMI-SAN?
PLEASE, WOULD YOU TURN THIS WAY?
HOW WOULD IZUMI-SAN KNOW ABOUT THAT?
OKAY, THANKS FOR WAITING EVERYONE!! NOW FOR THE FINAL COMPETITION!
CLAP
CLAP
CLAP
WHICH ONE OF THESE TWO WILL GET TO PARTNER UP WITH IZUMI-CHAN!?

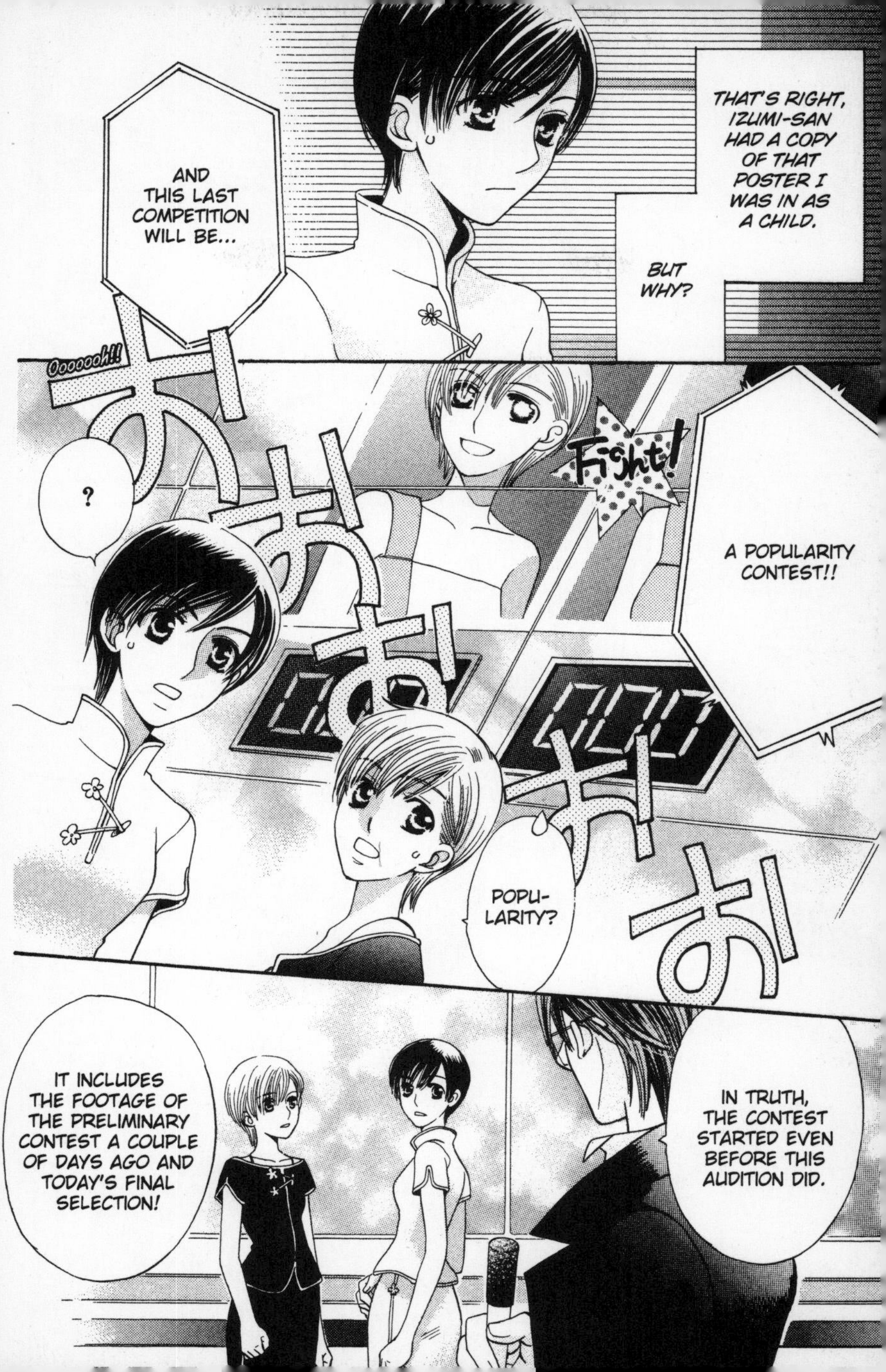
THAT'S RIGHT, IZUMI-SAN HAD A COPY OF THAT POSTER I WAS IN AS A CHILD.
BUT WHY?
AND THIS LAST COMPETITION WILL BE...
A POPULARITY CONTEST!!
Fight!
Oooooooh!!
?
POPU-LARITY?
IN TRUTH, THE CONTEST STARTED EVEN BEFORE THIS AUDITION DID.
IT INCLUDES THE FOOTAGE OF THE PRELIMINARY CONTEST A COUPLE OF DAYS AGO AND TODAY'S FINAL SELECTION!

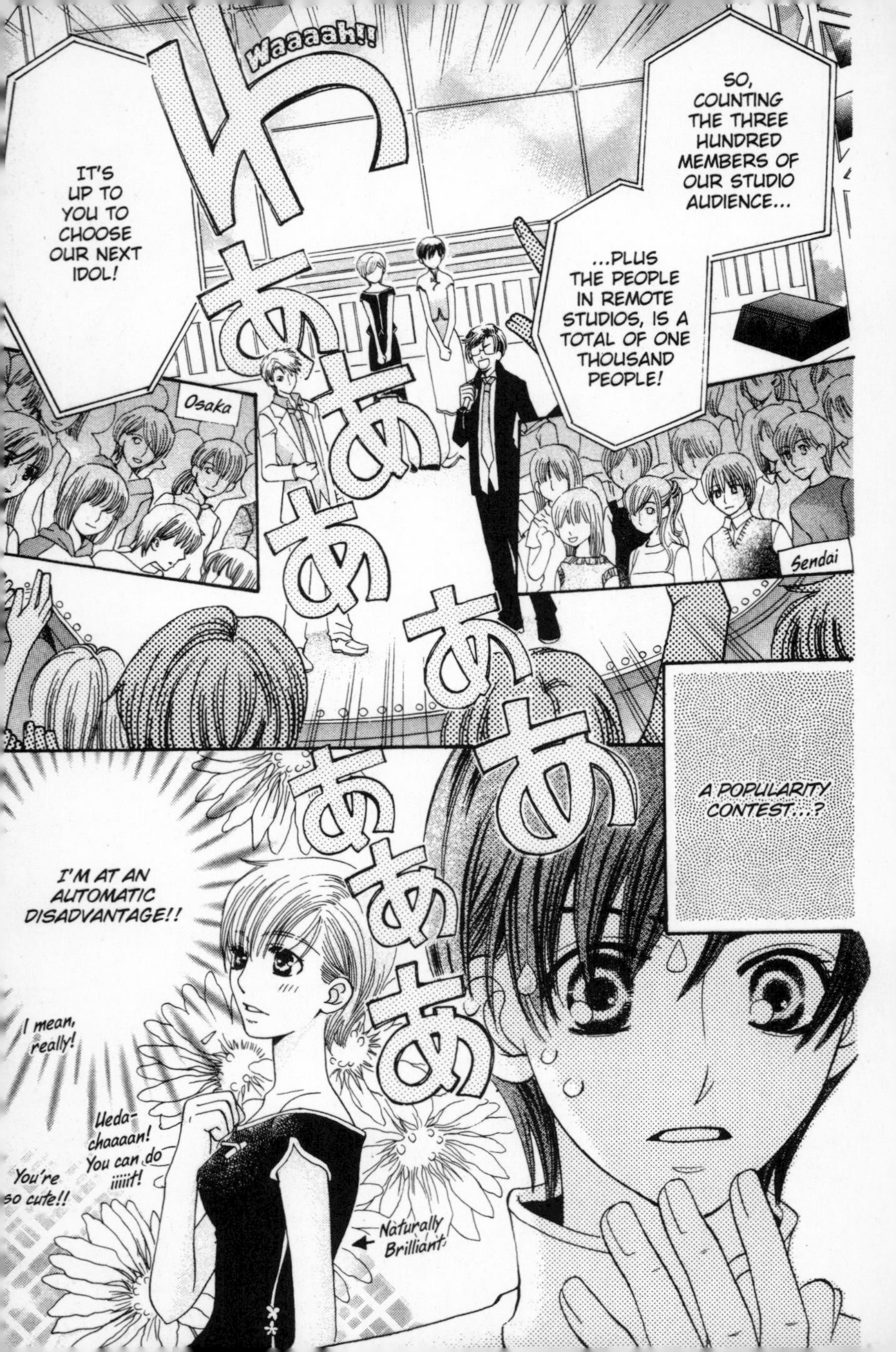
SO, COUNTING THE THREE HUNDRED MEMBERS OF OUR STUDIO AUDIENCE...
...PLUS THE PEOPLE IN REMOTE STUDIOS, IS A TOTAL OF ONE THOUSAND PEOPLE!
IT'S UP TO YOU TO CHOOSE OUR NEXT IDOL!
Waaaah!!
Sendai
Osaka
A POPULARITY CONTEST...?
I'M AT AN AUTOMATIC DISADVANTAGE!!
I mean, really!
Ueda-chaaaan! You can do iiiiit!
You're so cute!!
Naturally Brilliant

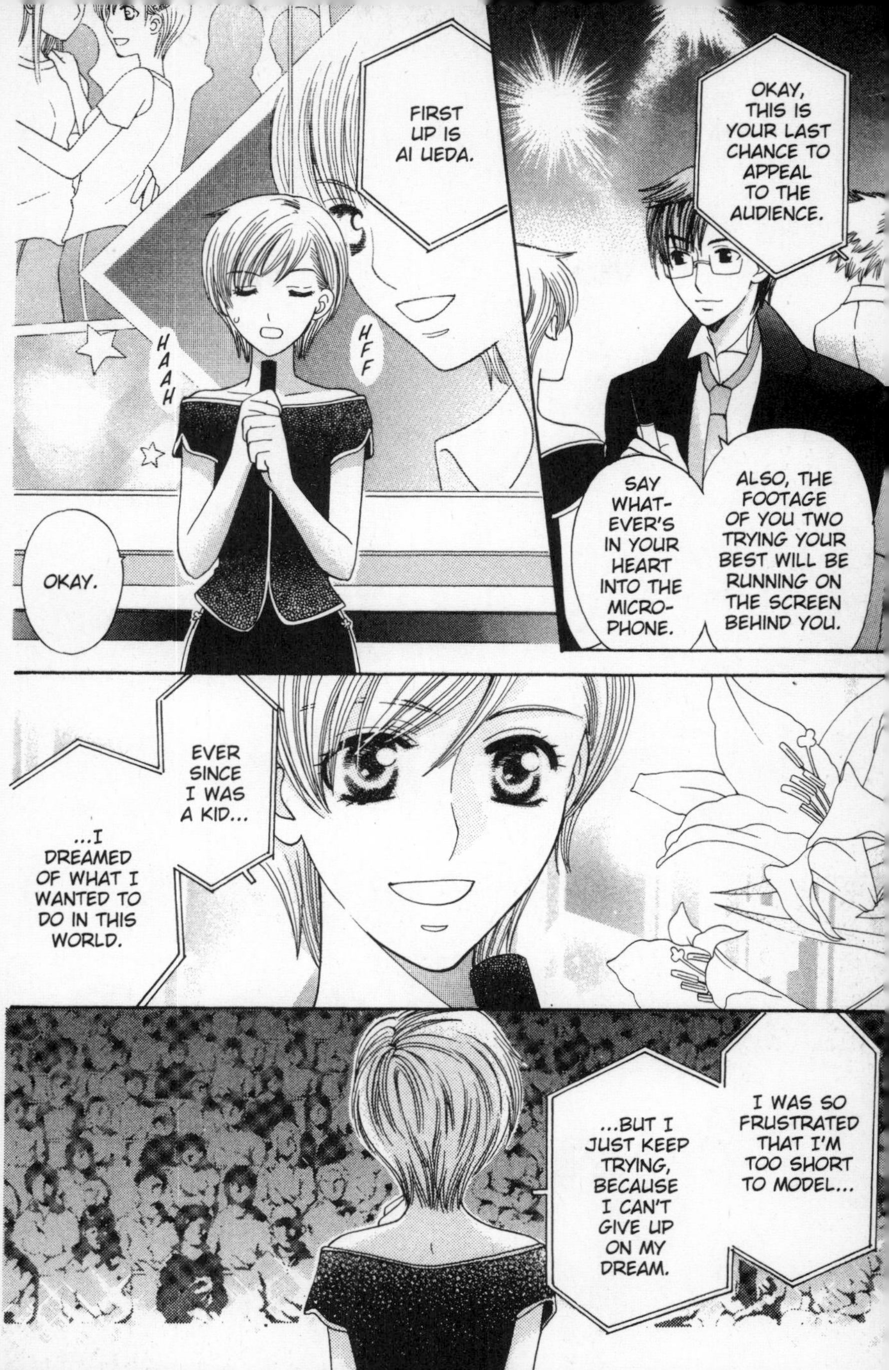
OKAY, THIS IS YOUR LAST CHANCE TO APPEAL TO THE AUDIENCE.
ALSO, THE FOOTAGE OF YOU TWO TRYING YOUR BEST WILL BE RUNNING ON THE SCREEN BEHIND YOU.
SAY WHAT-EVER'S IN YOUR HEART INTO THE MICRO-PHONE.
FIRST UP IS AI UEDA.
HFF
HAAH
OKAY.
EVER SINCE I WAS A KID...
...I DREAMED OF WHAT I WANTED TO DO IN THIS WORLD.
I WAS SO FRUSTRATED THAT I'M TOO SHORT TO MODEL...
...BUT I JUST KEEP TRYING, BECAUSE I CAN'T GIVE UP ON MY DREAM.

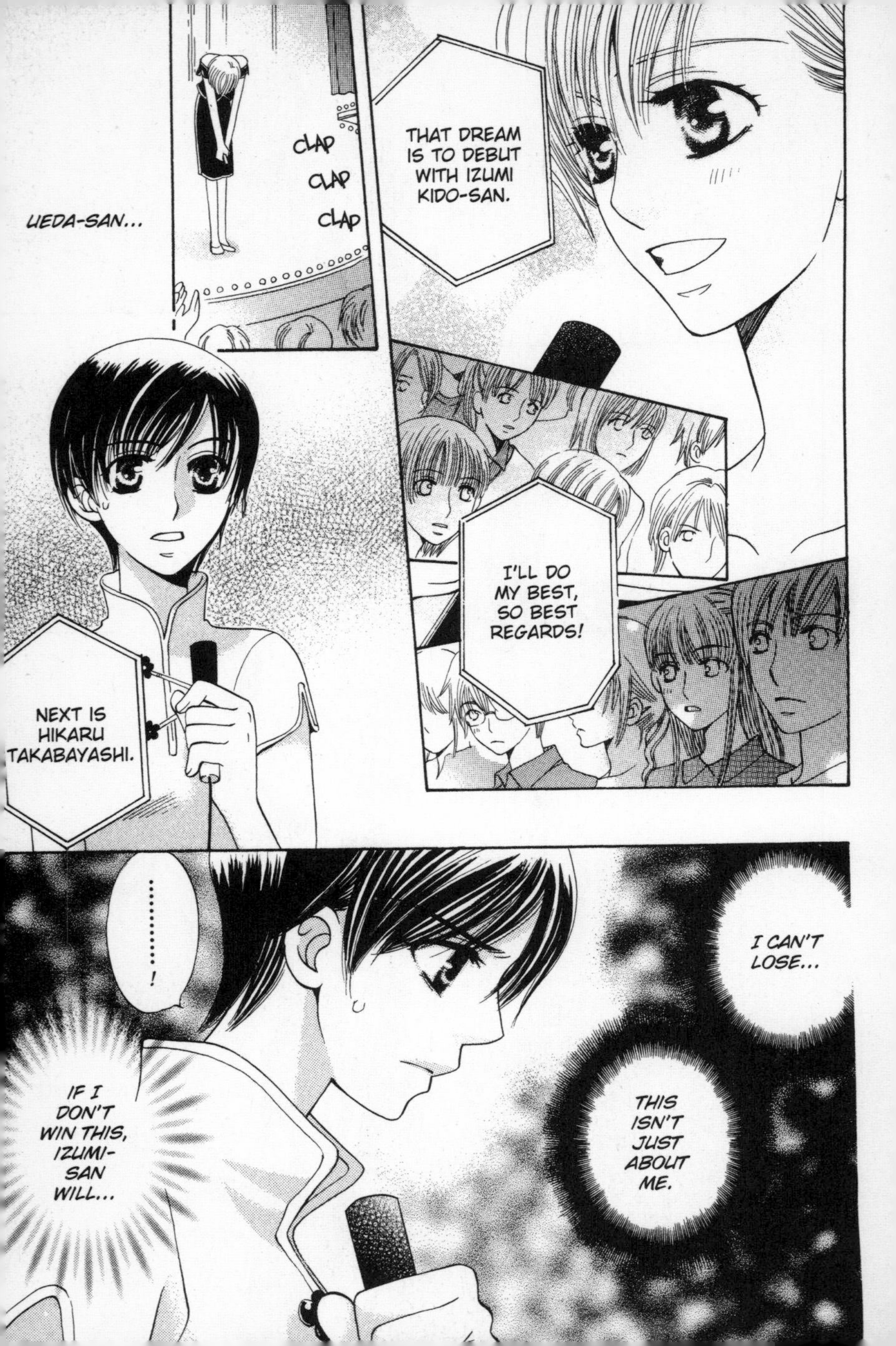
THAT DREAM IS TO DEBUT WITH IZUMI KIDO-SAN.
I'LL DO MY BEST, SO BEST REGARDS!
CLAP
CLAP
CLAP
UEDA-SAN...
NEXT IS HIKARU TAKABAYASHI.
I CAN'T LOSE...
THIS ISN'T JUST ABOUT ME.
......!
IF I DON'T WIN THIS, IZUMI-SAN WILL...

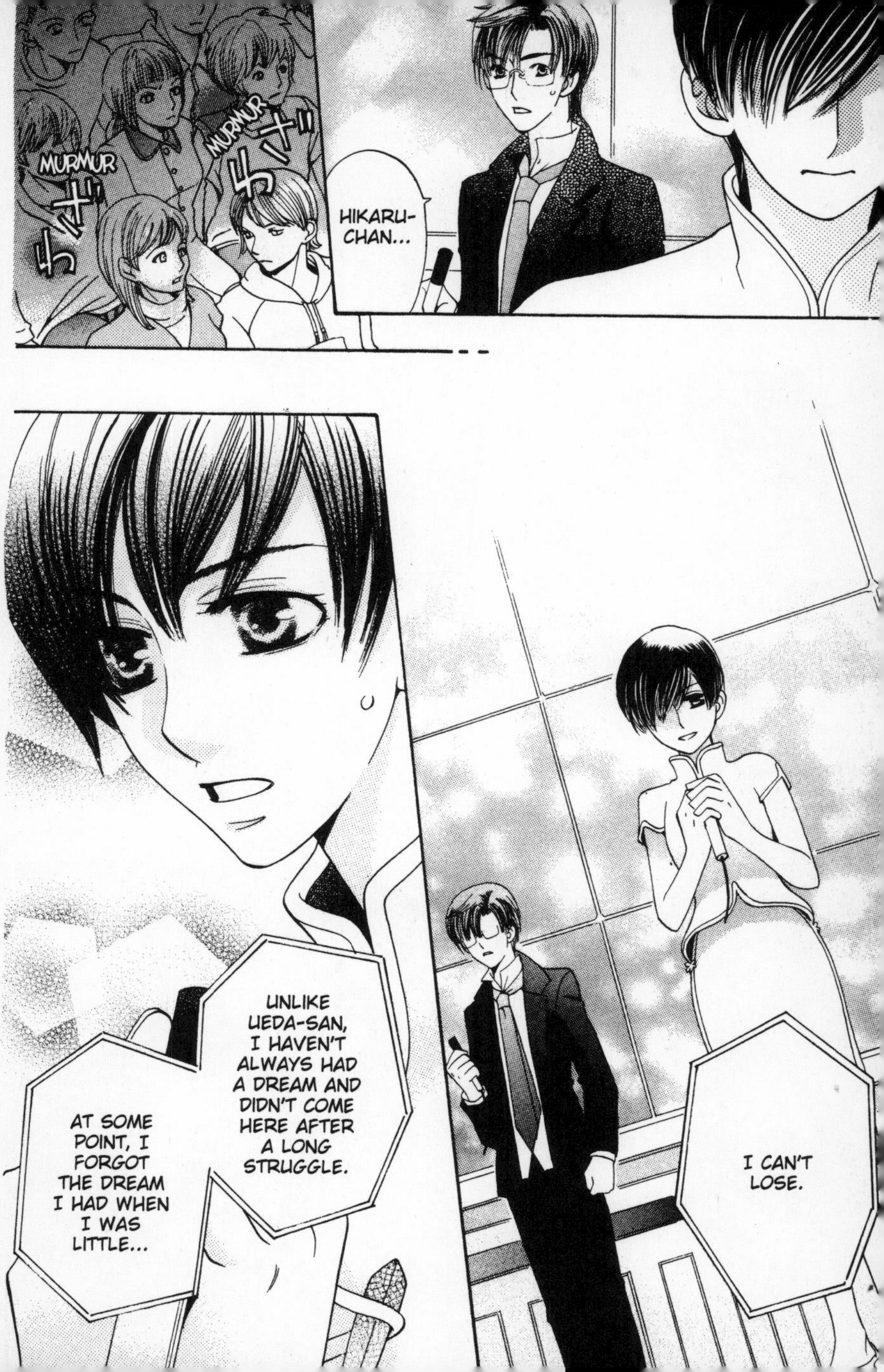
HIKARU-CHAN...
MURMUR
ざわ
MURMUR
ざわ
UNLIKE UEDA-SAN, I HAVEN'T ALWAYS HAD A DREAM AND DIDN'T COME HERE AFTER A LONG STRUGGLE.
AT SOME POINT, I FORGOT THE DREAM I HAD WHEN I WAS LITTLE...
I CAN'T LOSE.

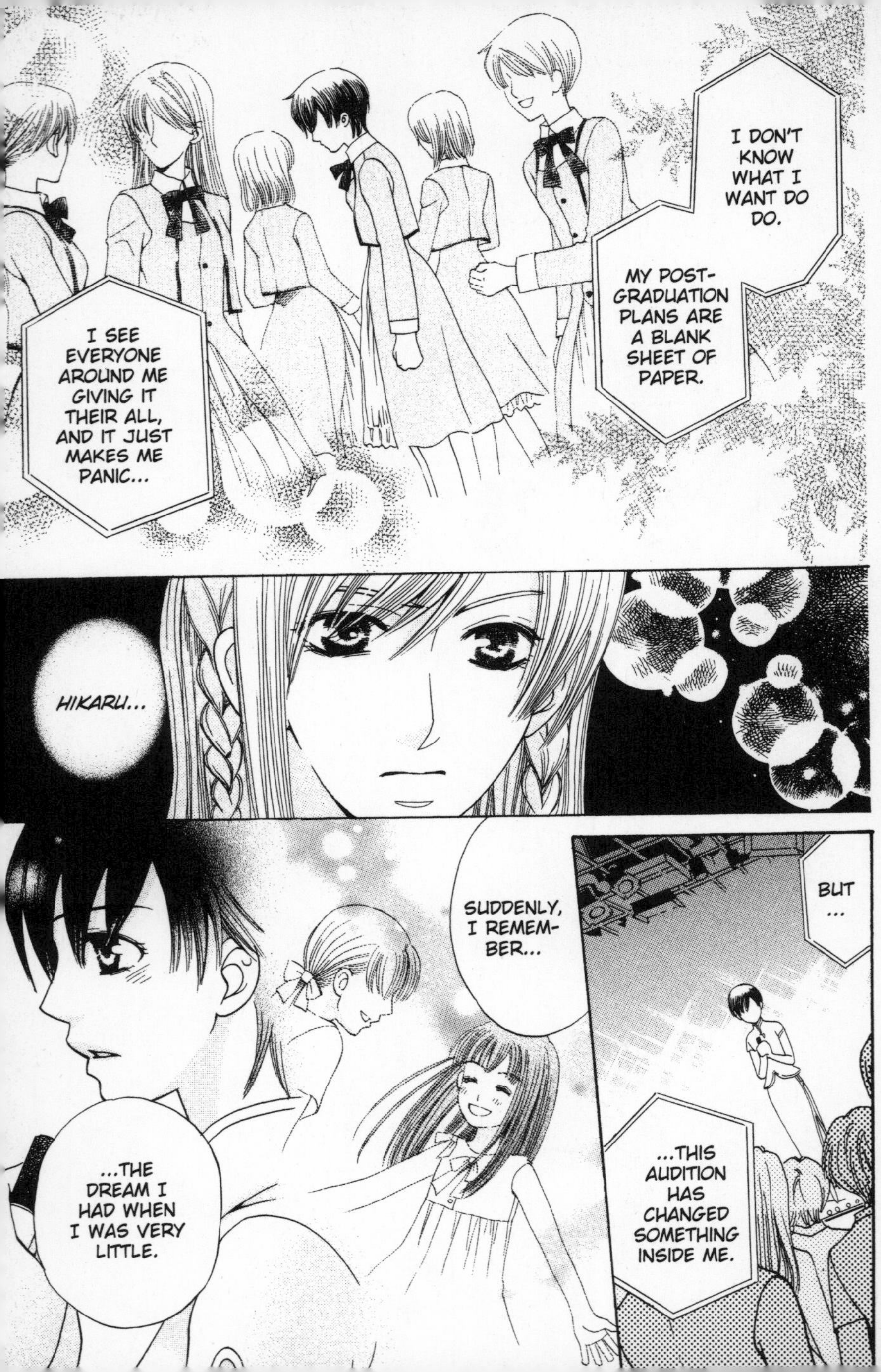
I DON'T KNOW WHAT I WANT DO DO.
MY POST-GRADUATION PLANS ARE A BLANK SHEET OF PAPER.
I SEE EVERYONE AROUND ME GIVING IT THEIR ALL, AND IT JUST MAKES ME PANIC...
HIKARU...
BUT ...
...THIS AUDITION HAS CHANGED SOMETHING INSIDE ME.
SUDDENLY, I REMEMBER...
...THE DREAM I HAD WHEN I WAS VERY LITTLE.

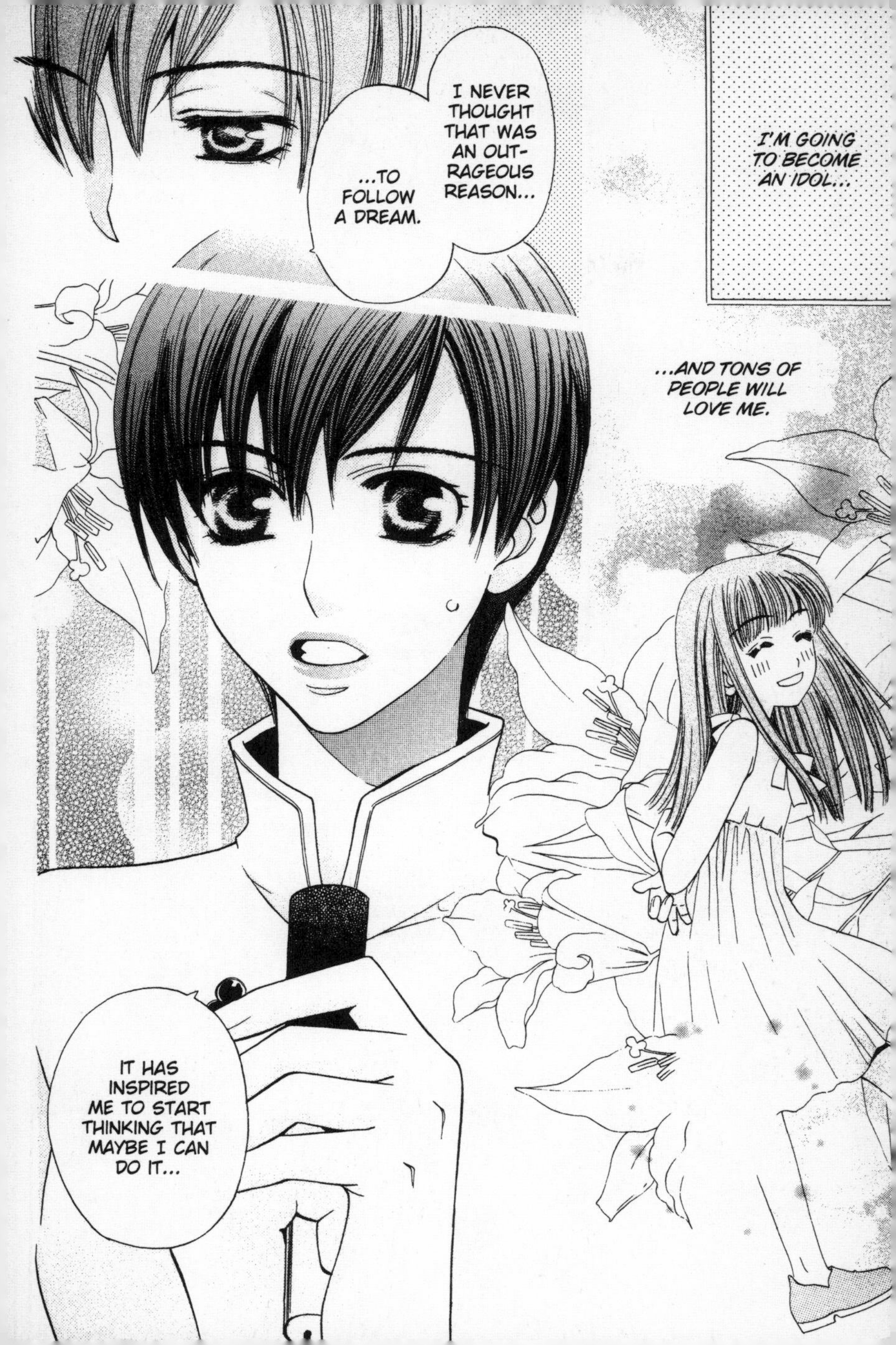
I'M GOING TO BECOME AN IDOL...
I NEVER THOUGHT THAT WAS AN OUTRAGEOUS REASON... ...TO FOLLOW A DREAM.
...AND TONS OF PEOPLE WILL LOVE ME.
IT HAS INSPIRED ME TO START THINKING THAT MAYBE I CAN DO IT...

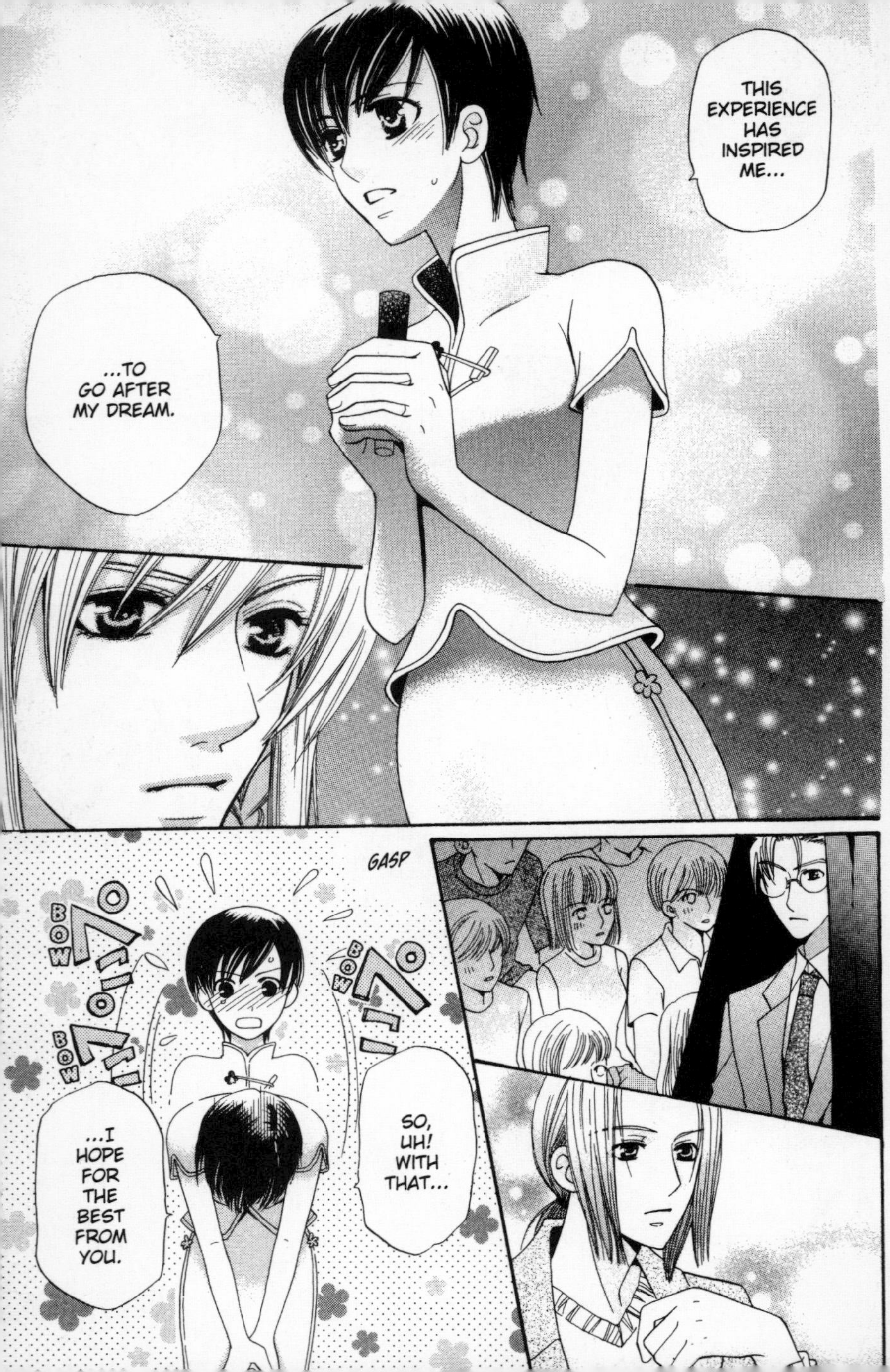
THIS EXPERIENCE HAS INSPIRED ME...
...TO GO AFTER MY DREAM.
GASP
BOW
BOW
BOW
SO, UH! WITH THAT...
...I HOPE FOR THE BEST FROM YOU.

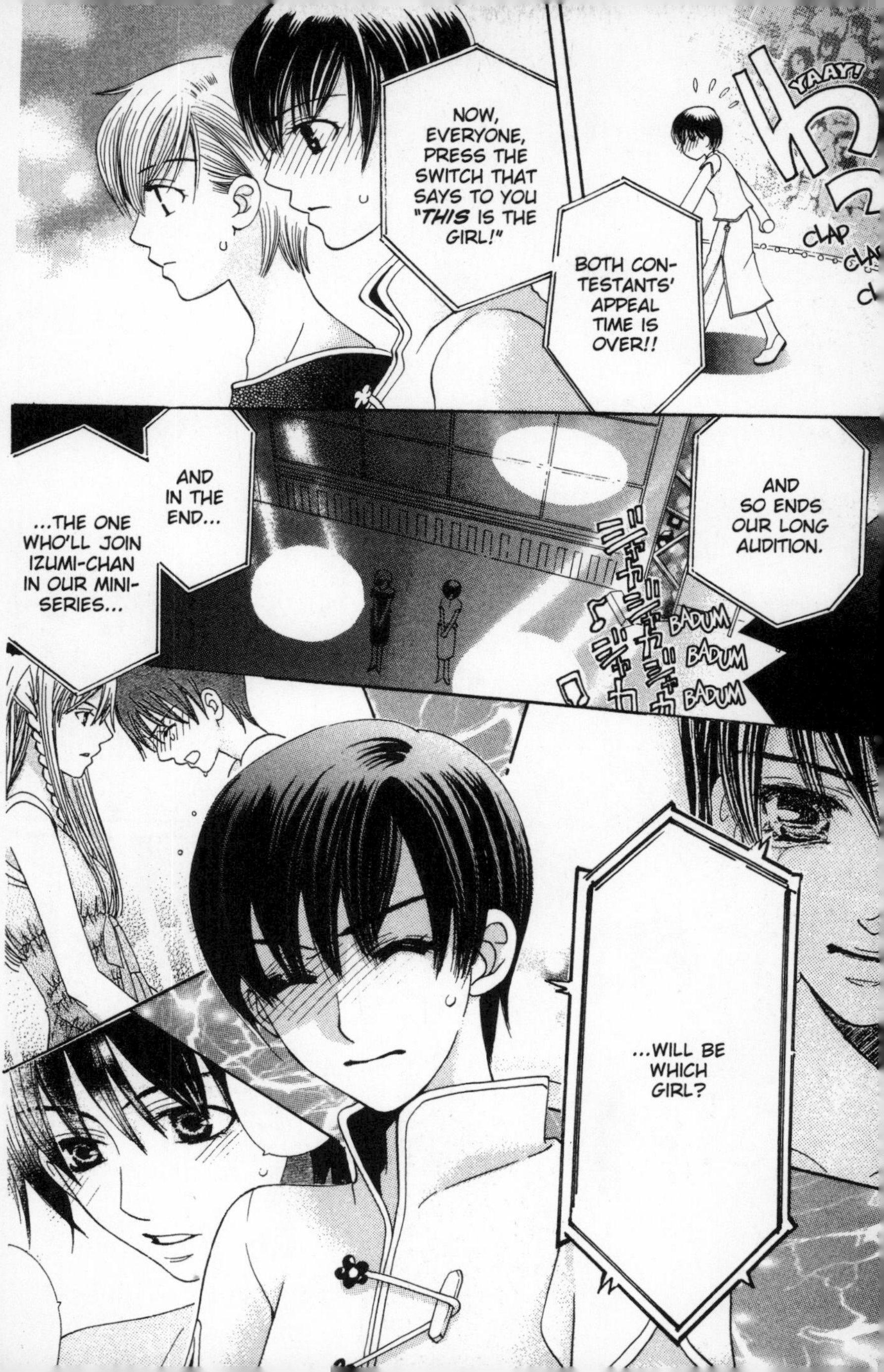
YAAY!
CLAP CLAP CLAP
BOTH CON-TESTANTS' APPEAL TIME IS OVER!!
NOW, EVERYONE, PRESS THE SWITCH THAT SAYS TO YOU "*THIS* IS THE GIRL!"
AND SO ENDS OUR LONG AUDITION.
BADUM BADUM BADUM
AND IN THE END...
...THE ONE WHO'LL JOIN IZUMI-CHAN IN OUR MINI-SERIES...
...WILL BE WHICH GIRL?

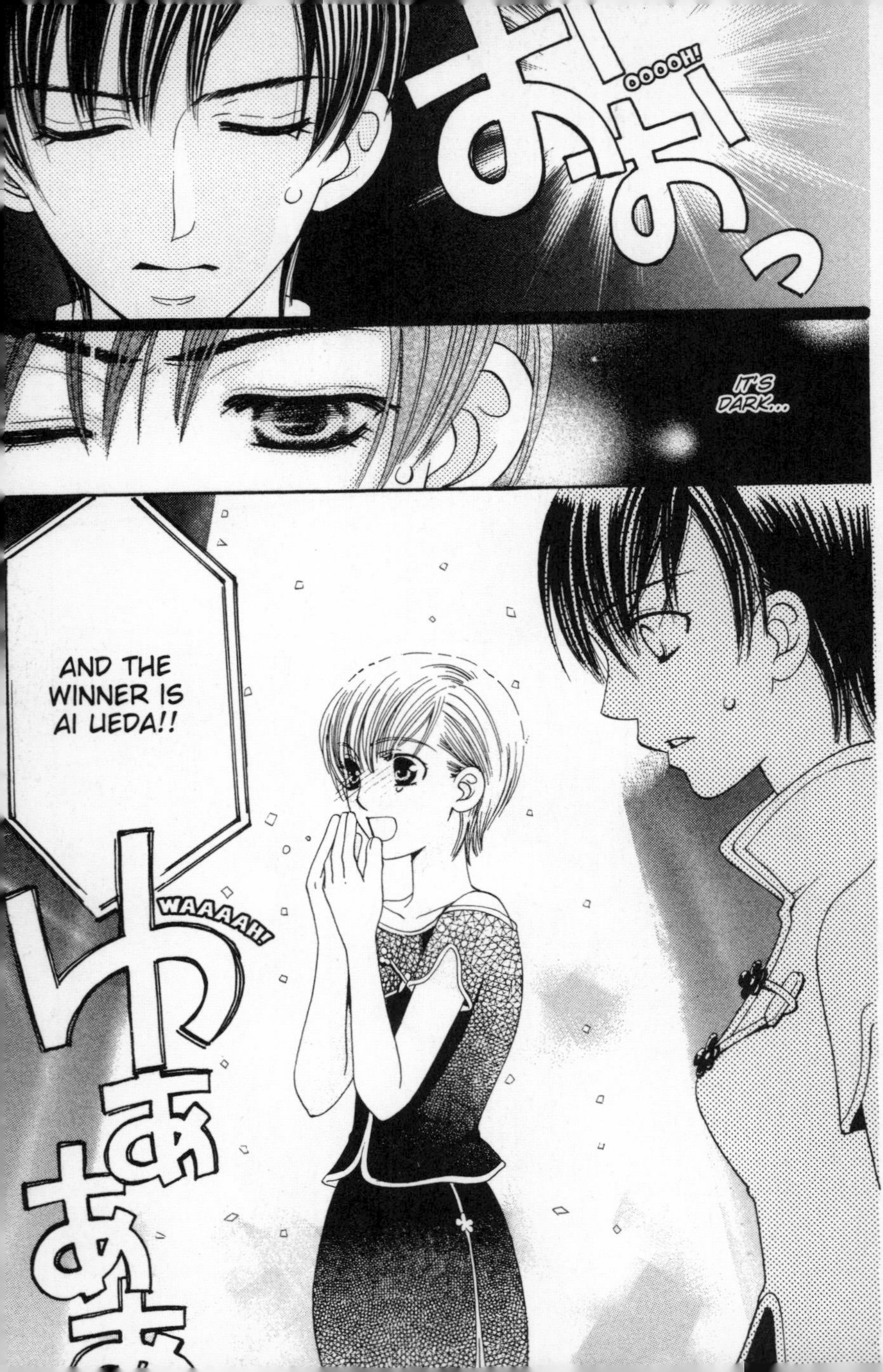
おおっ
OOOOH!
IT'S DARK...
AND THE WINNER IS AI UEDA!!
わああ
WAAAAH!

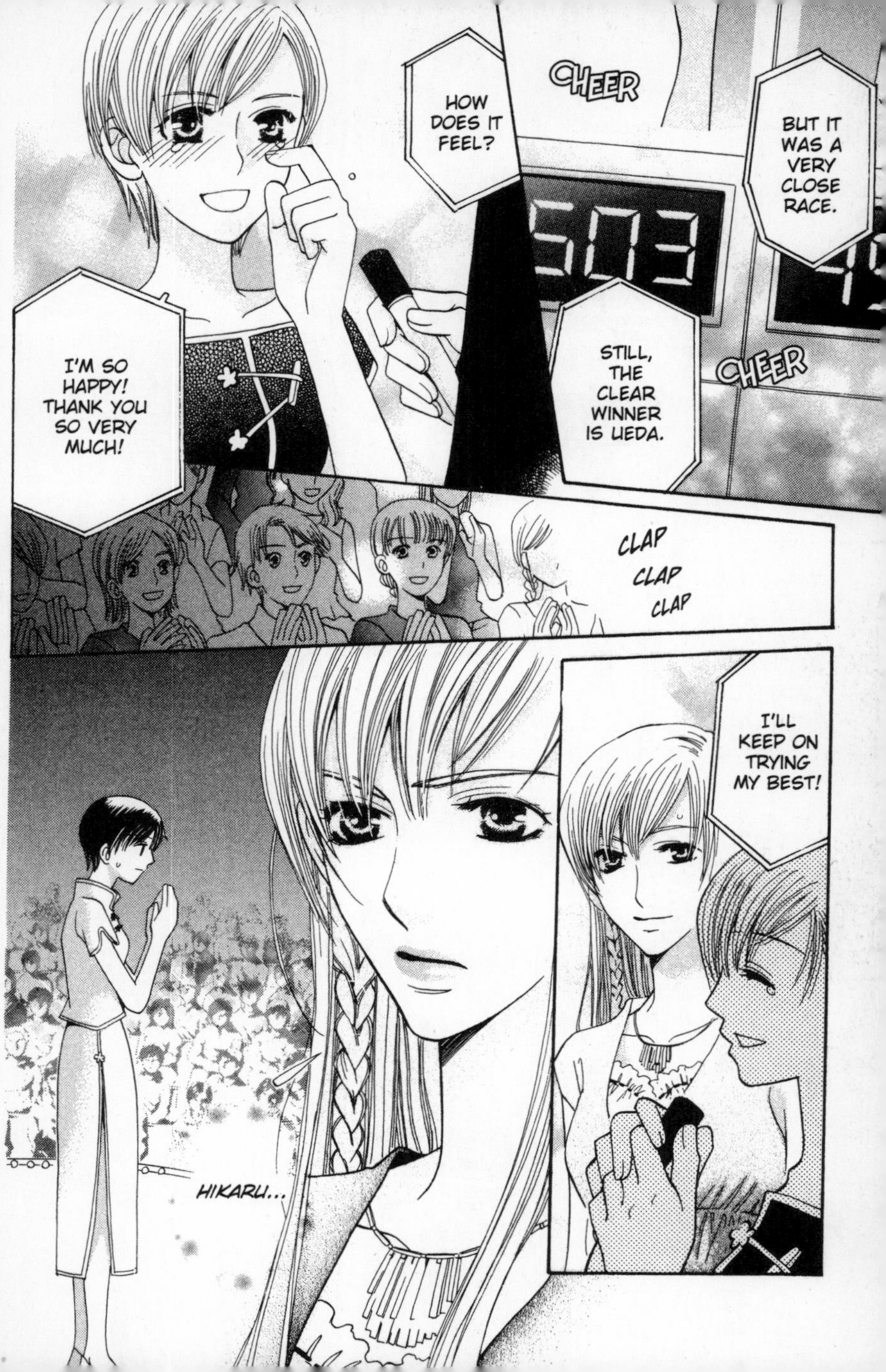
CHEER
BUT IT WAS A VERY CLOSE RACE.
STILL, THE CLEAR WINNER IS UEDA.
CHEER
HOW DOES IT FEEL?
I'M SO HAPPY! THANK YOU SO VERY MUCH!
CLAP CLAP CLAP
I'LL KEEP ON TRYING MY BEST!
HIKARU...

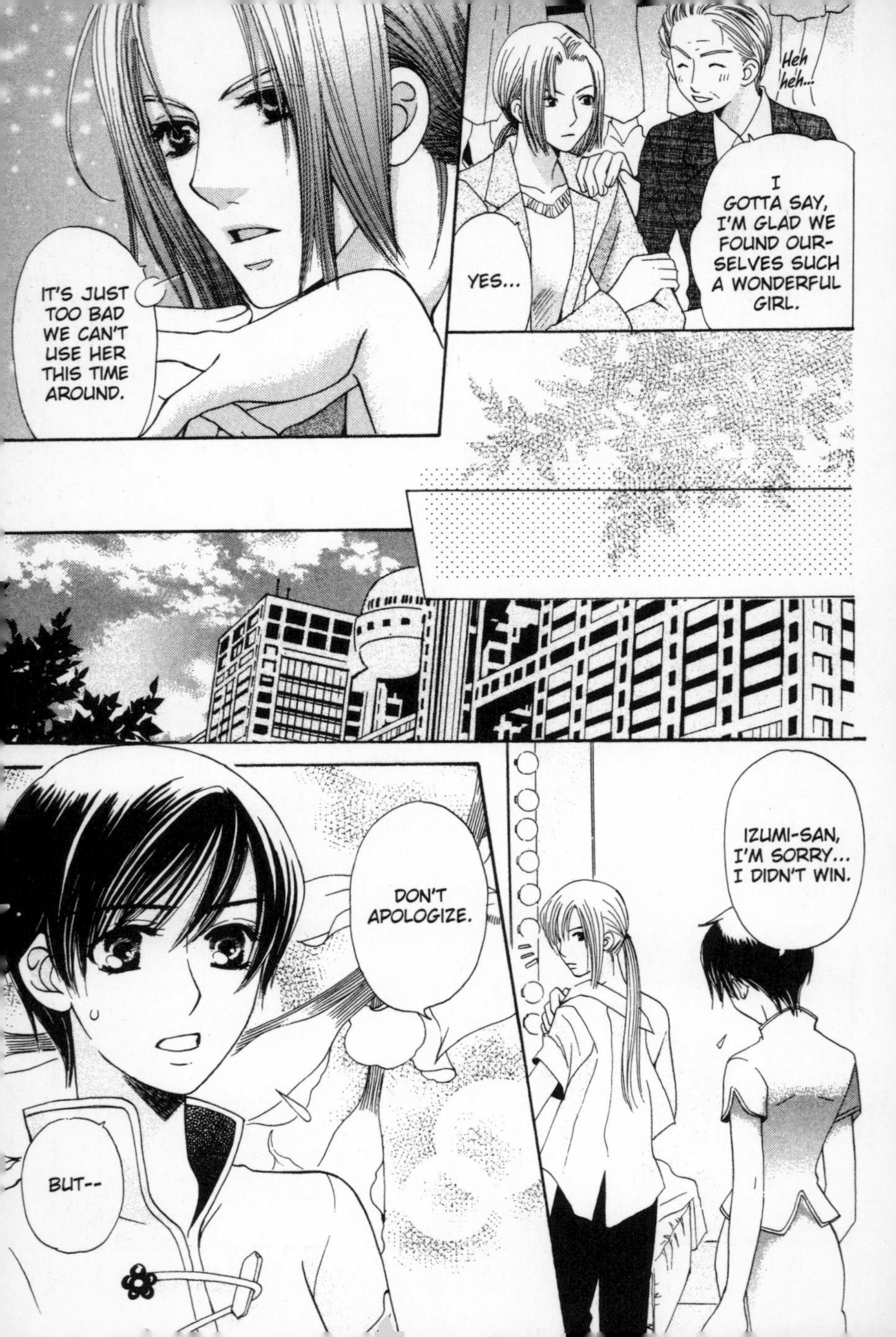
Heh heh...
I GOTTA SAY, I'M GLAD WE FOUND OURSELVES SUCH A WONDERFUL GIRL.
YES...
IT'S JUST TOO BAD WE CAN'T USE HER THIS TIME AROUND.
IZUMI-SAN, I'M SORRY... I DIDN'T WIN.
DON'T APOLOGIZE.
BUT--

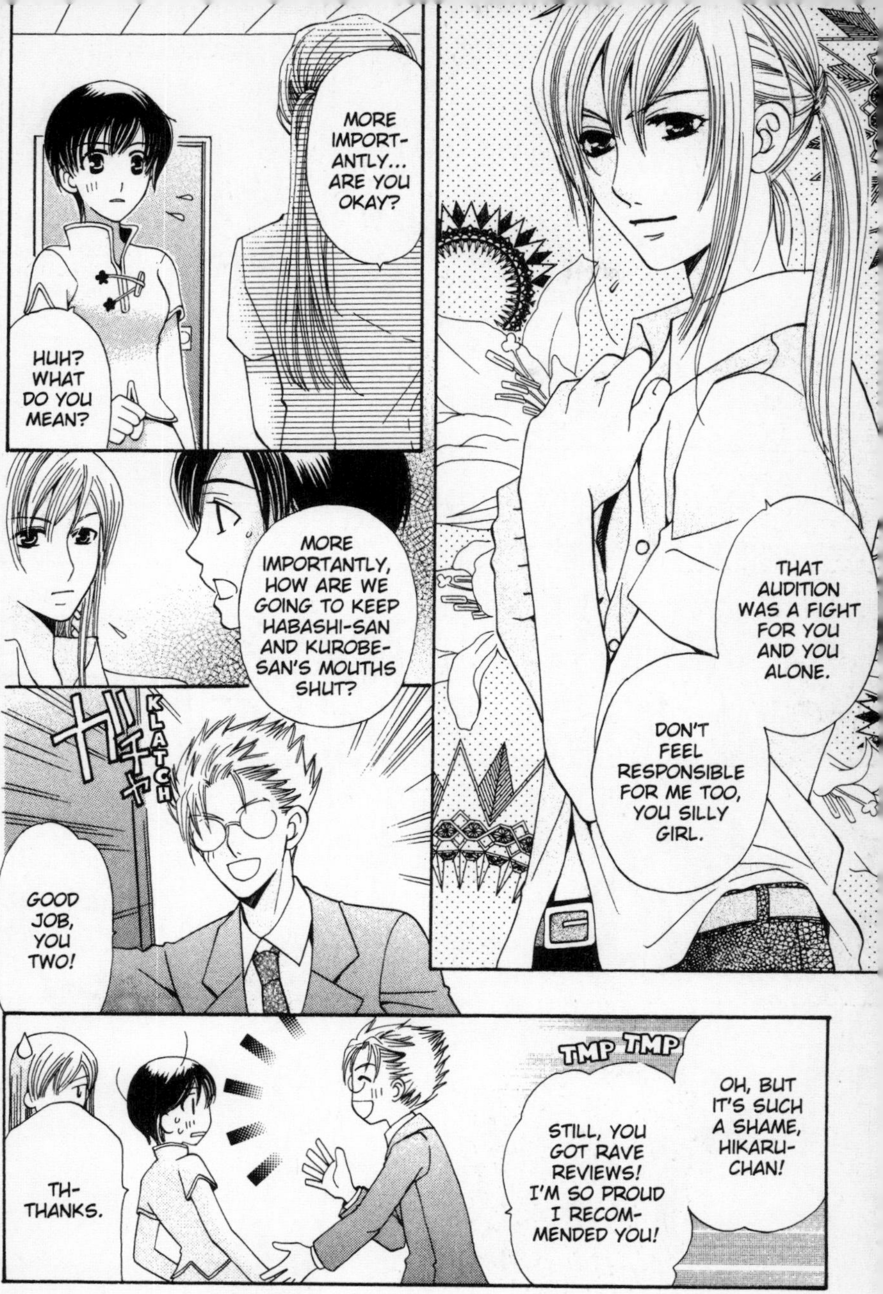
THAT AUDITION WAS A FIGHT FOR YOU AND YOU ALONE.
DON'T FEEL RESPONSIBLE FOR ME TOO, YOU SILLY GIRL.
MORE IMPORT-ANTLY... ARE YOU OKAY?
HUH? WHAT DO YOU MEAN?
MORE IMPORTANTLY, HOW ARE WE GOING TO KEEP HABASHI-SAN AND KUROBE-SAN'S MOUTHS SHUT?
ガチャ
KLATCH
GOOD JOB, YOU TWO!
OH, BUT IT'S SUCH A SHAME, HIKARU-CHAN!
TMP TMP
STILL, YOU GOT RAVE REVIEWS! I'M SO PROUD I RECOMMENDED YOU!
TH-THANKS.

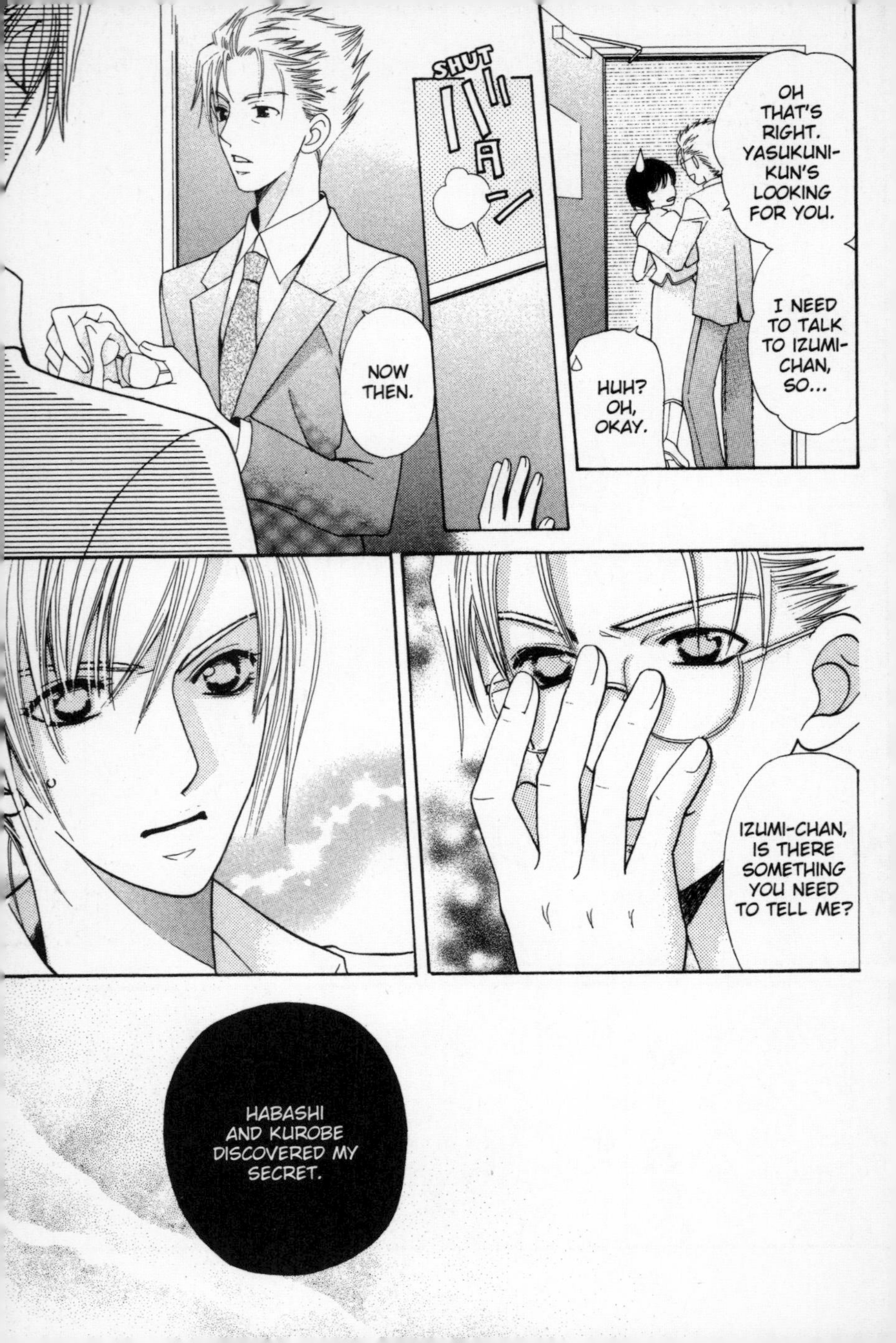
OH THAT'S RIGHT. YASUKUNI-KUN'S LOOKING FOR YOU.
I NEED TO TALK TO IZUMI-CHAN, SO...
HUH? OH, OKAY.
SHUT
NOW THEN.
IZUMI-CHAN, IS THERE SOMETHING YOU NEED TO TELL ME?
HABASHI AND KUROBE DISCOVERED MY SECRET.

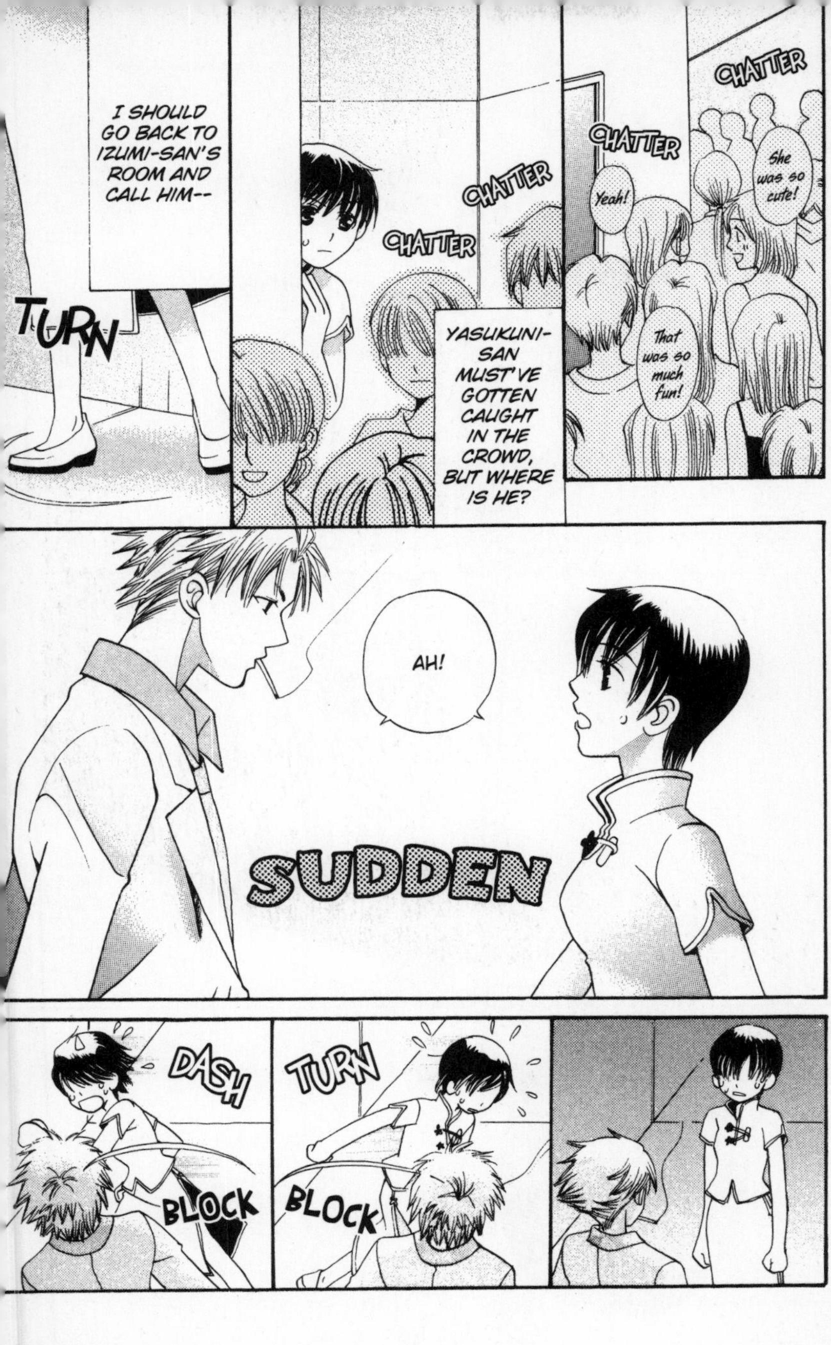
CHATTER
CHATTER
She was so cute!
Yeah!
That was so much fun!
CHATTER
CHATTER
YASUKUNI-SAN MUST'VE GOTTEN CAUGHT IN THE CROWD, BUT WHERE IS HE?
I SHOULD GO BACK TO IZUMI-SAN'S ROOM AND CALL HIM--
TURN
AH!
SUDDEN
TURN
BLOCK
DASH
BLOCK

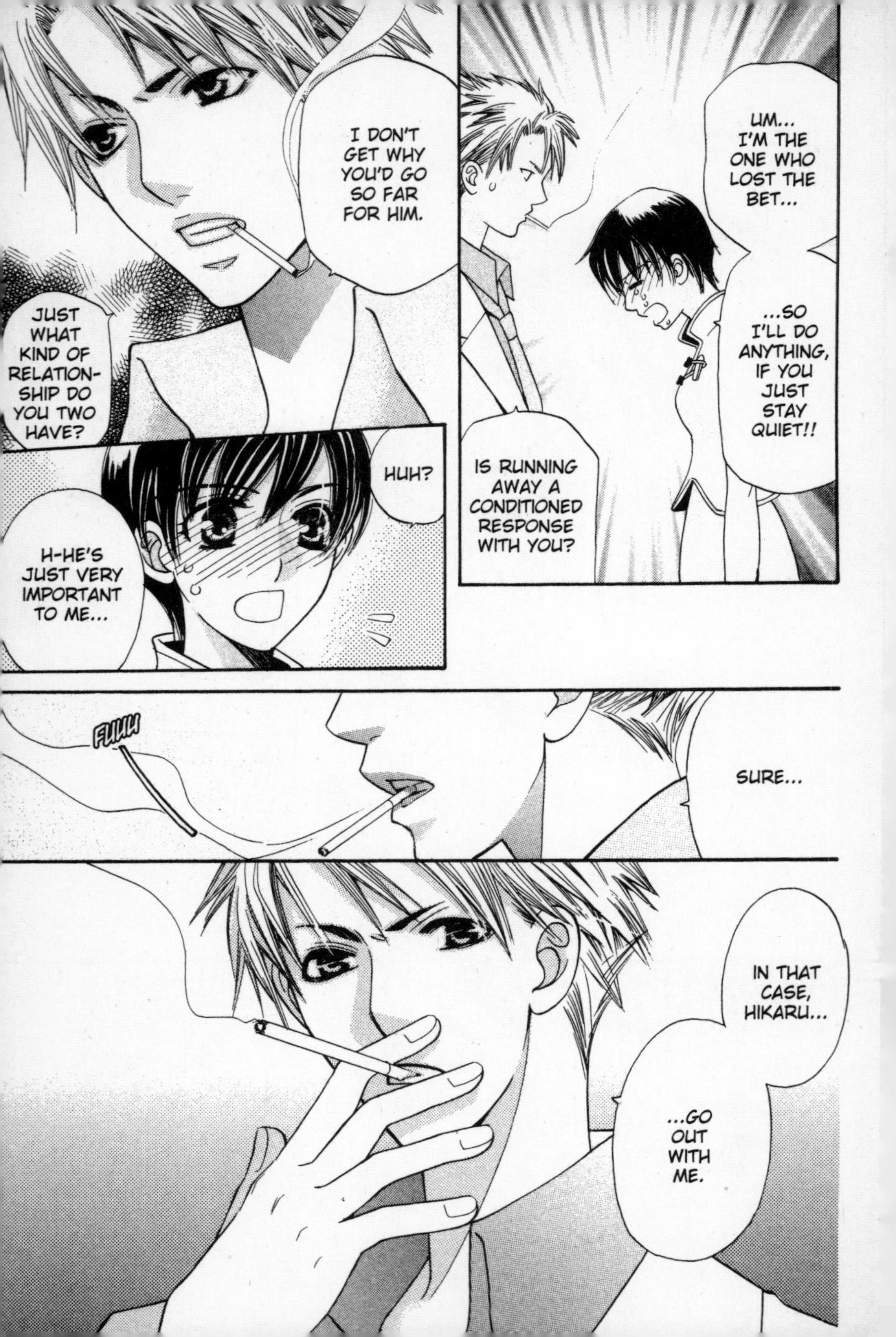
UM... I'M THE ONE WHO LOST THE BET...
...SO I'LL DO ANYTHING, IF YOU JUST STAY QUIET!!
IS RUNNING AWAY A CONDITIONED RESPONSE WITH YOU?
I DON'T GET WHY YOU'D GO SO FAR FOR HIM.
JUST WHAT KIND OF RELATION-SHIP DO YOU TWO HAVE?
HUH?
H-HE'S JUST VERY IMPORTANT TO ME...
SURE...
FUUU
IN THAT CASE, HIKARU...
...GO OUT WITH ME.

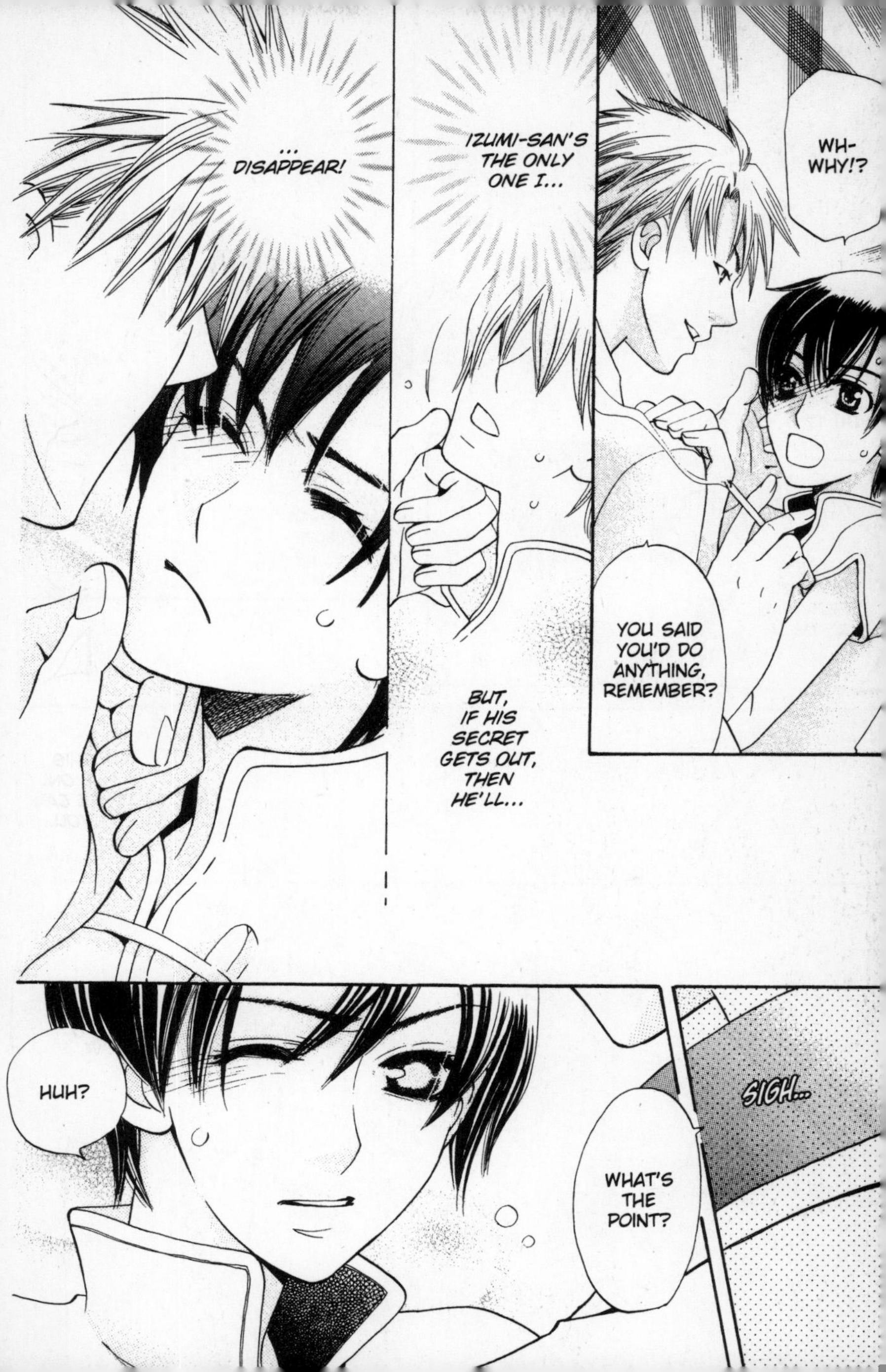
WH- WHY!?
YOU SAID YOU'D DO ANYTHING, REMEMBER?
IZUMI-SAN'S THE ONLY ONE I...
BUT, IF HIS SECRET GETS OUT, THEN HE'LL...
... DISAPPEAR!
SIGH...
WHAT'S THE POINT?
HUH?

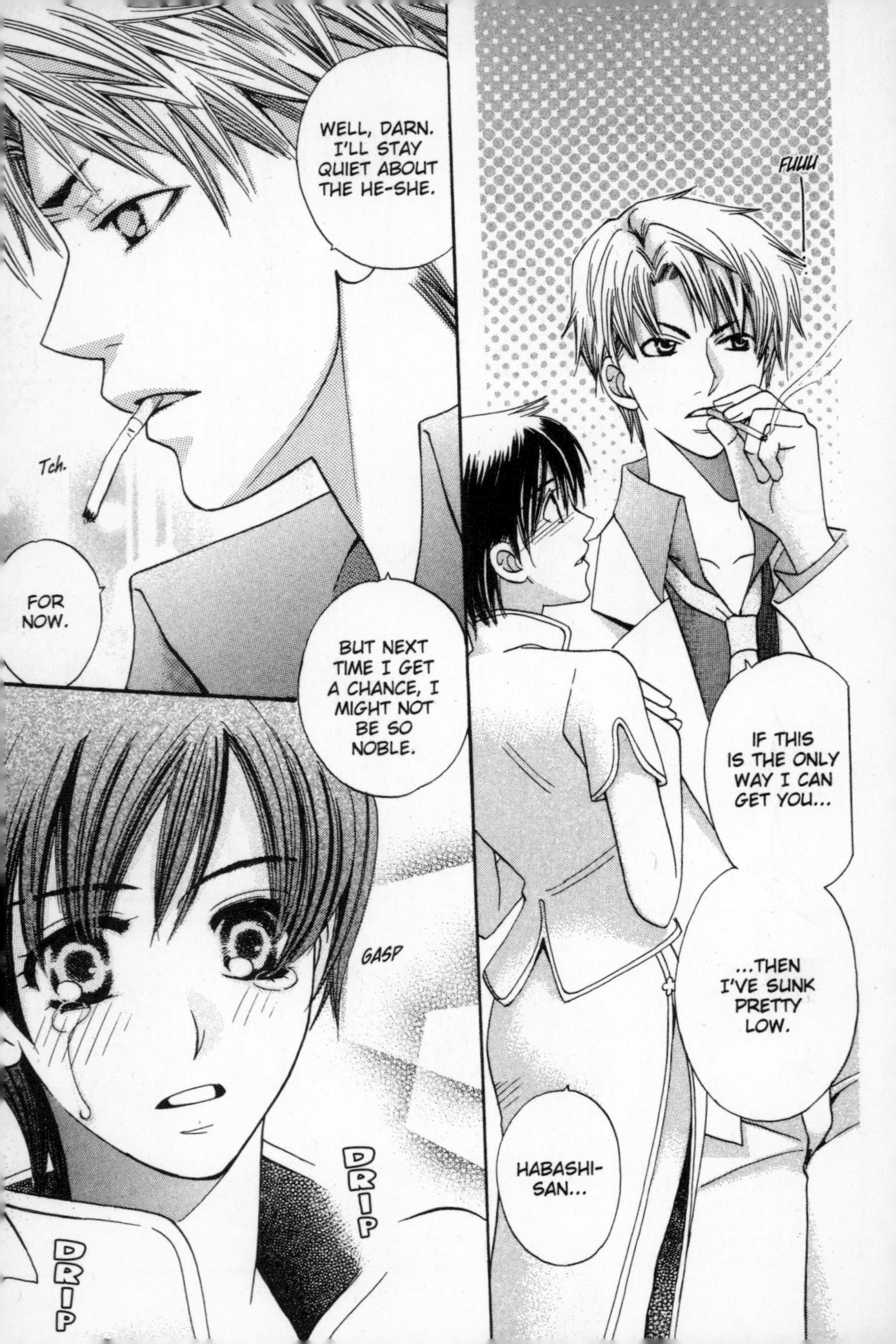
FUUU
IF THIS IS THE ONLY WAY I CAN GET YOU...
...THEN I'VE SUNK PRETTY LOW.
HABASHI-SAN...
WELL, DARN. I'LL STAY QUIET ABOUT THE HE-SHE.
Tch.
FOR NOW.
BUT NEXT TIME I GET A CHANCE, I MIGHT NOT BE SO NOBLE.
GASP
DRIP
DRIP

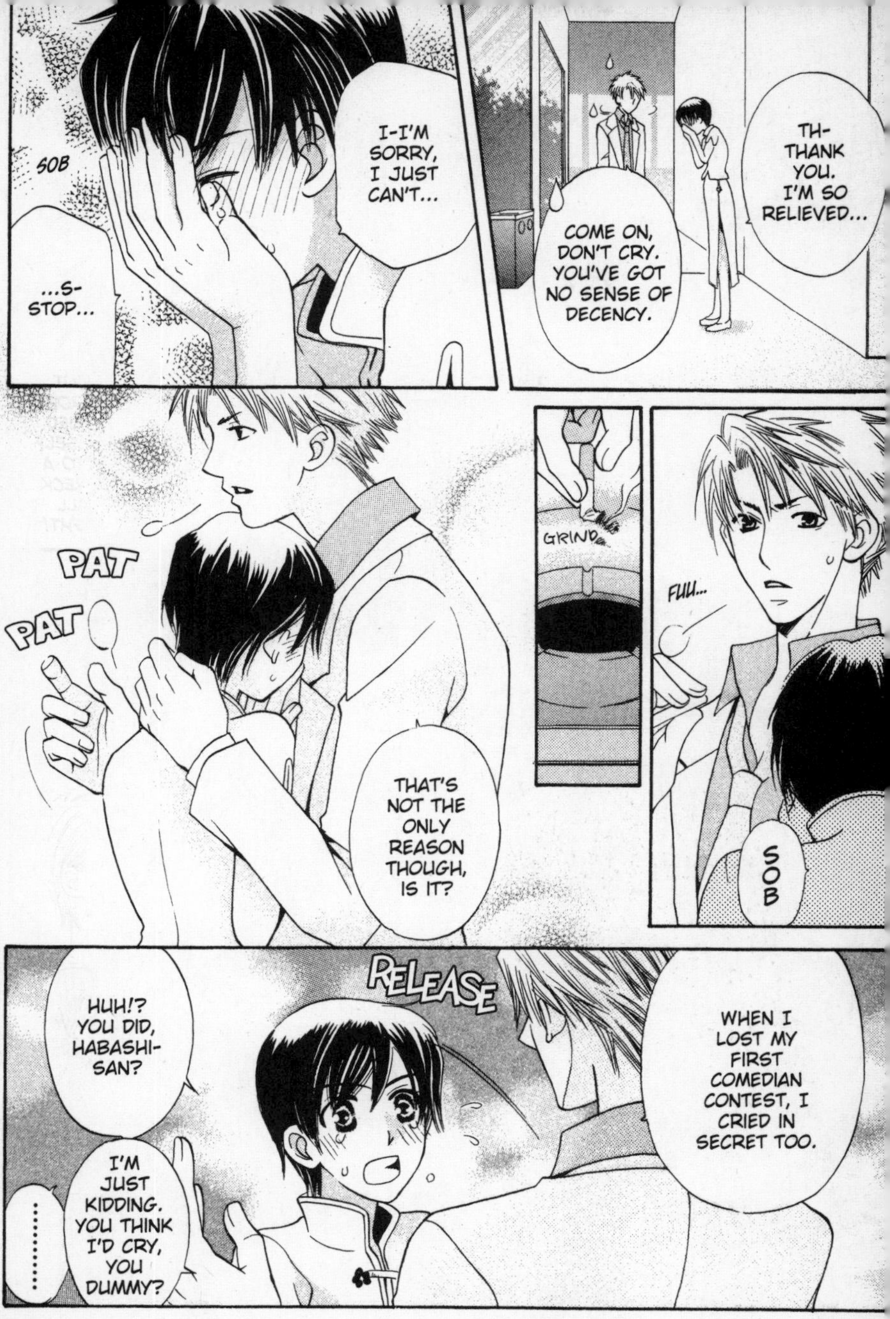
TH-THANK YOU. I'M SO RELIEVED...
COME ON, DON'T CRY. YOU'VE GOT NO SENSE OF DECENCY.
I-I'M SORRY, I JUST CAN'T...
SOB
...S-STOP...
FUU...
SOB
GRIND
PAT
PAT
THAT'S NOT THE ONLY REASON THOUGH, IS IT?
WHEN I LOST MY FIRST COMEDIAN CONTEST, I CRIED IN SECRET TOO.
RELEASE
HUH!? YOU DID, HABASHI-SAN?
I'M JUST KIDDING. YOU THINK I'D CRY, YOU DUMMY?
......

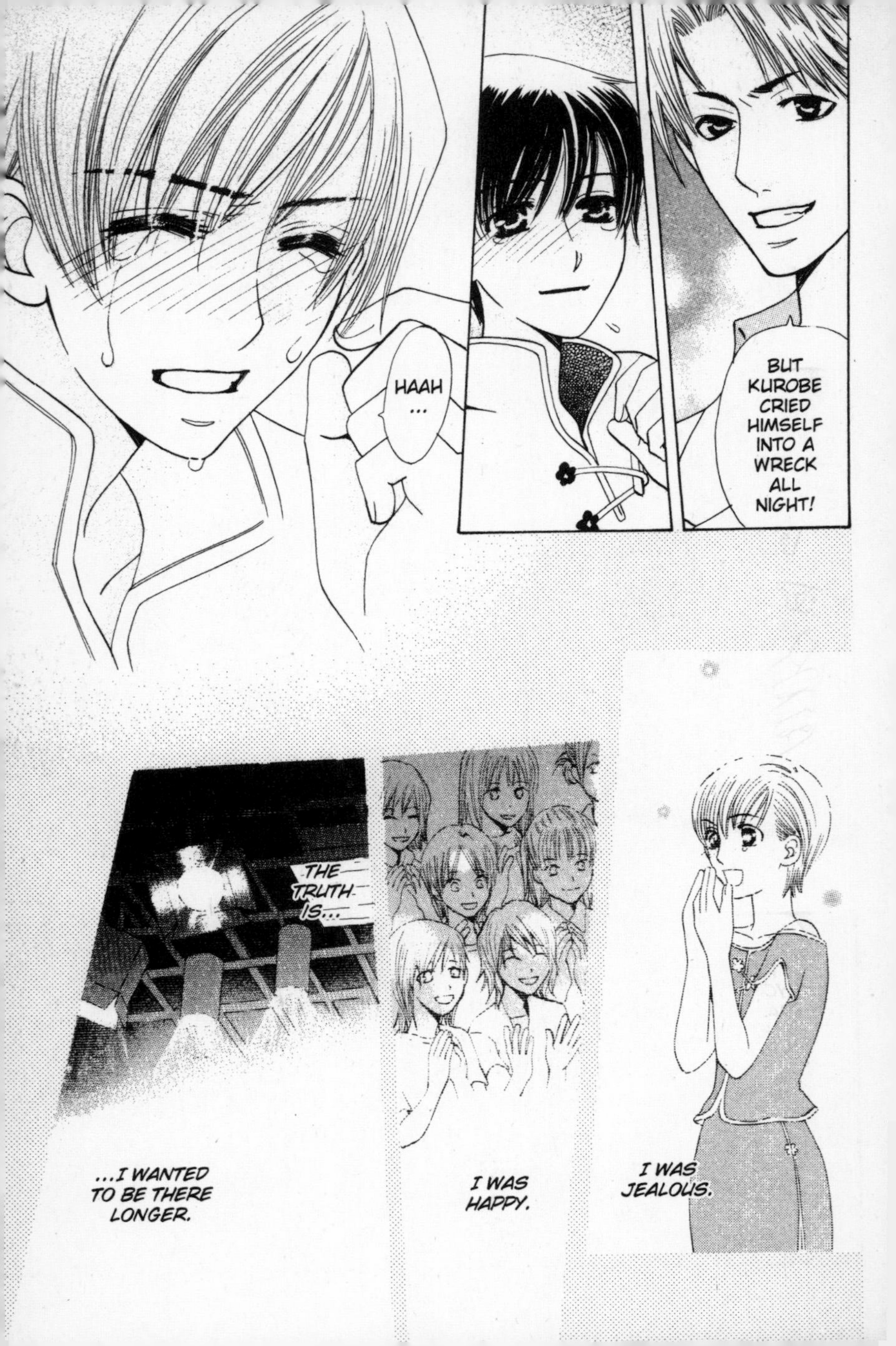
BUT KUROBE CRIED HIMSELF INTO A WRECK ALL NIGHT!
HAAH ...
I WAS JEALOUS.
I WAS HAPPY.
THE TRUTH IS...
...I WANTED TO BE THERE LONGER.

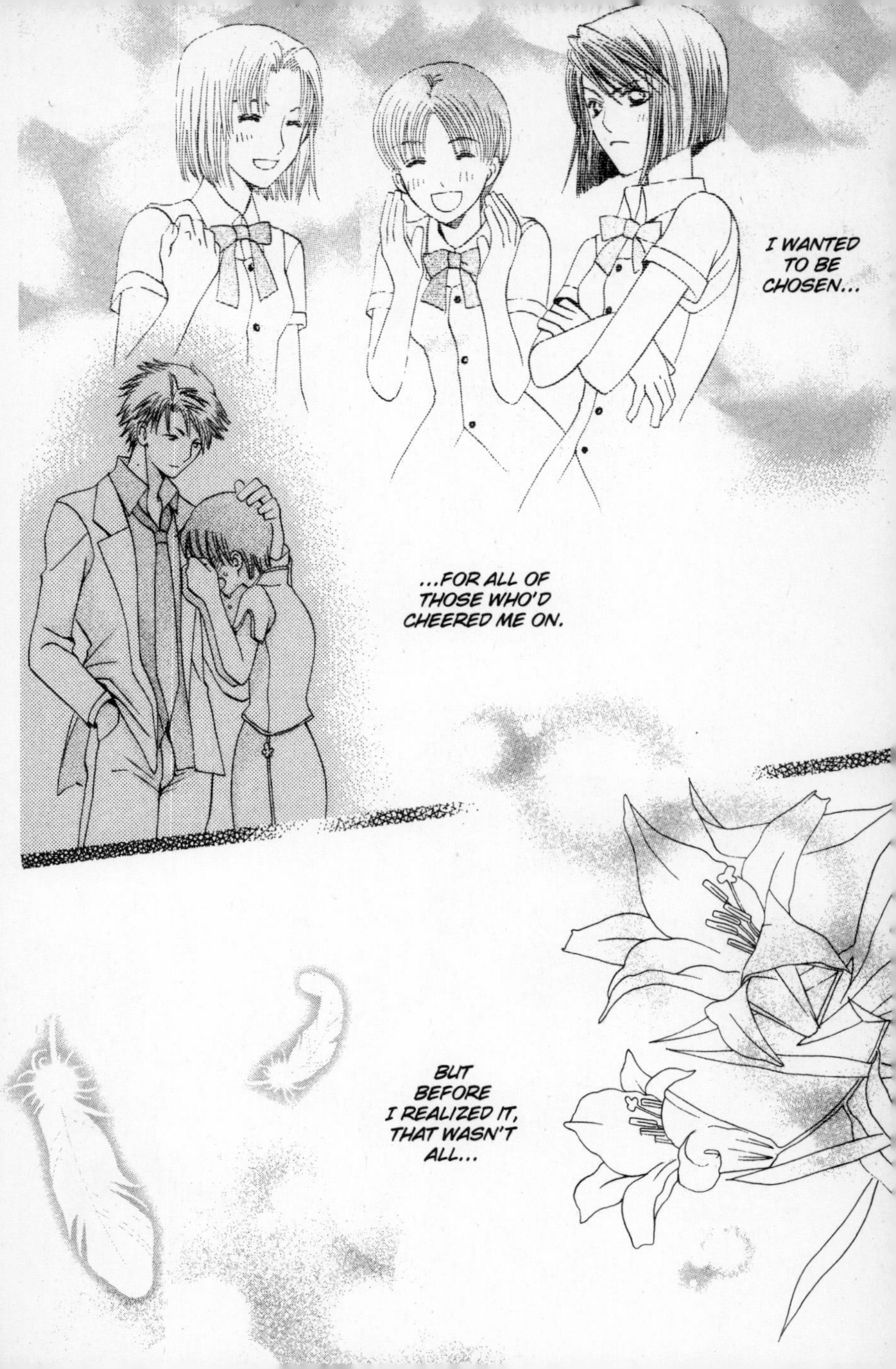
I WANTED TO BE CHOSEN...
...FOR ALL OF THOSE WHO'D CHEERED ME ON.
BUT BEFORE I REALIZED IT, THAT WASN'T ALL...

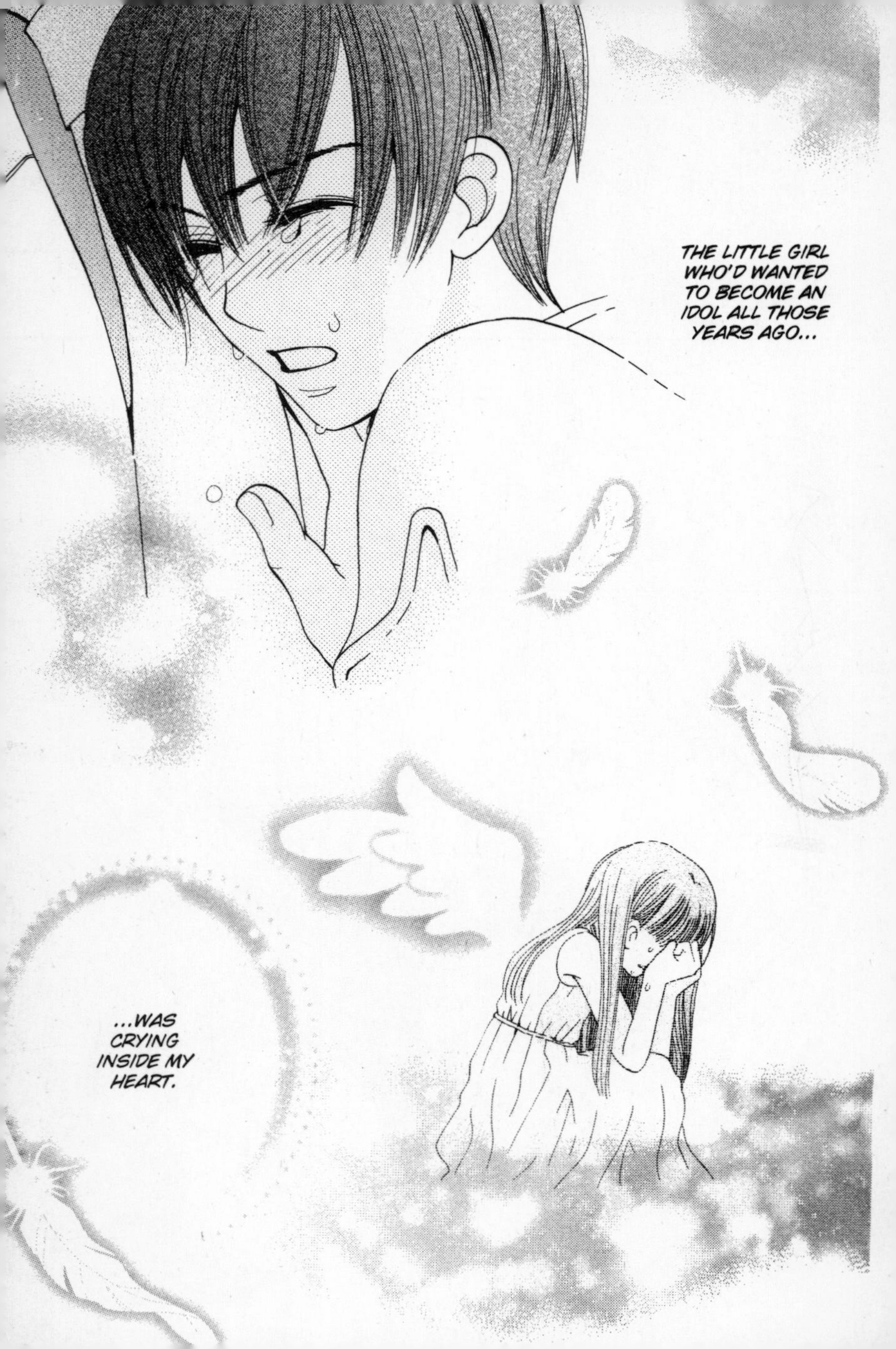
THE LITTLE GIRL WHO'D WANTED TO BECOME AN IDOL ALL THOSE YEARS AGO...
...WAS CRYING INSIDE MY HEART.

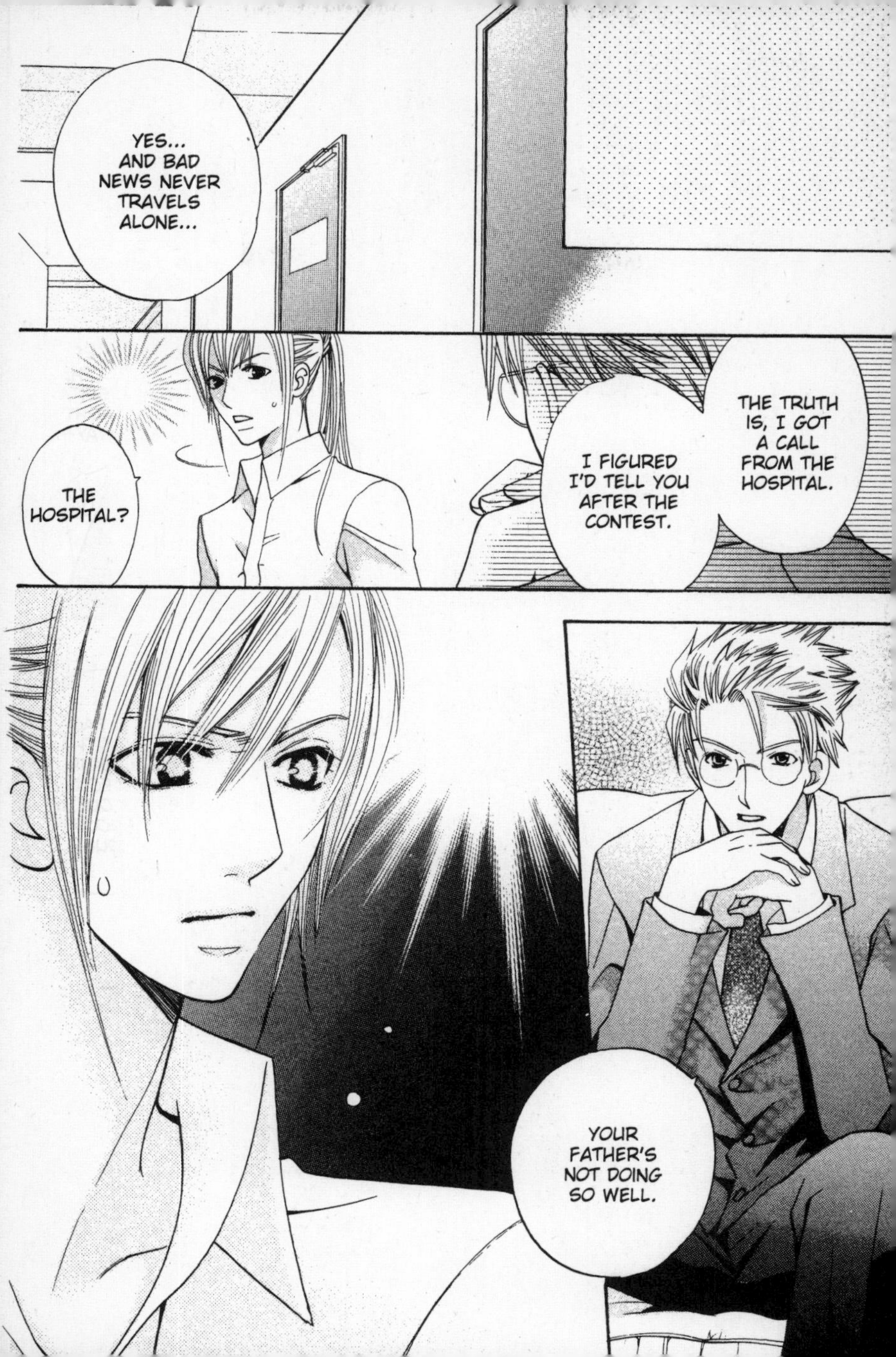
YES... AND BAD NEWS NEVER TRAVELS ALONE...
THE TRUTH IS, I GOT A CALL FROM THE HOSPITAL.
I FIGURED I'D TELL YOU AFTER THE CONTEST.
THE HOSPITAL?
YOUR FATHER'S NOT DOING SO WELL.

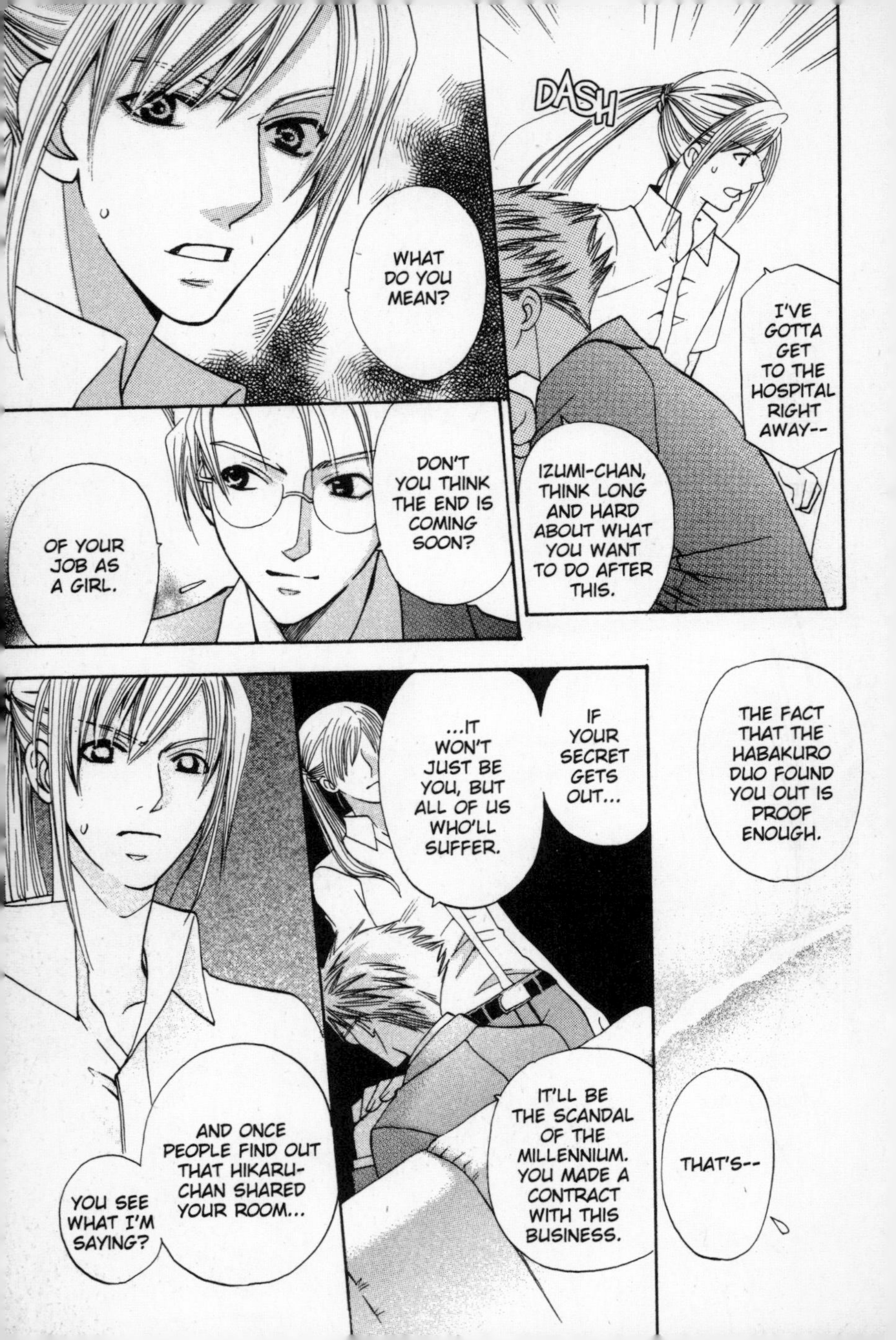
DASH
I'VE GOTTA GET TO THE HOSPITAL RIGHT AWAY--
IZUMI-CHAN, THINK LONG AND HARD ABOUT WHAT YOU WANT TO DO AFTER THIS.
WHAT DO YOU MEAN?
DON'T YOU THINK THE END IS COMING SOON?
OF YOUR JOB AS A GIRL.
THE FACT THAT THE HABAKURO DUO FOUND YOU OUT IS PROOF ENOUGH.
THAT'S--
IF YOUR SECRET GETS OUT...
...IT WON'T JUST BE YOU, BUT ALL OF US WHO'LL SUFFER.
IT'LL BE THE SCANDAL OF THE MILLENNIUM. YOU MADE A CONTRACT WITH THIS BUSINESS.
AND ONCE PEOPLE FIND OUT THAT HIKARU-CHAN SHARED YOUR ROOM...
YOU SEE WHAT I'M SAYING?

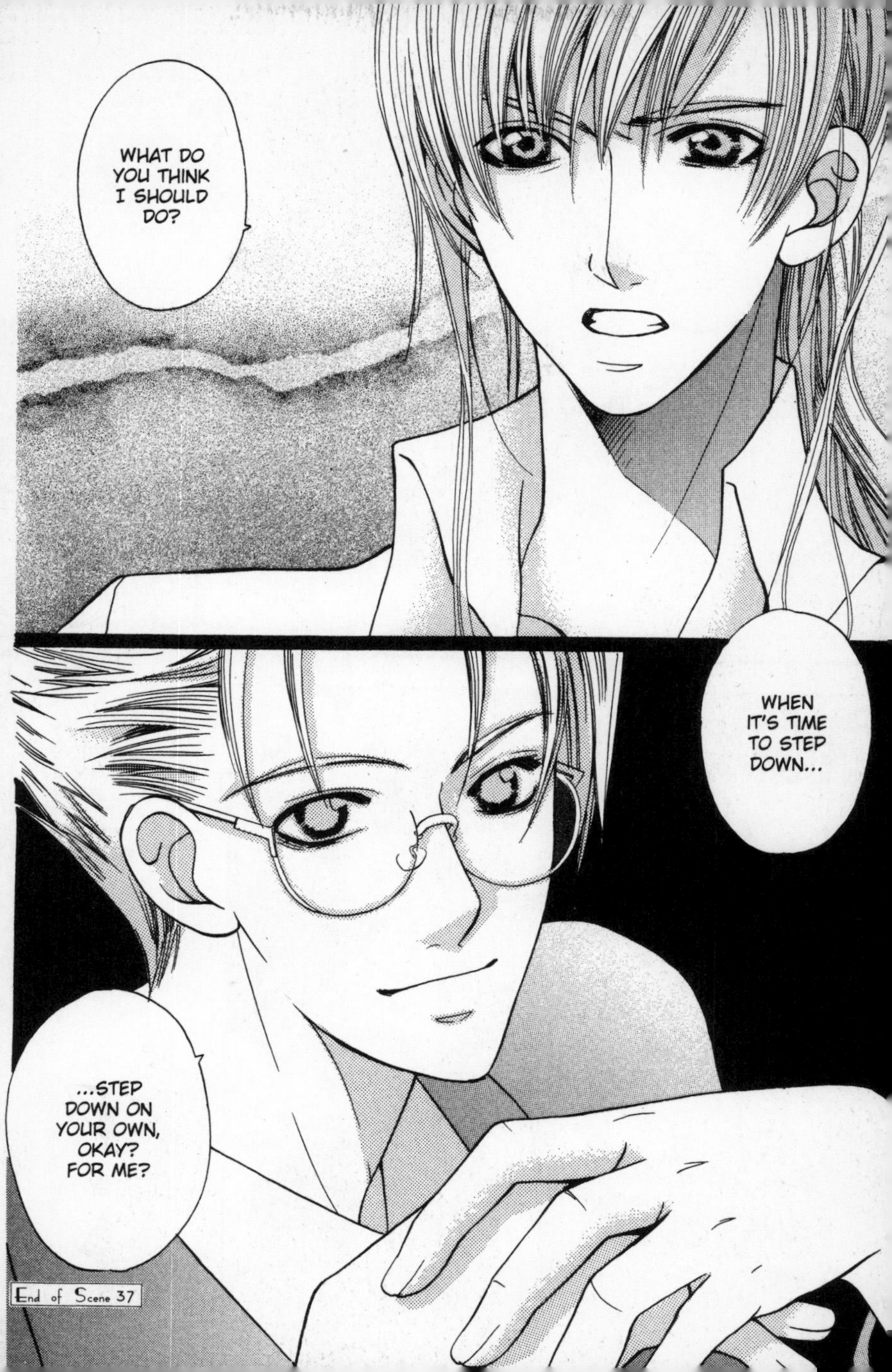
WHAT DO YOU THINK I SHOULD DO?
WHEN IT'S TIME TO STEP DOWN...
...STEP DOWN ON YOUR OWN, OKAY? FOR ME?
End of Scene 37

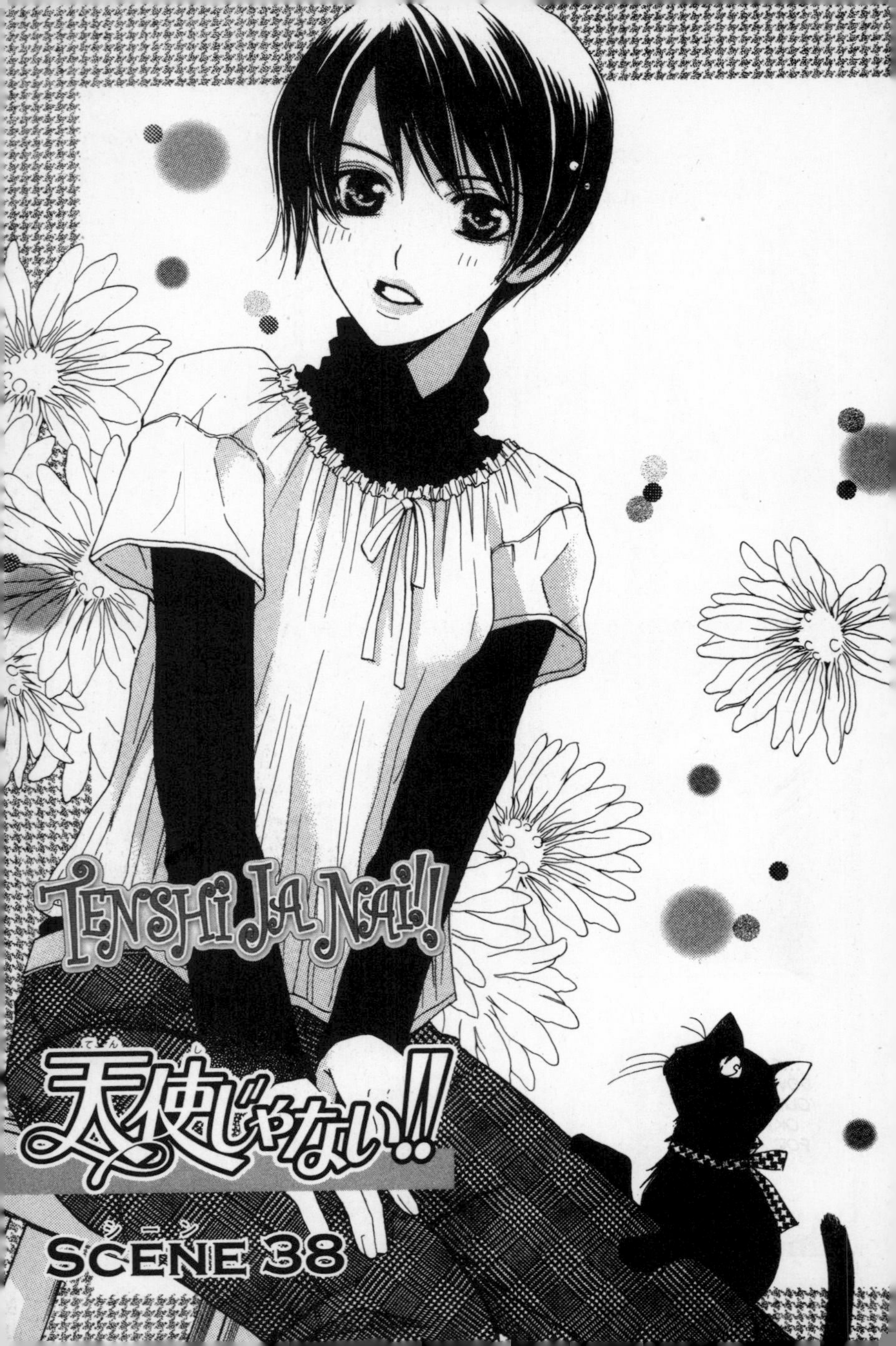
TENSHI JA NAI!!
天使じゃない!!
SCENE 38

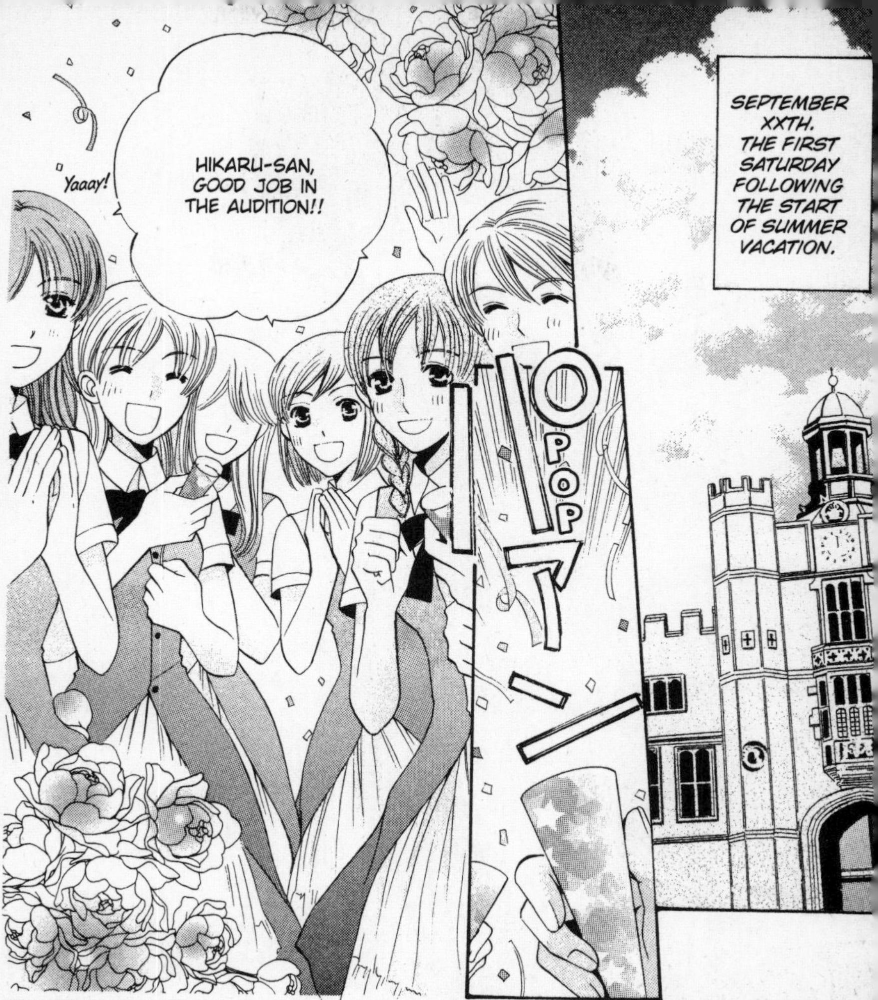
SEPTEMBER XXTH. THE FIRST SATURDAY FOLLOWING THE START OF SUMMER VACATION.
HIKARU-SAN, GOOD JOB IN THE AUDITION!!
Yaaay!
POP

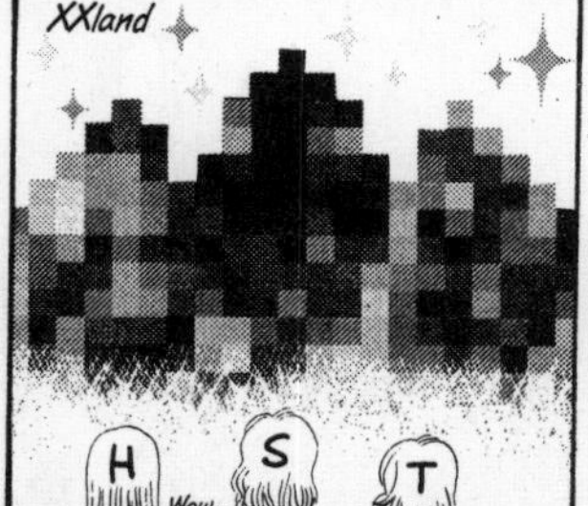
XXland
H
S
T
Wow...

*A Relaxing Trip ( 2 )*

*It was great weather at the Mouse Kingdom. Maybe because it was a weekday, we didn't have to stand in any lines for more than fifteen minutes, and by midday we'd ridden almost all the rides. The most fun thing had to be when we rode a rollercoaster and I got to hear my assistant T-san's scream. She even yelled "Die!" at one of the characters during the ride... (sweat)*

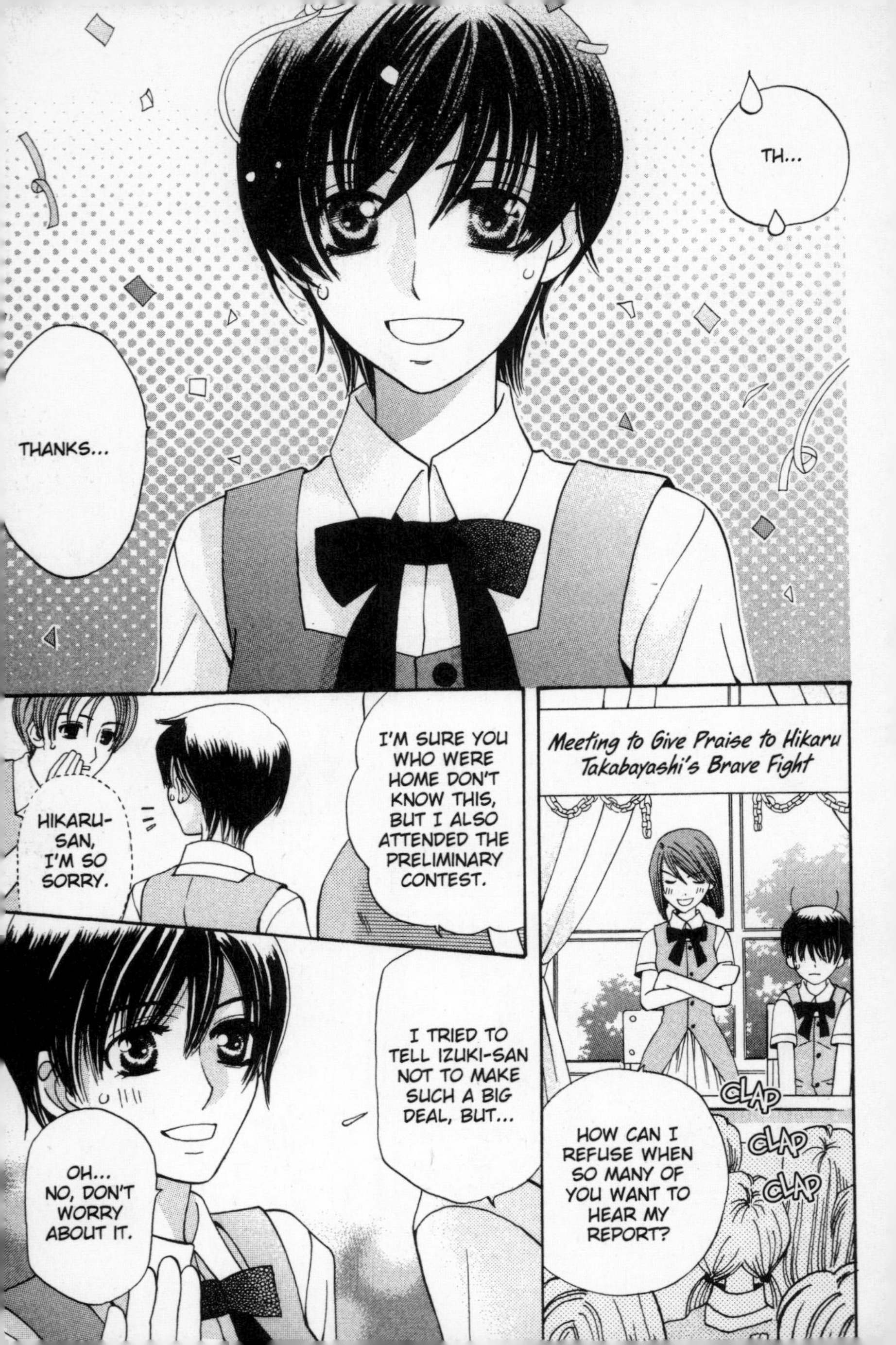
TH...
THANKS...
Meeting to Give Praise to Hikaru Takabayashi's Brave Fight
HOW CAN I REFUSE WHEN SO MANY OF YOU WANT TO HEAR MY REPORT?
CLAP
CLAP
CLAP
I'M SURE YOU WHO WERE HOME DON'T KNOW THIS, BUT I ALSO ATTENDED THE PRELIMINARY CONTEST.
HIKARU-SAN, I'M SO SORRY.
I TRIED TO TELL IZUKI-SAN NOT TO MAKE SUCH A BIG DEAL, BUT...
OH... NO, DON'T WORRY ABOUT IT.

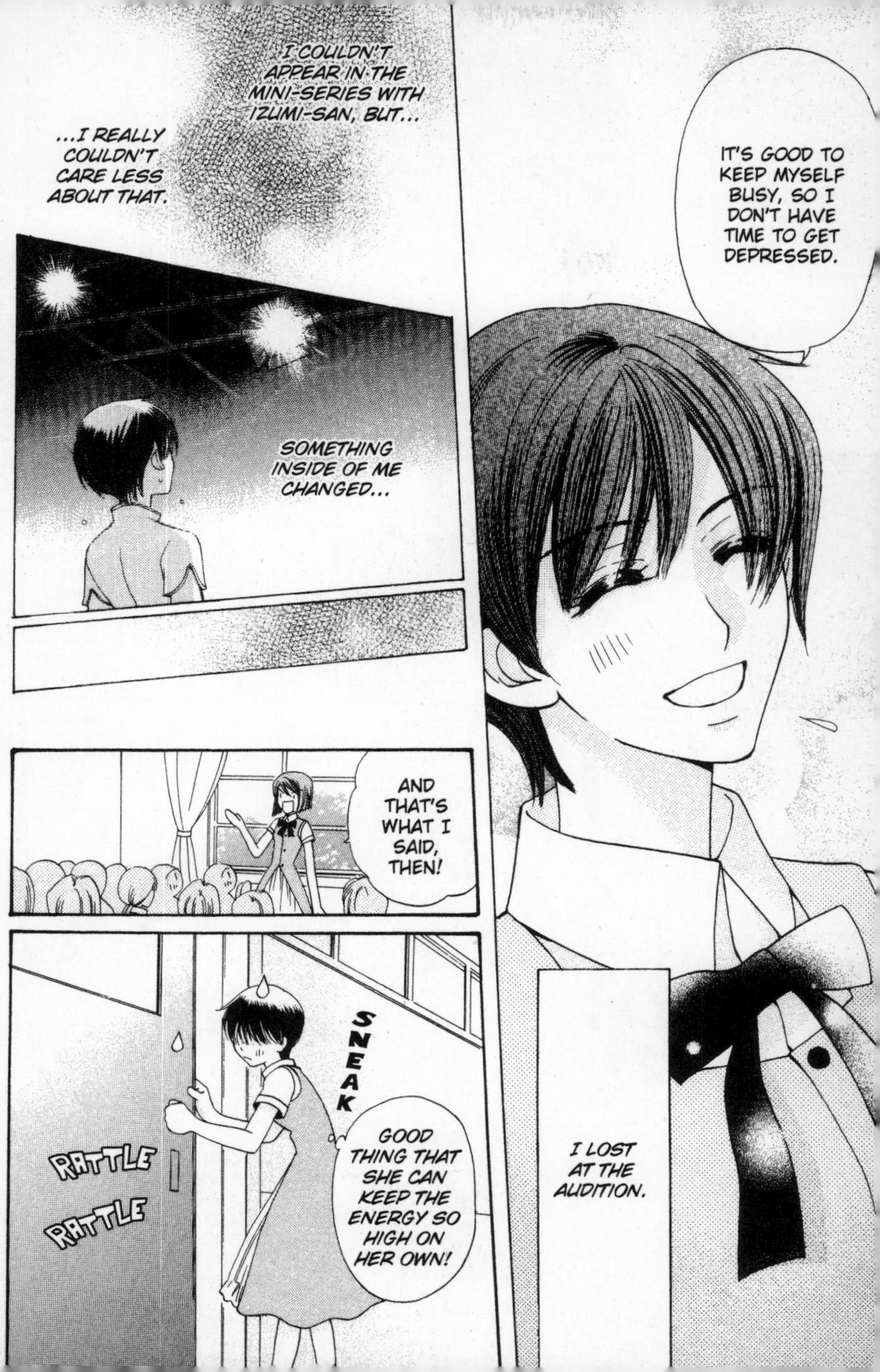
IT'S GOOD TO KEEP MYSELF BUSY, SO I DON'T HAVE TIME TO GET DEPRESSED.
I LOST AT THE AUDITION.
I COULDN'T APPEAR IN THE MINI-SERIES WITH IZUMI-SAN, BUT...
...I REALLY COULDN'T CARE LESS ABOUT THAT.
SOMETHING INSIDE OF ME CHANGED...
AND THAT'S WHAT I SAID, THEN!
SNEAK
GOOD THING THAT SHE CAN KEEP THE ENERGY SO HIGH ON HER OWN!
RATTLE
RATTLE

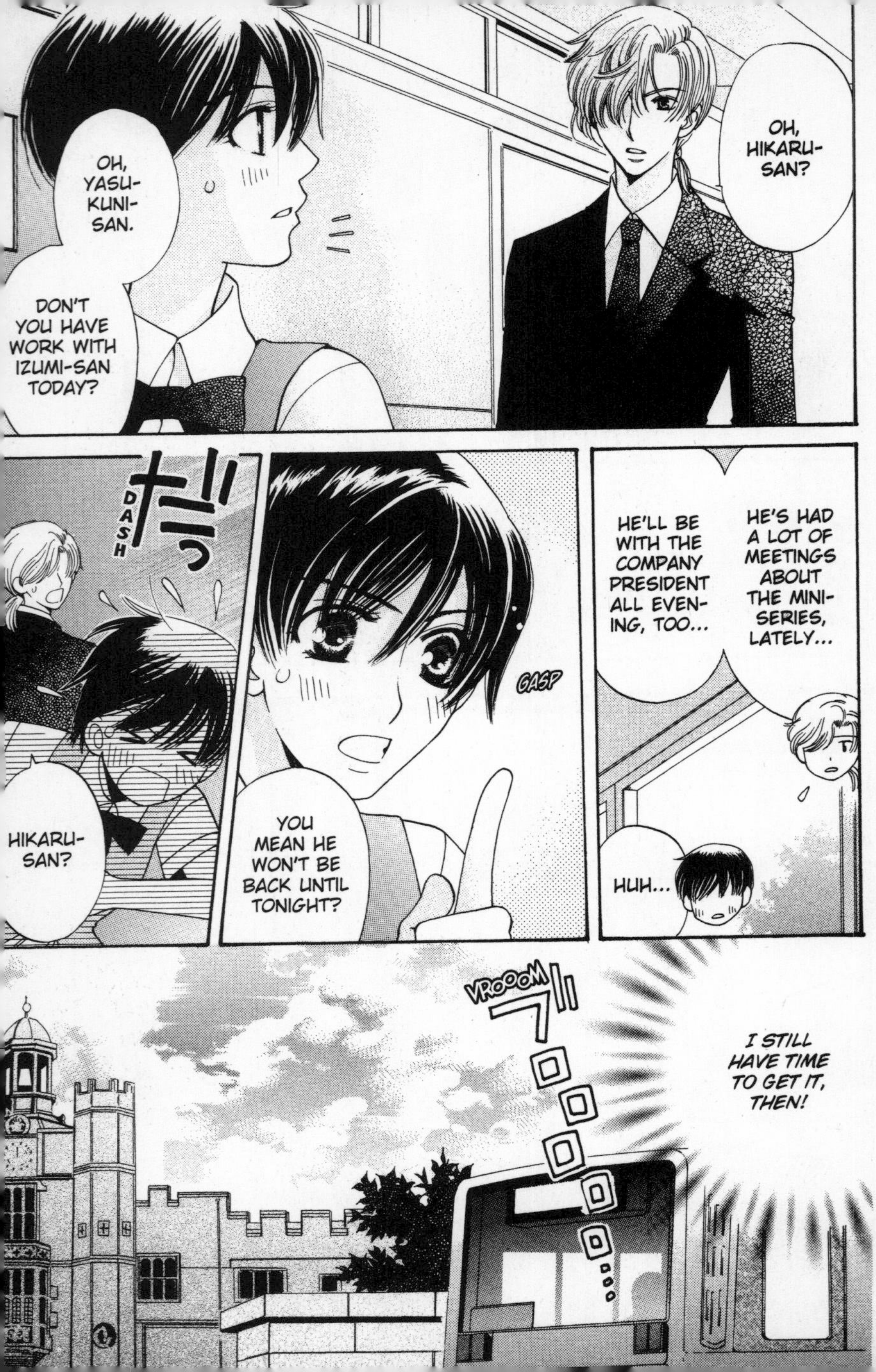
OH, HIKARU-SAN?
OH, YASU-KUNI-SAN.
DON'T YOU HAVE WORK WITH IZUMI-SAN TODAY?
HE'S HAD A LOT OF MEETINGS ABOUT THE MINI-SERIES, LATELY...
HE'LL BE WITH THE COMPANY PRESIDENT ALL EVENING, TOO...
HUH...
GASP
YOU MEAN HE WON'T BE BACK UNTIL TONIGHT?
DASH
HIKARU-SAN?
I STILL HAVE TIME TO GET IT, THEN!
VROOOM

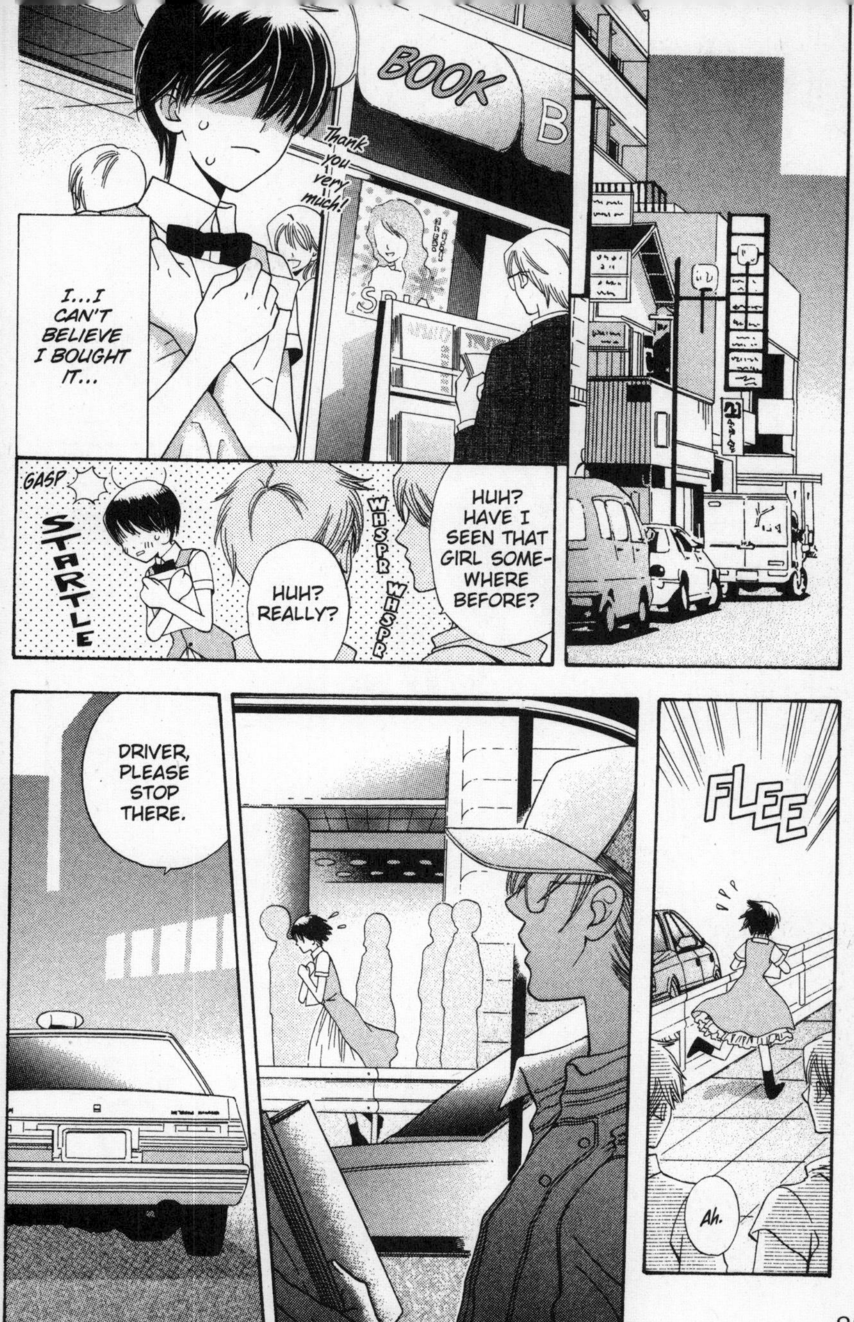
BOOK
Thank you very much!
I...I CAN'T BELIEVE I BOUGHT IT...
HUH? HAVE I SEEN THAT GIRL SOME-WHERE BEFORE?
WHSPR
WHSPR
HUH? REALLY?
STARTLE
GASP
FLEE
Ah.
DRIVER, PLEASE STOP THERE.

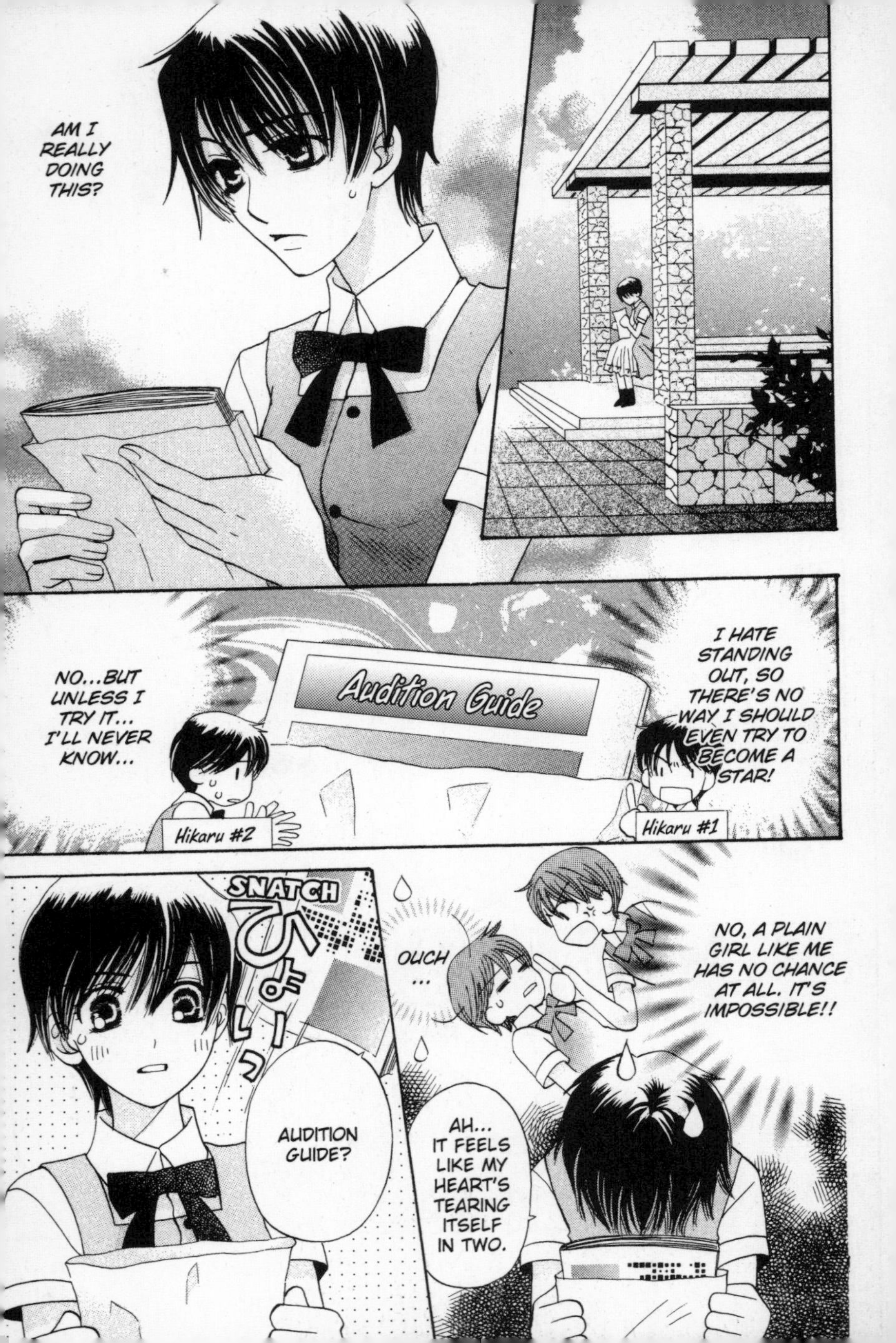
AM I REALLY DOING THIS?
I HATE STANDING OUT, SO THERE'S NO WAY I SHOULD EVEN TRY TO BECOME A STAR!
Hikaru #1
Audition Guide
NO...BUT UNLESS I TRY IT... I'LL NEVER KNOW...
Hikaru #2
NO, A PLAIN GIRL LIKE ME HAS NO CHANCE AT ALL. IT'S IMPOSSIBLE!!
OUCH ...
AH... IT FEELS LIKE MY HEART'S TEARING ITSELF IN TWO.
SNATCH
ひょいーっ
AUDITION GUIDE?

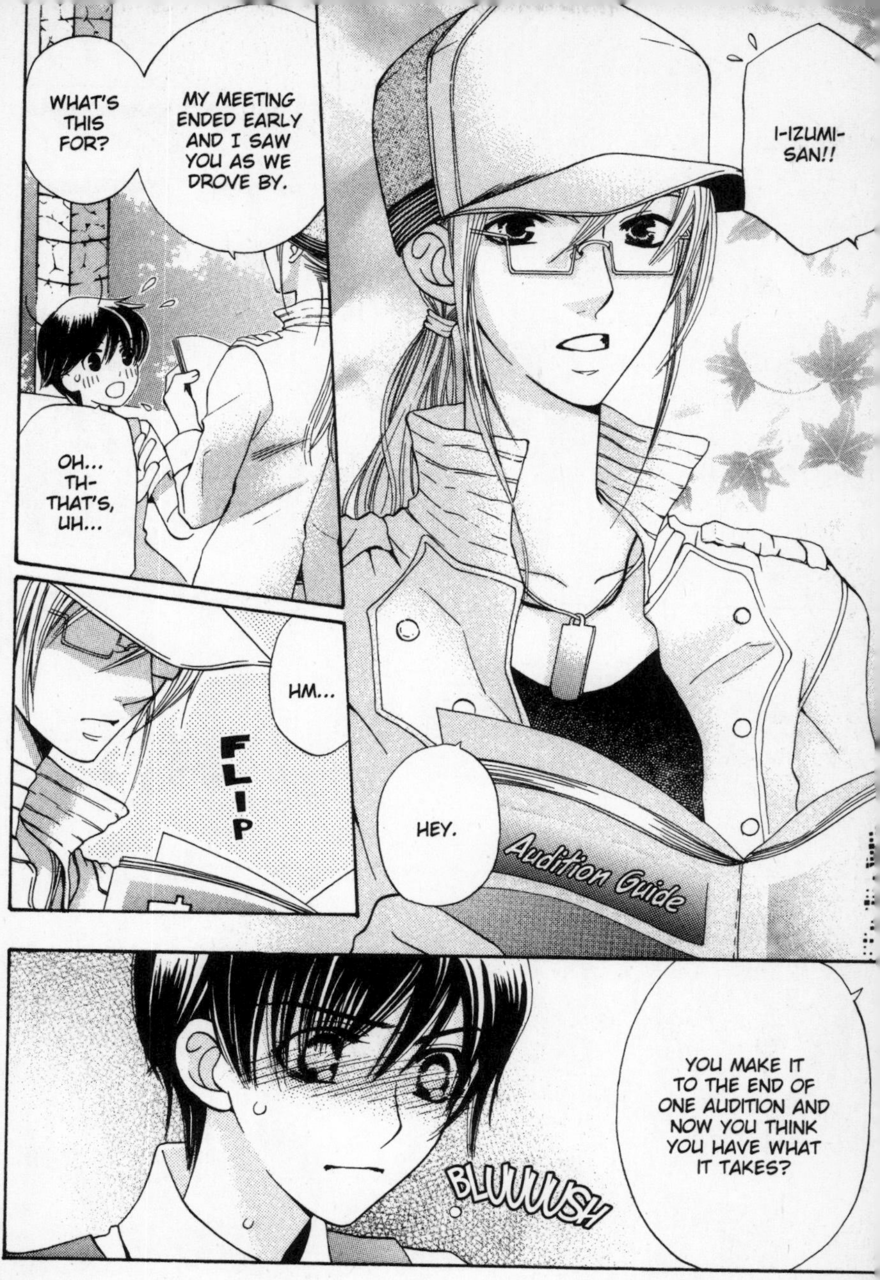
I-IZUMI-SAN!!
HEY.
Audition Guide
MY MEETING ENDED EARLY AND I SAW YOU AS WE DROVE BY.
WHAT'S THIS FOR?
OH... TH-THAT'S, UH...
HM...
FLIP
YOU MAKE IT TO THE END OF ONE AUDITION AND NOW YOU THINK YOU HAVE WHAT IT TAKES?
BLUUUUSH

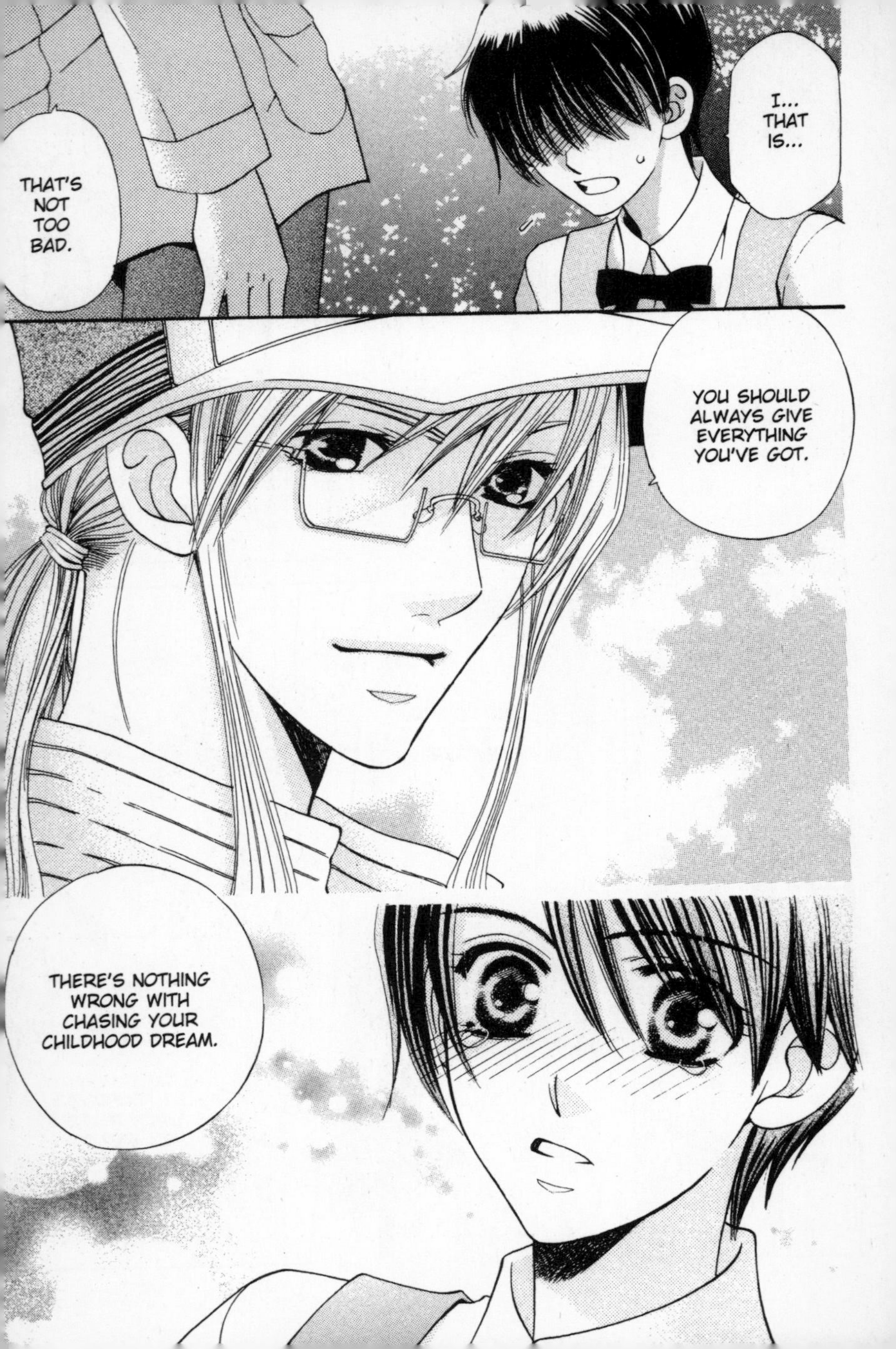
I... THAT IS...
THAT'S NOT TOO BAD.
YOU SHOULD ALWAYS GIVE EVERYTHING YOU'VE GOT.
THERE'S NOTHING WRONG WITH CHASING YOUR CHILDHOOD DREAM.

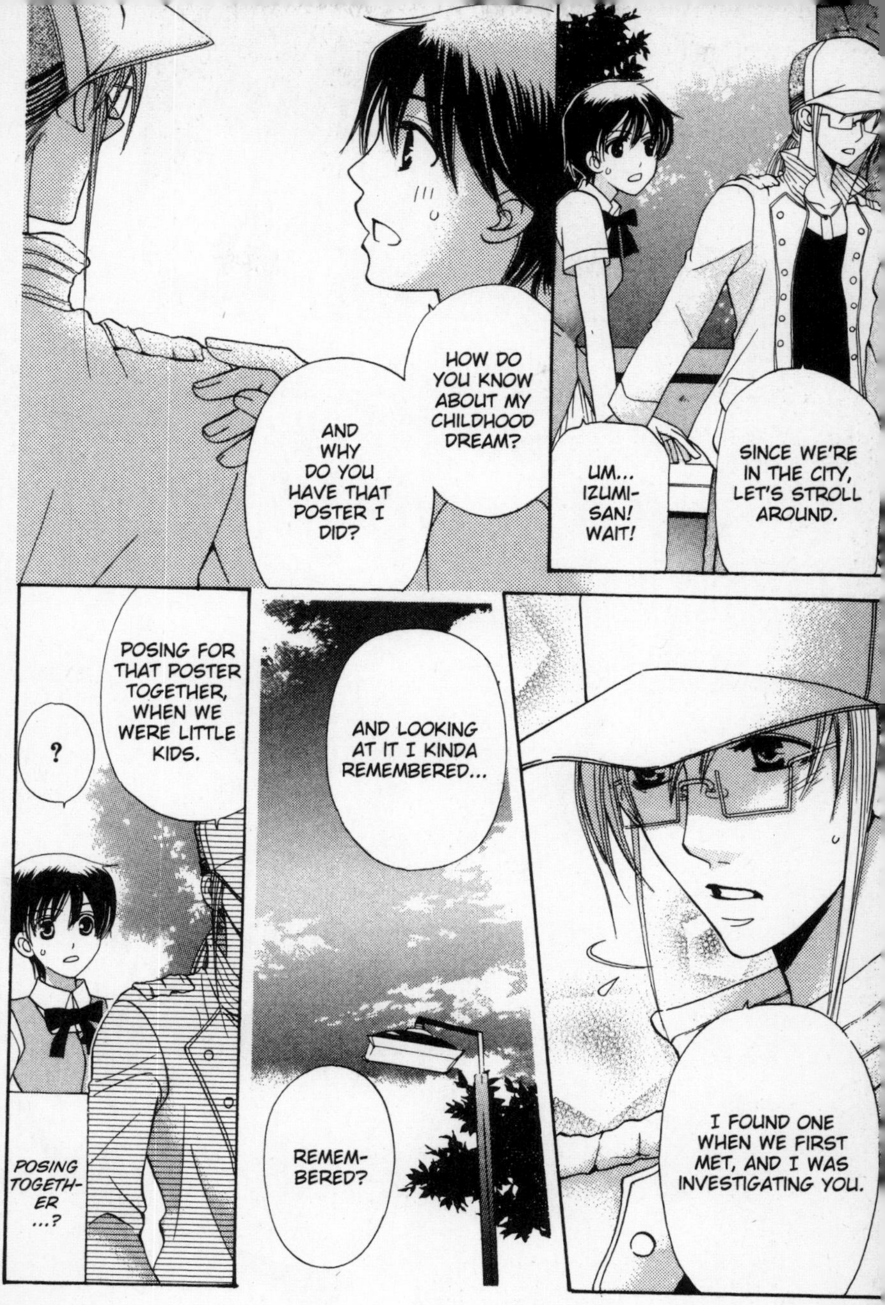
SINCE WE'RE IN THE CITY, LET'S STROLL AROUND.
UM... IZUMI-SAN! WAIT!
HOW DO YOU KNOW ABOUT MY CHILDHOOD DREAM?
AND WHY DO YOU HAVE THAT POSTER I DID?
I FOUND ONE WHEN WE FIRST MET, AND I WAS INVESTIGATING YOU.
AND LOOKING AT IT I KINDA REMEMBERED...
REMEM-BERED?
POSING FOR THAT POSTER TOGETHER, WHEN WE WERE LITTLE KIDS.
?
POSING TOGETH-ER ...?

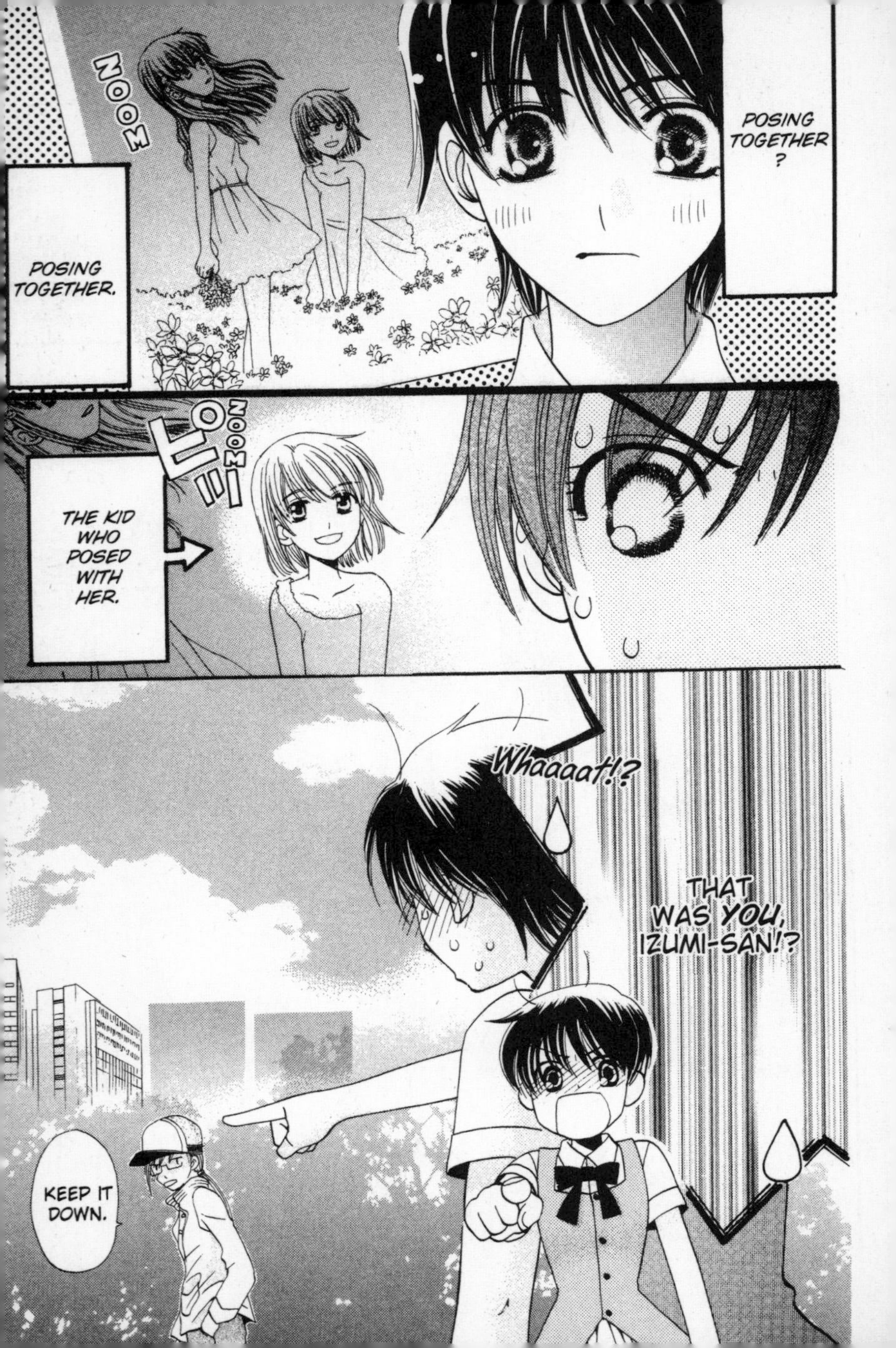
POSING TOGETHER ?
ZOOM
POSING TOGETHER.
ZOOM
THE KID WHO POSED WITH HER.
Whaaaat!?
THAT WAS YOU, IZUMI-SAN!?
KEEP IT DOWN.

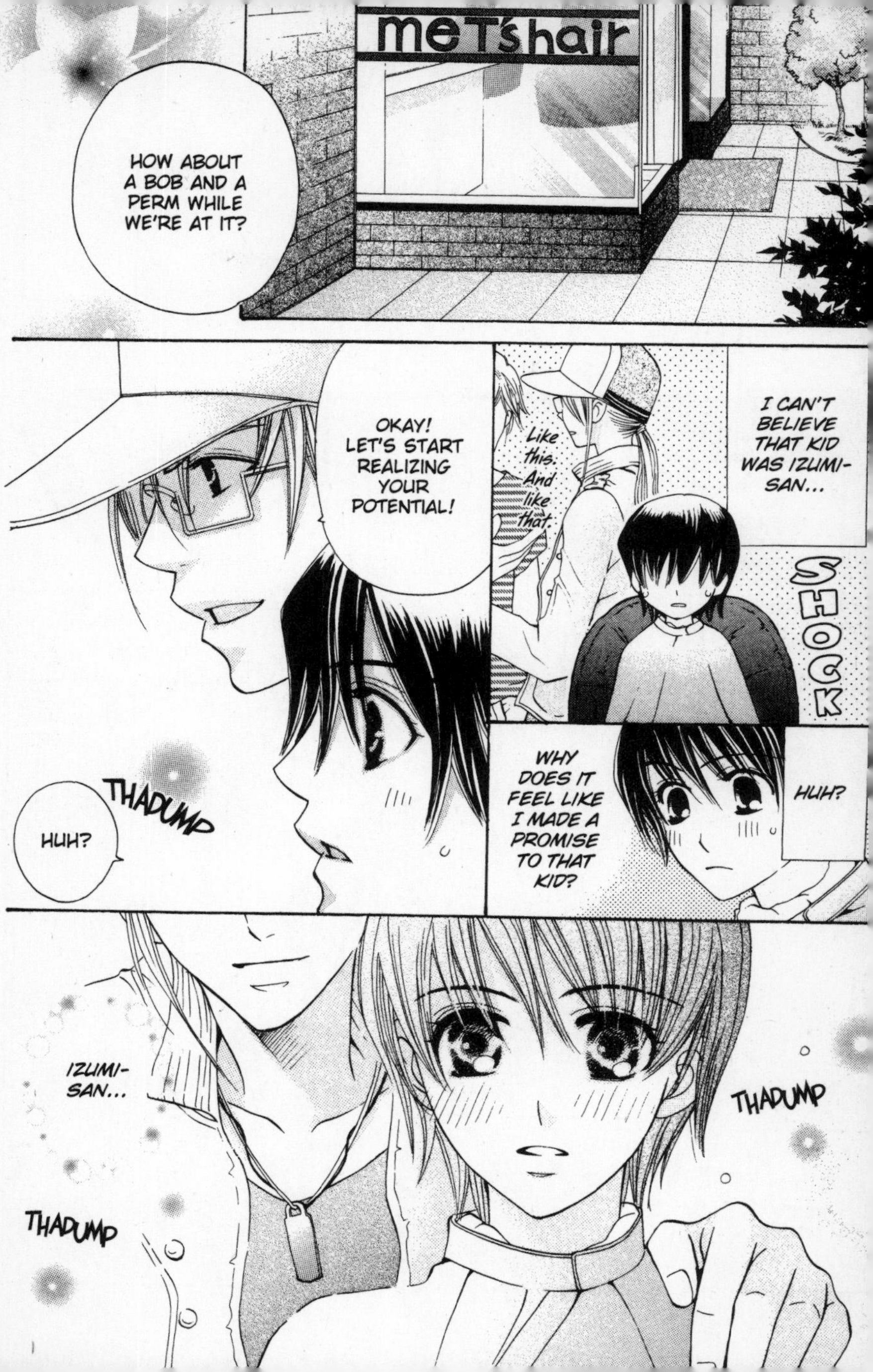
MET'S hair
HOW ABOUT A BOB AND A PERM WHILE WE'RE AT IT?
I CAN'T BELIEVE THAT KID WAS IZUMI-SAN...
SHOCK
Like this. And like that.
HUH?
WHY DOES IT FEEL LIKE I MADE A PROMISE TO THAT KID?
OKAY! LET'S START REALIZING YOUR POTENTIAL!
THADUMP
HUH?
THADUMP
IZUMI-SAN...
THADUMP

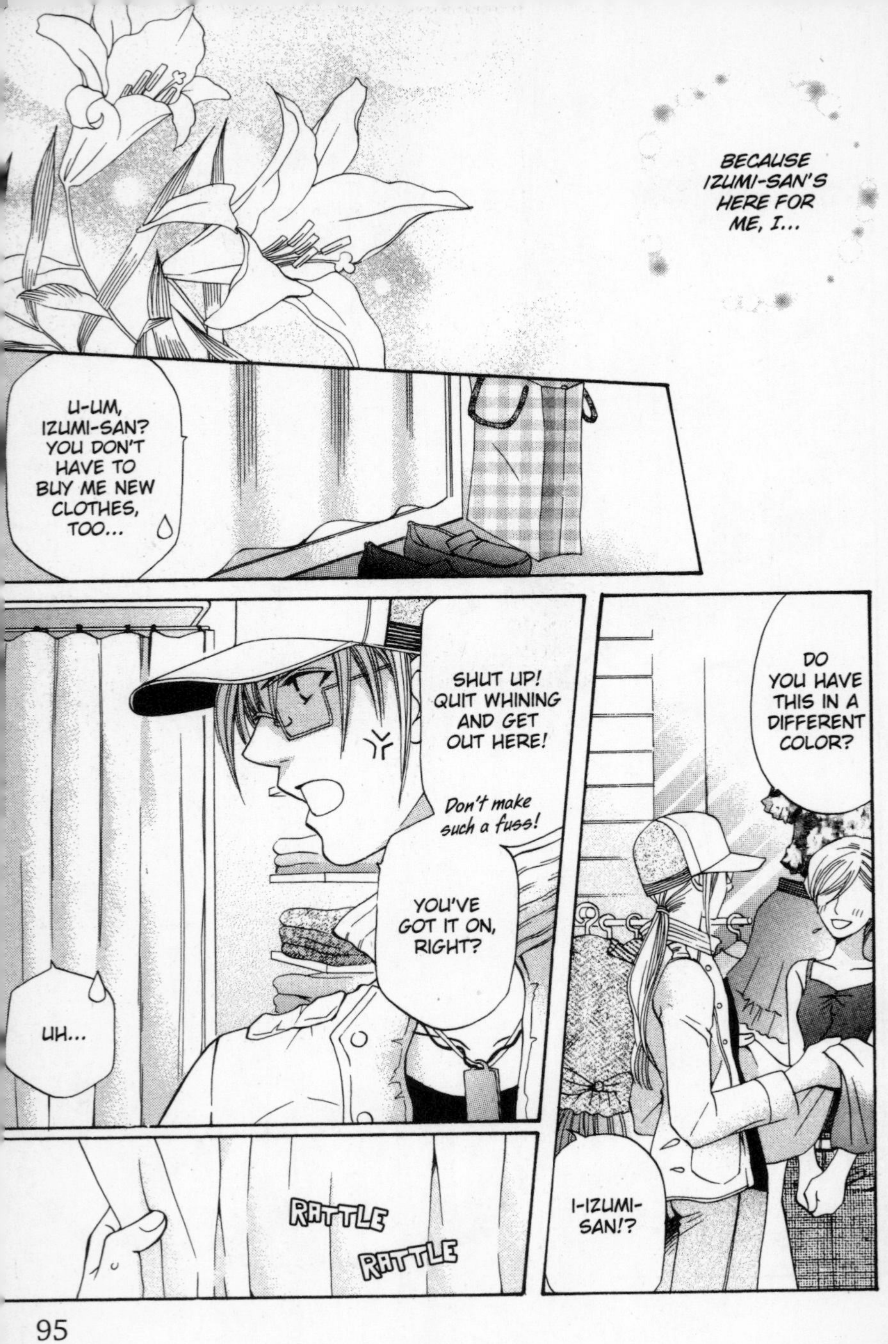
BECAUSE IZUMI-SAN'S HERE FOR ME, I...
U-UM, IZUMI-SAN? YOU DON'T HAVE TO BUY ME NEW CLOTHES, TOO...
DO YOU HAVE THIS IN A DIFFERENT COLOR?
I-IZUMI-SAN!?
SHUT UP! QUIT WHINING AND GET OUT HERE!
Don't make such a fuss!
YOU'VE GOT IT ON, RIGHT?
UH...
RATTLE
RATTLE

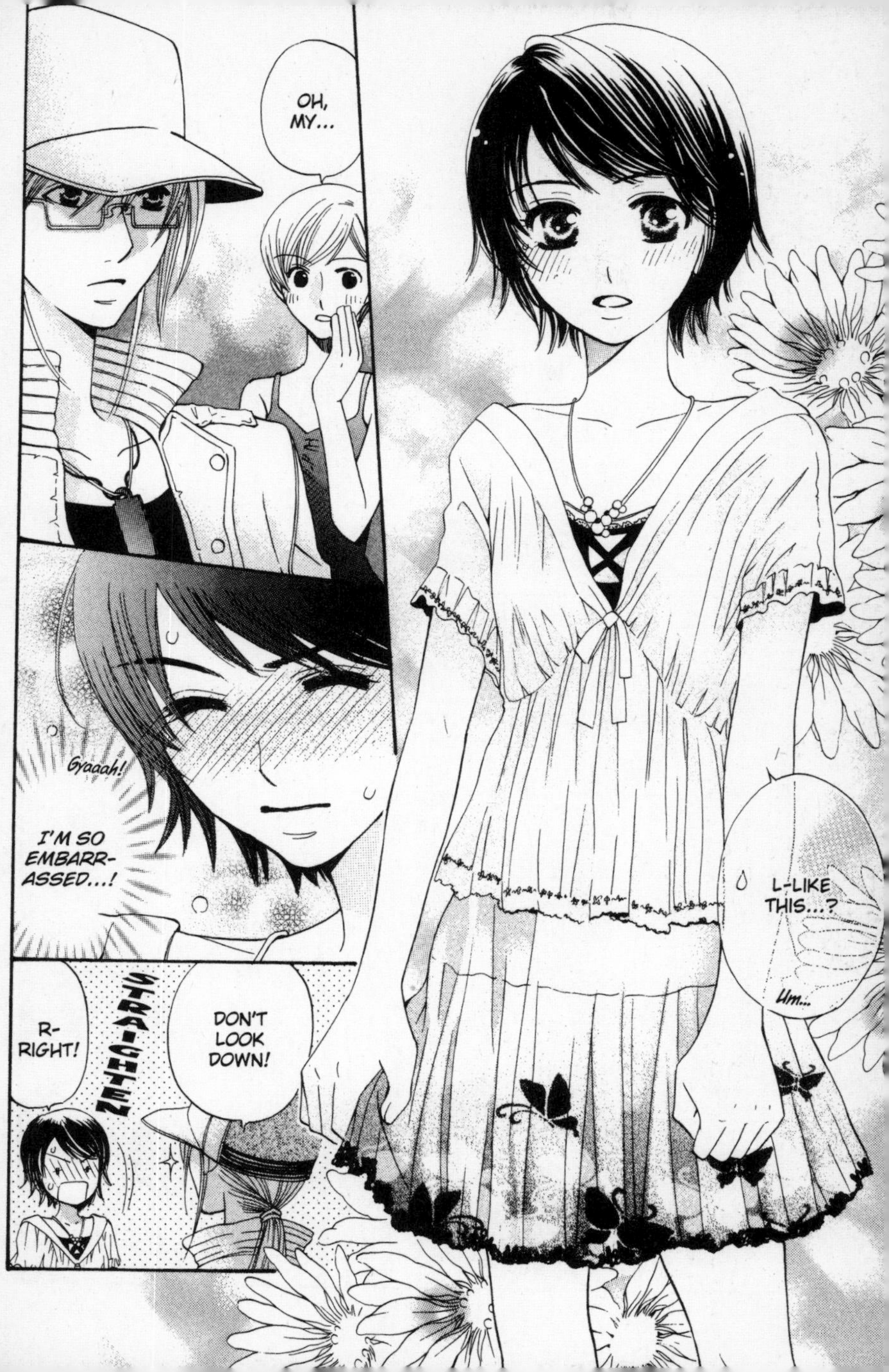
L-LIKE THIS...?
Um...
OH, MY...
Gyaaah!
I'M SO EMBARR-ASSED...!
DON'T LOOK DOWN!
STRAIGHTEN
R-RIGHT!

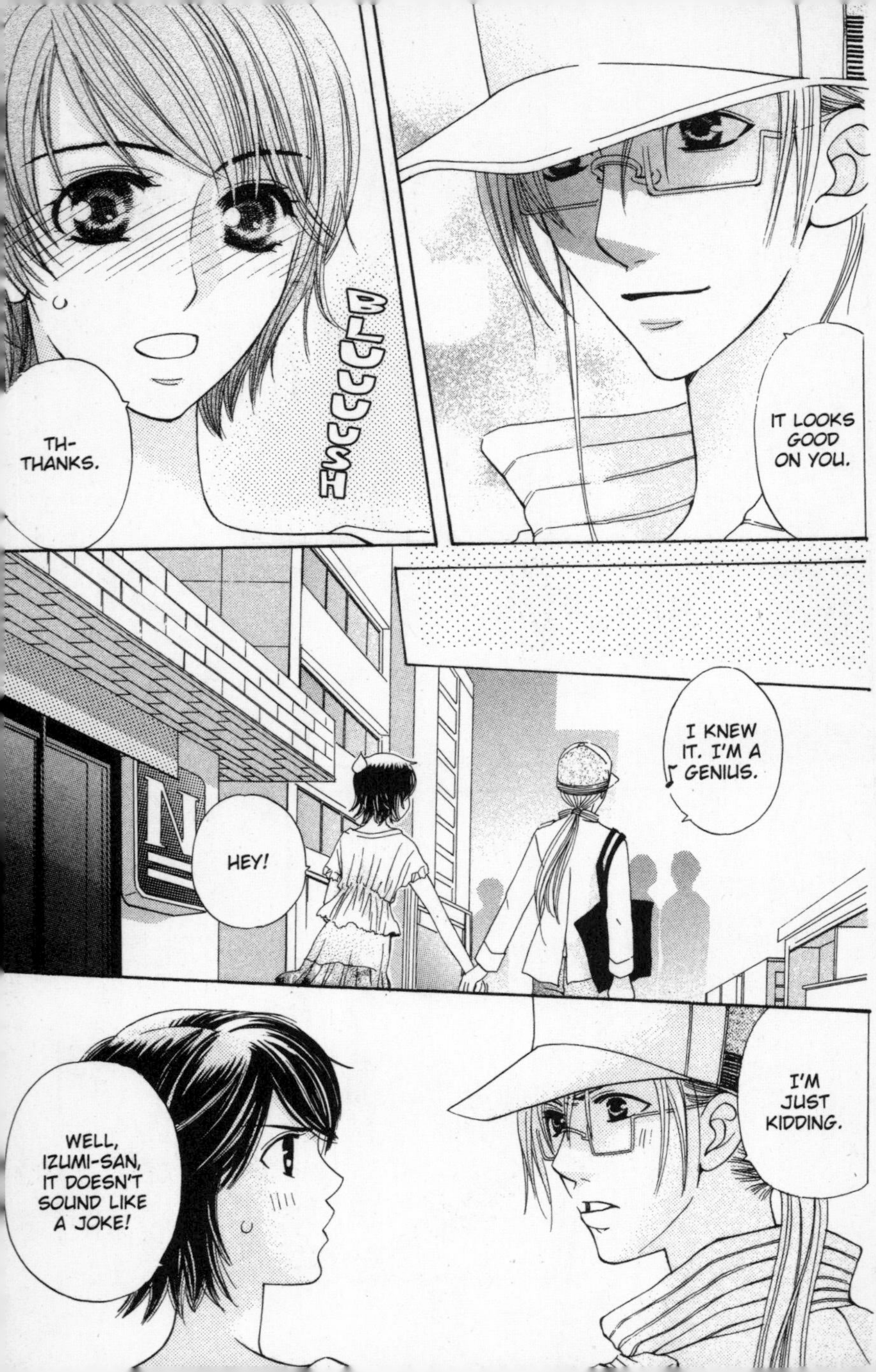
IT LOOKS GOOD ON YOU.
BLUUUUUSH
TH- THANKS.
I KNEW IT. I'M A GENIUS.
HEY!
I'M JUST KIDDING.
WELL, IZUMI-SAN, IT DOESN'T SOUND LIKE A JOKE!

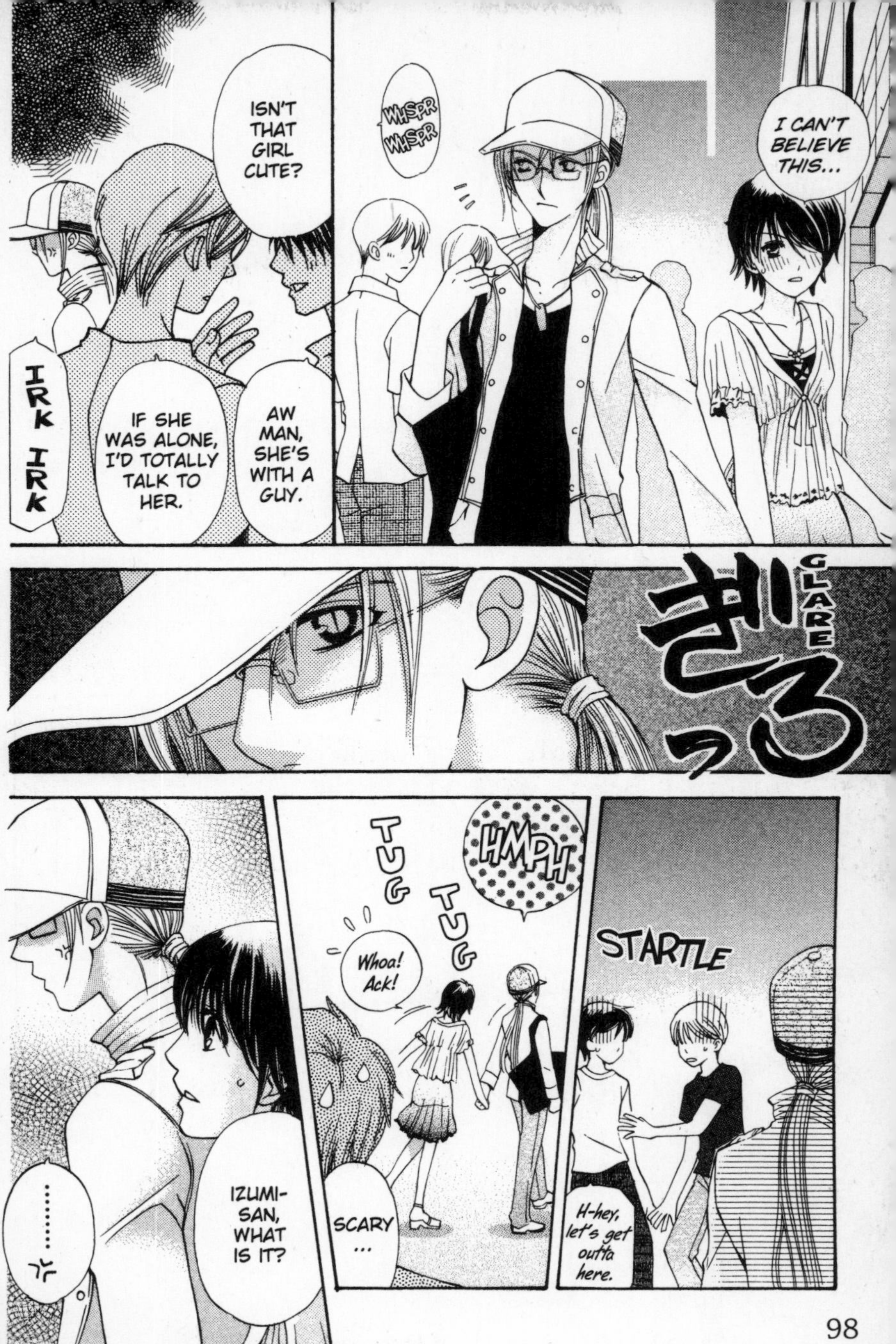
I CAN'T BELIEVE THIS...
WHSPR WHSPR
ISN'T THAT GIRL CUTE?
AW MAN, SHE'S WITH A GUY.
IF SHE WAS ALONE, I'D TOTALLY TALK TO HER.
IRK IRK
ぎろっ
GLARE
STARTLE
H-hey, let's get outta here.
HMPH
TUG TUG
Whoa! Ack!
SCARY ...
IZUMI-SAN, WHAT IS IT?
.......

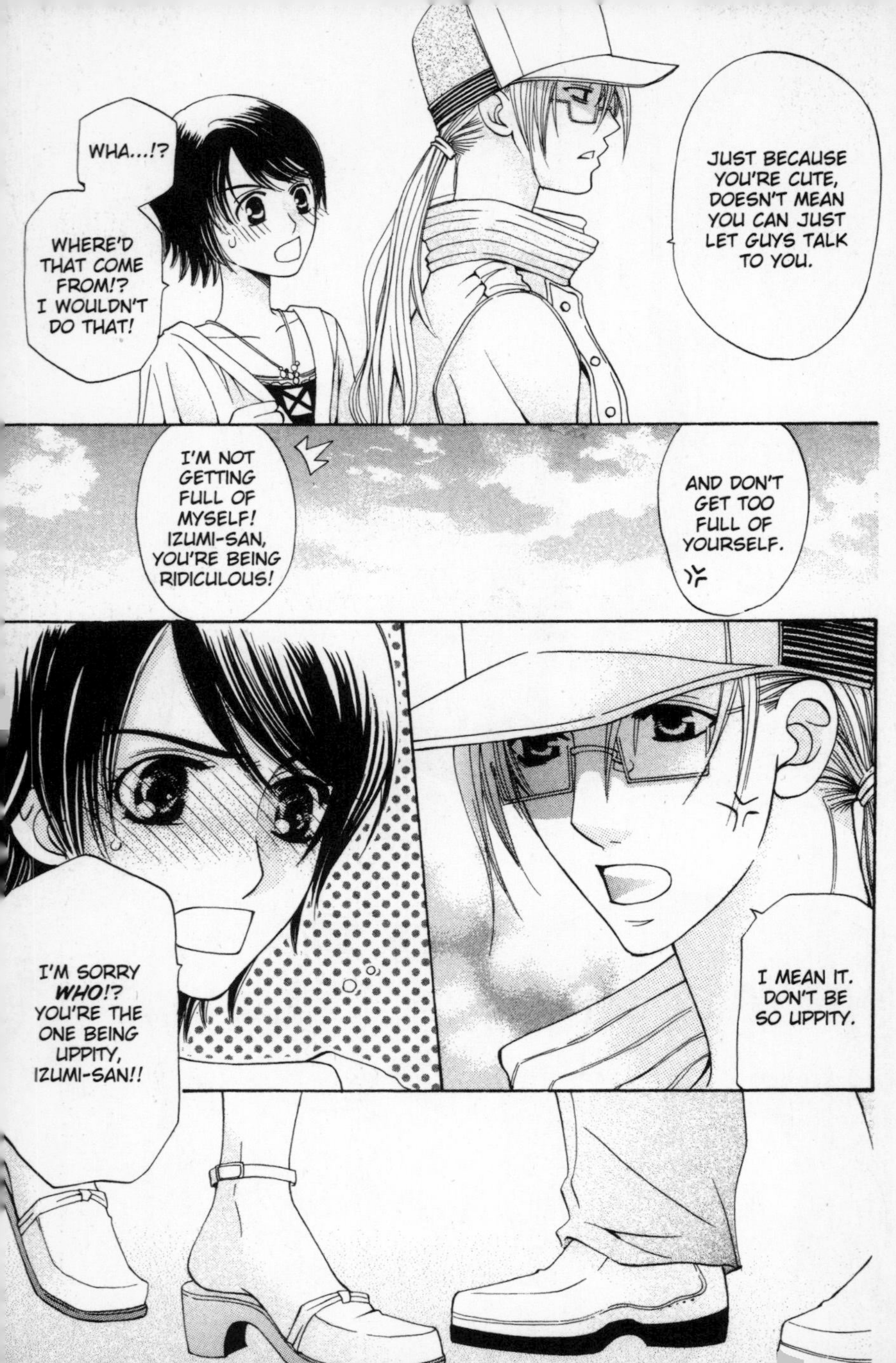
JUST BECAUSE YOU'RE CUTE, DOESN'T MEAN YOU CAN JUST LET GUYS TALK TO YOU.
WHA...!?
WHERE'D THAT COME FROM!? I WOULDN'T DO THAT!
AND DON'T GET TOO FULL OF YOURSELF.
I'M NOT GETTING FULL OF MYSELF! IZUMI-SAN, YOU'RE BEING RIDICULOUS!
I MEAN IT. DON'T BE SO UPPITY.
I'M SORRY ***WHO***!? YOU'RE THE ONE BEING UPPITY, IZUMI-SAN!!

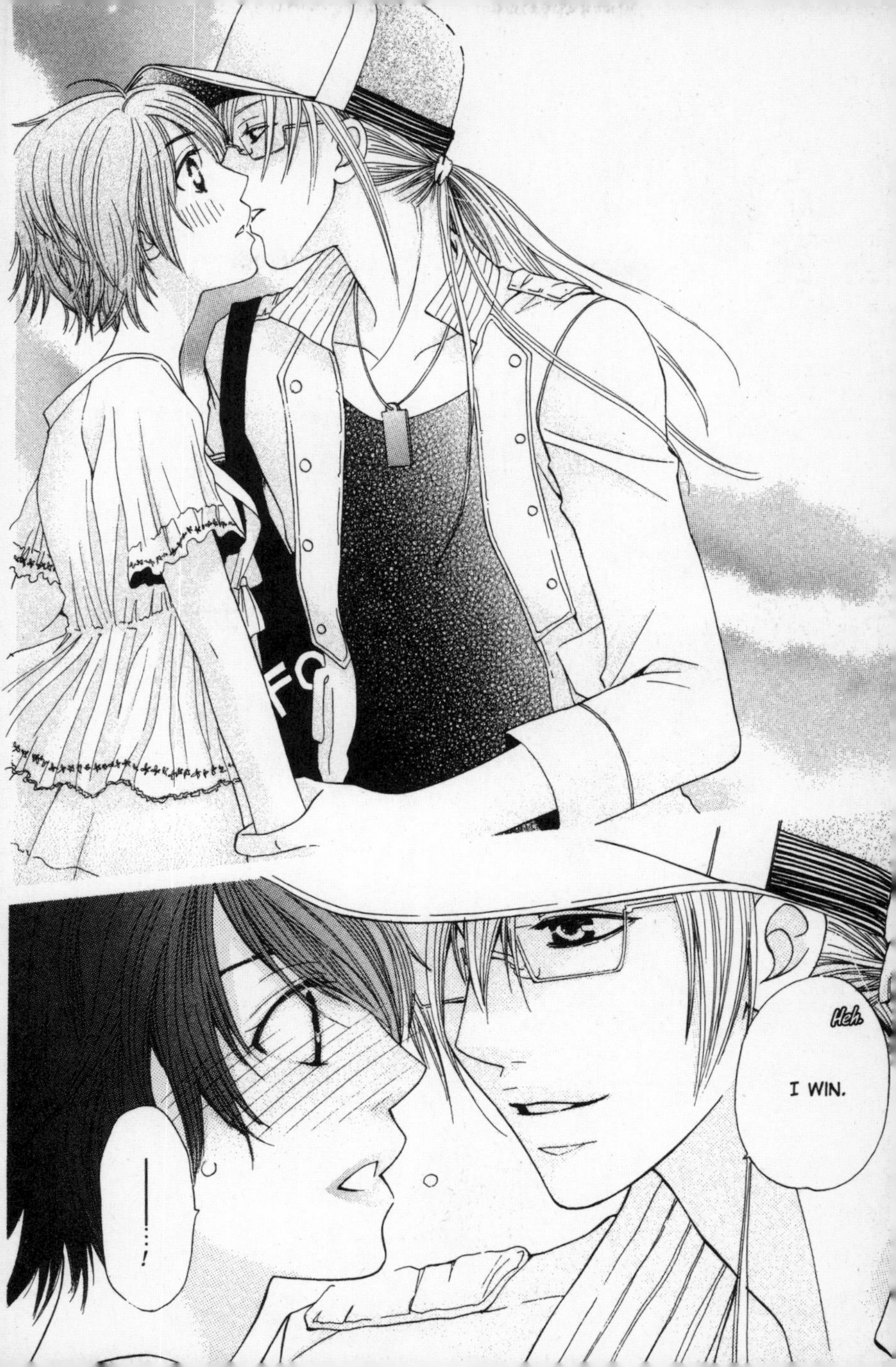
Heh.
I WIN.
—...!

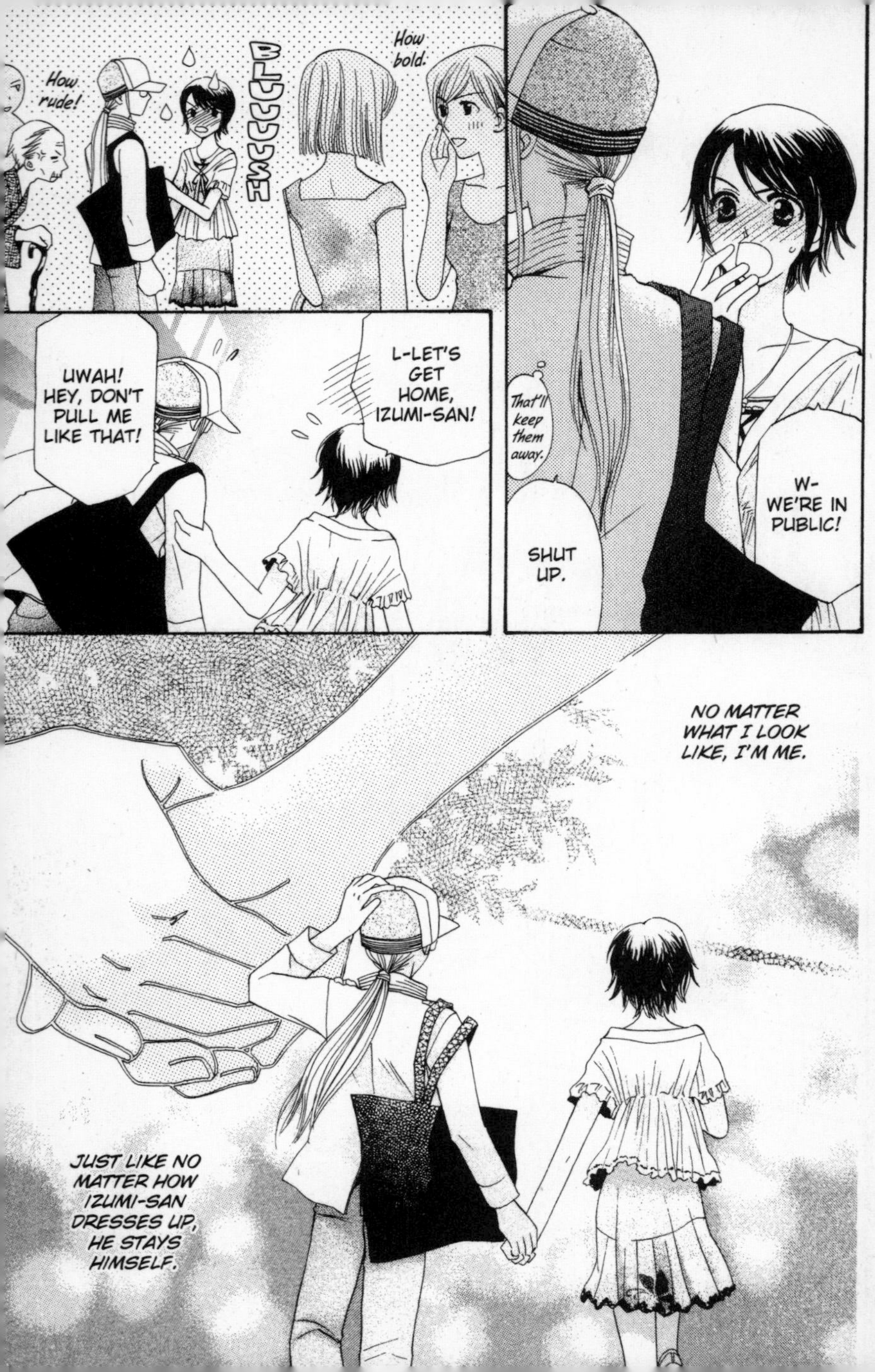
W- WE'RE IN PUBLIC!
SHUT UP.
That'll keep them away.
How bold.
BLUUSH
How rude!
L-LET'S GET HOME, IZUMI-SAN!
UWAH! HEY, DON'T PULL ME LIKE THAT!
NO MATTER WHAT I LOOK LIKE, I'M ME.
JUST LIKE NO MATTER HOW IZUMI-SAN DRESSES UP, HE STAYS HIMSELF.

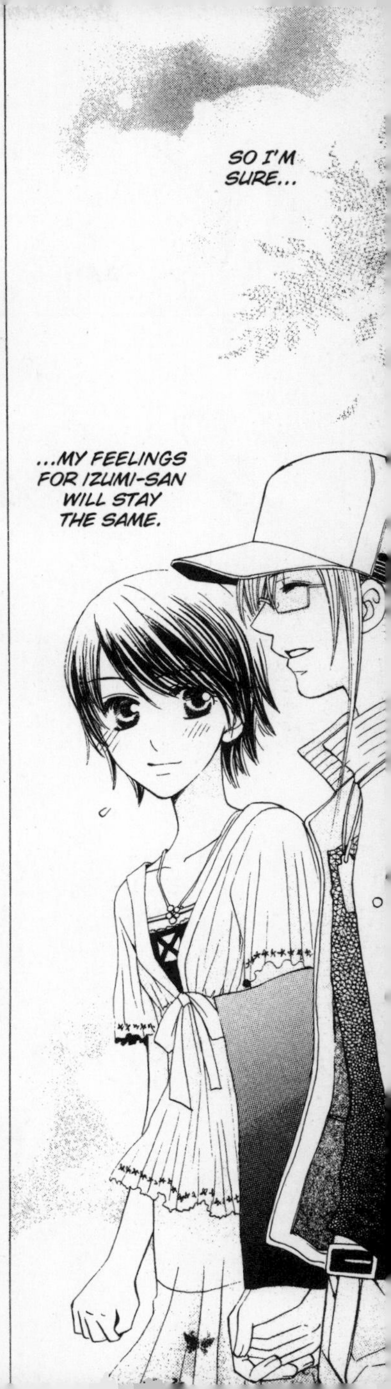
SO I'M SURE...
...MY FEELINGS FOR IZUMI-SAN WILL STAY THE SAME.

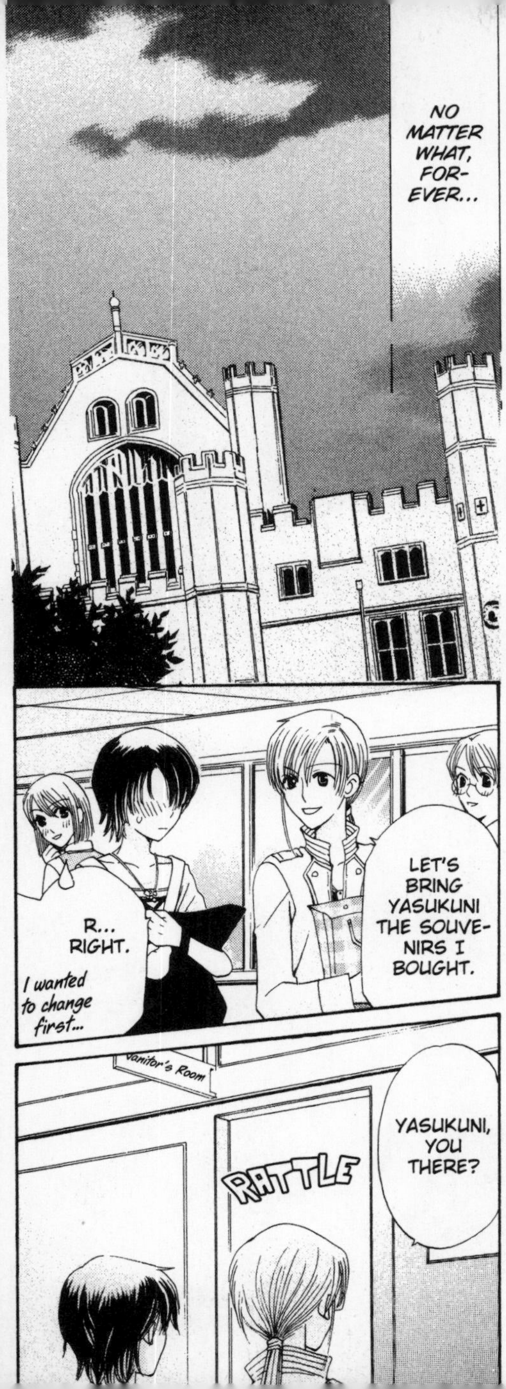
NO MATTER WHAT, FOR-EVER...
LET'S BRING YASUKUNI THE SOUVE-NIRS I BOUGHT.
R... RIGHT.
I wanted to change first...
YASUKUNI, YOU THERE?
Janitor's Room
RATTLE

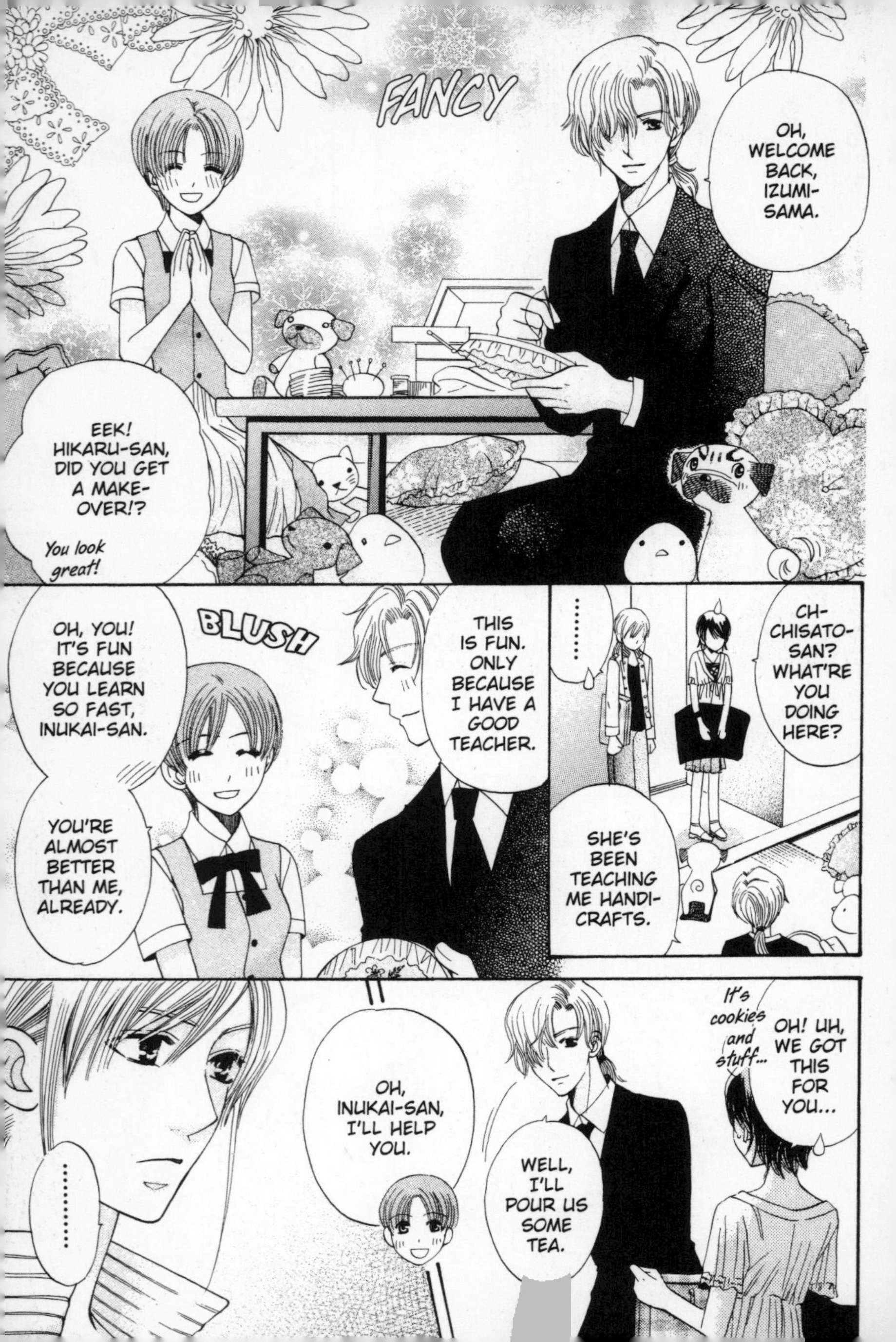

OH, WELCOME BACK, IZUMI-SAMA.
FANCY
EEK! HIKARU-SAN, DID YOU GET A MAKE-OVER!?
You look great!
CH-CHISATO-SAN? WHAT'RE YOU DOING HERE?
......
SHE'S BEEN TEACHING ME HANDI-CRAFTS.
THIS IS FUN. ONLY BECAUSE I HAVE A GOOD TEACHER.
BLUSH
OH, YOU! IT'S FUN BECAUSE YOU LEARN SO FAST, INUKAI-SAN.
YOU'RE ALMOST BETTER THAN ME, ALREADY.
OH! UH, WE GOT THIS FOR YOU...
It's cookies and stuff...
WELL, I'LL POUR US SOME TEA.
OH, INUKAI-SAN, I'LL HELP YOU.
......

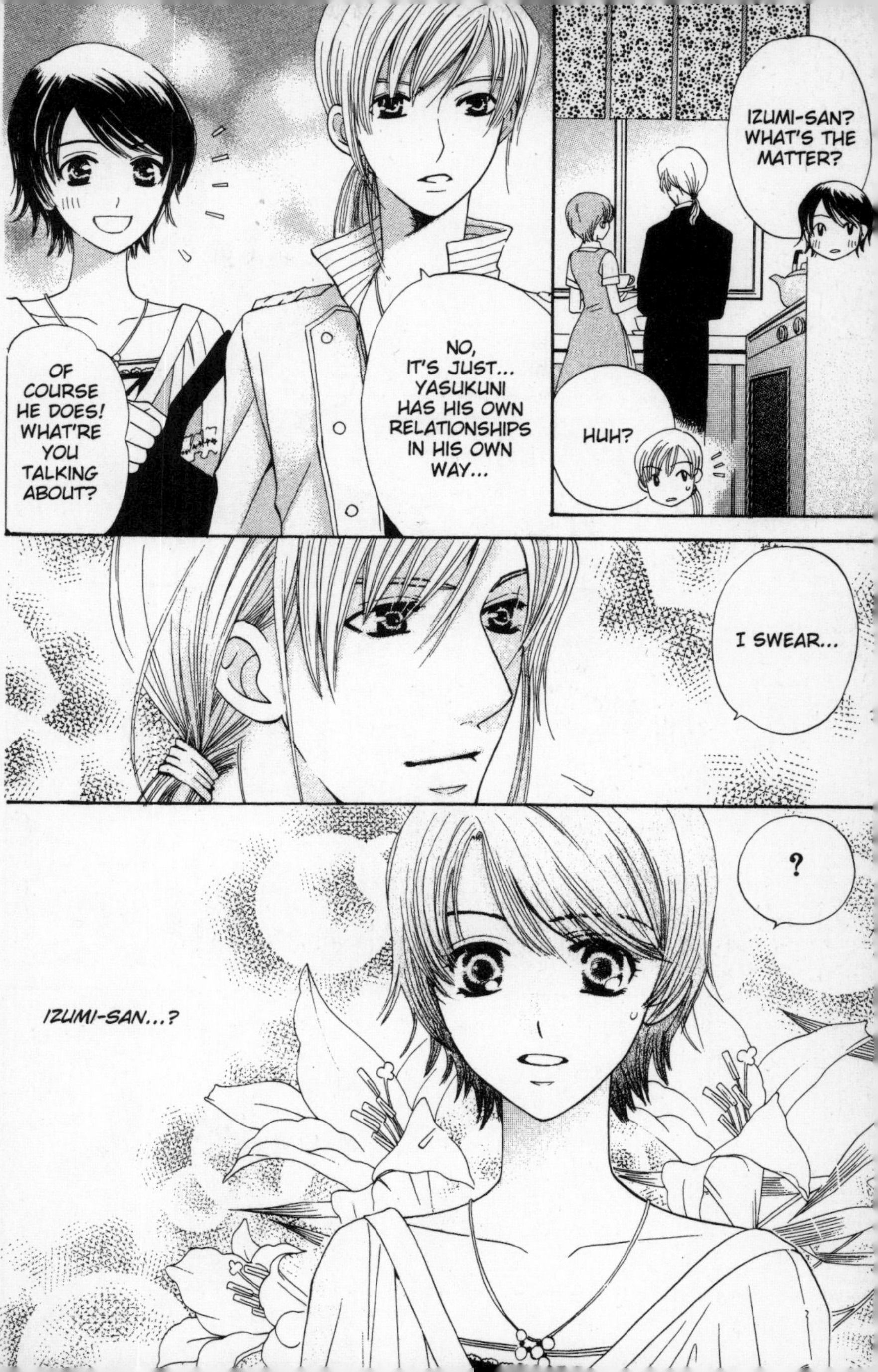
IZUMI-SAN? WHAT'S THE MATTER?
HUH?
NO, IT'S JUST... YASUKUNI HAS HIS OWN RELATIONSHIPS IN HIS OWN WAY...
OF COURSE HE DOES! WHAT'RE YOU TALKING ABOUT?
I SWEAR...
?
IZUMI-SAN...?

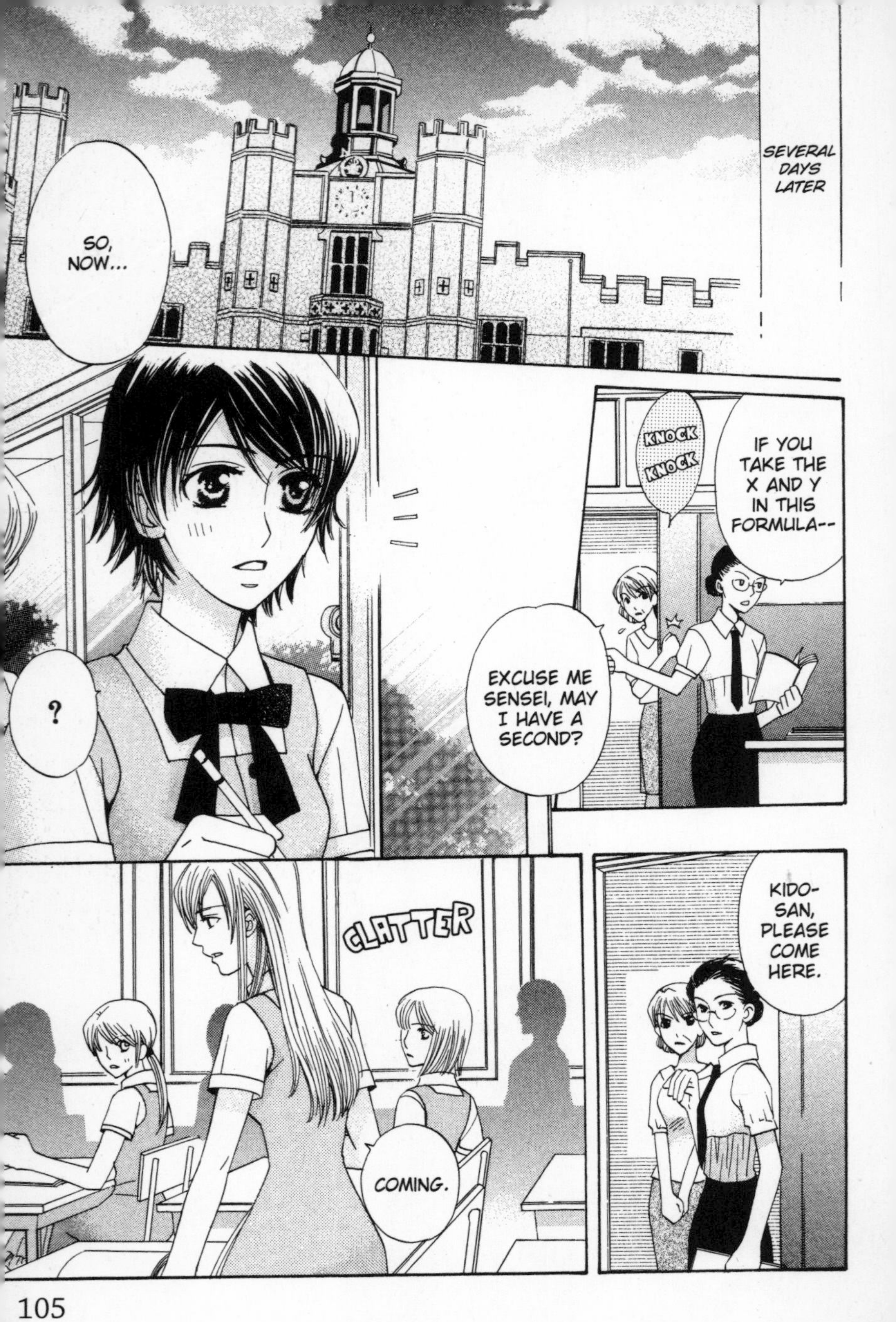
SEVERAL DAYS LATER
SO, NOW...
IF YOU TAKE THE X AND Y IN THIS FORMULA--
KNOCK KNOCK
EXCUSE ME SENSEI, MAY I HAVE A SECOND?
?
KIDO-SAN, PLEASE COME HERE.
CLATTER
COMING.

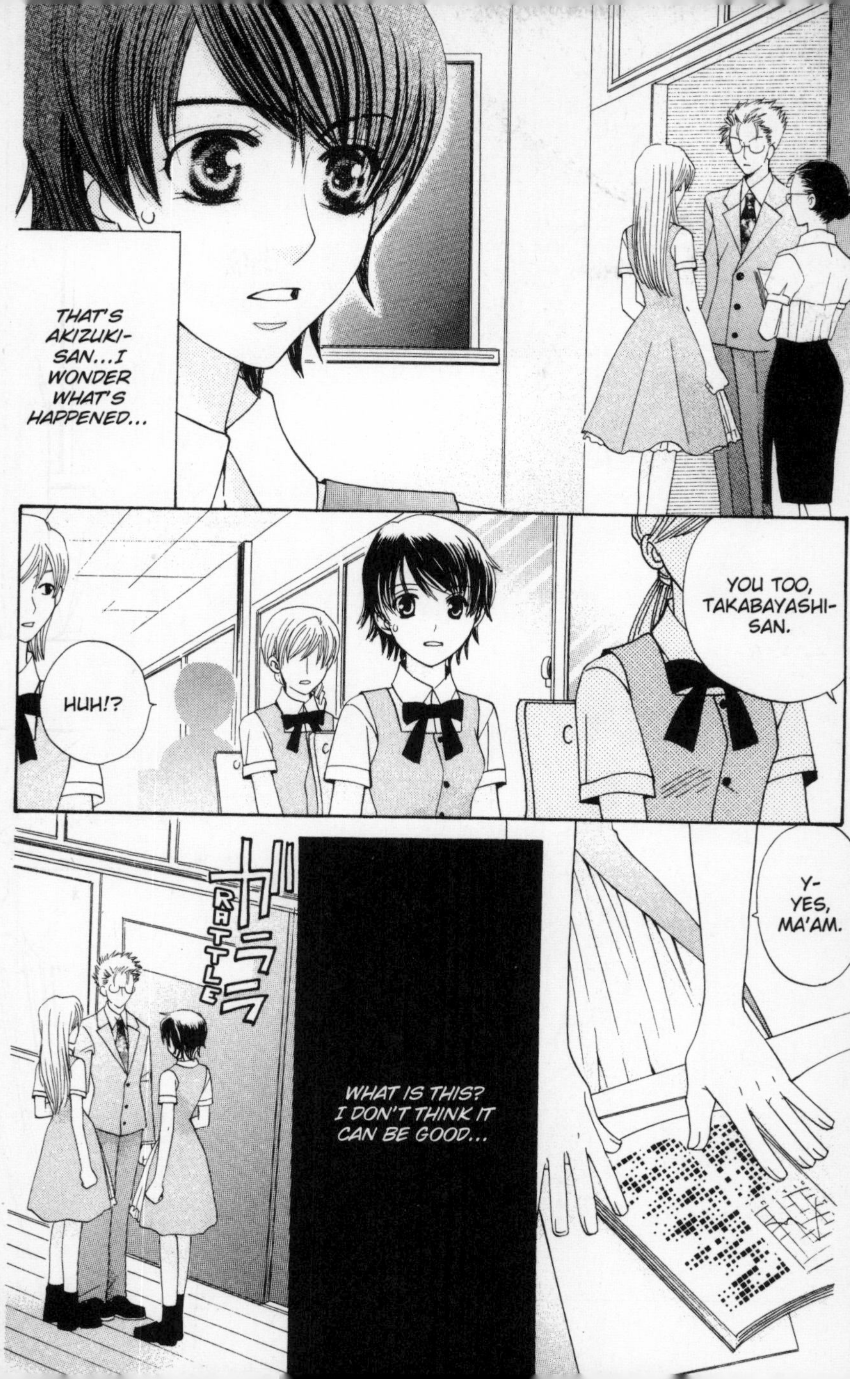
THAT'S AKIZUKI-SAN...I WONDER WHAT'S HAPPENED...
YOU TOO, TAKABAYASHI-SAN.
HUH!?
Y-YES, MA'AM.
WHAT IS THIS? I DON'T THINK IT CAN BE GOOD...
RATTLE

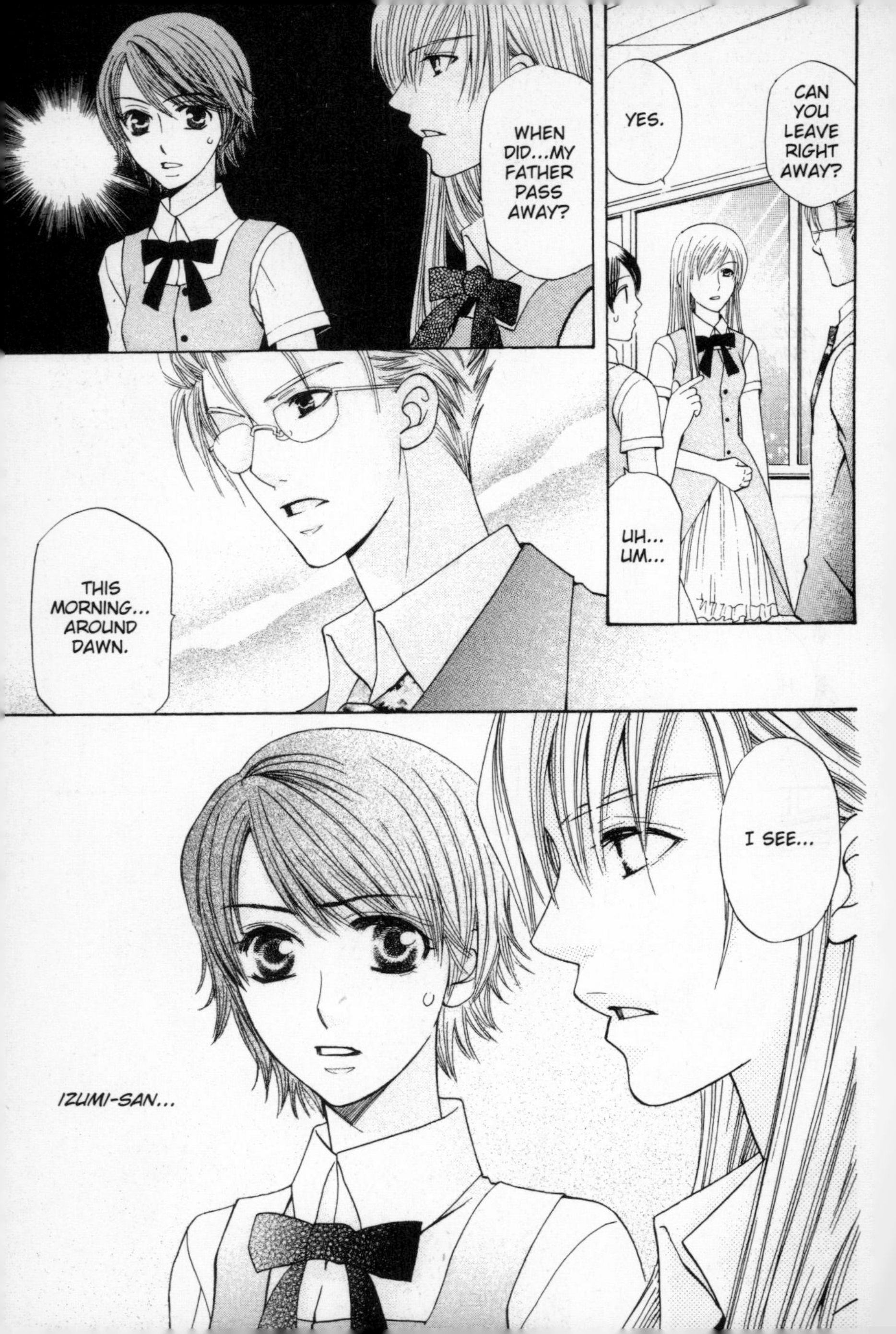
CAN YOU LEAVE RIGHT AWAY?
YES.
UH... UM...
WHEN DID...MY FATHER PASS AWAY?
THIS MORNING... AROUND DAWN.
I SEE...
IZUMI-SAN...

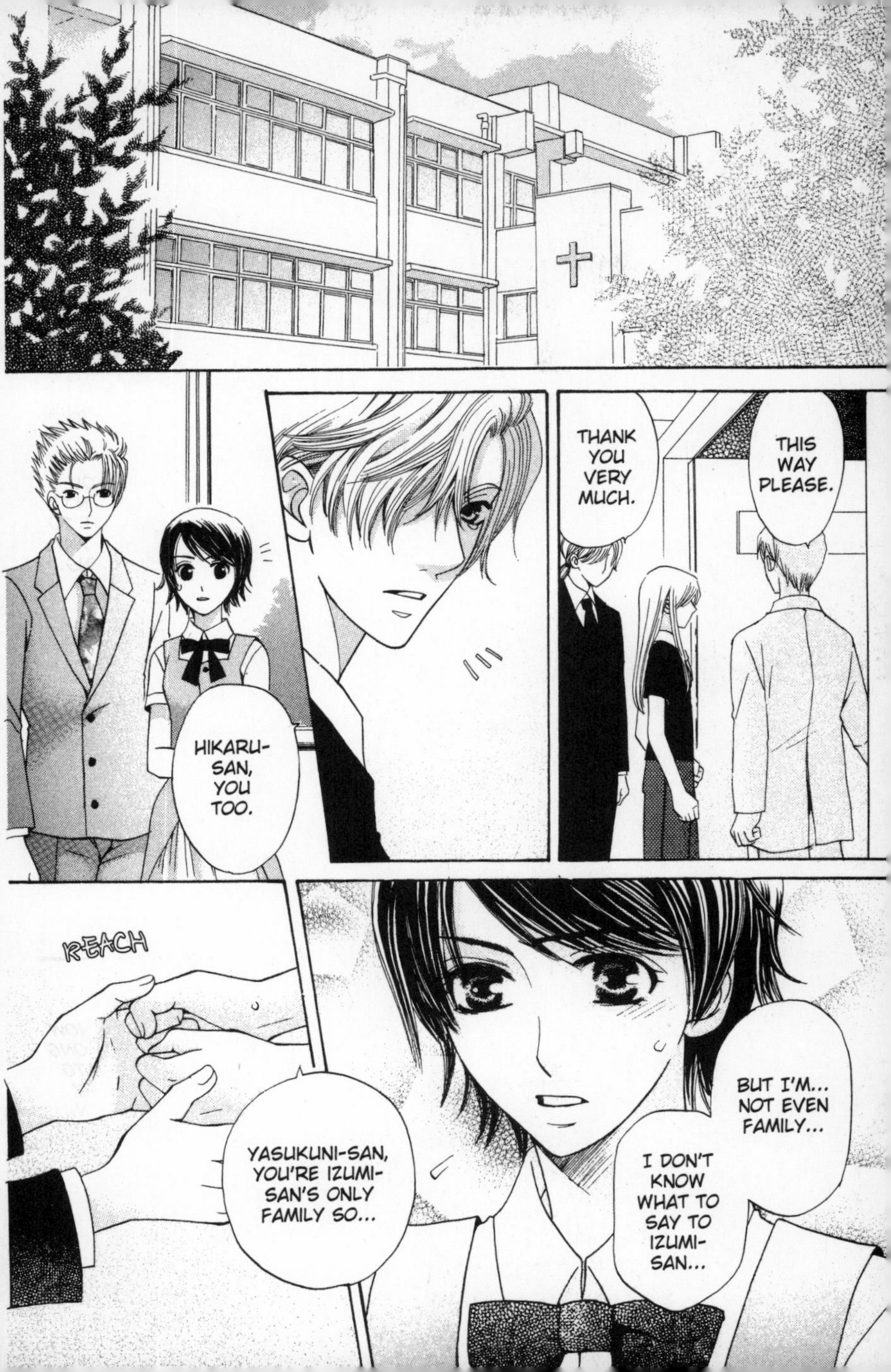
THIS WAY PLEASE.
THANK YOU VERY MUCH.
HIKARU-SAN, YOU TOO.
BUT I'M... NOT EVEN FAMILY...
I DON'T KNOW WHAT TO SAY TO IZUMI-SAN...
REACH
YASUKUNI-SAN, YOU'RE IZUMI-SAN'S ONLY FAMILY SO...

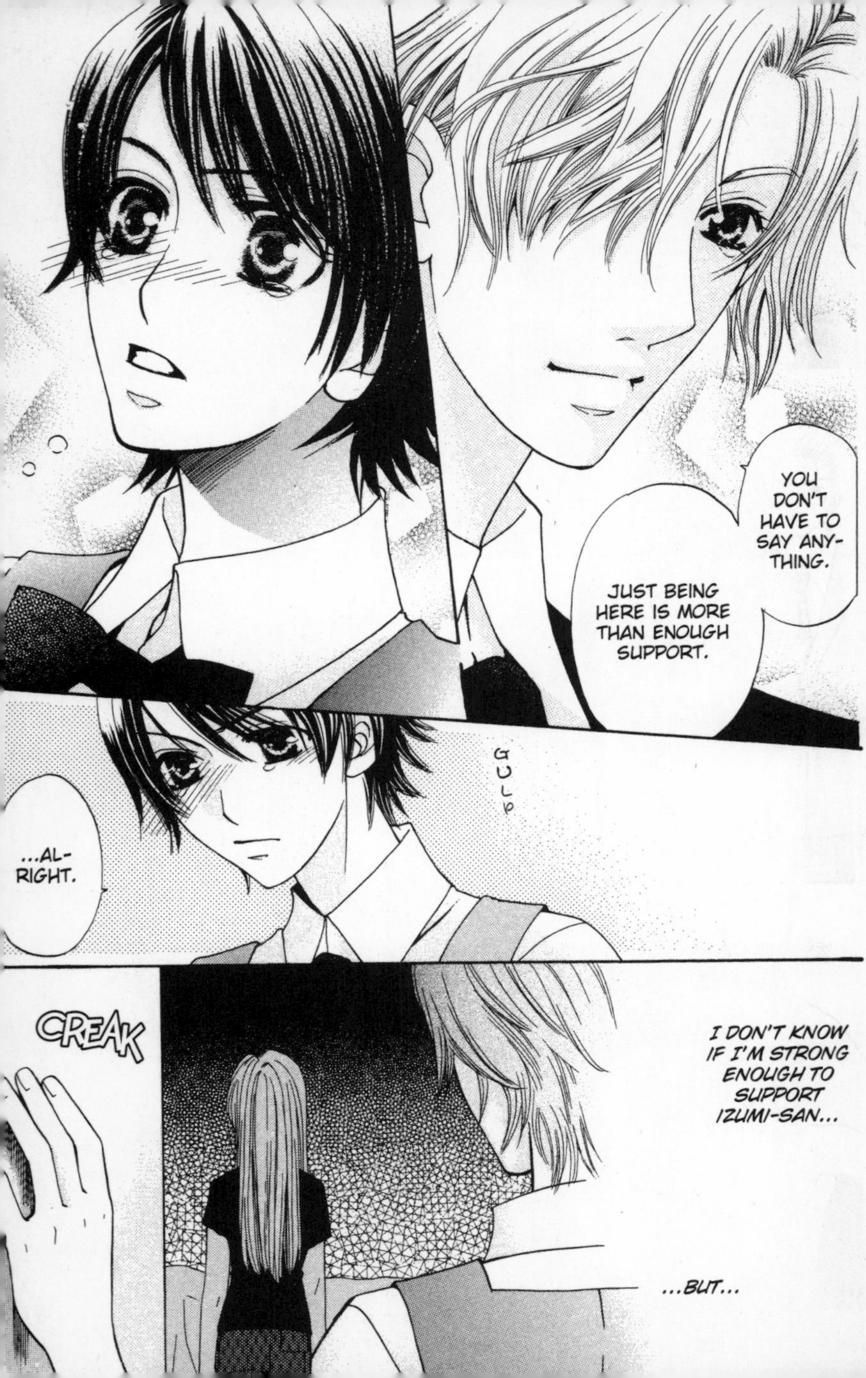
YOU DON'T HAVE TO SAY ANY-THING.
JUST BEING HERE IS MORE THAN ENOUGH SUPPORT.
GULP
...AL-RIGHT.
I DON'T KNOW IF I'M STRONG ENOUGH TO SUPPORT IZUMI-SAN...
CREAK
...BUT...

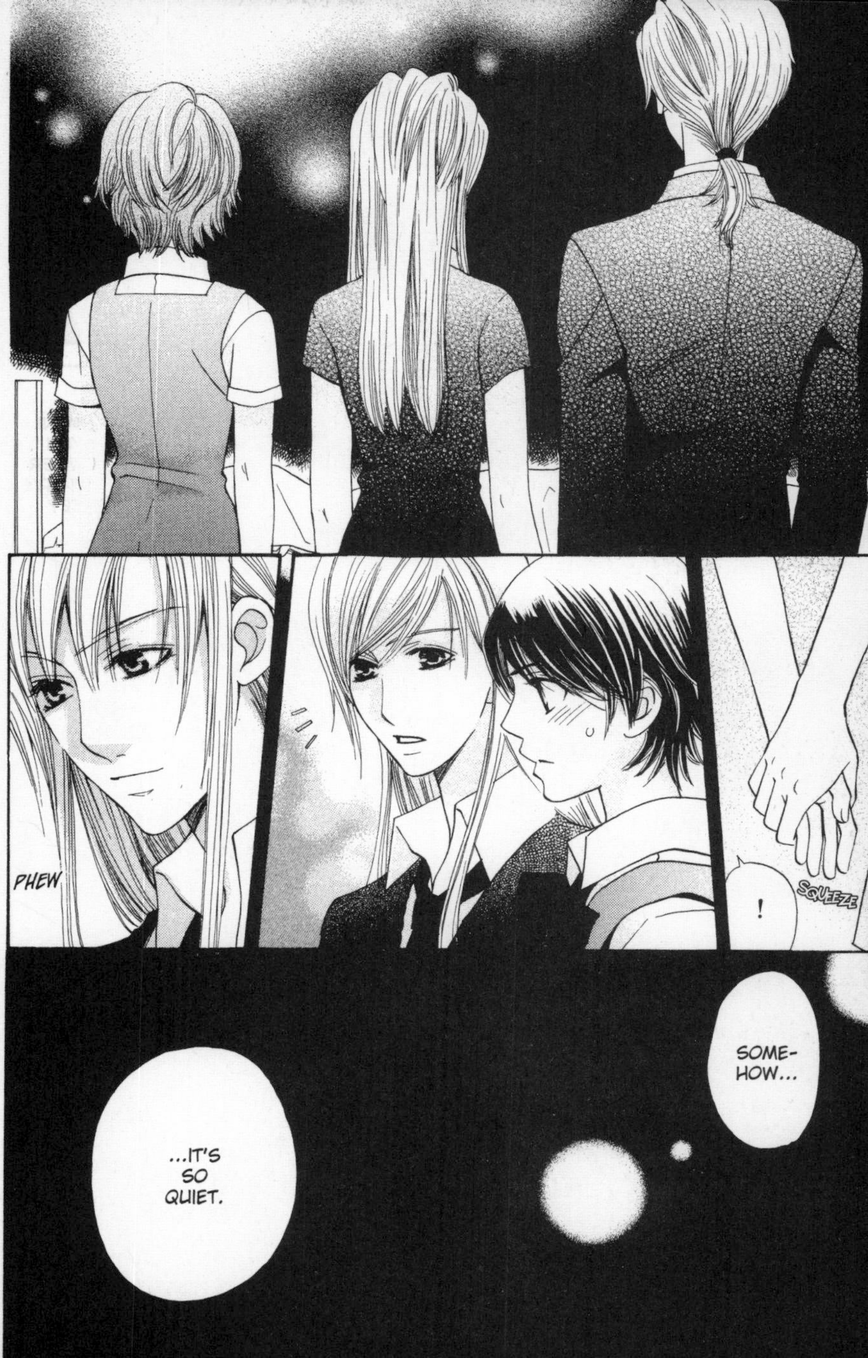
SQUEEZE
!
PHEW
SOME-HOW...
...IT'S SO QUIET.

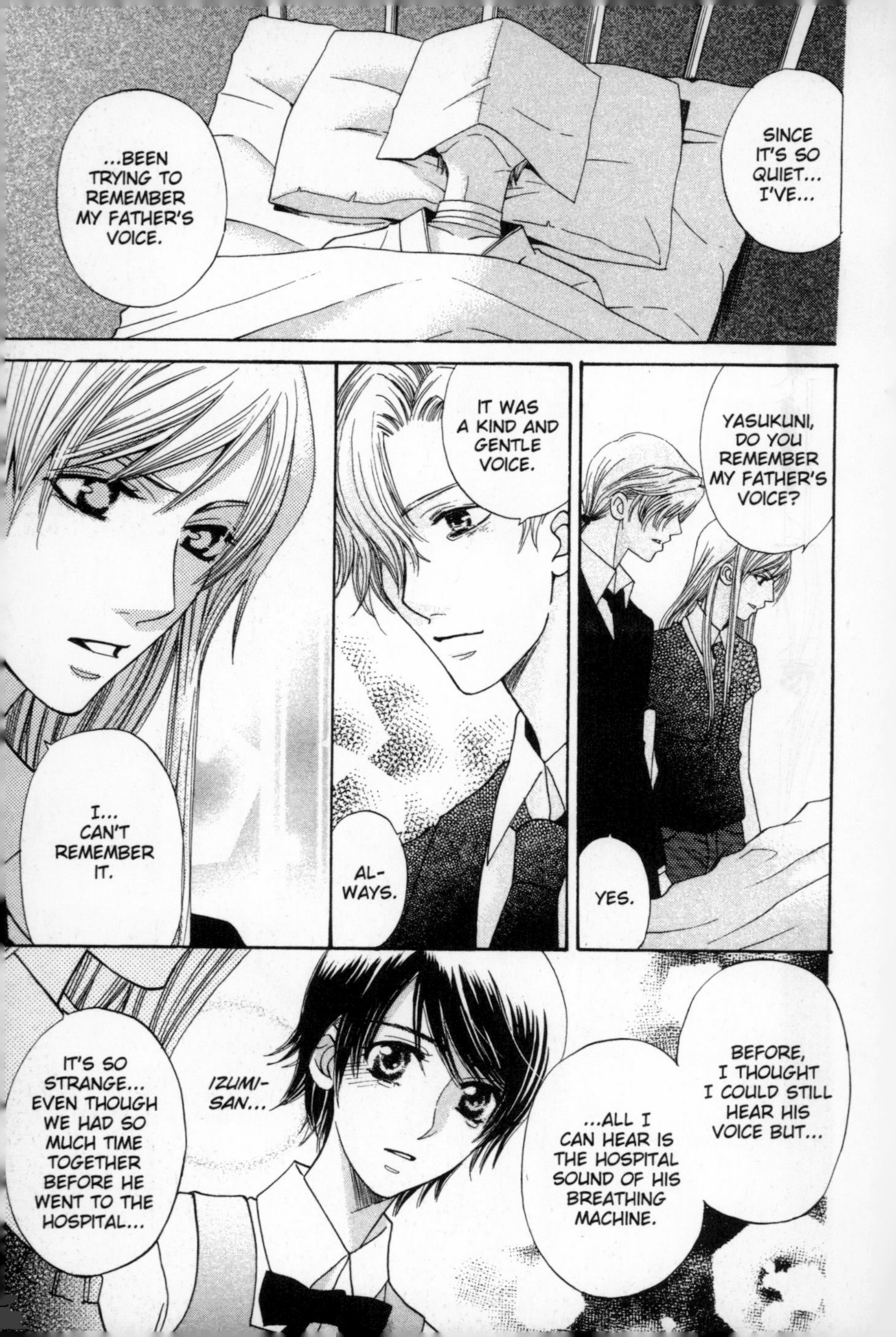
SINCE IT'S SO QUIET... I'VE...
...BEEN TRYING TO REMEMBER MY FATHER'S VOICE.
YASUKUNI, DO YOU REMEMBER MY FATHER'S VOICE?
YES.
IT WAS A KIND AND GENTLE VOICE.
AL-WAYS.
I... CAN'T REMEMBER IT.
BEFORE, I THOUGHT I COULD STILL HEAR HIS VOICE BUT...
...ALL I CAN HEAR IS THE HOSPITAL SOUND OF HIS BREATHING MACHINE.
IZUMI-SAN...
IT'S SO STRANGE... EVEN THOUGH WE HAD SO MUCH TIME TOGETHER BEFORE HE WENT TO THE HOSPITAL...

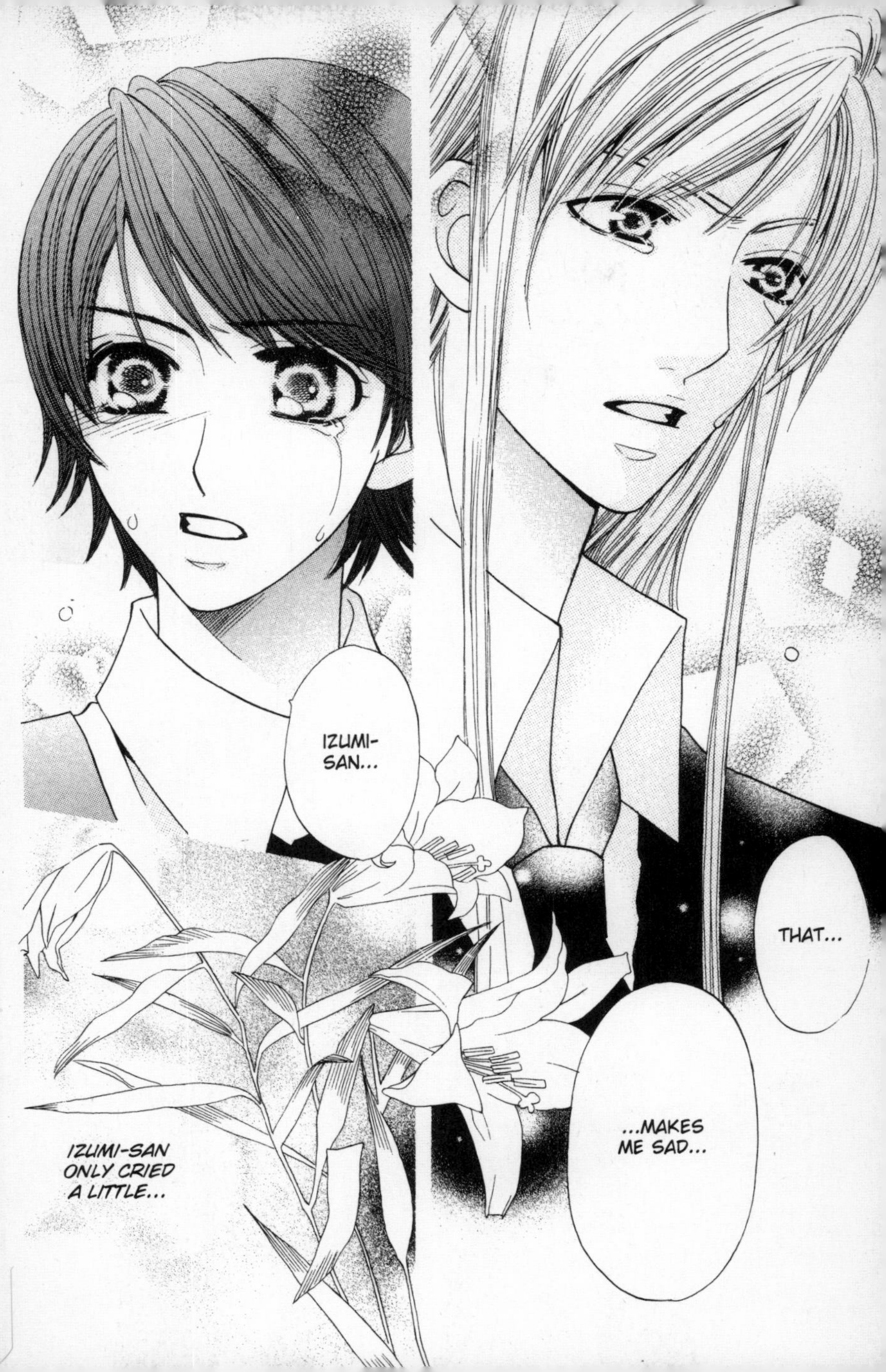
THAT...
...MAKES ME SAD...
IZUMI-SAN...
IZUMI-SAN ONLY CRIED A LITTLE...

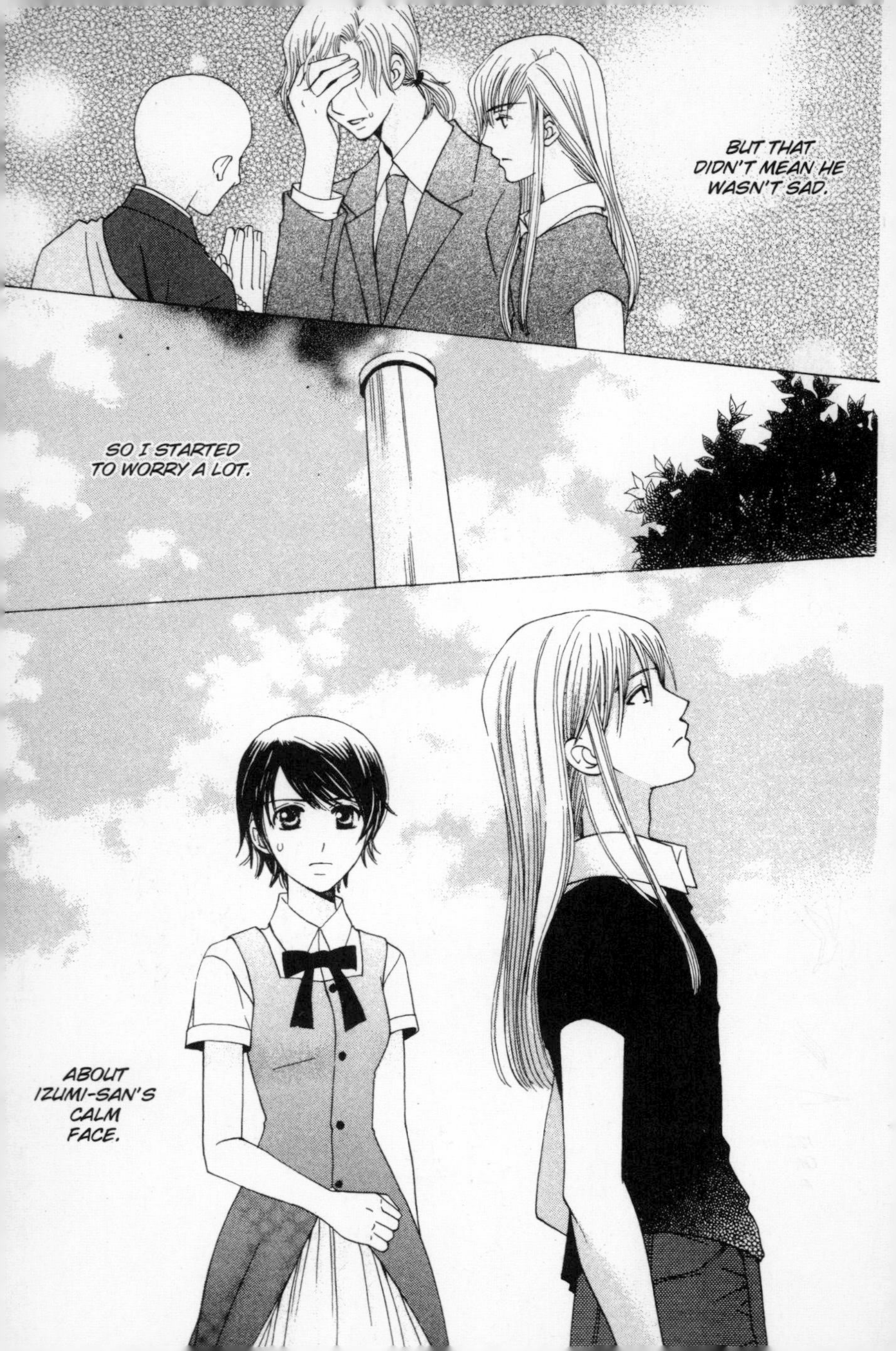
BUT THAT DIDN'T MEAN HE WASN'T SAD.
SO I STARTED TO WORRY A LOT.
ABOUT IZUMI-SAN'S CALM FACE.

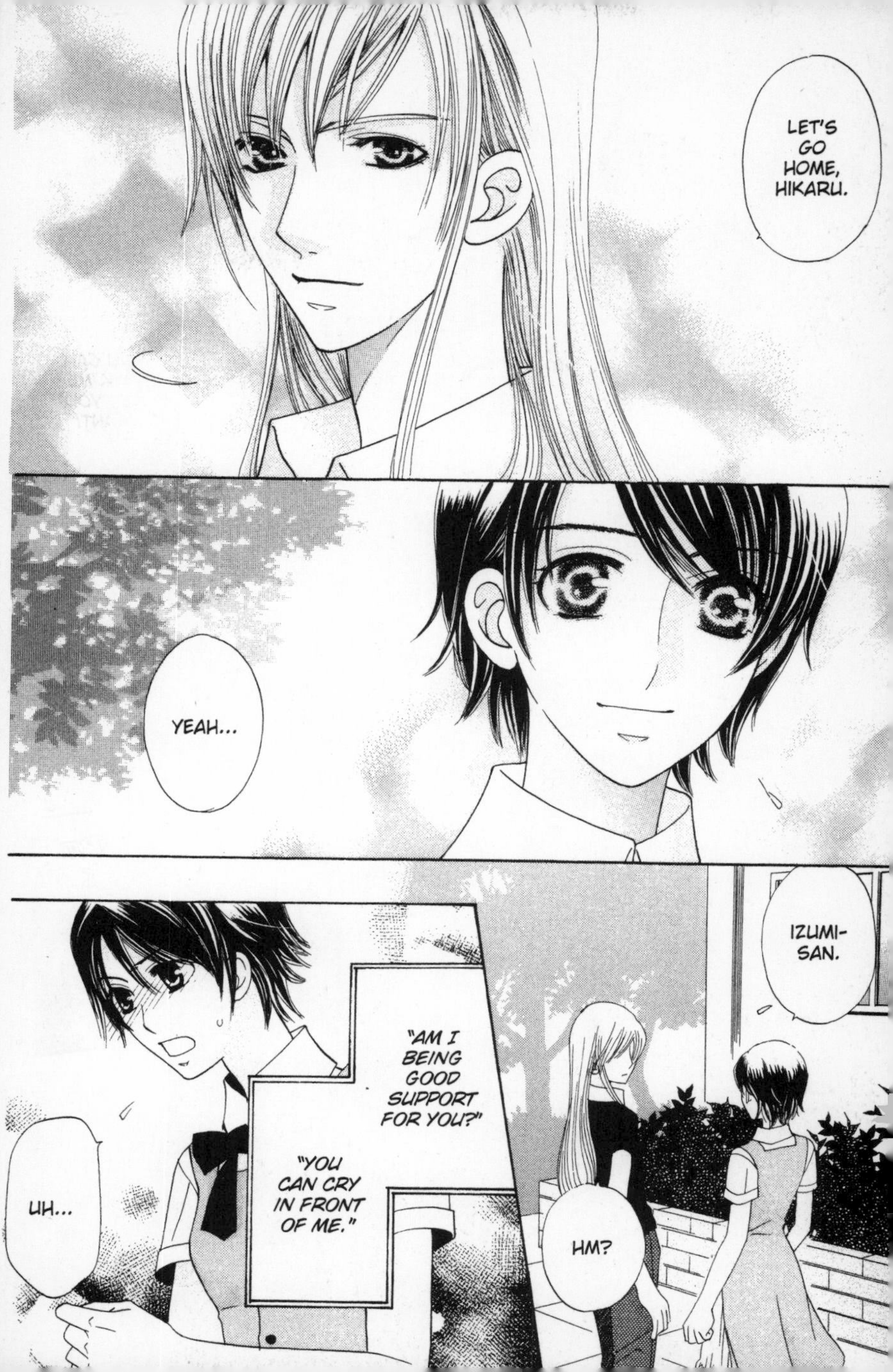
LET'S GO HOME, HIKARU.
YEAH...
IZUMI-SAN.
HM?
"AM I BEING GOOD SUPPORT FOR YOU?"
"YOU CAN CRY IN FRONT OF ME."
UH...

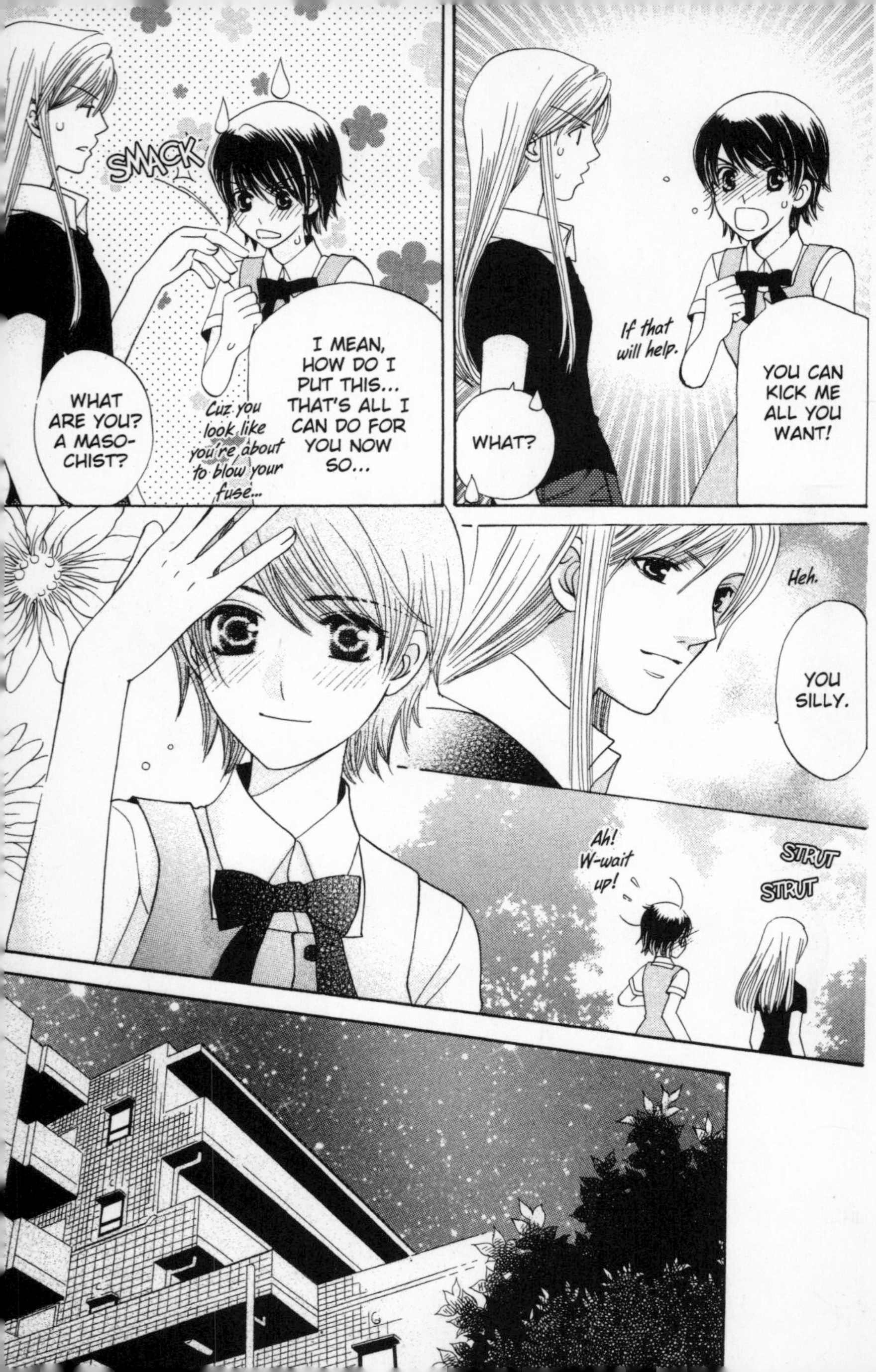
YOU CAN KICK ME ALL YOU WANT!
If that will help.
WHAT?
SMACK
I MEAN, HOW DO I PUT THIS... THAT'S ALL I CAN DO FOR YOU NOW SO...
Cuz you look like you're about to blow your fuse...
WHAT ARE YOU? A MASO-CHIST?
Heh.
YOU SILLY.
STRUT
STRUT
Ah! W-wait up!

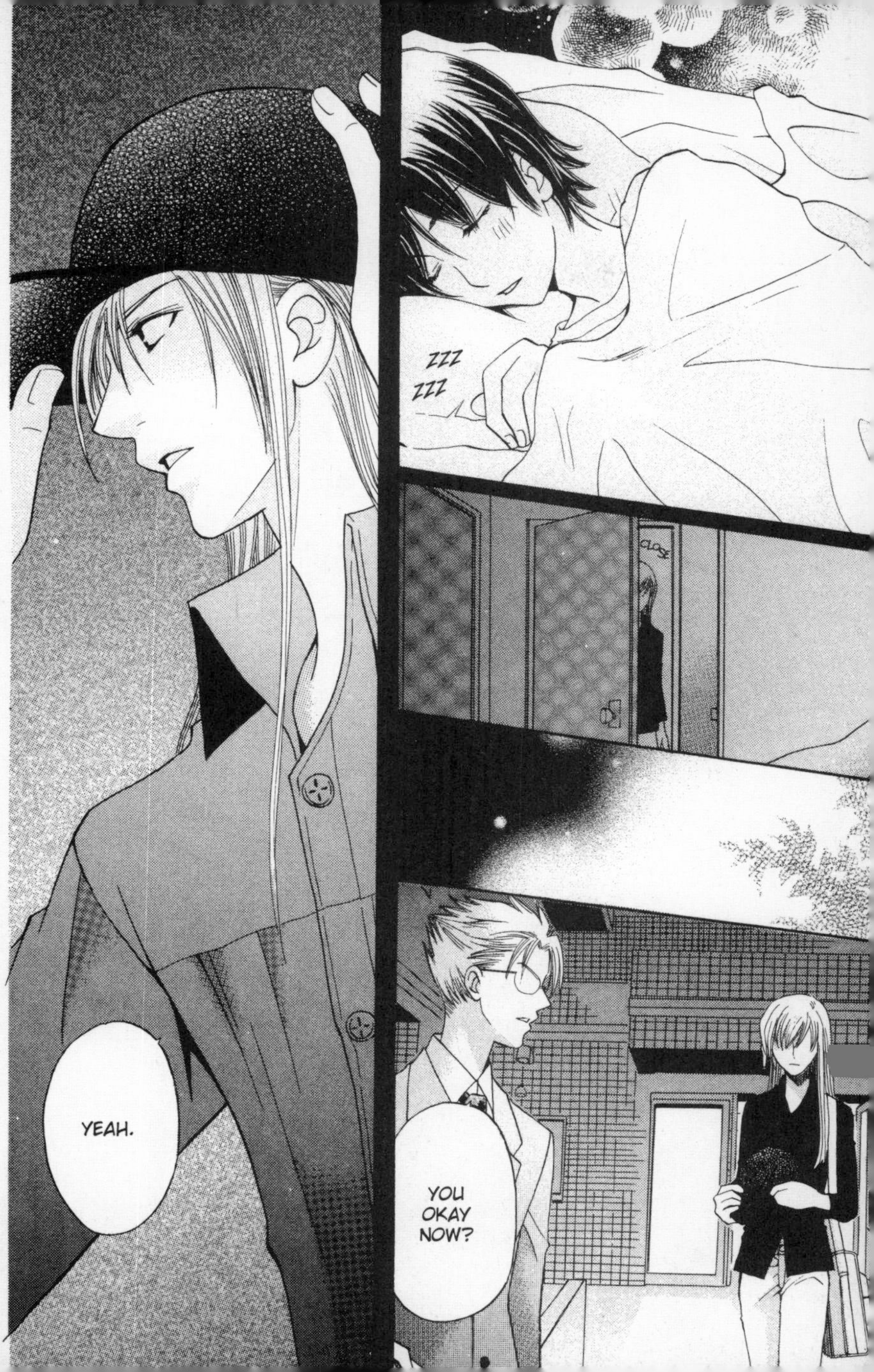
ZZZ
ZZZ
CLOSE
YOU OKAY NOW?
YEAH.

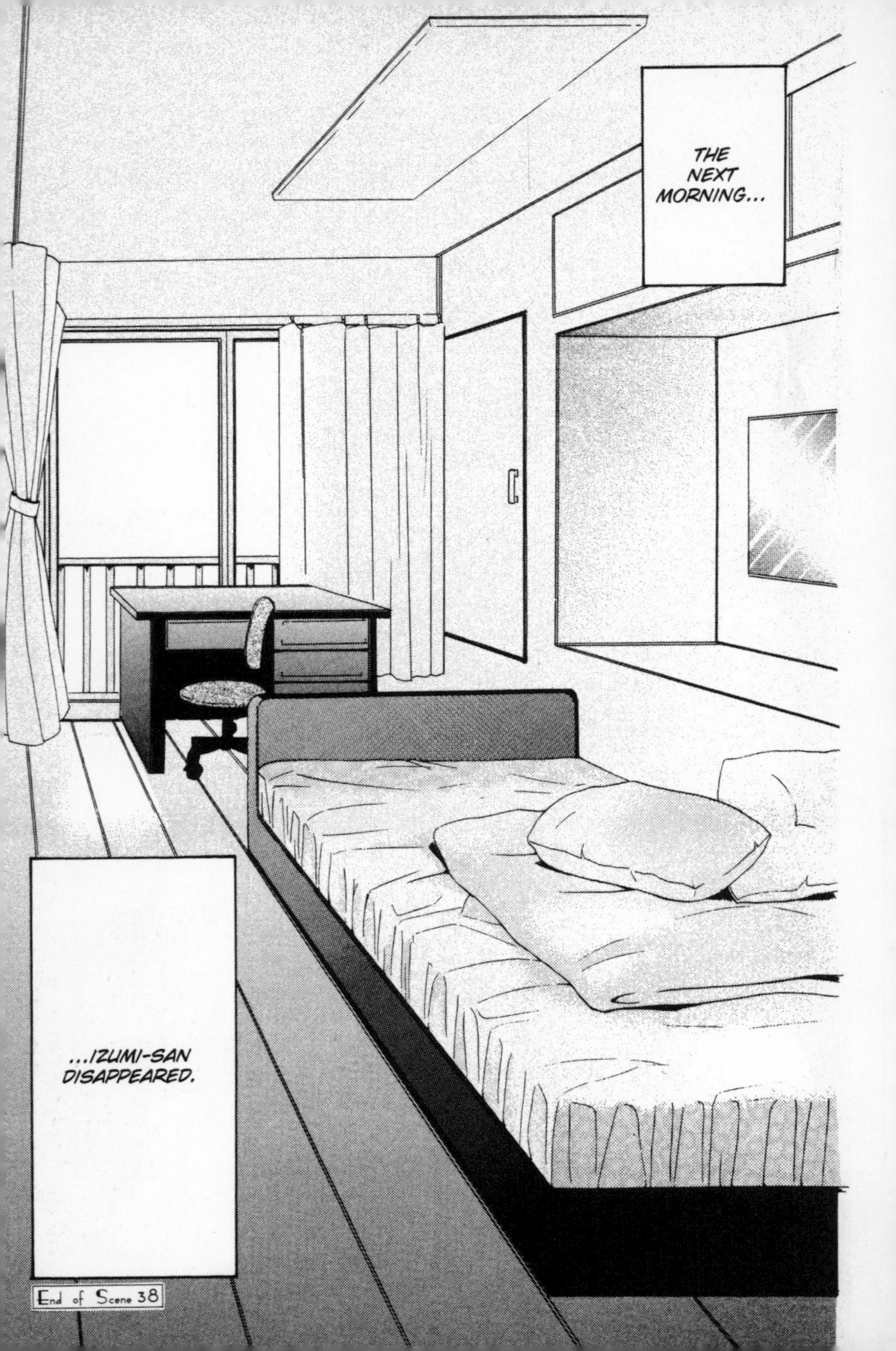
THE NEXT MORNING...
...IZUMI-SAN DISAPPEARED.
End of Scene 38

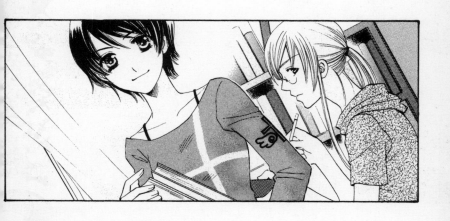

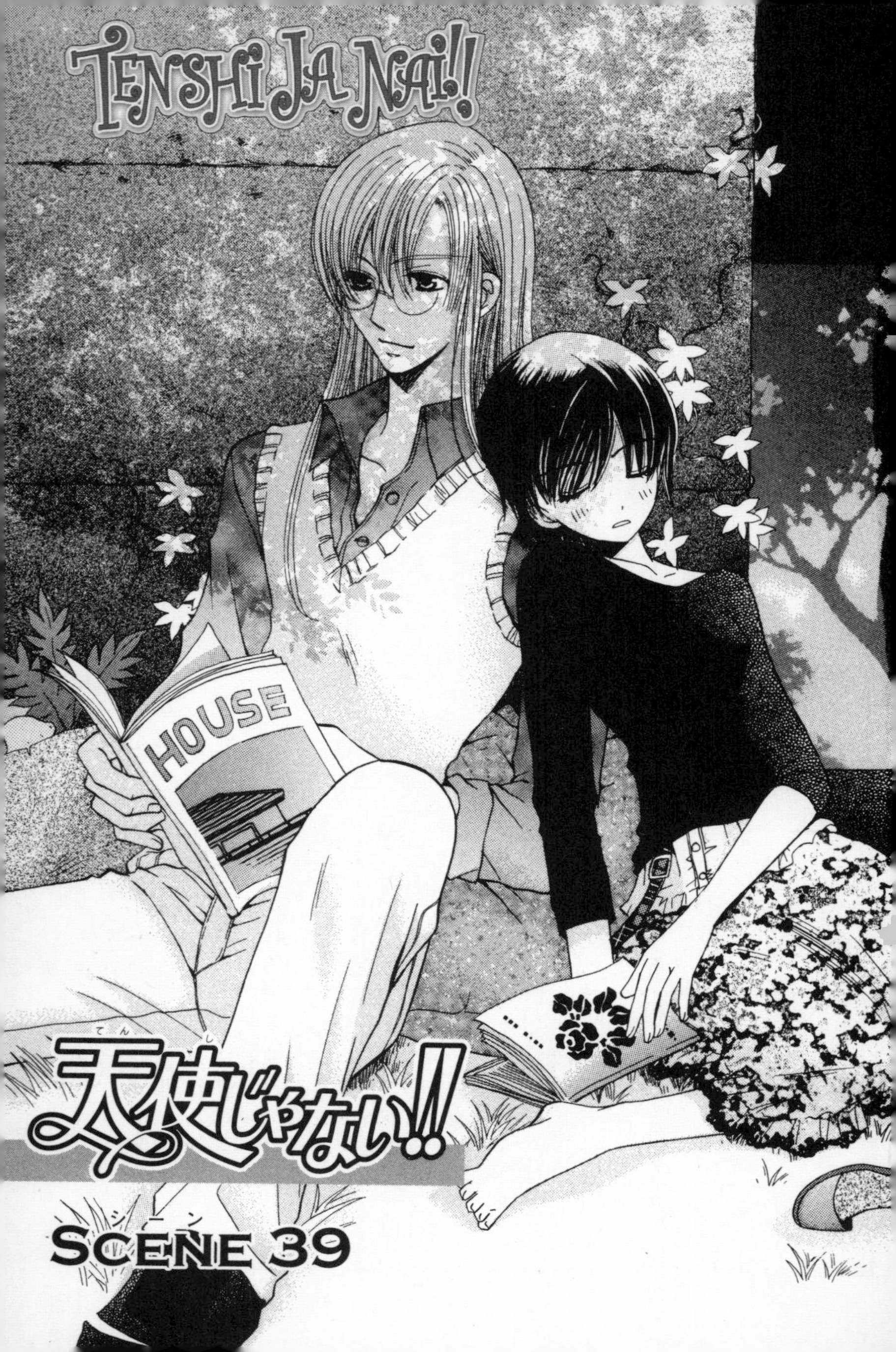
TENSHI JA NAI!!
HOUSE
天使じゃない!!
SCENE 39

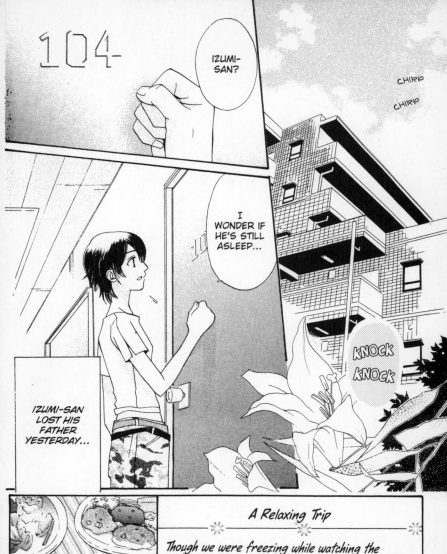

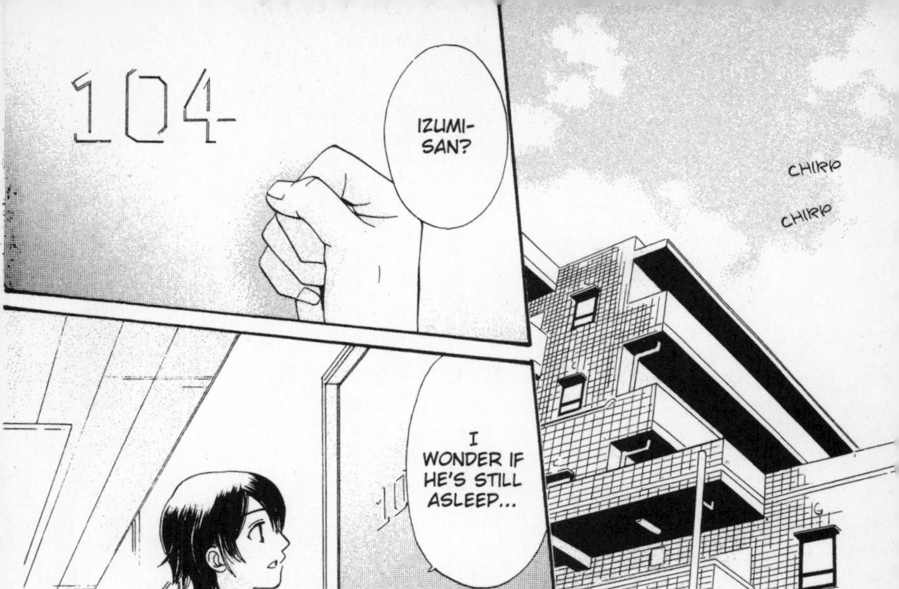
CHIRP
CHIRP
104
IZUMI-SAN?
I WONDER IF HE'S STILL ASLEEP...
KNOCK
KNOCK
IZUMI-SAN LOST HIS FATHER YESTERDAY...

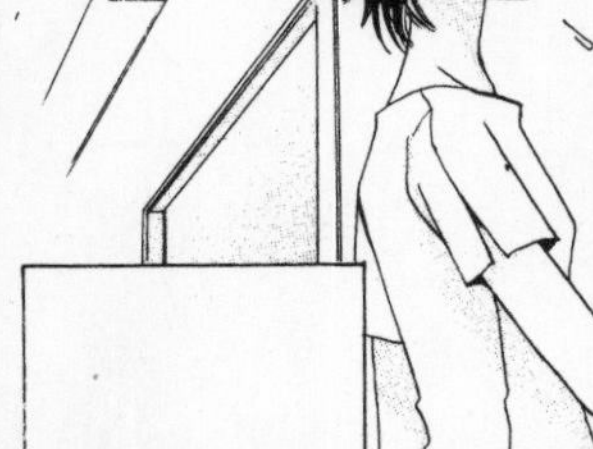
T-san's
H-san's
Mine

### A Relaxing Trip

*Though we were freezing while watching the night parade, we were in high spirits when we got to a Bush Restaurant. Strangely enough H-san had the best arrangement of side dishes, all her favorite foods! Mine and T-san's were all brown... but come on T-san, you didn't have to try so many different curries...*

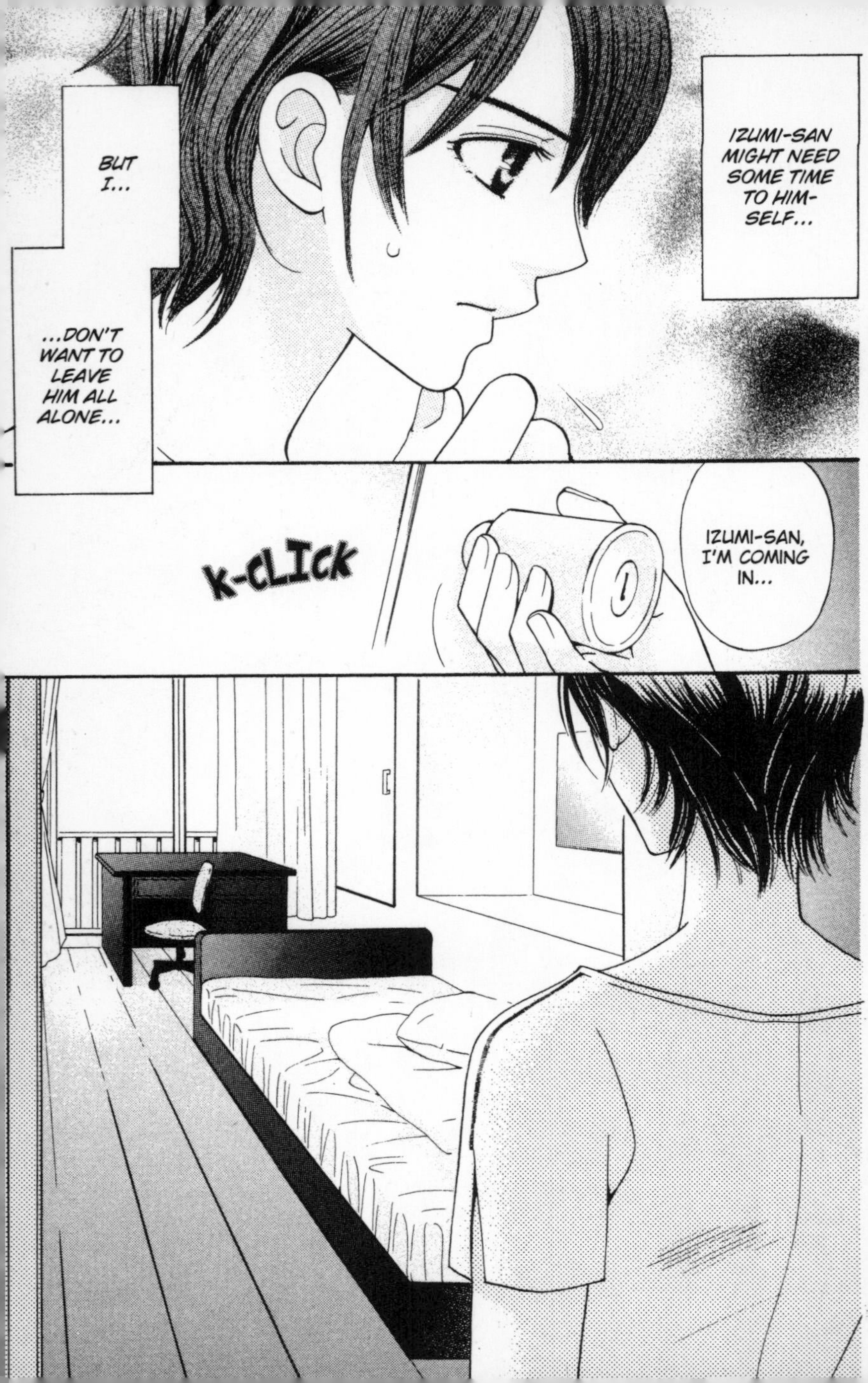
IZUMI-SAN MIGHT NEED SOME TIME TO HIM-SELF...
BUT I...
...DON'T WANT TO LEAVE HIM ALL ALONE...
IZUMI-SAN, I'M COMING IN...
K-CLICK

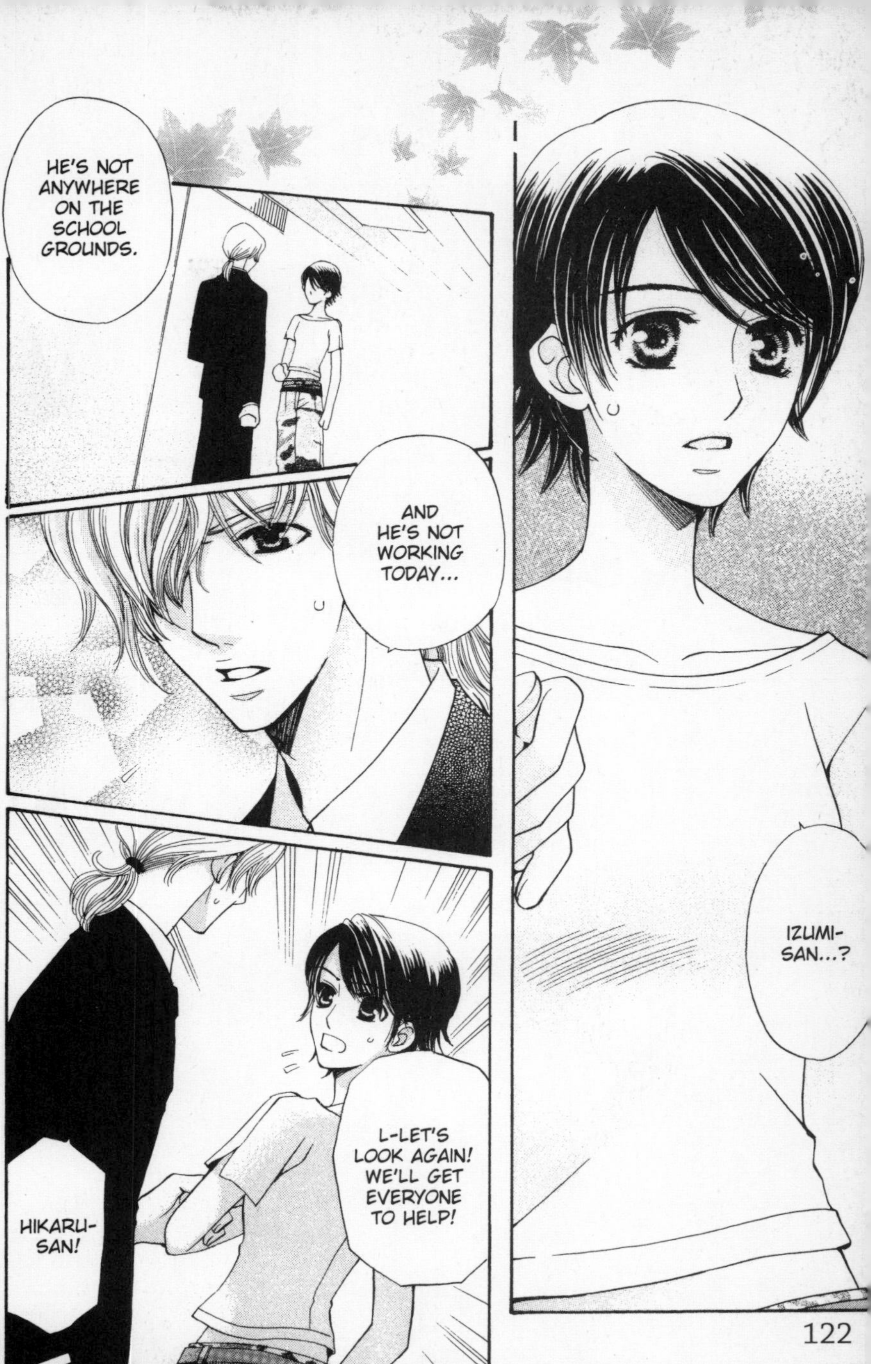
IZUMI-SAN...?
HE'S NOT ANYWHERE ON THE SCHOOL GROUNDS.
AND HE'S NOT WORKING TODAY...
L-LET'S LOOK AGAIN! WE'LL GET EVERYONE TO HELP!
HIKARU-SAN!

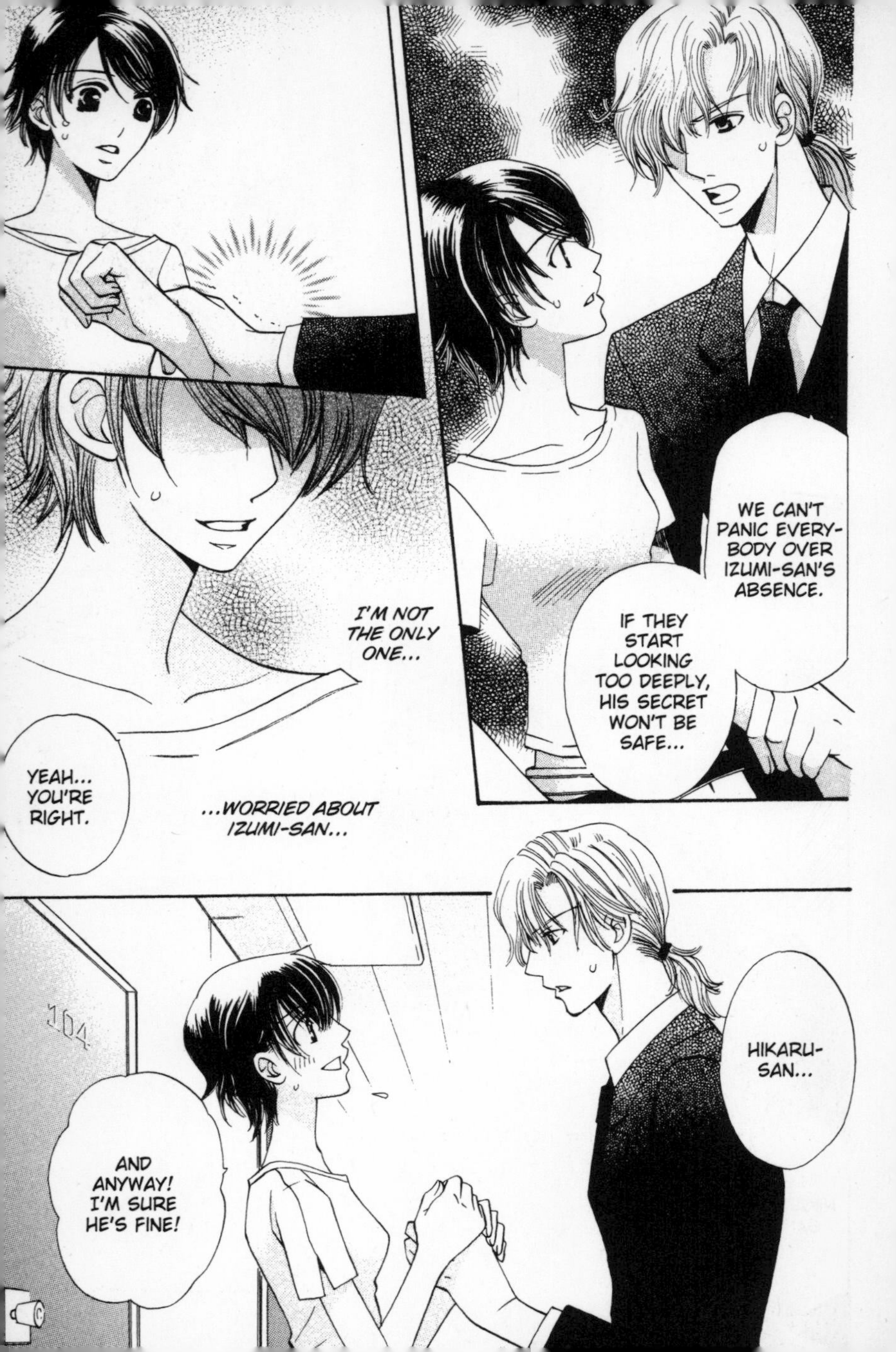
WE CAN'T PANIC EVERY-BODY OVER IZUMI-SAN'S ABSENCE.
IF THEY START LOOKING TOO DEEPLY, HIS SECRET WON'T BE SAFE...
I'M NOT THE ONLY ONE...
...WORRIED ABOUT IZUMI-SAN...
YEAH... YOU'RE RIGHT.
HIKARU-SAN...
AND ANYWAY! I'M SURE HE'S FINE!

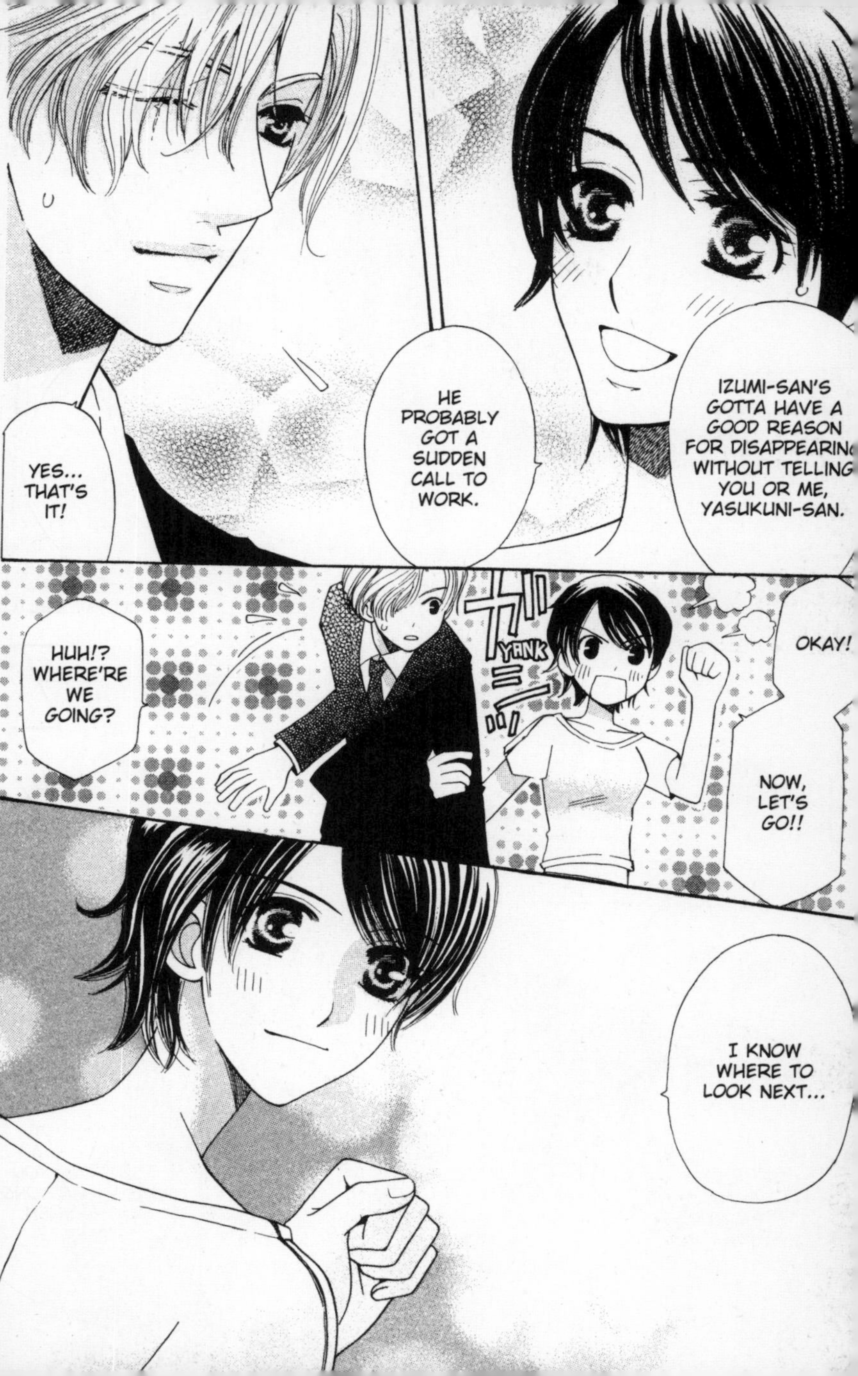

IZUMI-SAN'S GOTTA HAVE A GOOD REASON FOR DISAPPEARING WITHOUT TELLING YOU OR ME, YASUKUNI-SAN.
HE PROBABLY GOT A SUDDEN CALL TO WORK.
YES... THAT'S IT!
OKAY!
NOW, LET'S GO!!
YANK
HUH!? WHERE'RE WE GOING?
I KNOW WHERE TO LOOK NEXT...

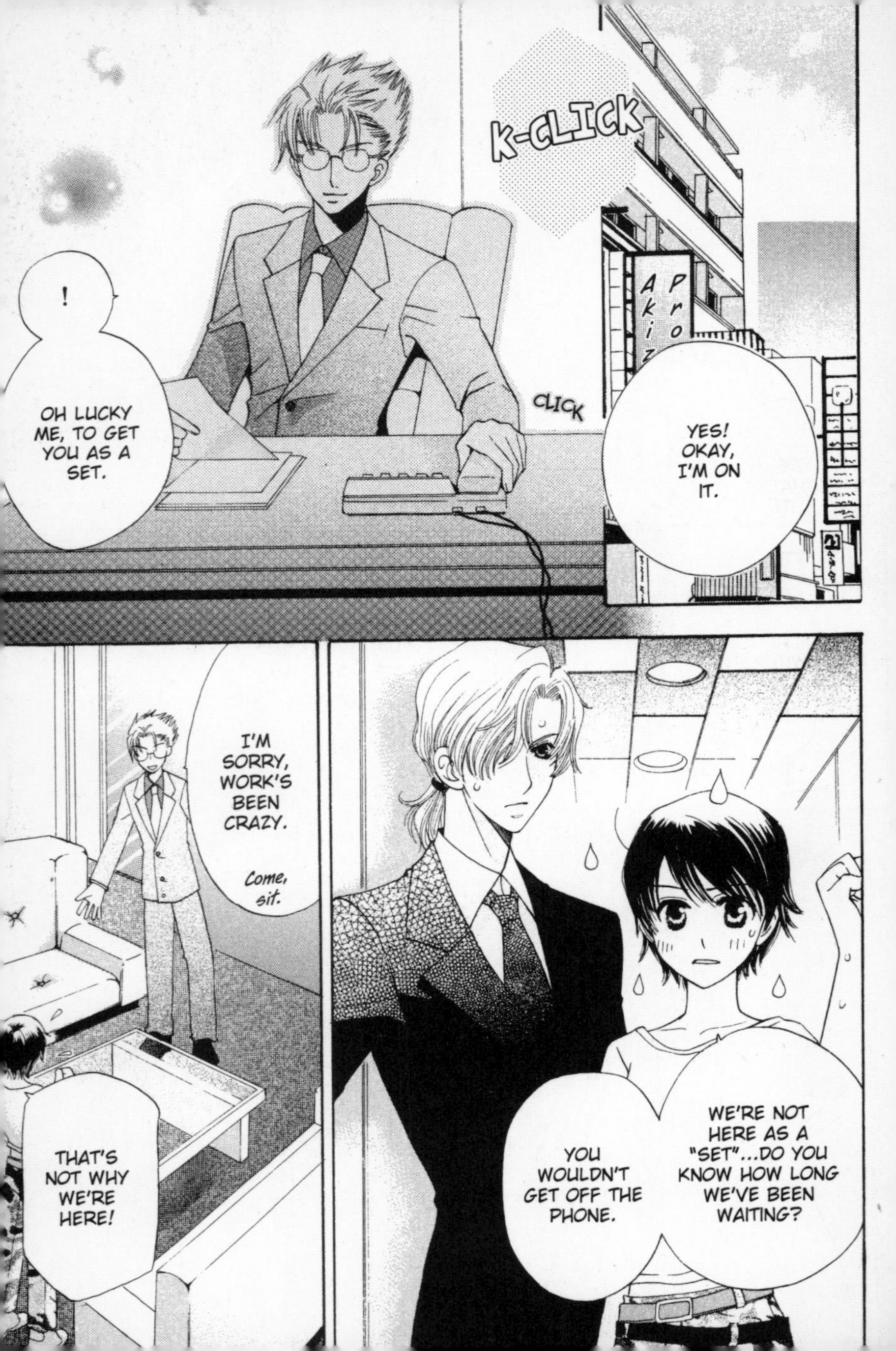
K-CLICK
YES! OKAY, I'M ON IT.
Akiz Pro
CLICK
!
OH LUCKY ME, TO GET YOU AS A SET.
WE'RE NOT HERE AS A "SET"...DO YOU KNOW HOW LONG WE'VE BEEN WAITING?
YOU WOULDN'T GET OFF THE PHONE.
I'M SORRY, WORK'S BEEN CRAZY.
Come, sit.
THAT'S NOT WHY WE'RE HERE!

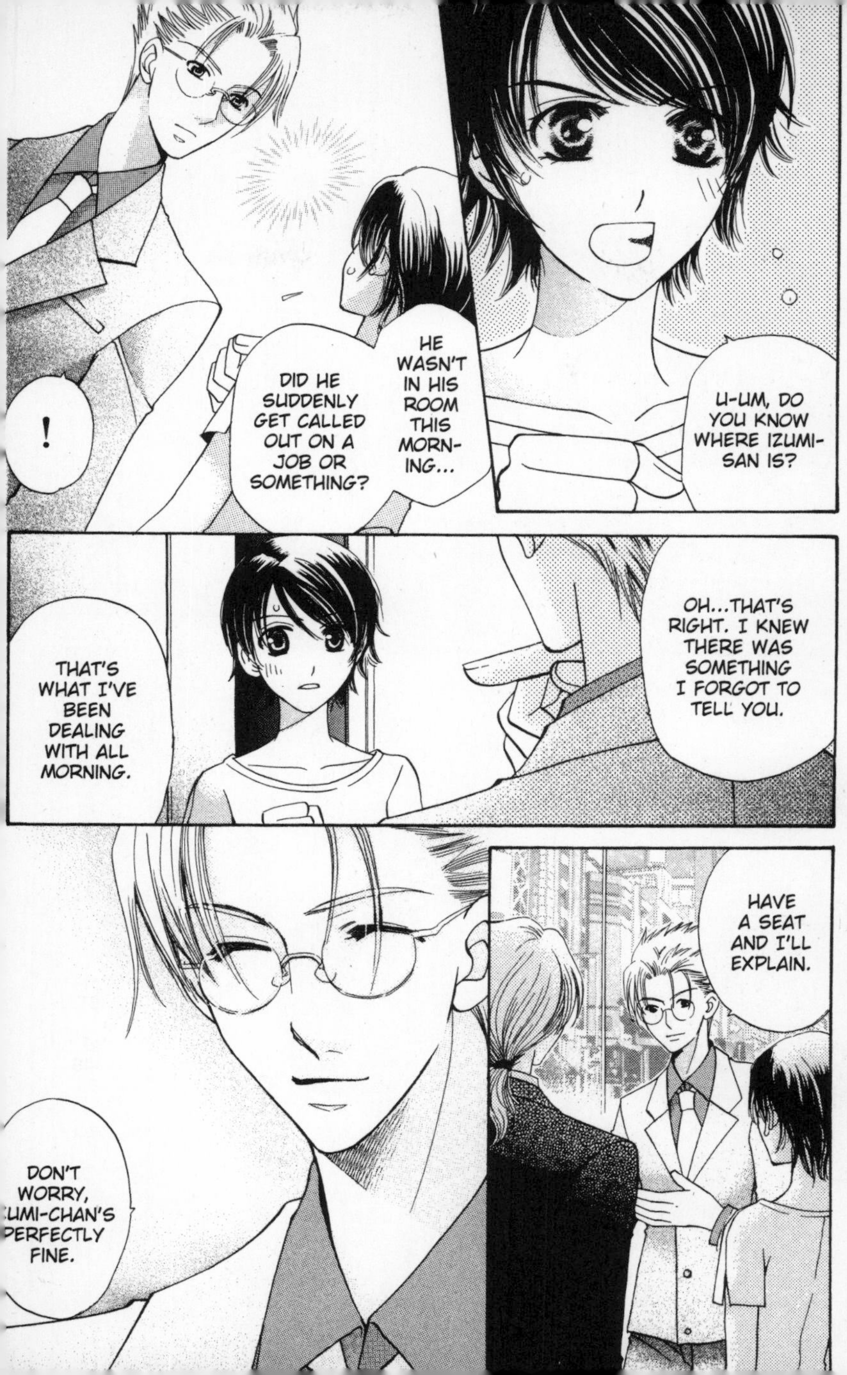
U-UM, DO YOU KNOW WHERE IZUMI-SAN IS?
HE WASN'T IN HIS ROOM THIS MORNING...
DID HE SUDDENLY GET CALLED OUT ON A JOB OR SOMETHING?
!
OH...THAT'S RIGHT. I KNEW THERE WAS SOMETHING I FORGOT TO TELL YOU.
THAT'S WHAT I'VE BEEN DEALING WITH ALL MORNING.
HAVE A SEAT AND I'LL EXPLAIN.
DON'T WORRY, UMI-CHAN'S PERFECTLY FINE.

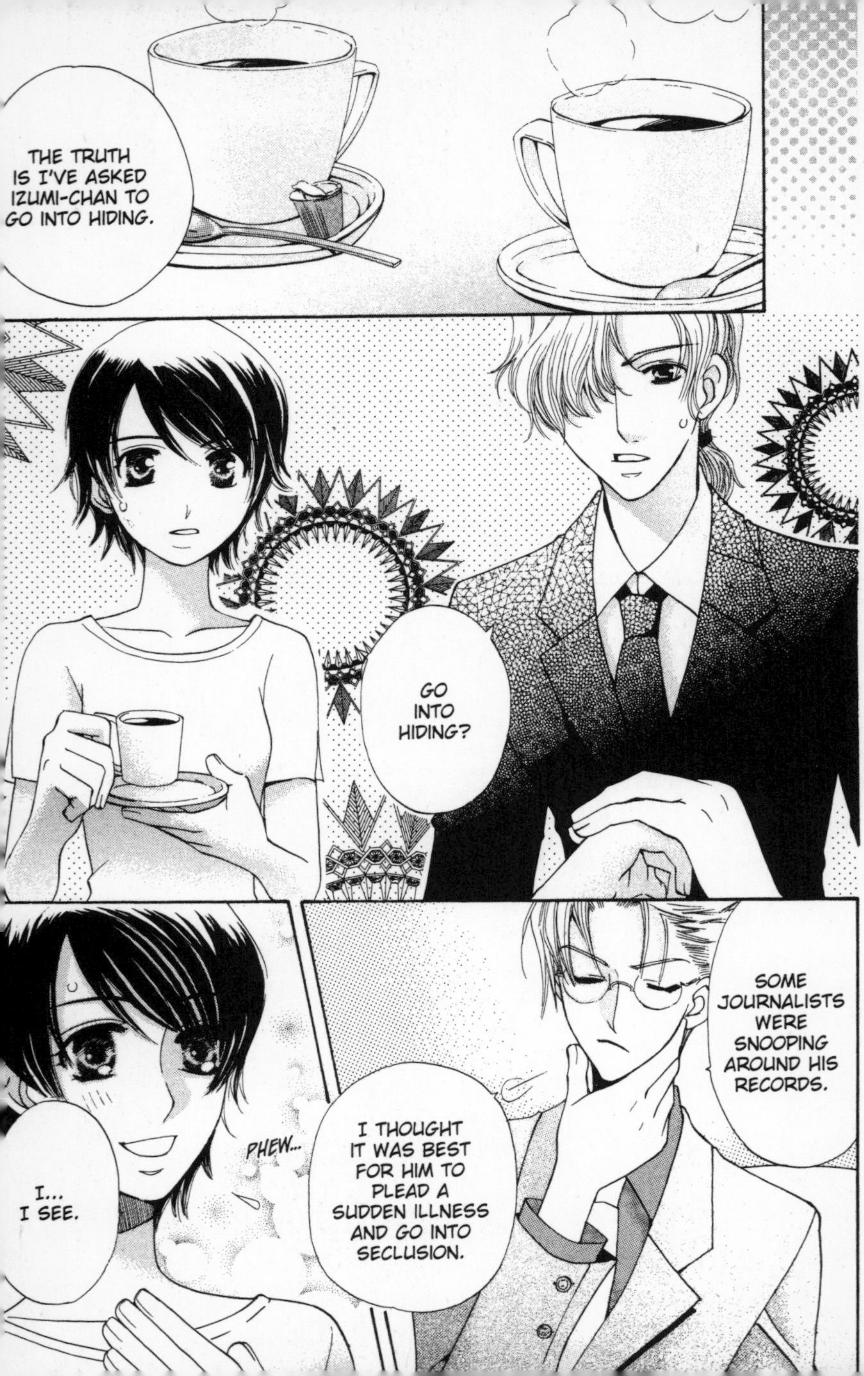
THE TRUTH IS I'VE ASKED IZUMI-CHAN TO GO INTO HIDING.
GO INTO HIDING?
SOME JOURNALISTS WERE SNOOPING AROUND HIS RECORDS.
I THOUGHT IT WAS BEST FOR HIM TO PLEAD A SUDDEN ILLNESS AND GO INTO SECLUSION.
PHEW...
I... I SEE.

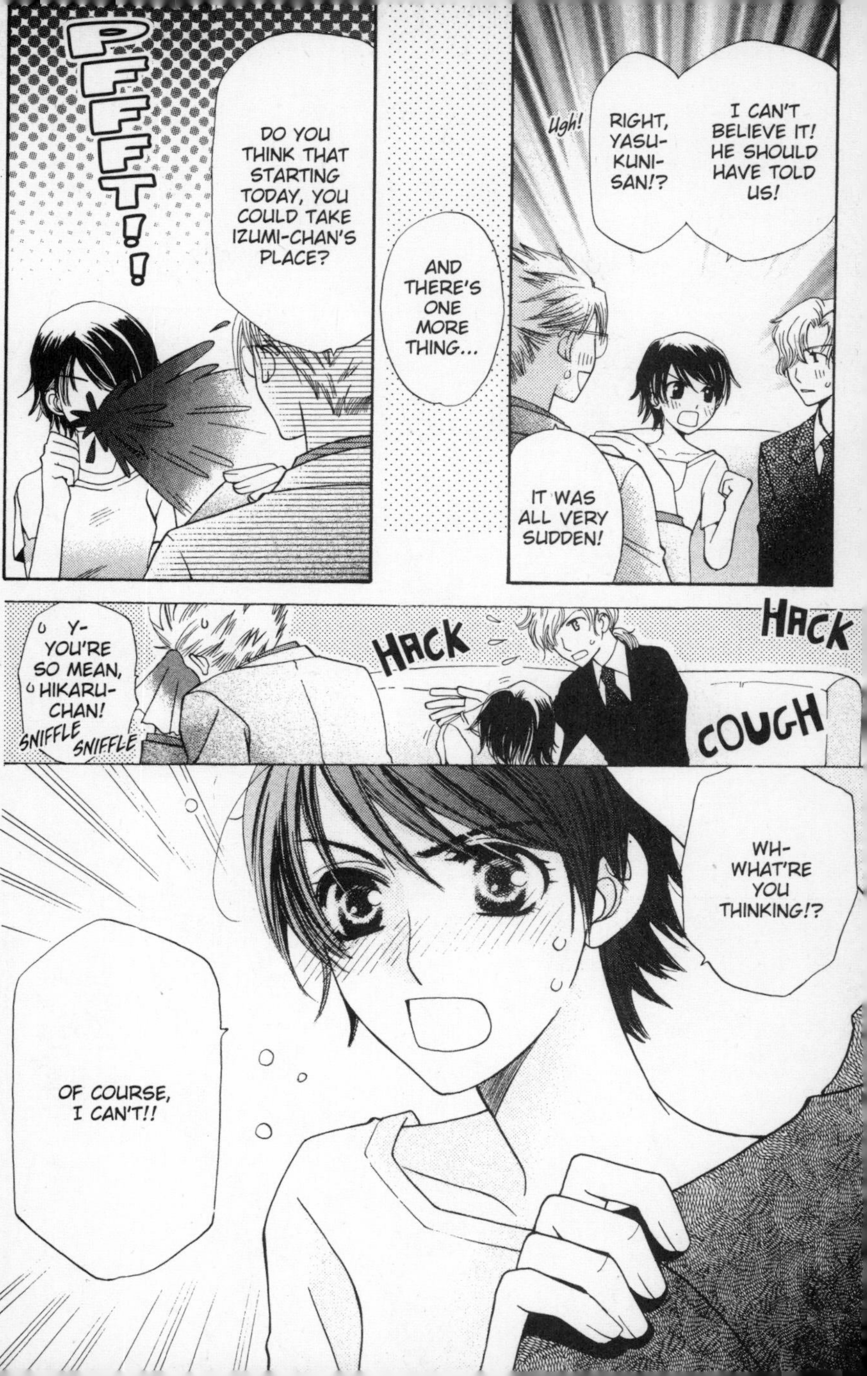
I CAN'T BELIEVE IT! HE SHOULD HAVE TOLD US!
RIGHT, YASUKUNI-SAN!?
Ugh!
IT WAS ALL VERY SUDDEN!
AND THERE'S ONE MORE THING...
DO YOU THINK THAT STARTING TODAY, YOU COULD TAKE IZUMI-CHAN'S PLACE?
PFFFT!!
HACK
COUGH
HACK
Y-YOU'RE SO MEAN, HIKARU-CHAN!
SNIFFLE SNIFFLE
WH-WHAT'RE YOU THINKING!?
OF COURSE, I CAN'T!!

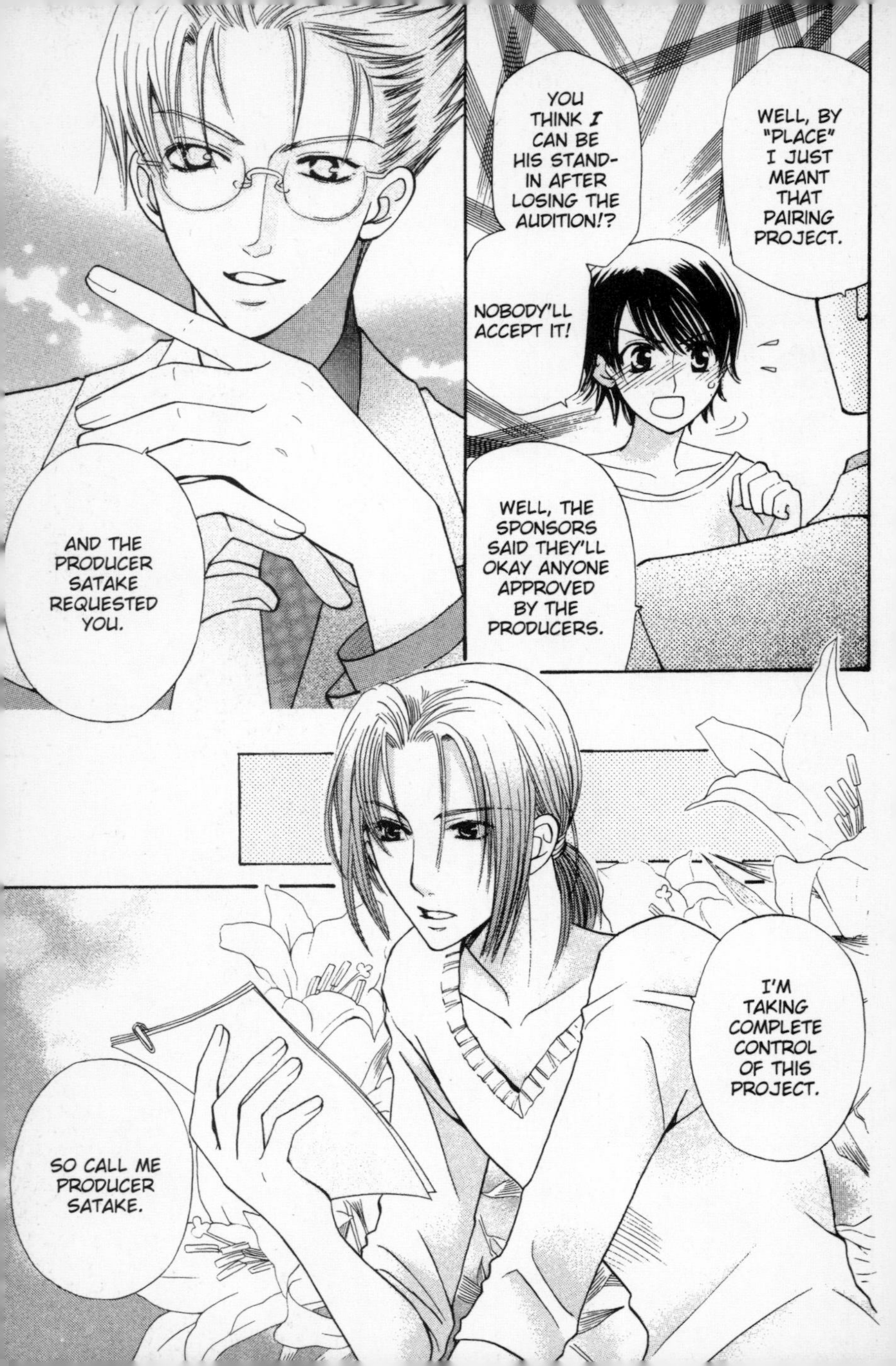
WELL, BY "PLACE" I JUST MEANT THAT PAIRING PROJECT.
YOU THINK *I* CAN BE HIS STAND-IN AFTER LOSING THE AUDITION!?
NOBODY'LL ACCEPT IT!
WELL, THE SPONSORS SAID THEY'LL OKAY ANYONE APPROVED BY THE PRODUCERS.
AND THE PRODUCER SATAKE REQUESTED YOU.
I'M TAKING COMPLETE CONTROL OF THIS PROJECT.
SO CALL ME PRODUCER SATAKE.

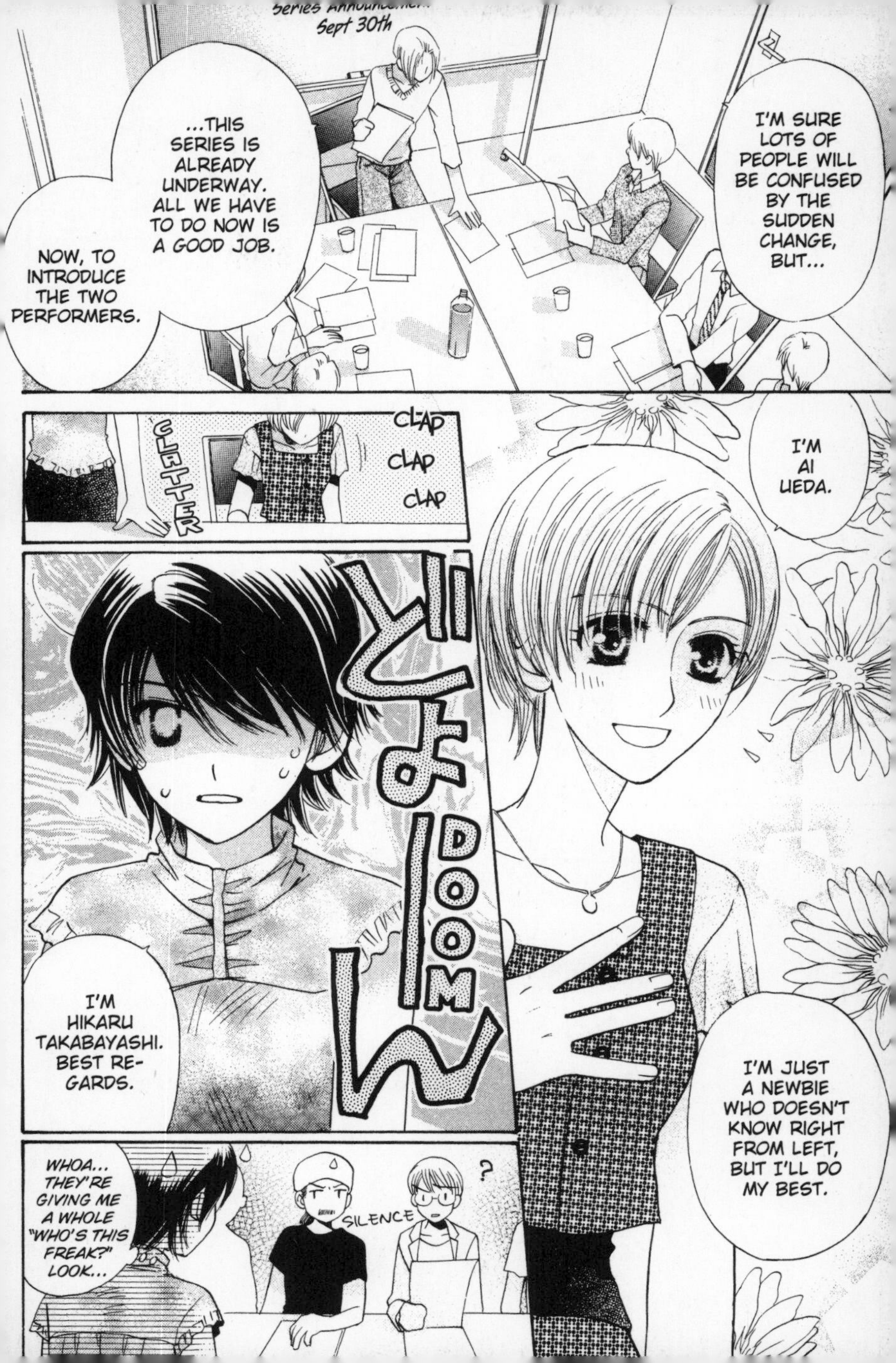
Series
Sept 30th
I'M SURE LOTS OF PEOPLE WILL BE CONFUSED BY THE SUDDEN CHANGE, BUT...
...THIS SERIES IS ALREADY UNDERWAY. ALL WE HAVE TO DO NOW IS A GOOD JOB.
NOW, TO INTRODUCE THE TWO PERFORMERS.
I'M AI UEDA.
I'M JUST A NEWBIE WHO DOESN'T KNOW RIGHT FROM LEFT, BUT I'LL DO MY BEST.
CLAP
CLAP
CLAP
CLATTER
DOOOM
I'M HIKARU TAKABAYASHI. BEST RE-GARDS.
?
SILENCE
WHOA... THEY'RE GIVING ME A WHOLE "WHO'S THIS FREAK?" LOOK...

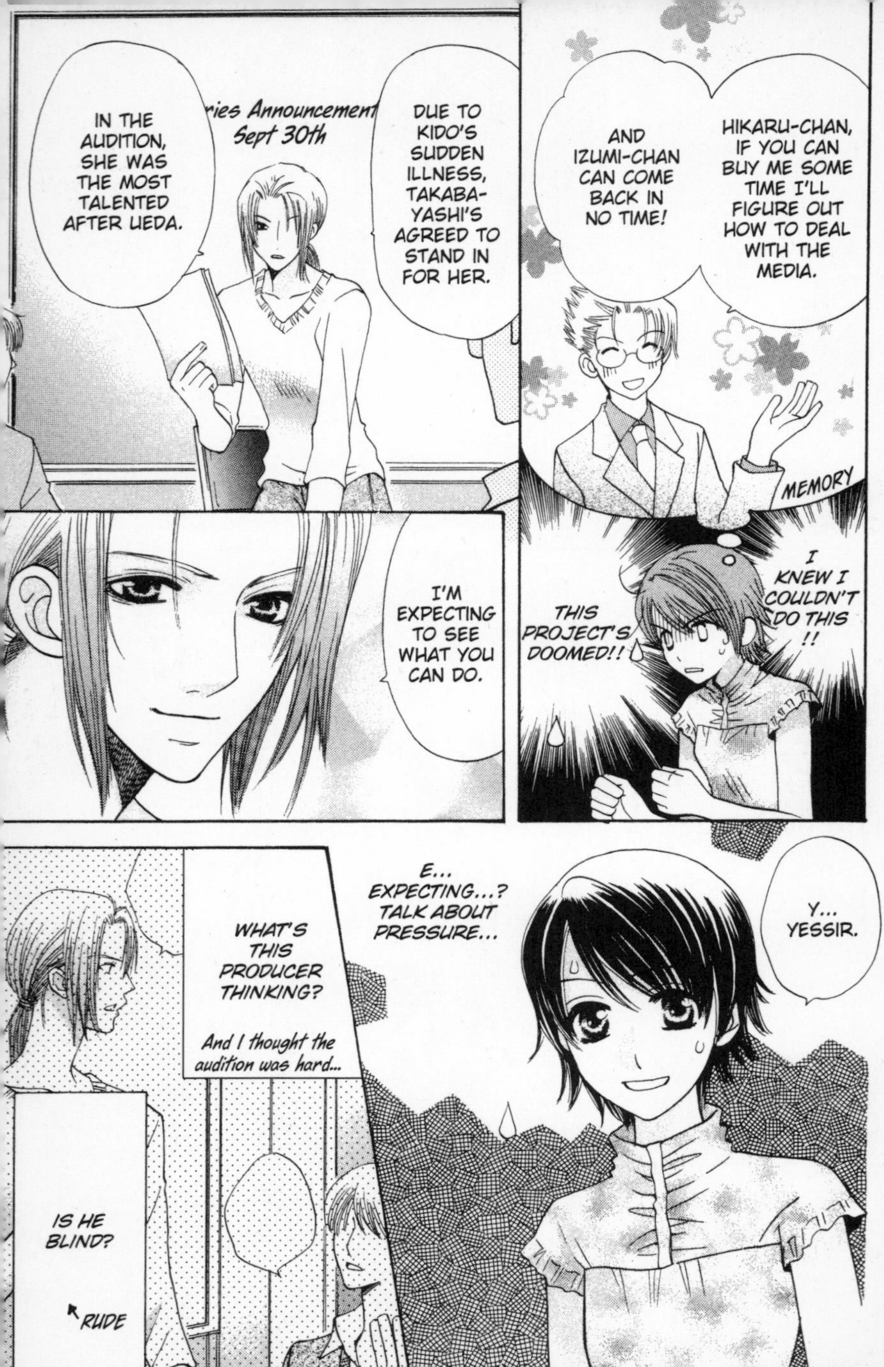
HIKARU-CHAN, IF YOU CAN BUY ME SOME TIME I'LL FIGURE OUT HOW TO DEAL WITH THE MEDIA.
AND IZUMI-CHAN CAN COME BACK IN NO TIME!
MEMORY
ries Announcement Sept 30th
DUE TO KIDO'S SUDDEN ILLNESS, TAKABA-YASHI'S AGREED TO STAND IN FOR HER.
IN THE AUDITION, SHE WAS THE MOST TALENTED AFTER UEDA.
I KNEW I COULDN'T DO THIS!!
THIS PROJECT'S DOOMED!!
I'M EXPECTING TO SEE WHAT YOU CAN DO.
Y... YESSIR.
E... EXPECTING...? TALK ABOUT PRESSURE...
WHAT'S THIS PRODUCER THINKING?
And I thought the audition was hard...
IS HE BLIND?
RUDE

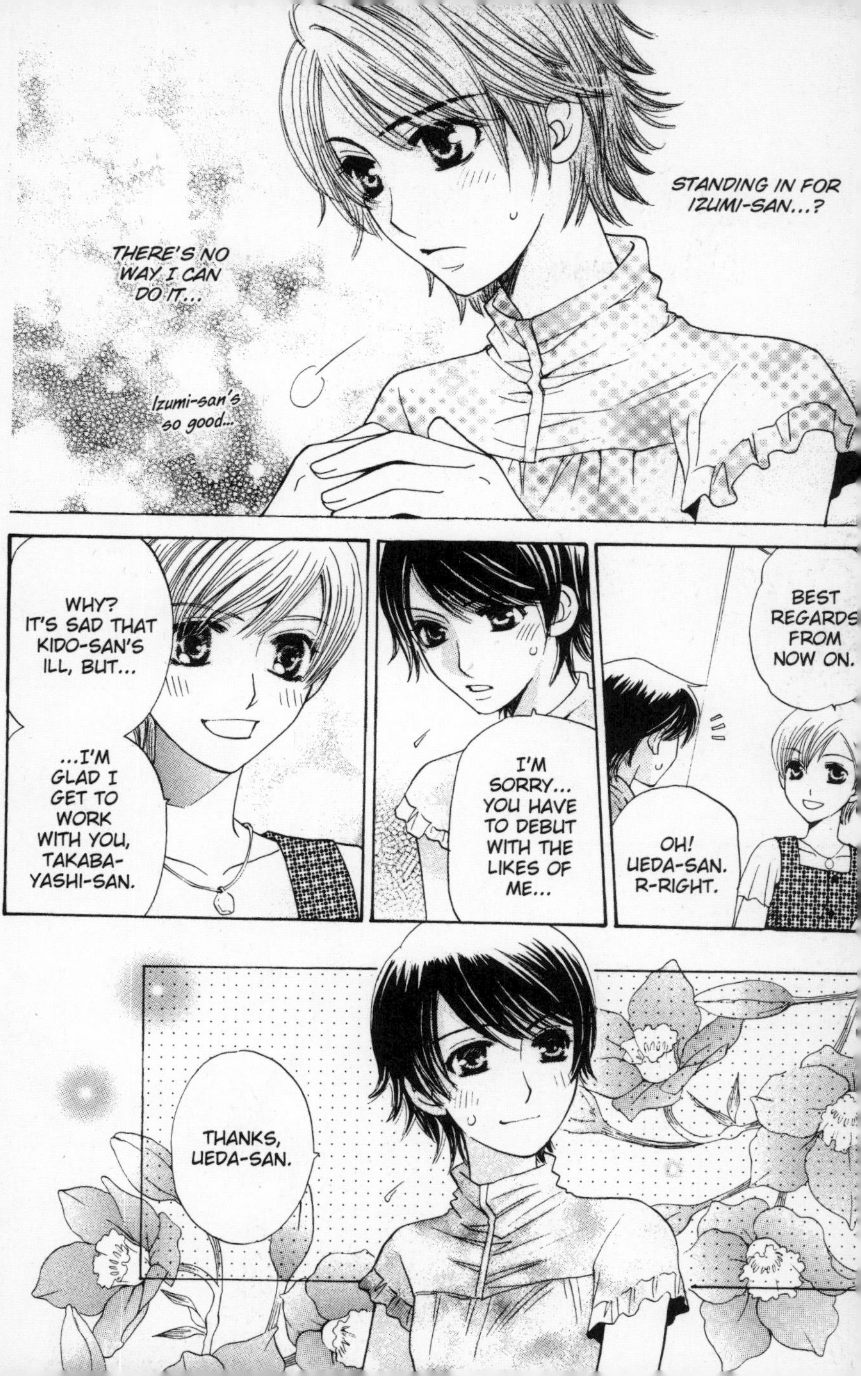

STANDING IN FOR IZUMI-SAN...?
THERE'S NO WAY I CAN DO IT...
Izumi-san's so good...
BEST REGARDS FROM NOW ON.
OH! UEDA-SAN. R-RIGHT.
I'M SORRY... YOU HAVE TO DEBUT WITH THE LIKES OF ME...
WHY? IT'S SAD THAT KIDO-SAN'S ILL, BUT...
...I'M GLAD I GET TO WORK WITH YOU, TAKABA-YASHI-SAN.
THANKS, UEDA-SAN.

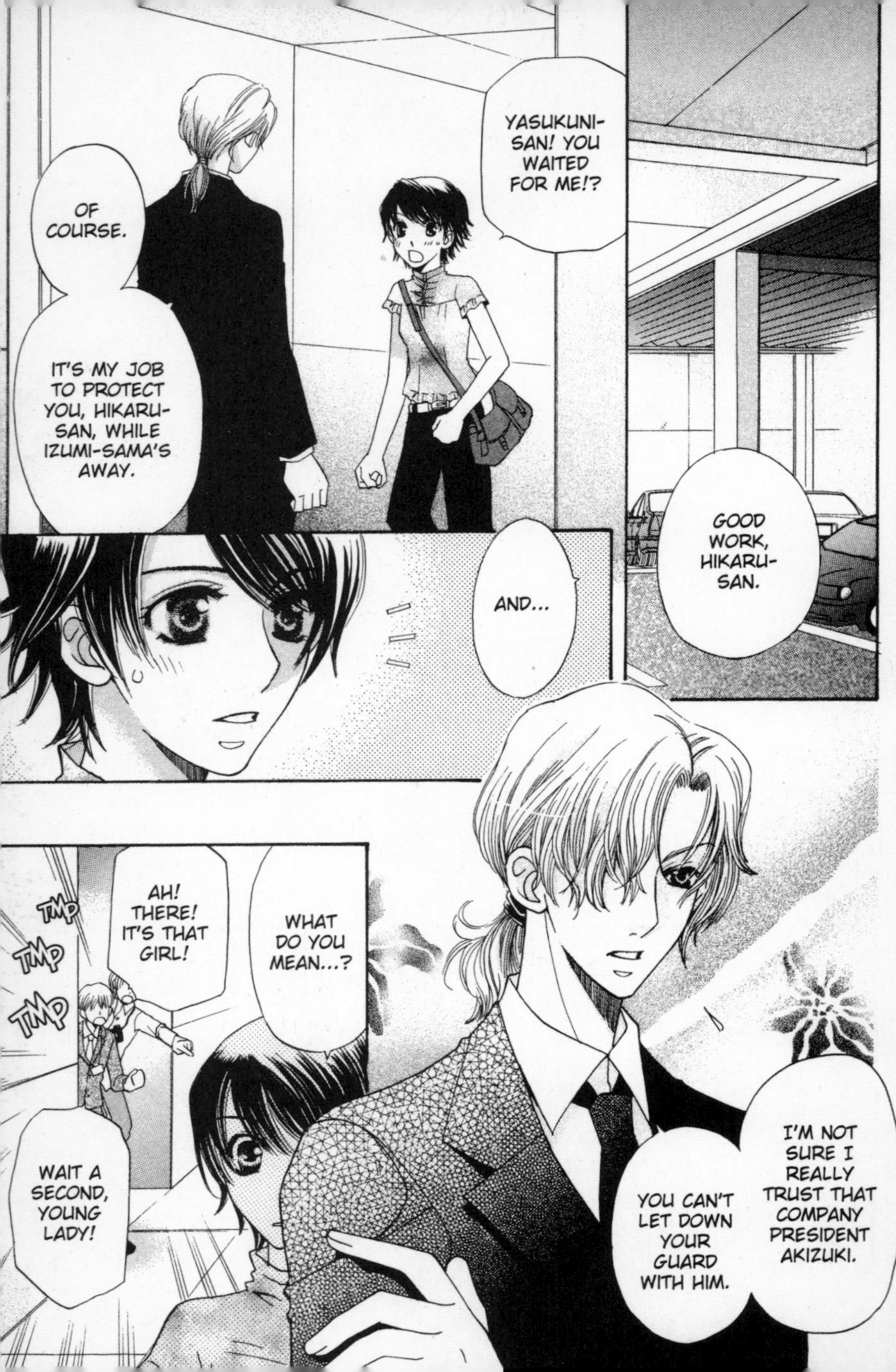
GOOD WORK, HIKARU-SAN.
YASUKUNI-SAN! YOU WAITED FOR ME!?
OF COURSE.
IT'S MY JOB TO PROTECT YOU, HIKARU-SAN, WHILE IZUMI-SAMA'S AWAY.
AND...
I'M NOT SURE I REALLY TRUST THAT COMPANY PRESIDENT AKIZUKI.
YOU CAN'T LET DOWN YOUR GUARD WITH HIM.
WHAT DO YOU MEAN...?
AH! THERE! IT'S THAT GIRL!
TMP
TMP
TMP
WAIT A SECOND, YOUNG LADY!

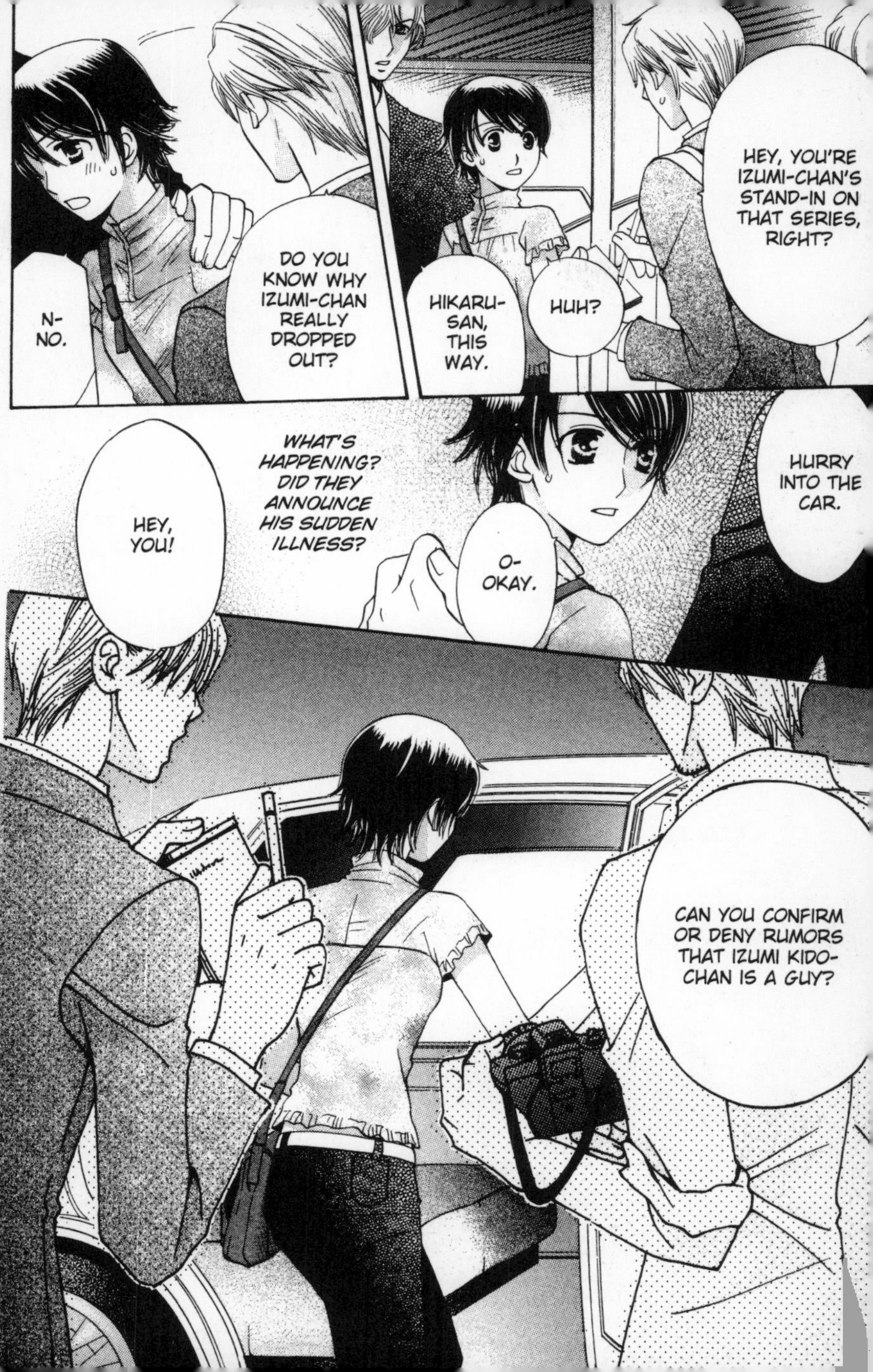
HEY, YOU'RE IZUMI-CHAN'S STAND-IN ON THAT SERIES, RIGHT?
HUH?
HIKARU-SAN, THIS WAY.
DO YOU KNOW WHY IZUMI-CHAN REALLY DROPPED OUT?
N-NO.
HURRY INTO THE CAR.
O-OKAY.
WHAT'S HAPPENING? DID THEY ANNOUNCE HIS SUDDEN ILLNESS?
HEY, YOU!
CAN YOU CONFIRM OR DENY RUMORS THAT IZUMI KIDO-CHAN IS A GUY?

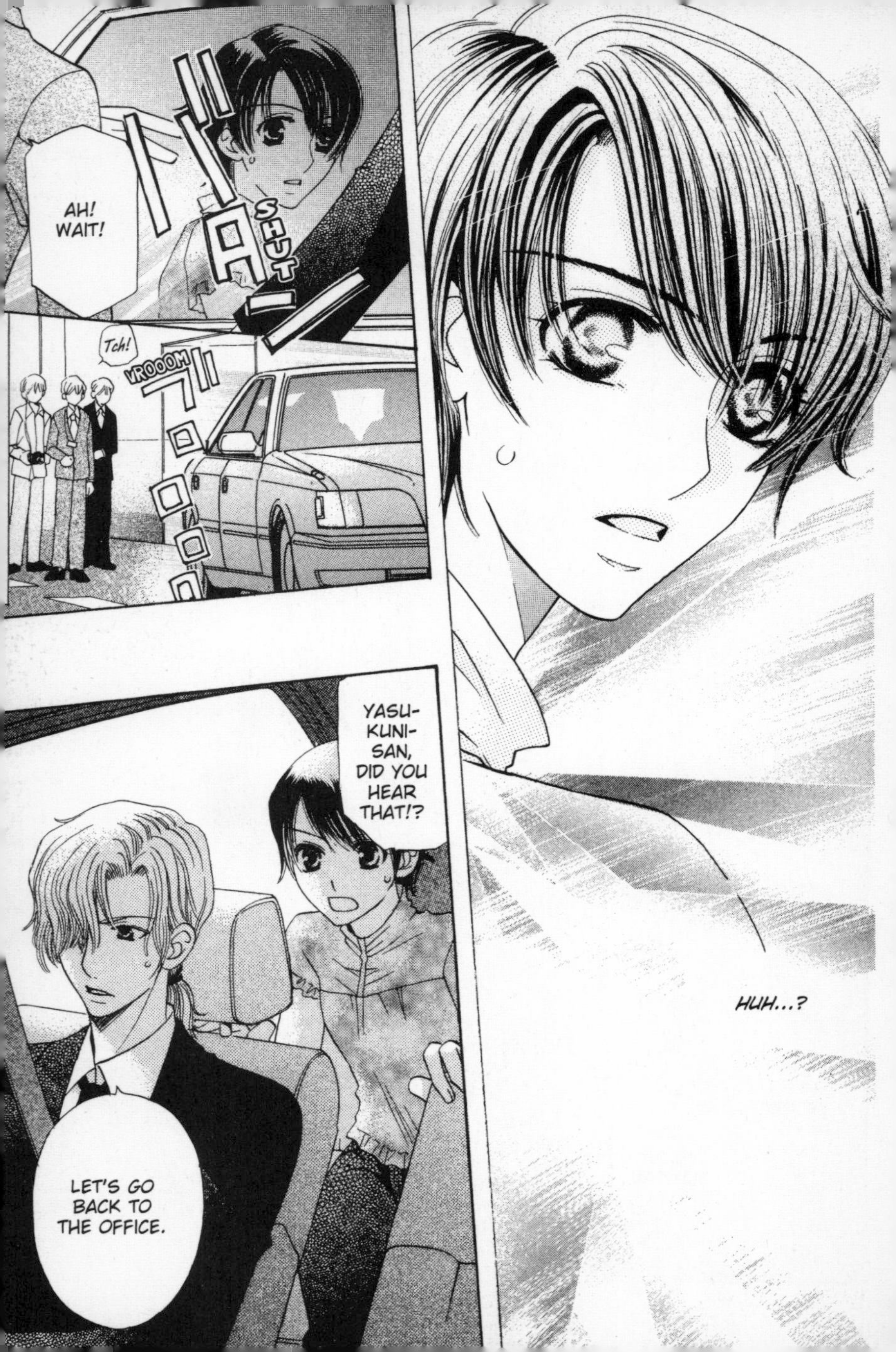
HUH...?
AH! WAIT!
SHUT
Tch!
VROOOM
YASU-KUNI-SAN, DID YOU HEAR THAT!?
LET'S GO BACK TO THE OFFICE.

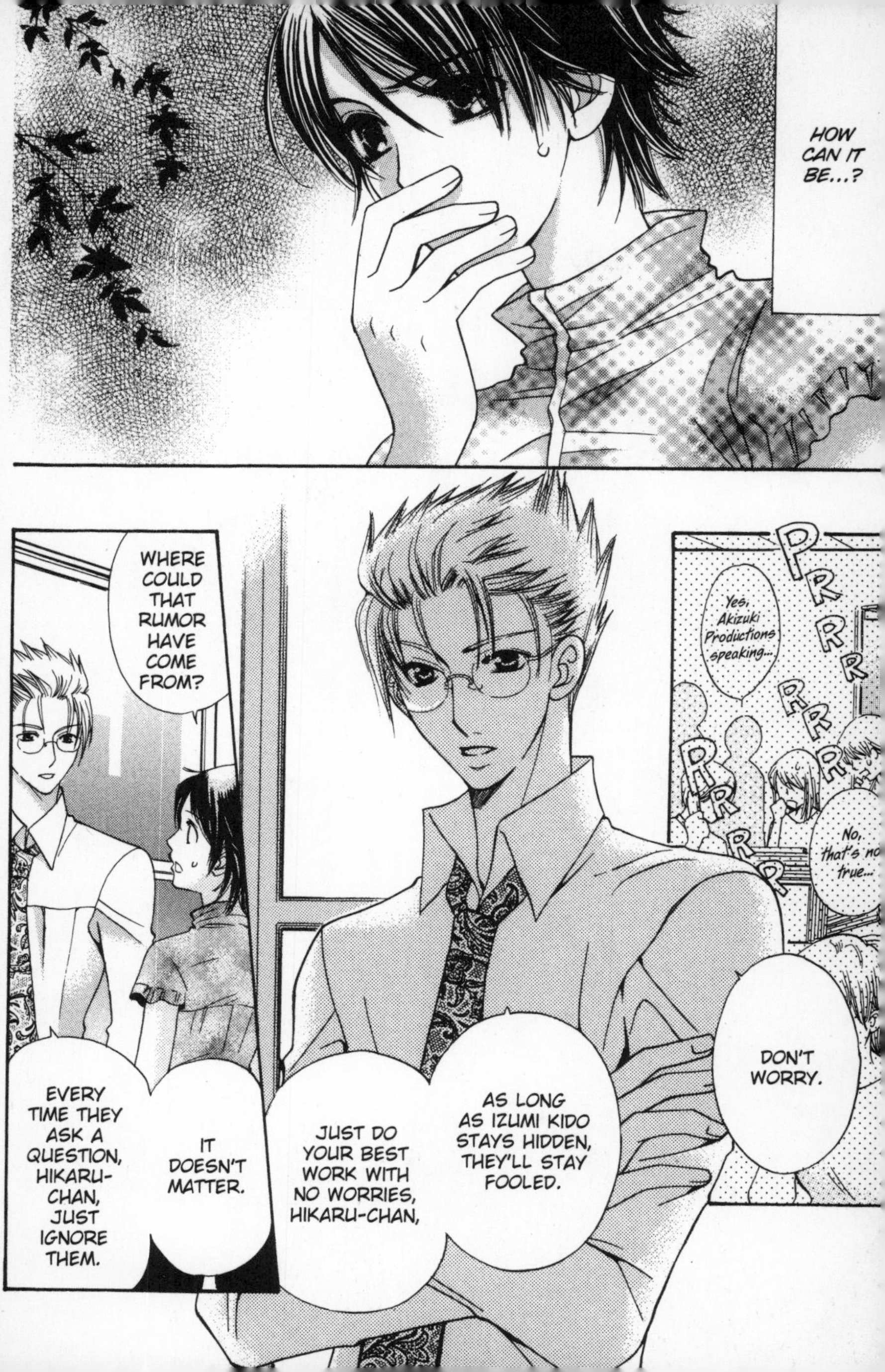
HOW CAN IT BE...?
PRRR
Yes, Akizuki Productions speaking...
No, that's no true...
WHERE COULD THAT RUMOR HAVE COME FROM?
DON'T WORRY.
AS LONG AS IZUMI KIDO STAYS HIDDEN, THEY'LL STAY FOOLED.
JUST DO YOUR BEST WORK WITH NO WORRIES, HIKARU-CHAN,
IT DOESN'T MATTER.
EVERY TIME THEY ASK A QUESTION, HIKARU-CHAN, JUST IGNORE THEM.

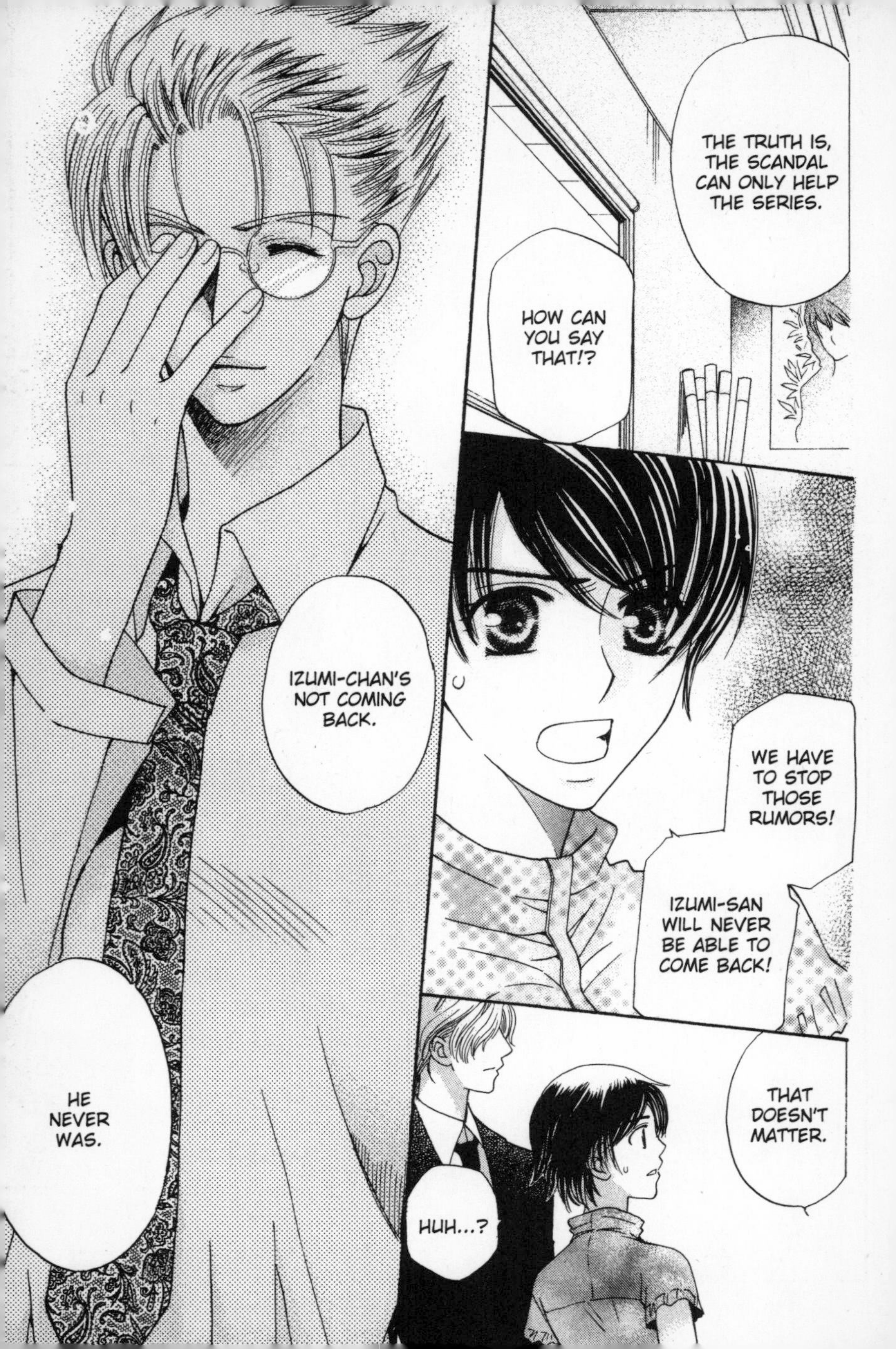
THE TRUTH IS, THE SCANDAL CAN ONLY HELP THE SERIES.
HOW CAN YOU SAY THAT!?
WE HAVE TO STOP THOSE RUMORS!
IZUMI-SAN WILL NEVER BE ABLE TO COME BACK!
THAT DOESN'T MATTER.
HUH...?
IZUMI-CHAN'S NOT COMING BACK.
HE NEVER WAS.

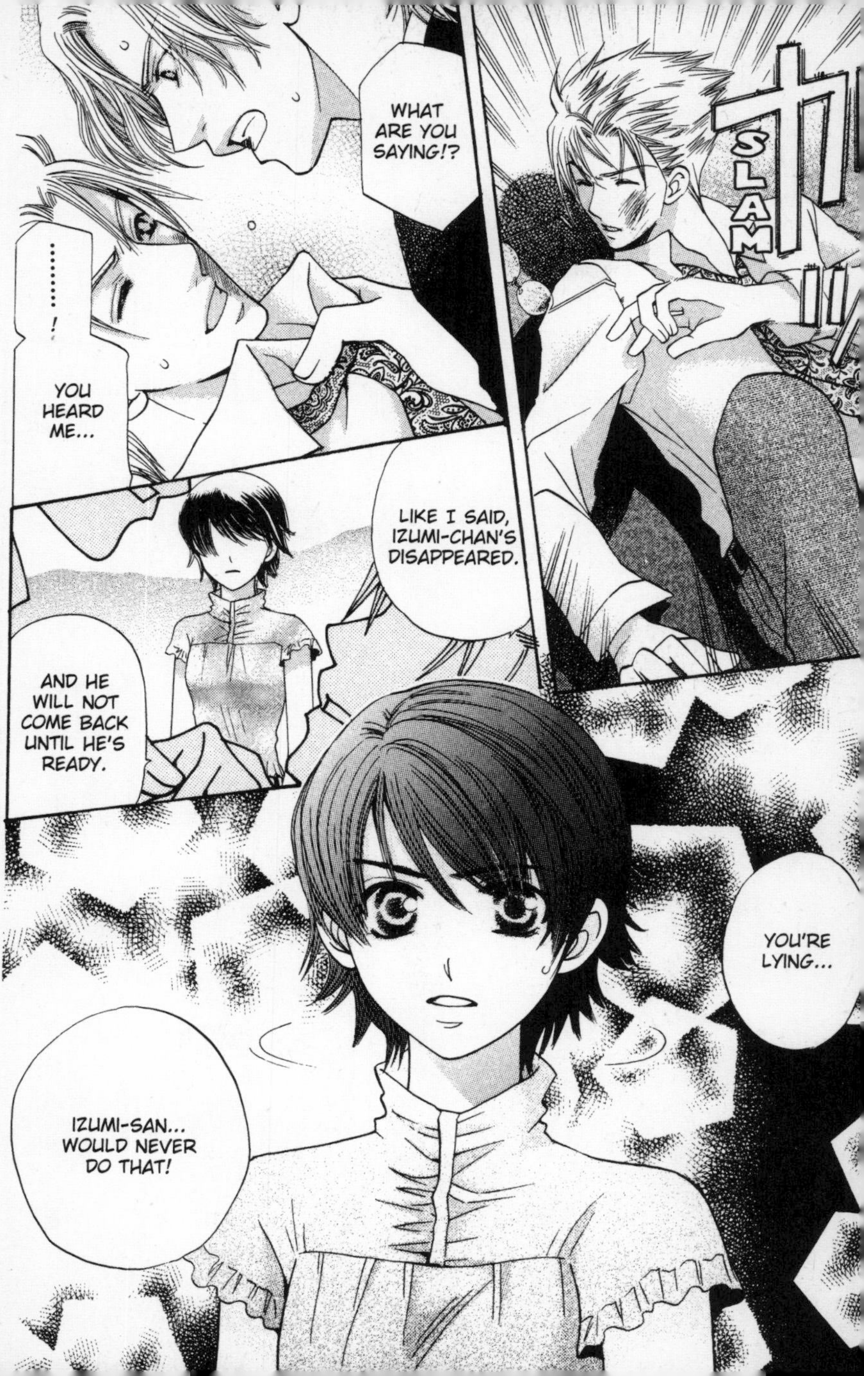
SLAM
WHAT ARE YOU SAYING!?
........!
YOU HEARD ME...
LIKE I SAID, IZUMI-CHAN'S DISAPPEARED.
AND HE WILL NOT COME BACK UNTIL HE'S READY.
YOU'RE LYING...
IZUMI-SAN... WOULD NEVER DO THAT!

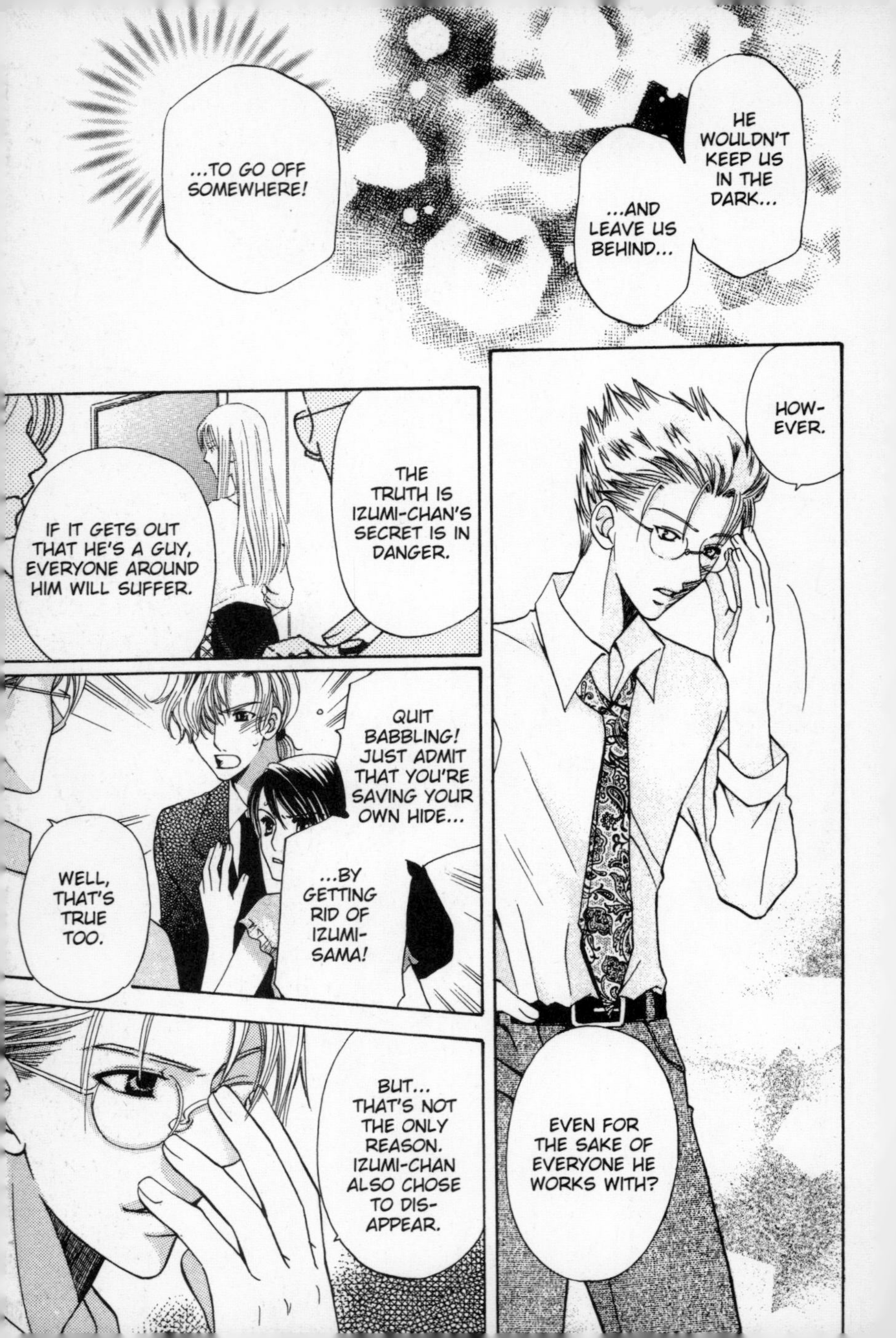
HE WOULDN'T KEEP US IN THE DARK...
...AND LEAVE US BEHIND...
...TO GO OFF SOMEWHERE!
HOW-EVER.
EVEN FOR THE SAKE OF EVERYONE HE WORKS WITH?
THE TRUTH IS IZUMI-CHAN'S SECRET IS IN DANGER.
IF IT GETS OUT THAT HE'S A GUY, EVERYONE AROUND HIM WILL SUFFER.
QUIT BABBLING! JUST ADMIT THAT YOU'RE SAVING YOUR OWN HIDE...
...BY GETTING RID OF IZUMI-SAMA!
WELL, THAT'S TRUE TOO.
BUT... THAT'S NOT THE ONLY REASON. IZUMI-CHAN ALSO CHOSE TO DIS-APPEAR.

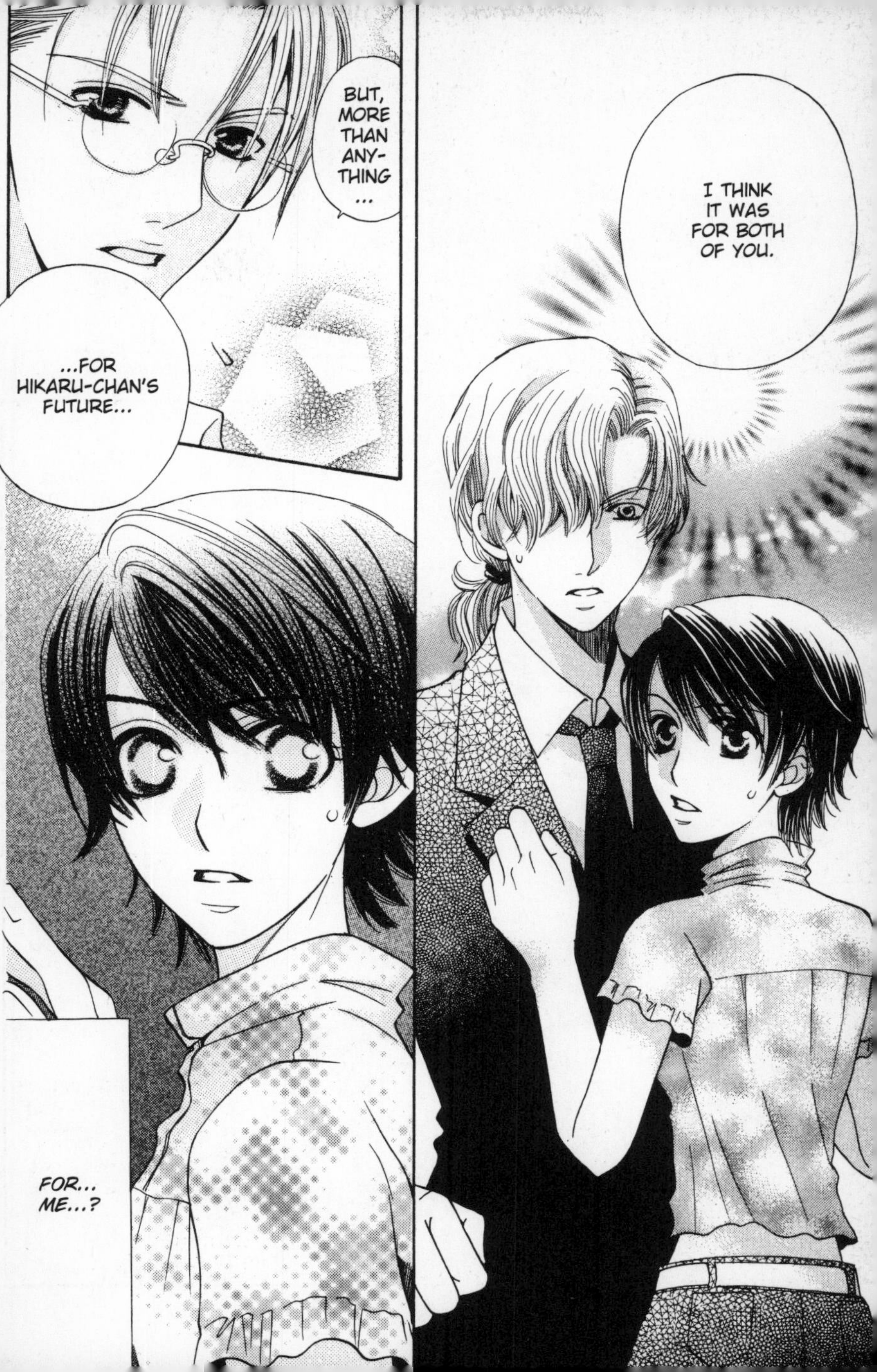
BUT, MORE THAN ANY-THING...
...FOR HIKARU-CHAN'S FUTURE...
FOR... ME...?
I THINK IT WAS FOR BOTH OF YOU.

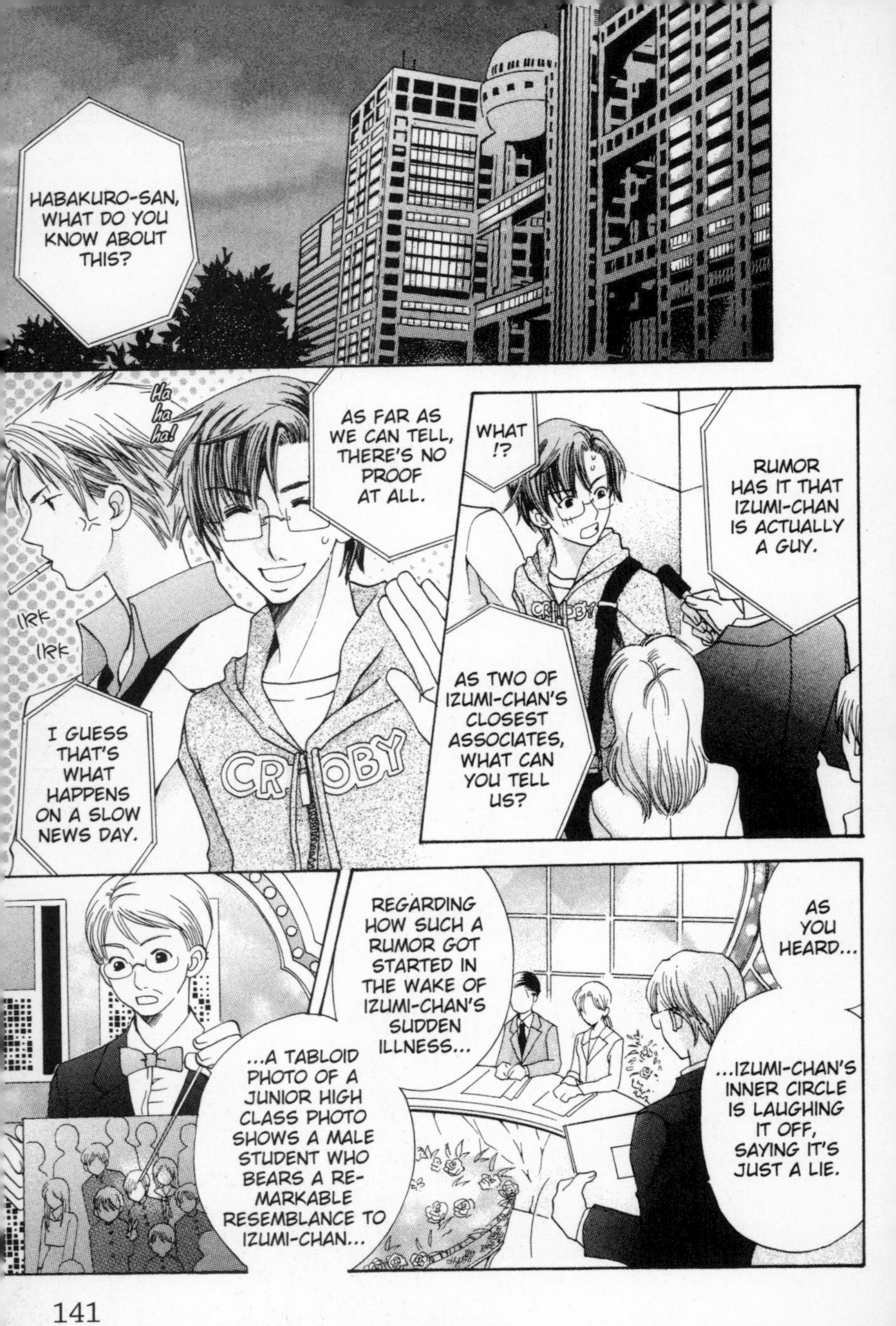
HABAKURO-SAN, WHAT DO YOU KNOW ABOUT THIS?
RUMOR HAS IT THAT IZUMI-CHAN IS ACTUALLY A GUY.
WHAT !?
AS TWO OF IZUMI-CHAN'S CLOSEST ASSOCIATES, WHAT CAN YOU TELL US?
AS FAR AS WE CAN TELL, THERE'S NO PROOF AT ALL.
Ha ha ha!
IRK
IRK
I GUESS THAT'S WHAT HAPPENS ON A SLOW NEWS DAY.
AS YOU HEARD...
...IZUMI-CHAN'S INNER CIRCLE IS LAUGHING IT OFF, SAYING IT'S JUST A LIE.
REGARDING HOW SUCH A RUMOR GOT STARTED IN THE WAKE OF IZUMI-CHAN'S SUDDEN ILLNESS...
...A TABLOID PHOTO OF A JUNIOR HIGH CLASS PHOTO SHOWS A MALE STUDENT WHO BEARS A RE-MARKABLE RESEMBLANCE TO IZUMI-CHAN...

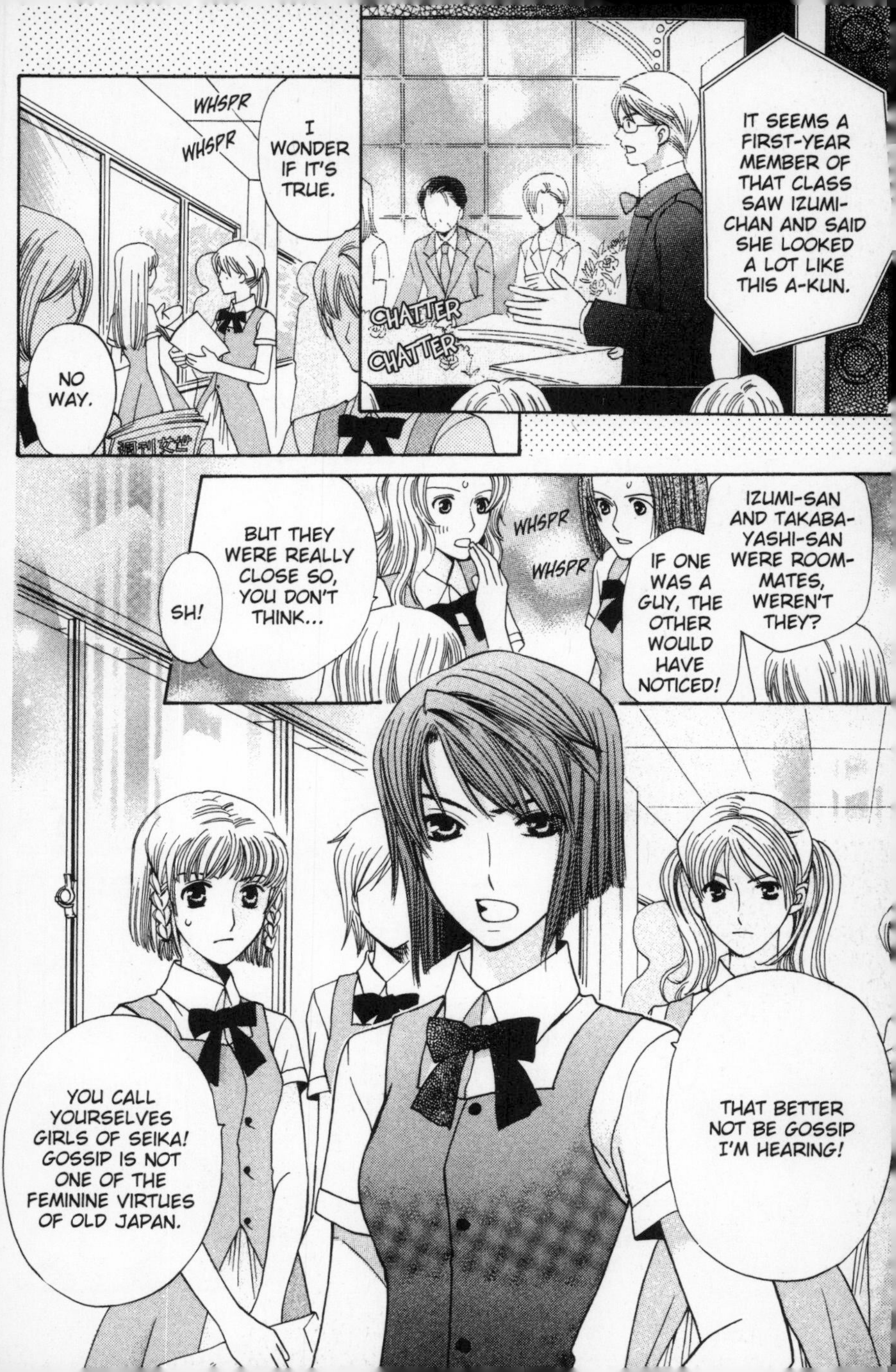
IT SEEMS A FIRST-YEAR MEMBER OF THAT CLASS SAW IZUMI-CHAN AND SAID SHE LOOKED A LOT LIKE THIS A-KUN.
CHATTER
CHATTER
WHSPR
WHSPR
I WONDER IF IT'S TRUE.
NO WAY.
IZUMI-SAN AND TAKABAYASHI-SAN WERE ROOMMATES, WEREN'T THEY?
IF ONE WAS A GUY, THE OTHER WOULD HAVE NOTICED!
WHSPR
WHSPR
BUT THEY WERE REALLY CLOSE SO, YOU DON'T THINK...
SH!
THAT BETTER NOT BE GOSSIP I'M HEARING!
YOU CALL YOURSELVES GIRLS OF SEIKA! GOSSIP IS NOT ONE OF THE FEMININE VIRTUES OF OLD JAPAN.

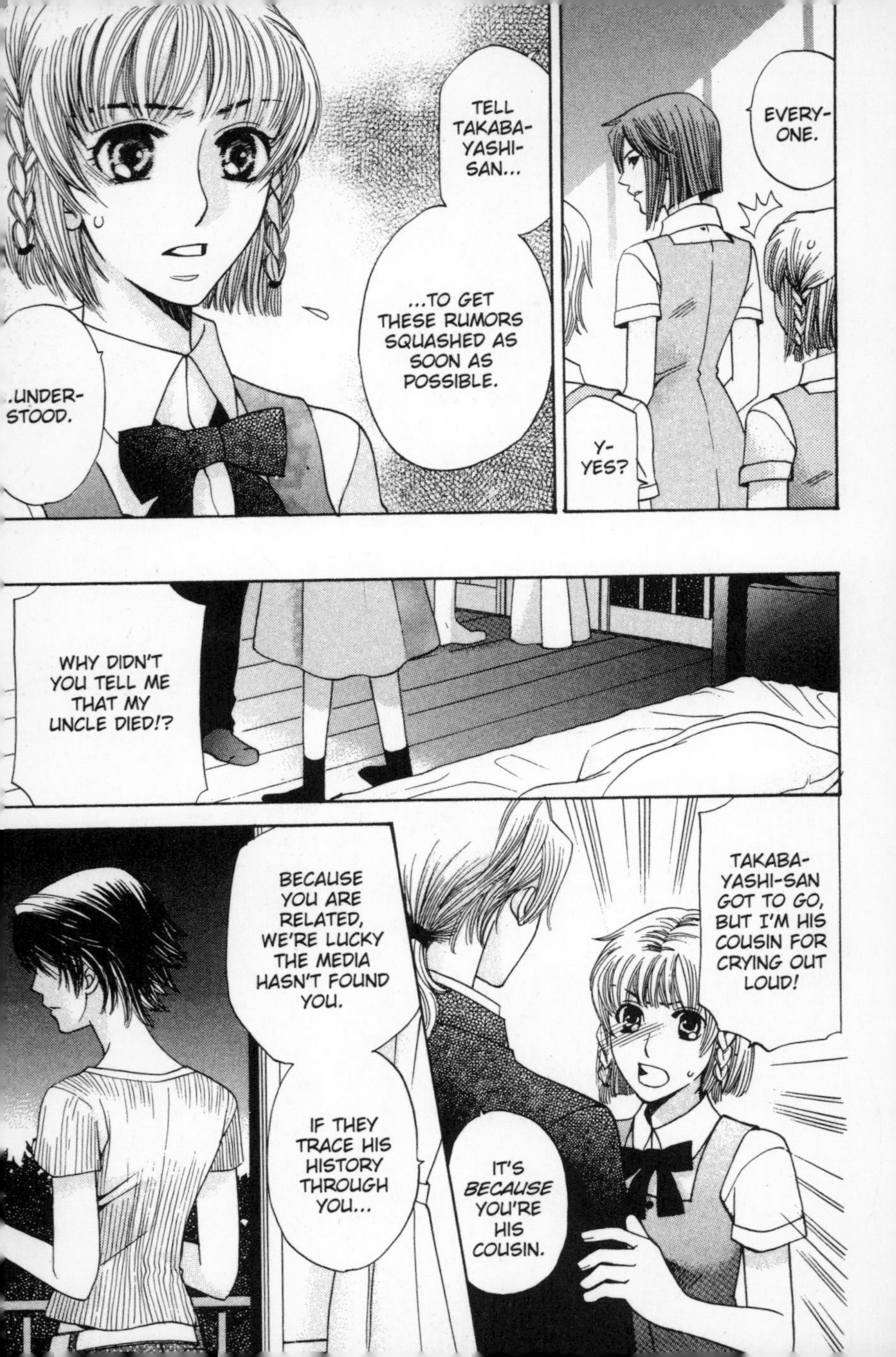

EVERY-ONE.
Y-YES?
TELL TAKABA-YASHI-SAN...
...TO GET THESE RUMORS SQUASHED AS SOON AS POSSIBLE.
.UNDER-STOOD.
WHY DIDN'T YOU TELL ME THAT MY UNCLE DIED!?
TAKABA-YASHI-SAN GOT TO GO, BUT I'M HIS COUSIN FOR CRYING OUT LOUD!
IT'S *BECAUSE* YOU'RE HIS COUSIN.
BECAUSE YOU ARE RELATED, WE'RE LUCKY THE MEDIA HASN'T FOUND YOU.
IF THEY TRACE HIS HISTORY THROUGH YOU...

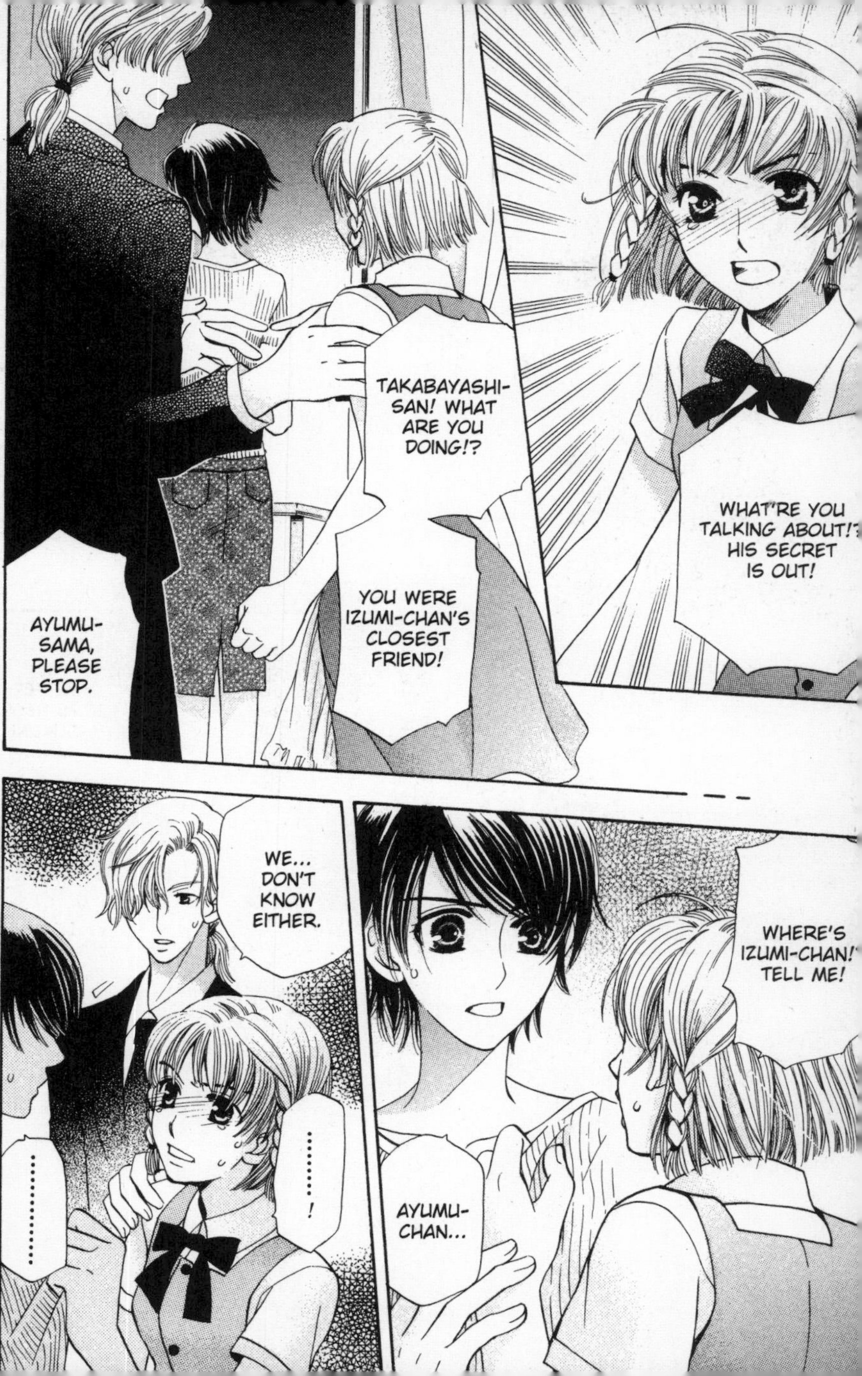
WHAT'RE YOU TALKING ABOUT!? HIS SECRET IS OUT!
TAKABAYASHI-SAN! WHAT ARE YOU DOING!?
YOU WERE IZUMI-CHAN'S CLOSEST FRIEND!
AYUMU-SAMA, PLEASE STOP.
WHERE'S IZUMI-CHAN! TELL ME!
AYUMU-CHAN...
WE... DON'T KNOW EITHER.
......!
........

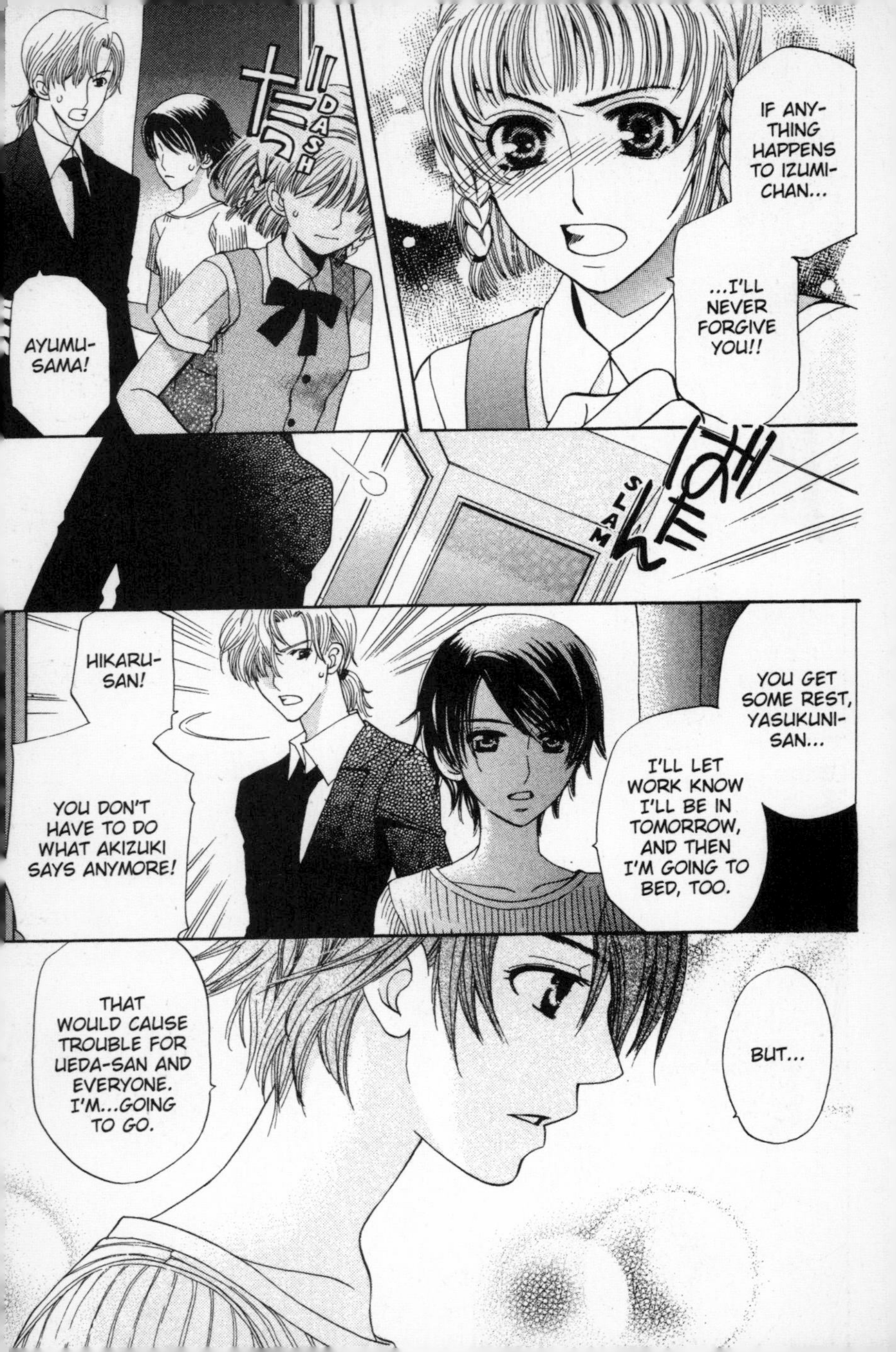
IF ANYTHING HAPPENS TO IZUMI-CHAN...
...I'LL NEVER FORGIVE YOU!!
DASH
AYUMU-SAMA!
SLAM
YOU GET SOME REST, YASUKUNI-SAN...
I'LL LET WORK KNOW I'LL BE IN TOMORROW, AND THEN I'M GOING TO BED, TOO.
HIKARU-SAN!
YOU DON'T HAVE TO DO WHAT AKIZUKI SAYS ANYMORE!
BUT...
THAT WOULD CAUSE TROUBLE FOR UEDA-SAN AND EVERYONE. I'M...GOING TO GO.

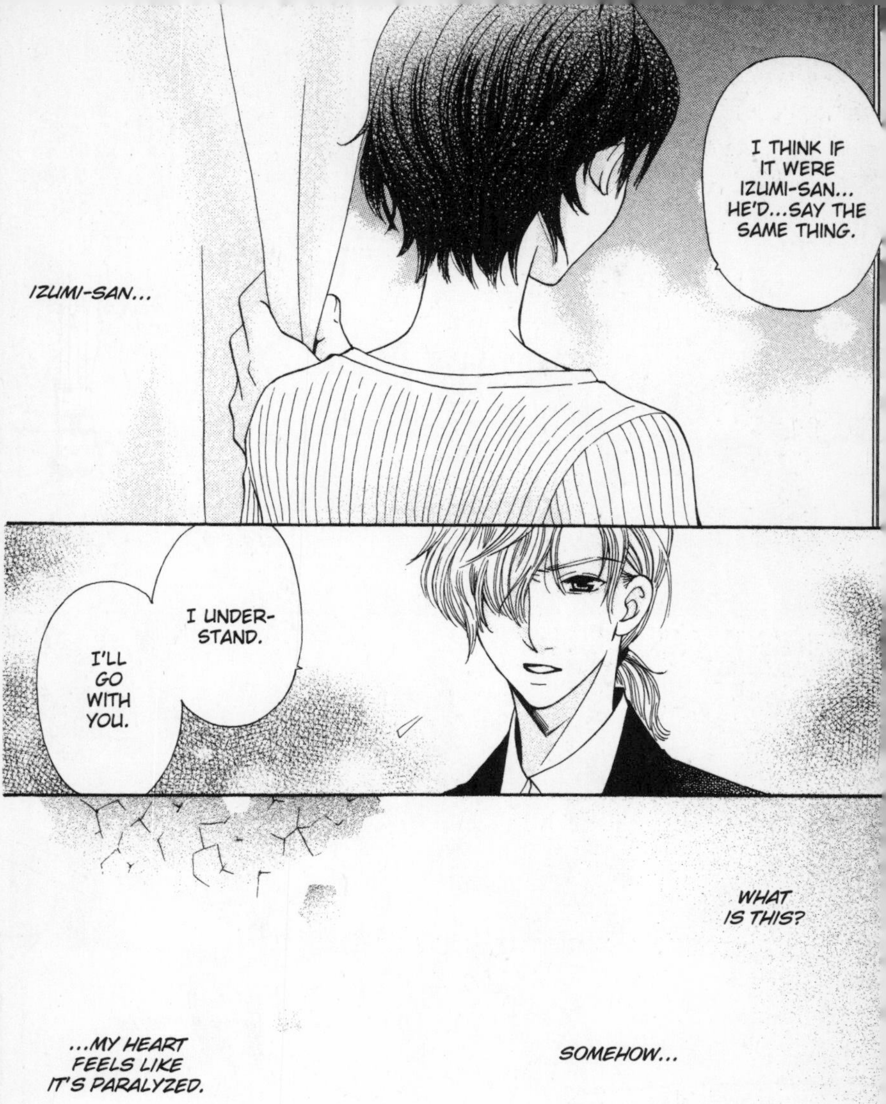
I THINK IF IT WERE IZUMI-SAN... HE'D...SAY THE SAME THING.
IZUMI-SAN...
I UNDER-STAND.
I'LL GO WITH YOU.
WHAT IS THIS?
SOMEHOW...
...MY HEART FEELS LIKE IT'S PARALYZED.

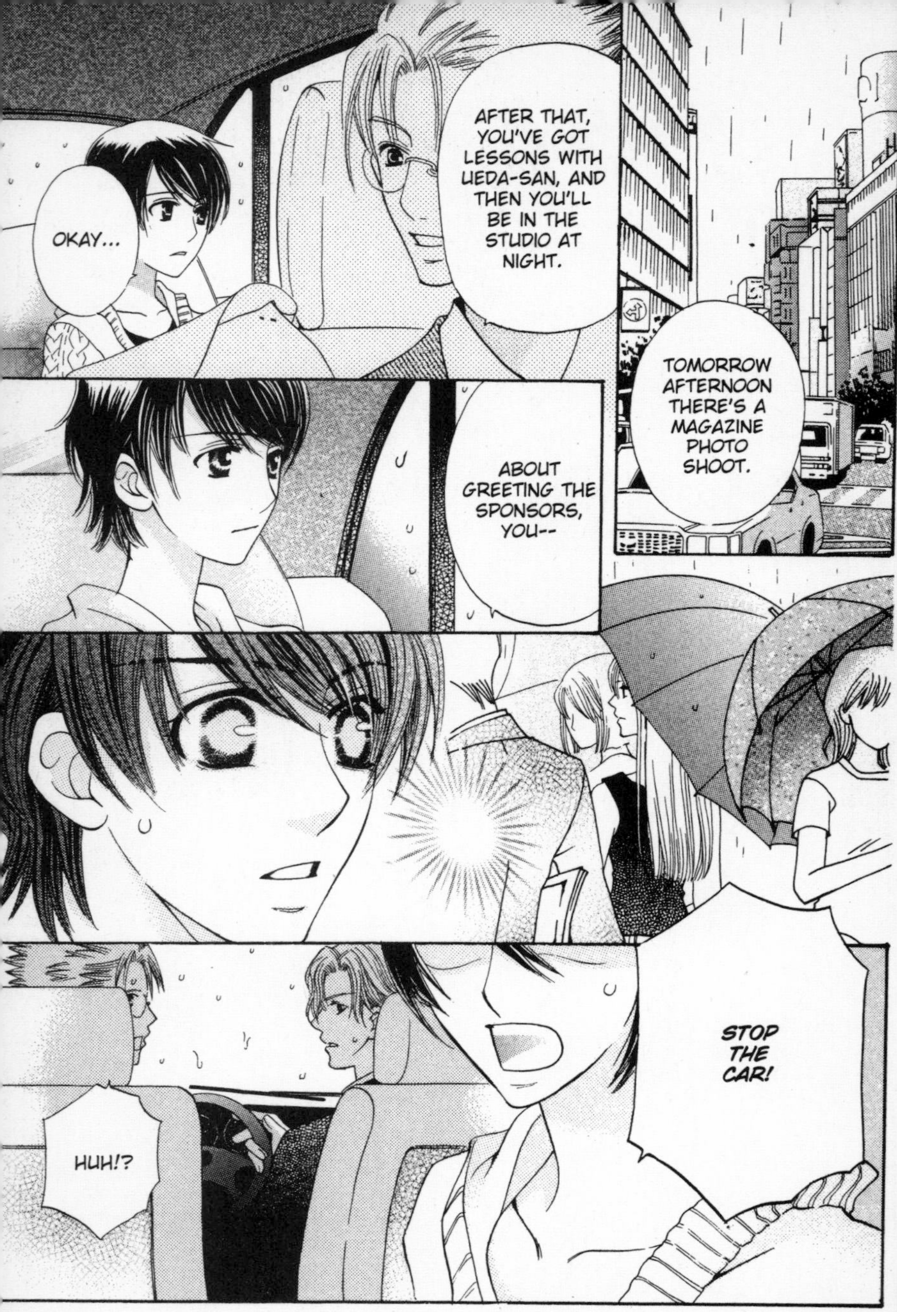
TOMORROW AFTERNOON THERE'S A MAGAZINE PHOTO SHOOT.
AFTER THAT, YOU'VE GOT LESSONS WITH UEDA-SAN, AND THEN YOU'LL BE IN THE STUDIO AT NIGHT.
OKAY...
ABOUT GREETING THE SPONSORS, YOU--
STOP THE CAR!
HUH!?

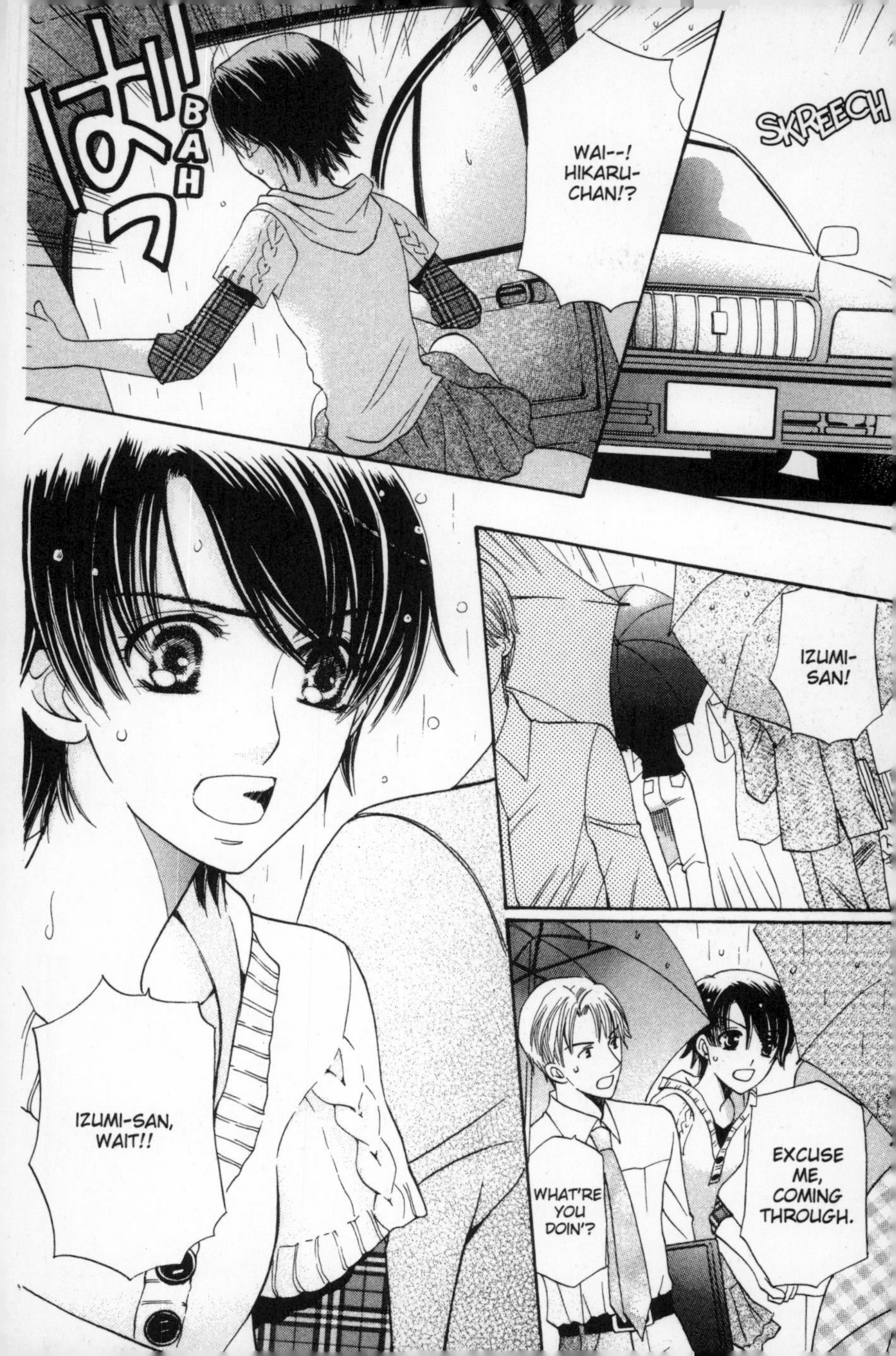
SKREECH
WAI--! HIKARU-CHAN!?
はっ
BAH
IZUMI-SAN!
EXCUSE ME, COMING THROUGH.
WHAT'RE YOU DOIN'?
IZUMI-SAN, WAIT!!

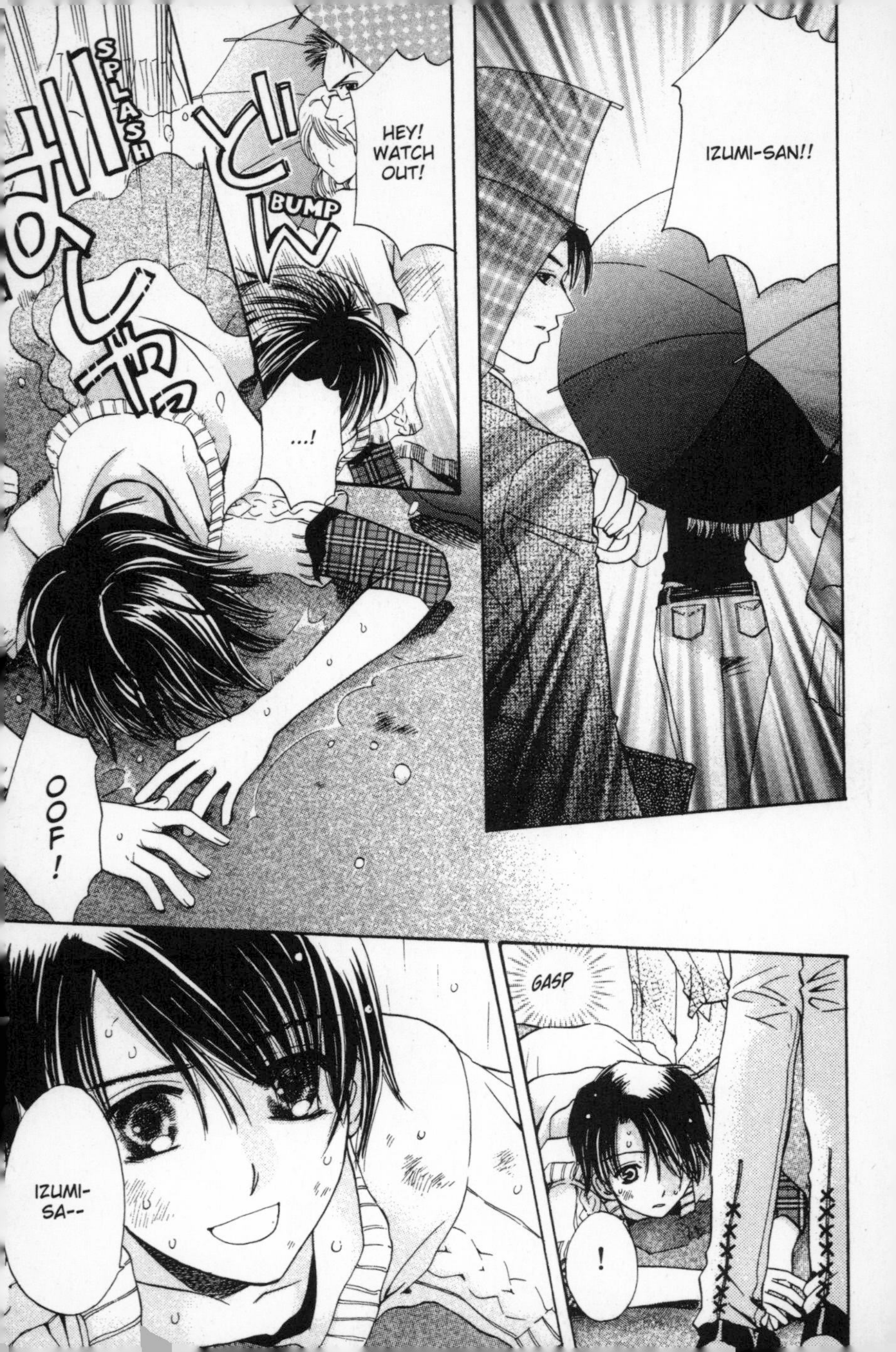
IZUMI-SAN!!
HEY! WATCH OUT!
BUMP
SPLASH
...!
OOF!
GASP
!
IZUMI-SA--

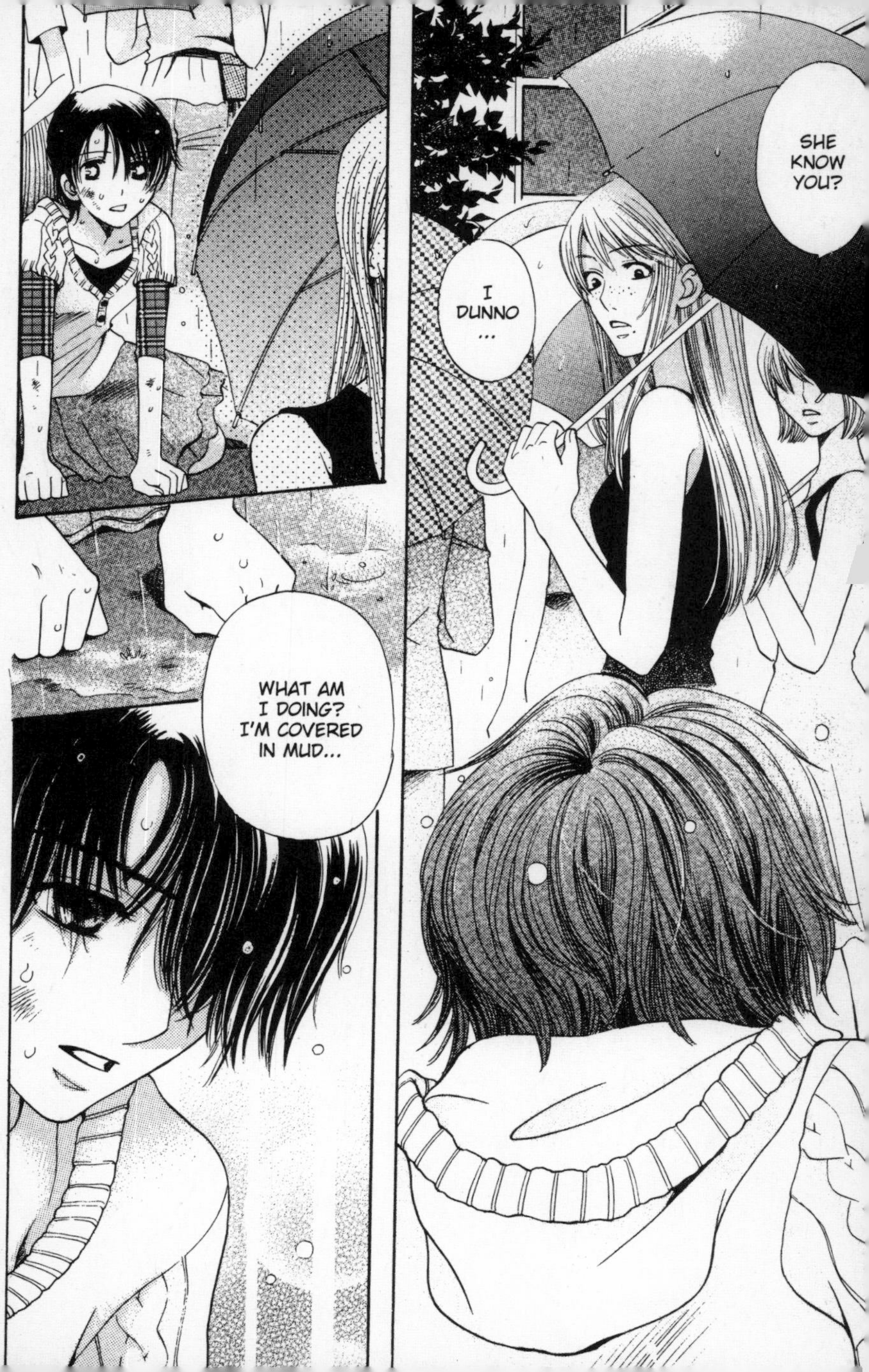
SHE KNOW YOU?
I DUNNO ...
WHAT AM I DOING? I'M COVERED IN MUD...

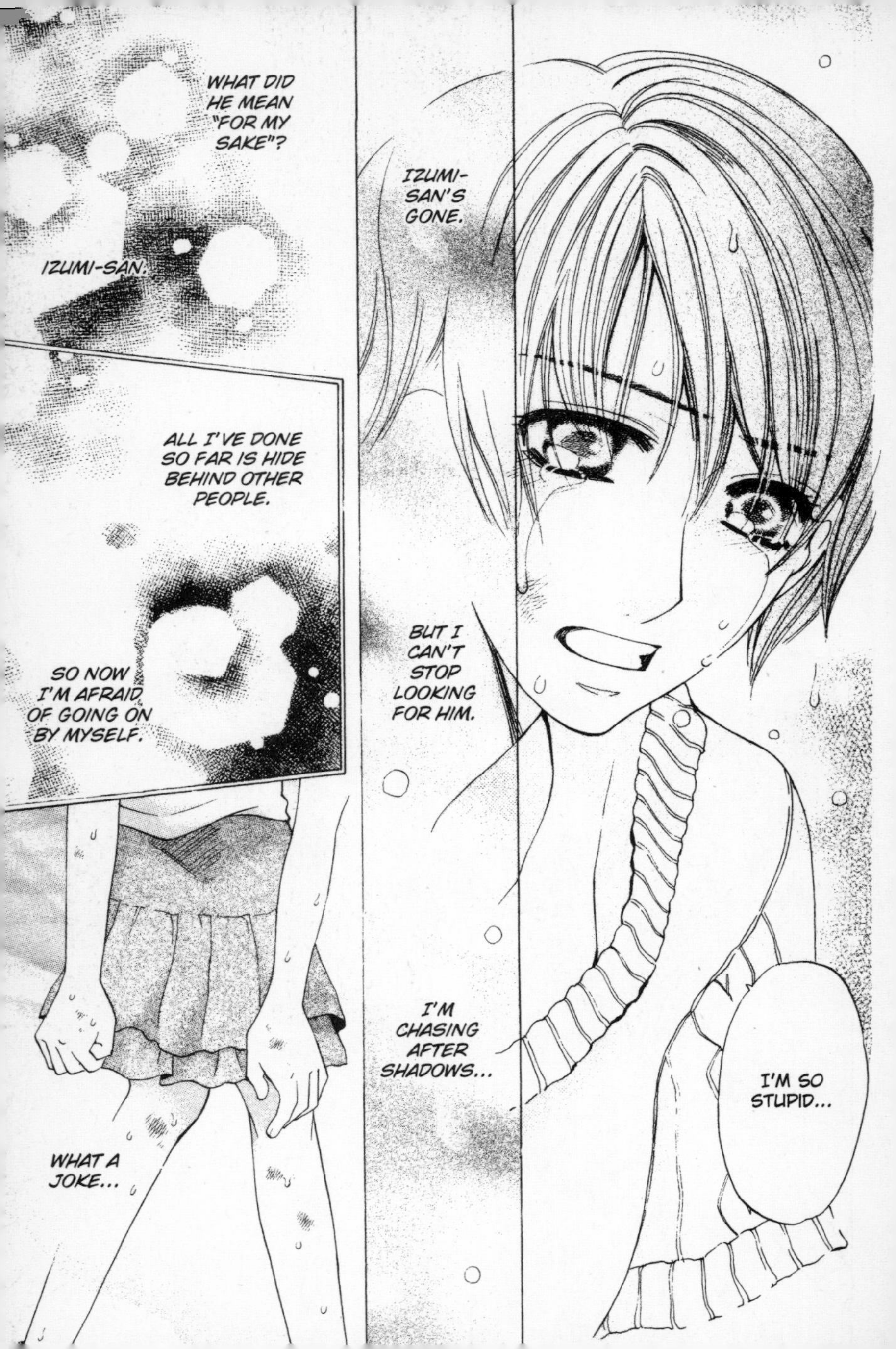
I'M SO STUPID...
IZUMI-SAN'S GONE.
BUT I CAN'T STOP LOOKING FOR HIM.
I'M CHASING AFTER SHADOWS...
WHAT DID HE MEAN "FOR MY SAKE"?
IZUMI-SAN.
ALL I'VE DONE SO FAR IS HIDE BEHIND OTHER PEOPLE.
SO NOW I'M AFRAID OF GOING ON BY MYSELF.
WHAT A JOKE...

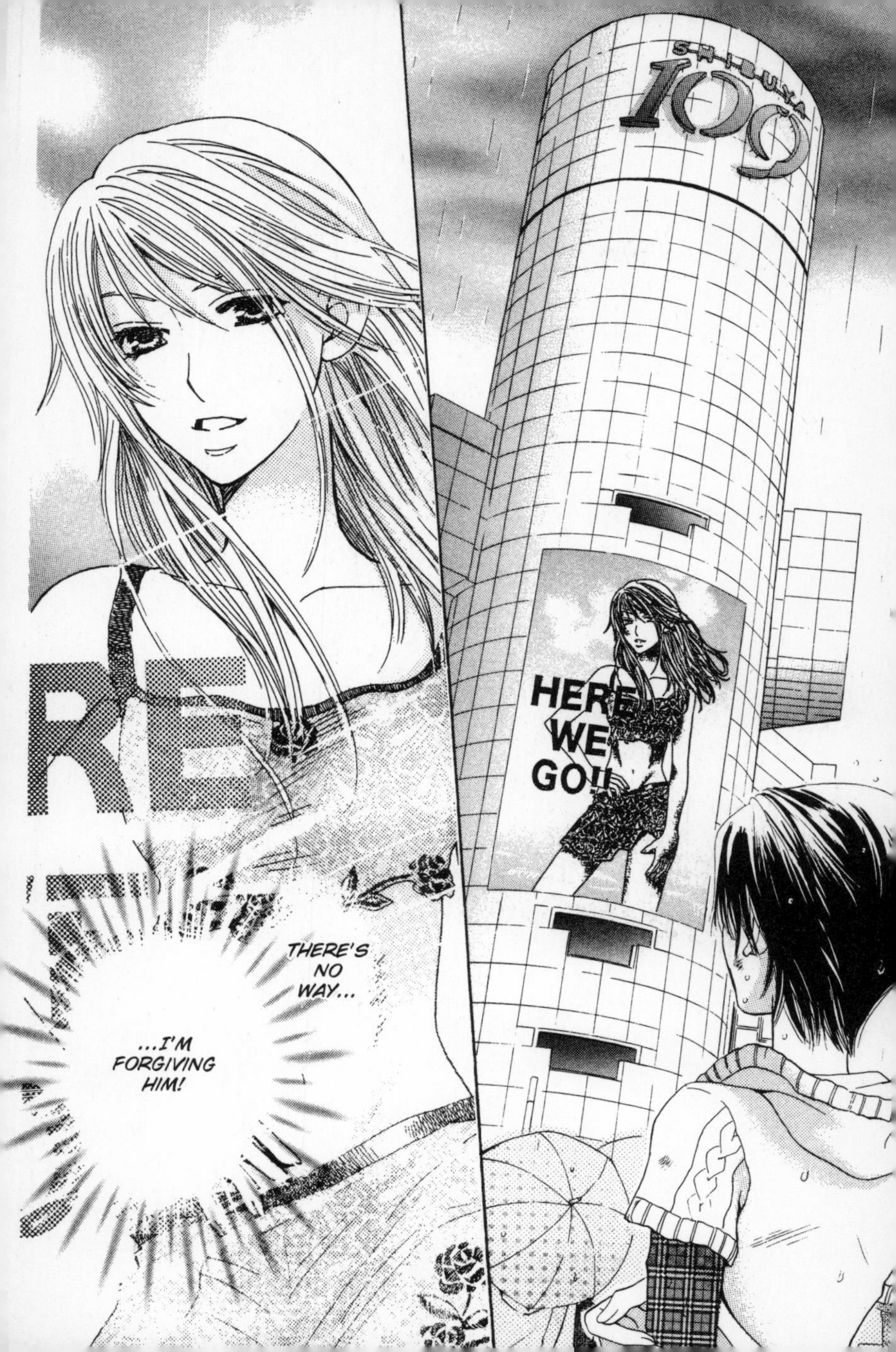
SHIBUYA 109
HERE WE GO!!
THERE'S NO WAY...
...I'M FORGIVING HIM!

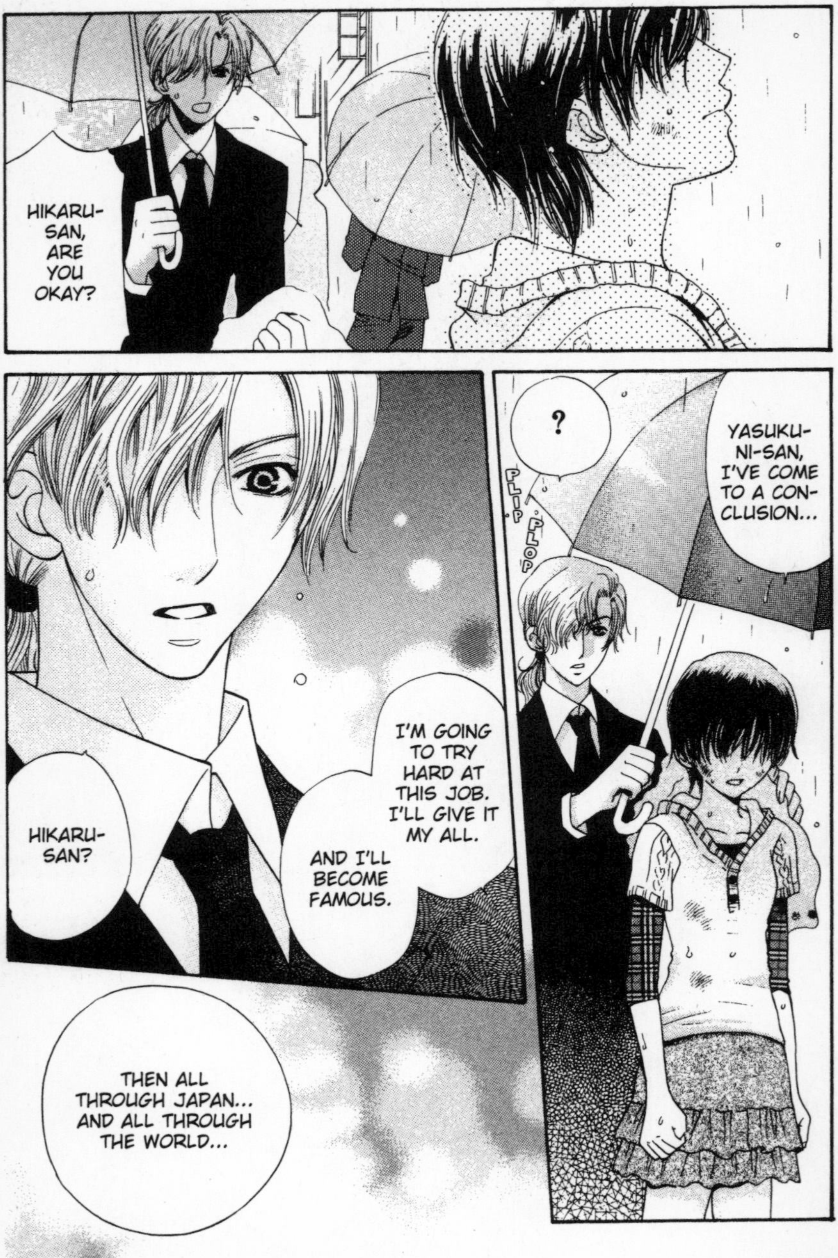
HIKARU-SAN, ARE YOU OKAY?
YASUKUNI-SAN, I'VE COME TO A CONCLUSION...
?
FLIP FLOP
I'M GOING TO TRY HARD AT THIS JOB. I'LL GIVE IT MY ALL.
AND I'LL BECOME FAMOUS.
HIKARU-SAN?
THEN ALL THROUGH JAPAN... AND ALL THROUGH THE WORLD...

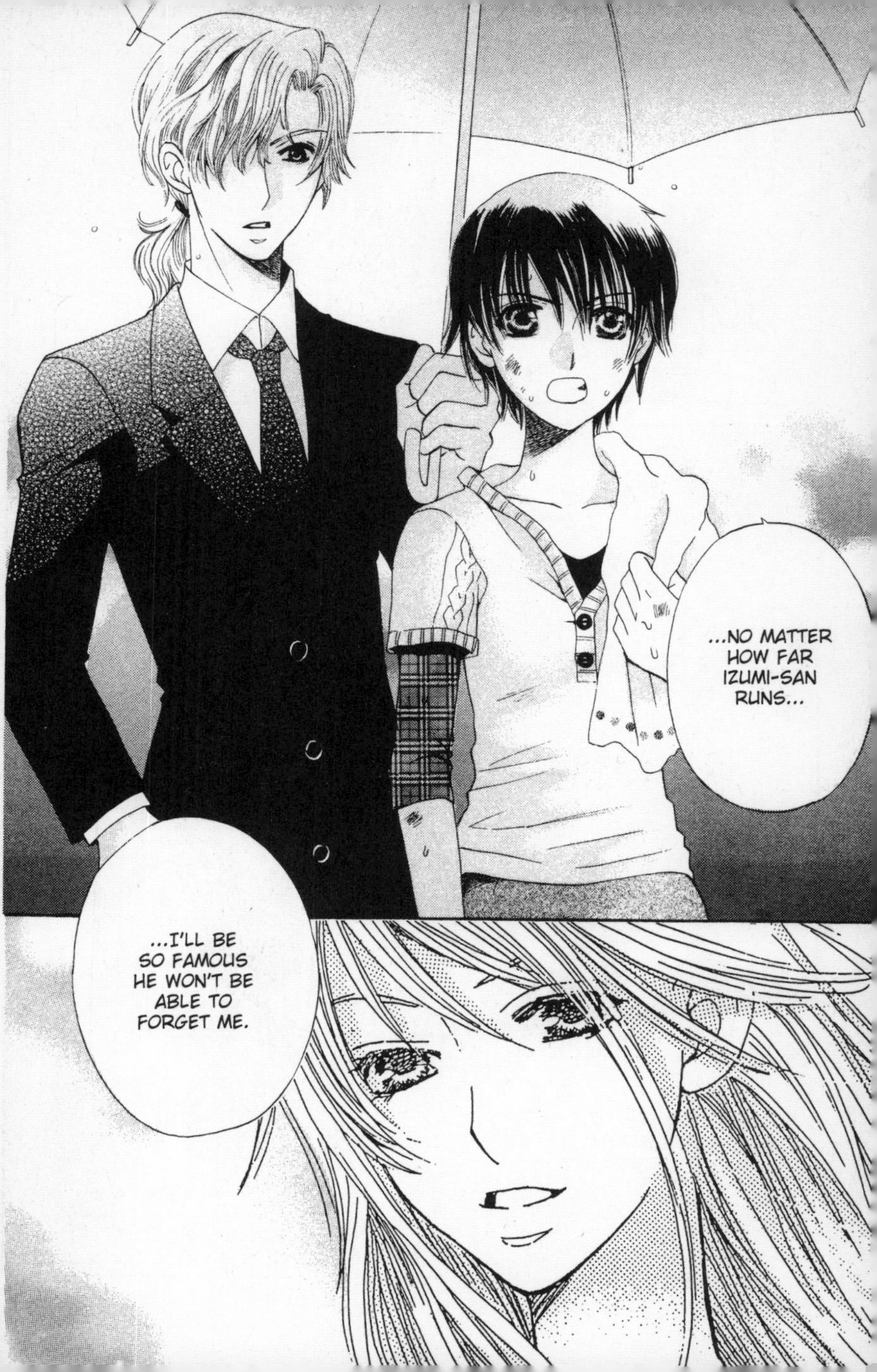
...NO MATTER HOW FAR IZUMI-SAN RUNS...
...I'LL BE SO FAMOUS HE WON'T BE ABLE TO FORGET ME.

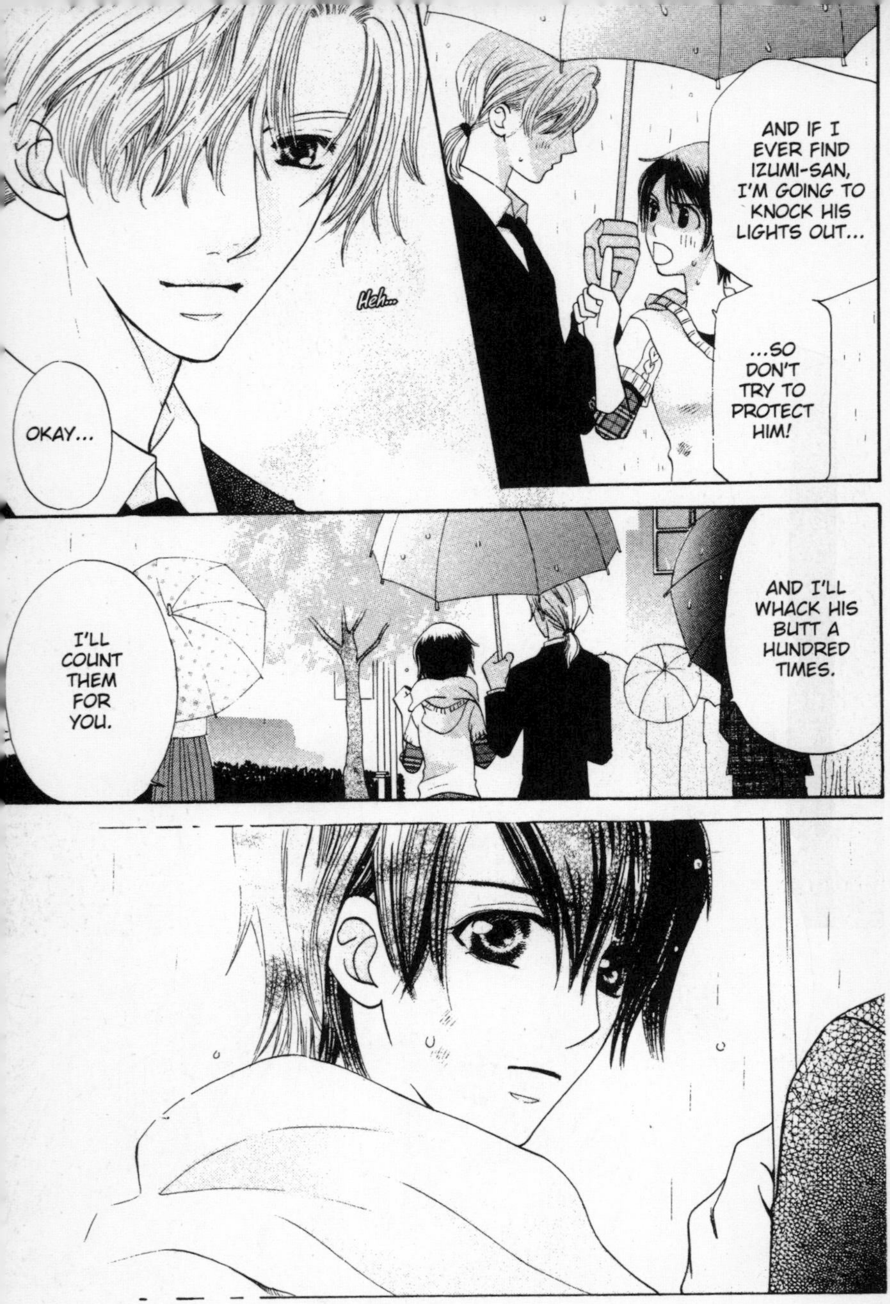
AND IF I EVER FIND IZUMI-SAN, I'M GOING TO KNOCK HIS LIGHTS OUT...
...SO DON'T TRY TO PROTECT HIM!
Heh...
OKAY...
AND I'LL WHACK HIS BUTT A HUNDRED TIMES.
I'LL COUNT THEM FOR YOU.

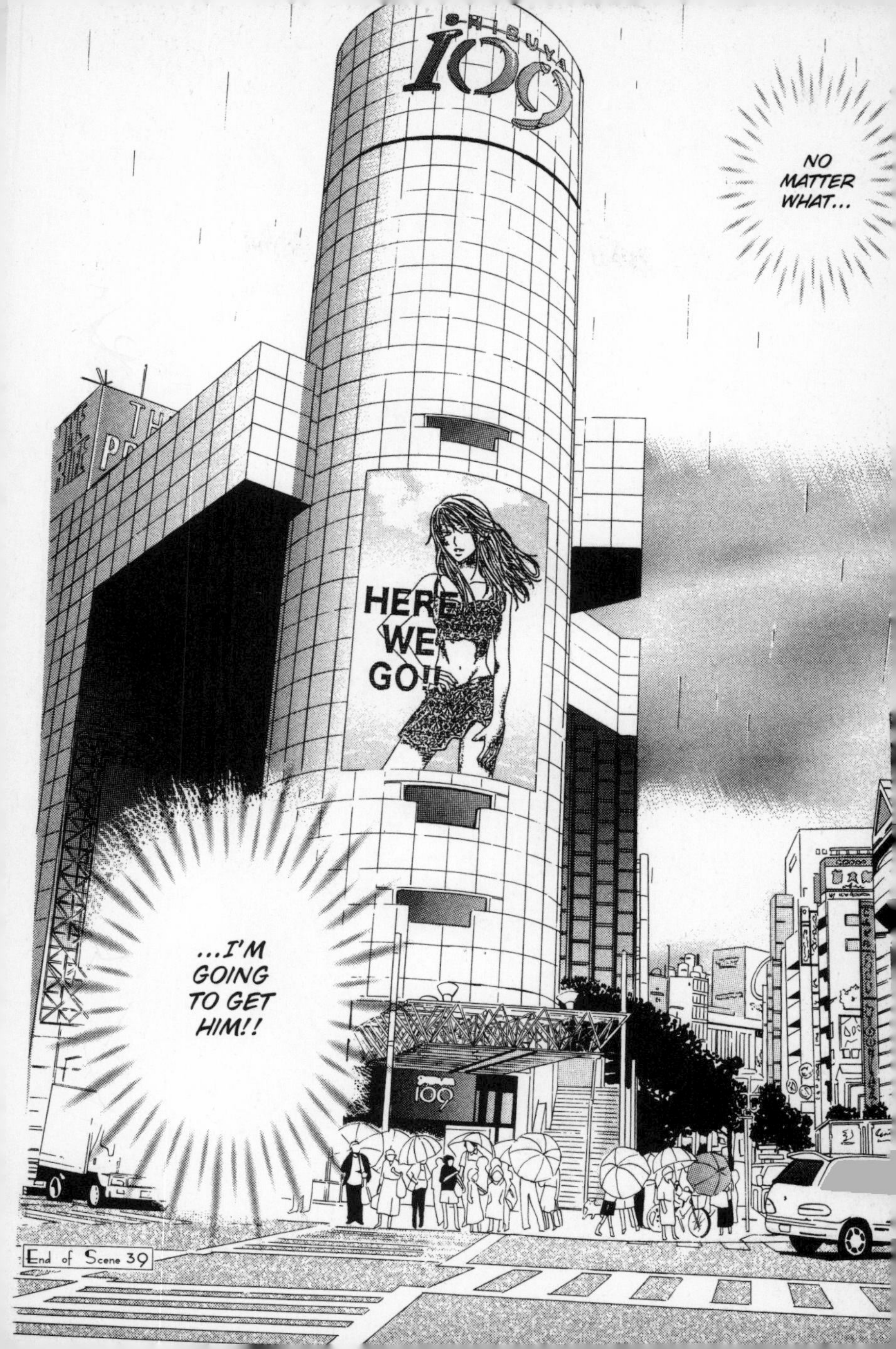
NO MATTER WHAT...
SHIBUYA 109
HERE WE GO!!
...I'M GOING TO GET HIM!!
109
End of Scene 39

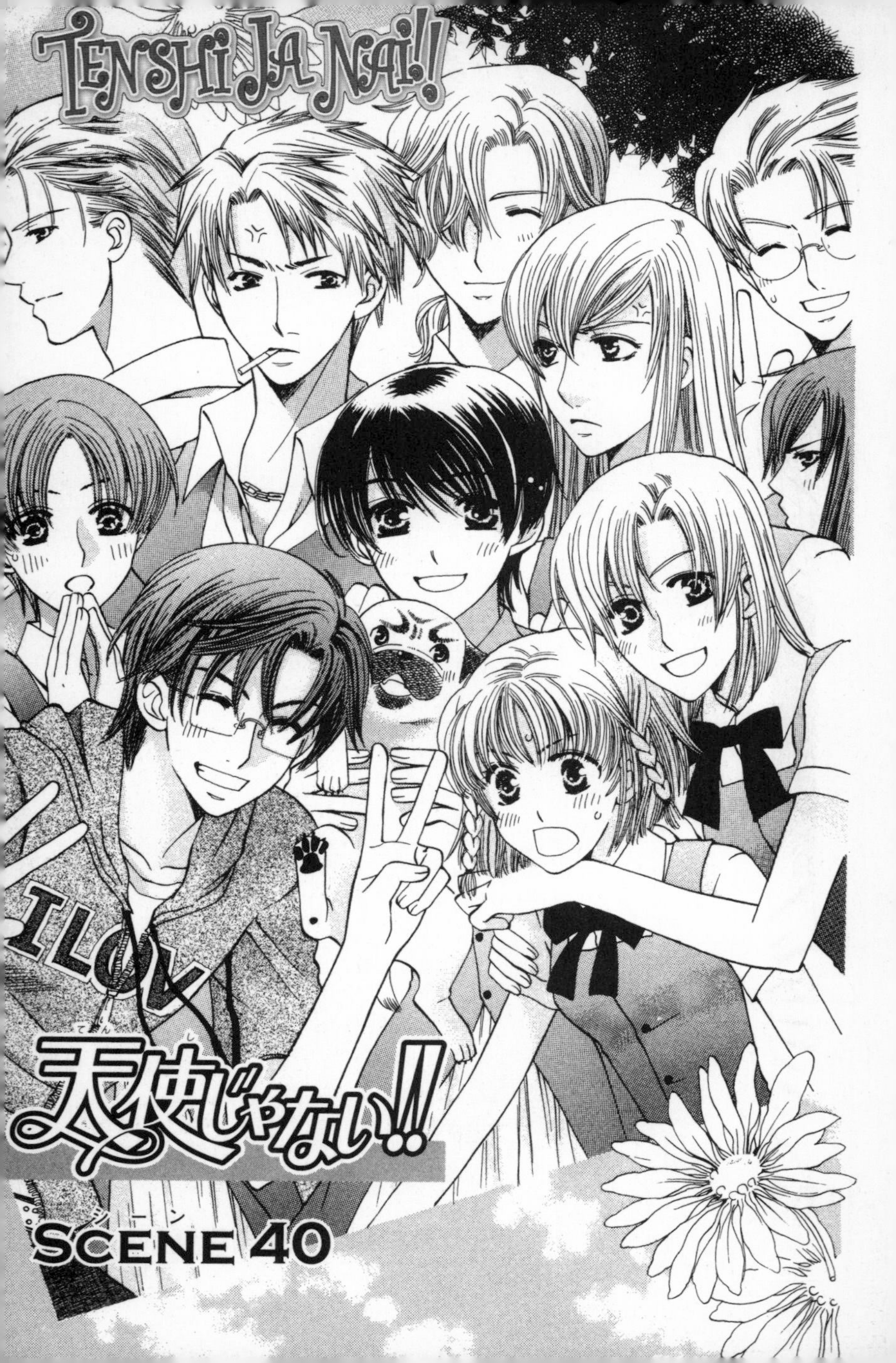
TENSHI JA NAI!!
天使じゃない!!
SCENE 40

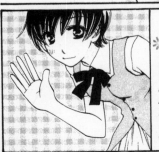

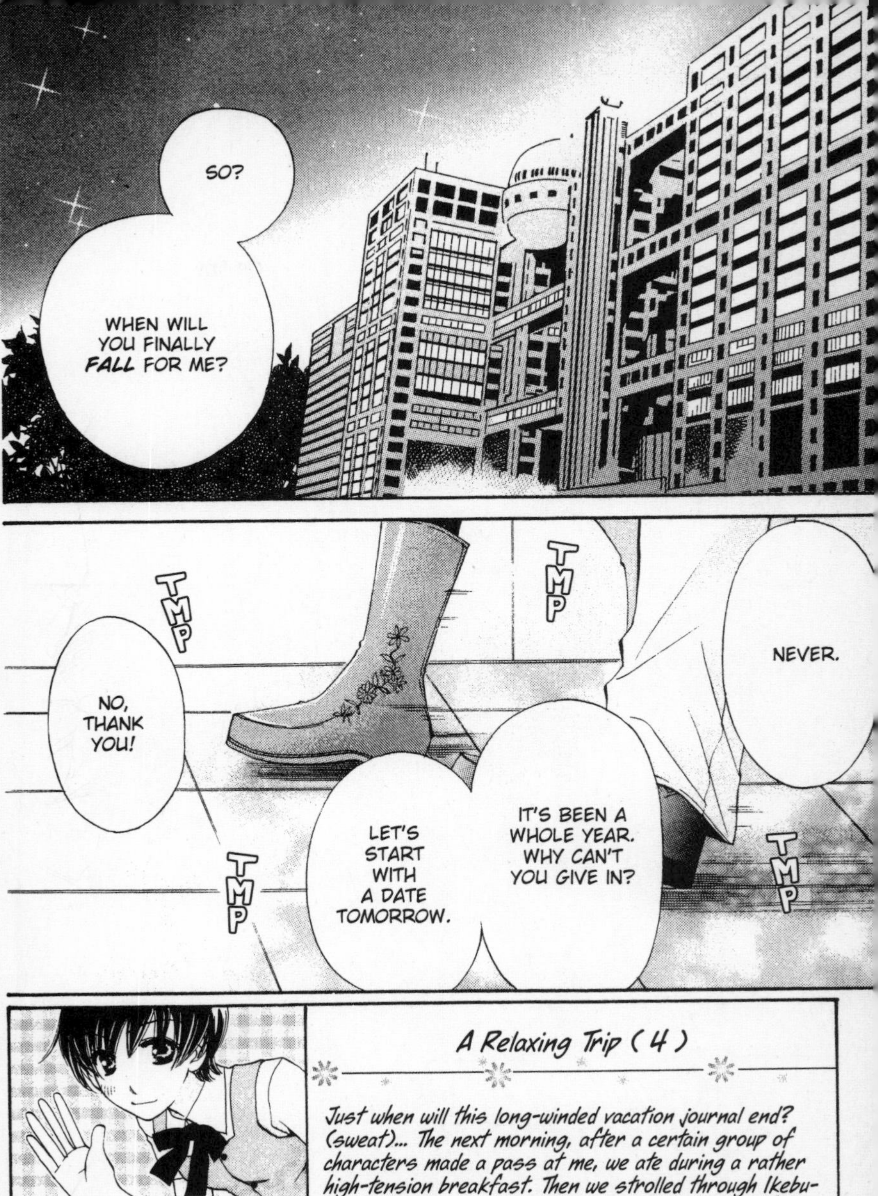
SO?
WHEN WILL YOU FINALLY FALL FOR ME?
TMP
NEVER.
TMP
IT'S BEEN A WHOLE YEAR. WHY CAN'T YOU GIVE IN?
LET'S START WITH A DATE TOMORROW.
TMP
TMP
NO, THANK YOU!
A Relaxing Trip ( 4 )
Just when will this long-winded vacation journal end? (sweat)... The next morning, after a certain group of characters made a pass at me, we ate during a rather high-tension breakfast. Then we strolled through Ikebukuro, ate as we walked, and made it back home safely. Talk about anti-climactic...♢♢ So to both my assistants and all you who read this far: good job and thanks!

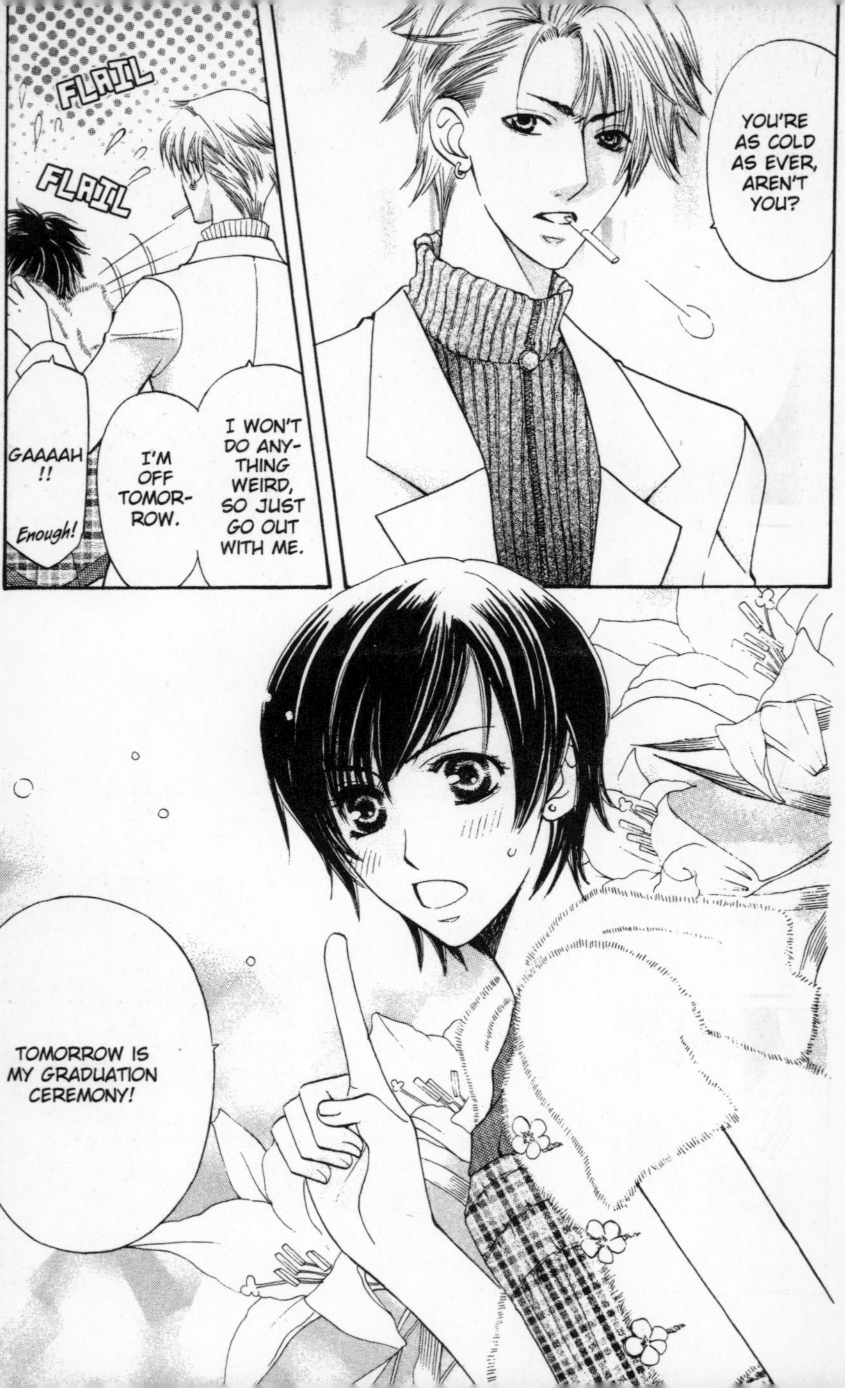
YOU'RE AS COLD AS EVER, AREN'T YOU?
FLAIL
FLAIL
I WON'T DO ANY-THING WEIRD, SO JUST GO OUT WITH ME.
I'M OFF TOMOR-ROW.
GAAAAH !!
Enough!
TOMORROW IS MY GRADUATION CEREMONY!

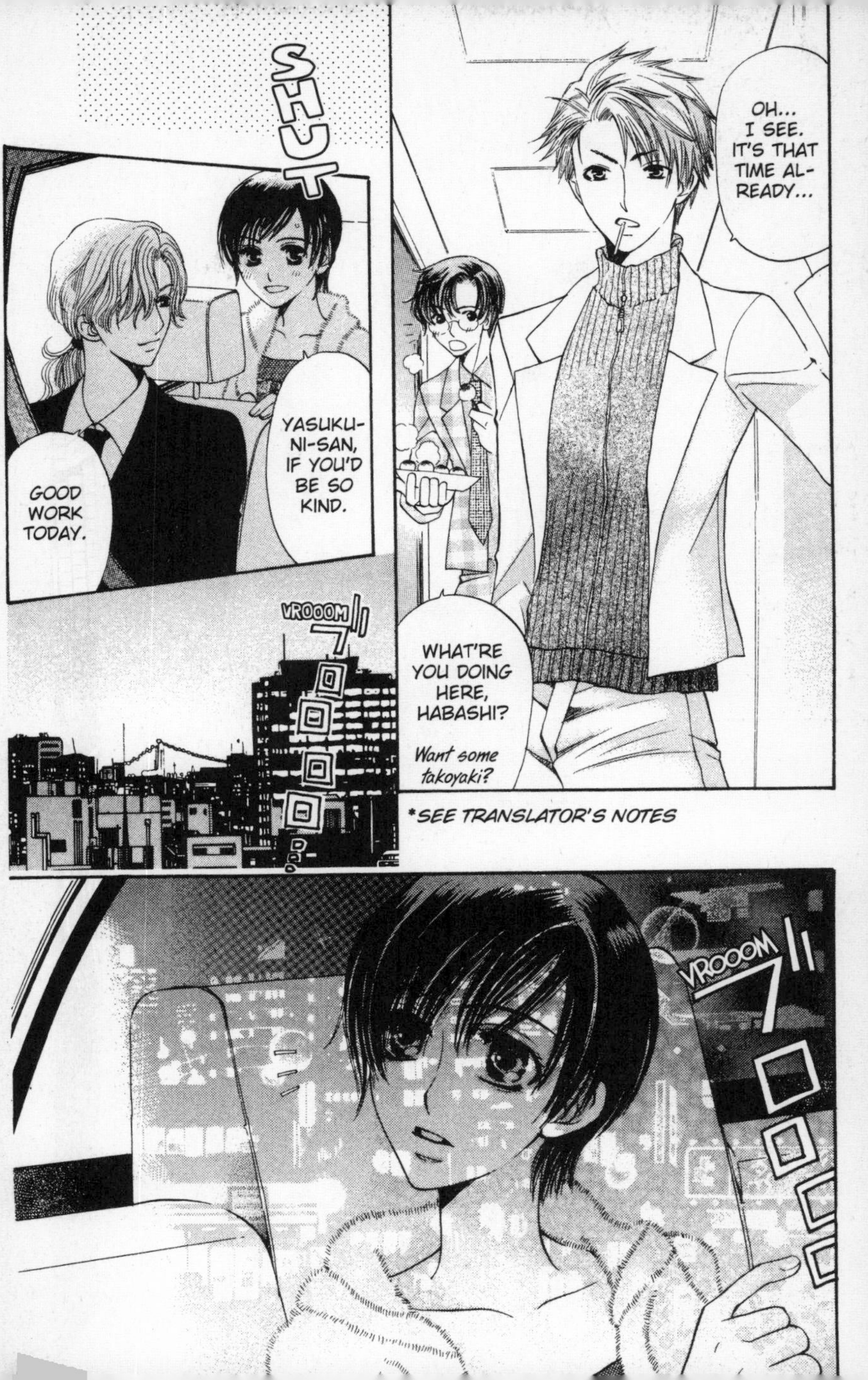
OH... I SEE. IT'S THAT TIME AL-READY...
WHAT'RE YOU DOING HERE, HABASHI?
Want some takoyaki?
SHUT
YASUKU-NI-SAN, IF YOU'D BE SO KIND.
GOOD WORK TODAY.
VROOOM
VROOOM

*SEE TRANSLATOR'S NOTES

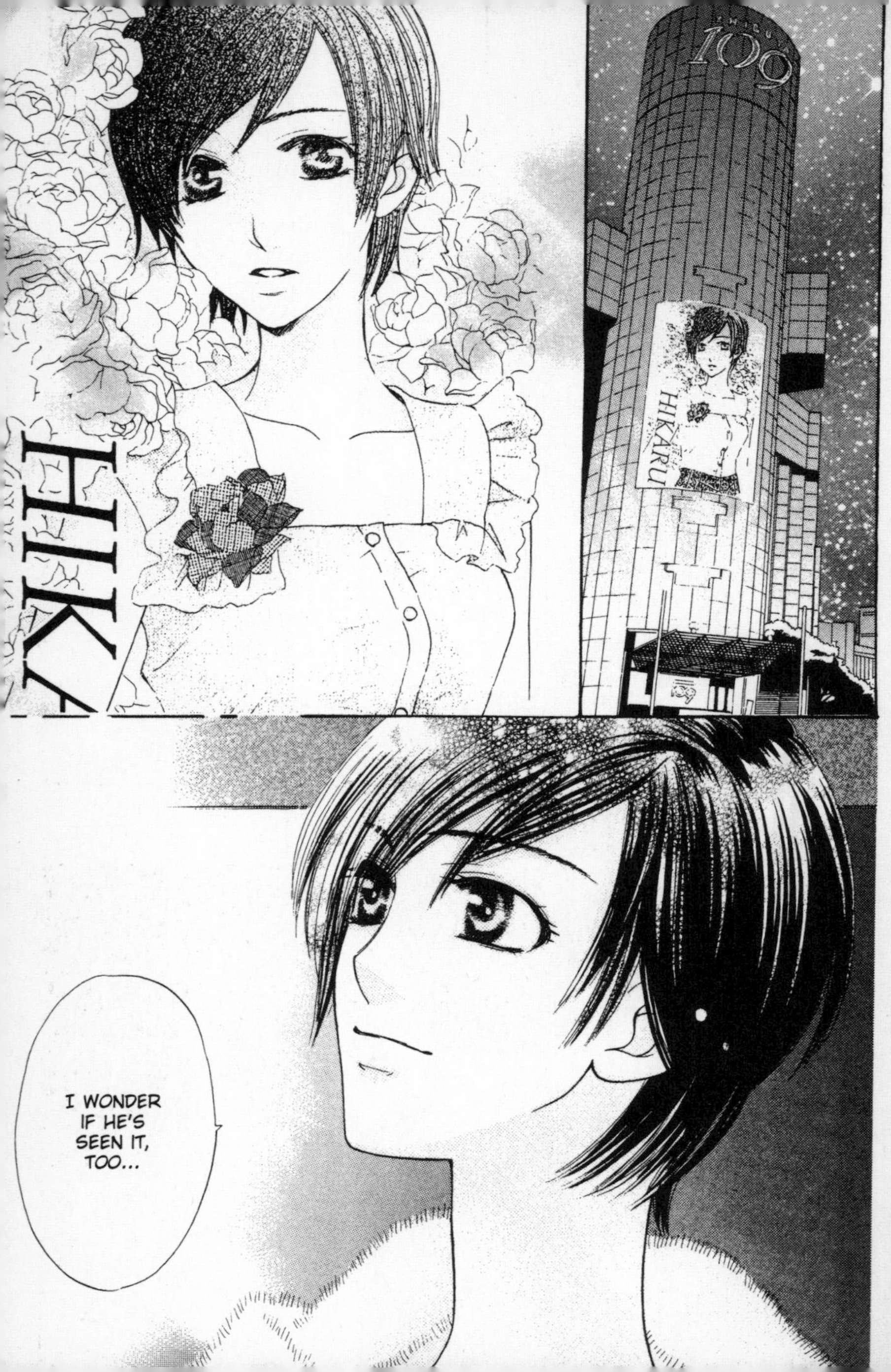
109
HIKARU
HIK
I WONDER IF HE'S SEEN IT, TOO...

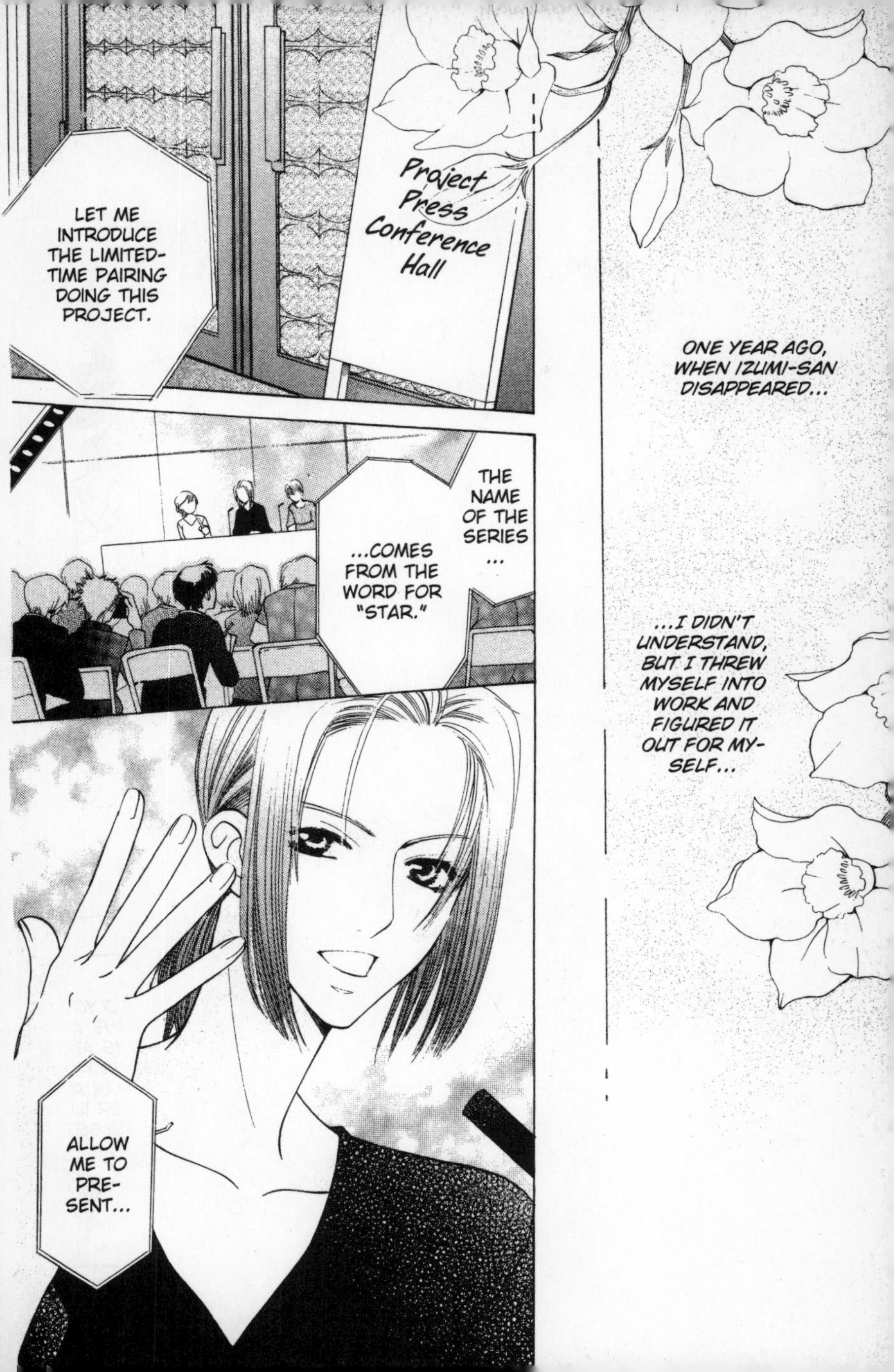
ONE YEAR AGO, WHEN IZUMI-SAN DISAPPEARED...
...I DIDN'T UNDERSTAND, BUT I THREW MYSELF INTO WORK AND FIGURED IT OUT FOR MY-SELF...
Project Press Conference Hall
LET ME INTRODUCE THE LIMITED-TIME PAIRING DOING THIS PROJECT.
THE NAME OF THE SERIES...
...COMES FROM THE WORD FOR "STAR."
ALLOW ME TO PRE-SENT...

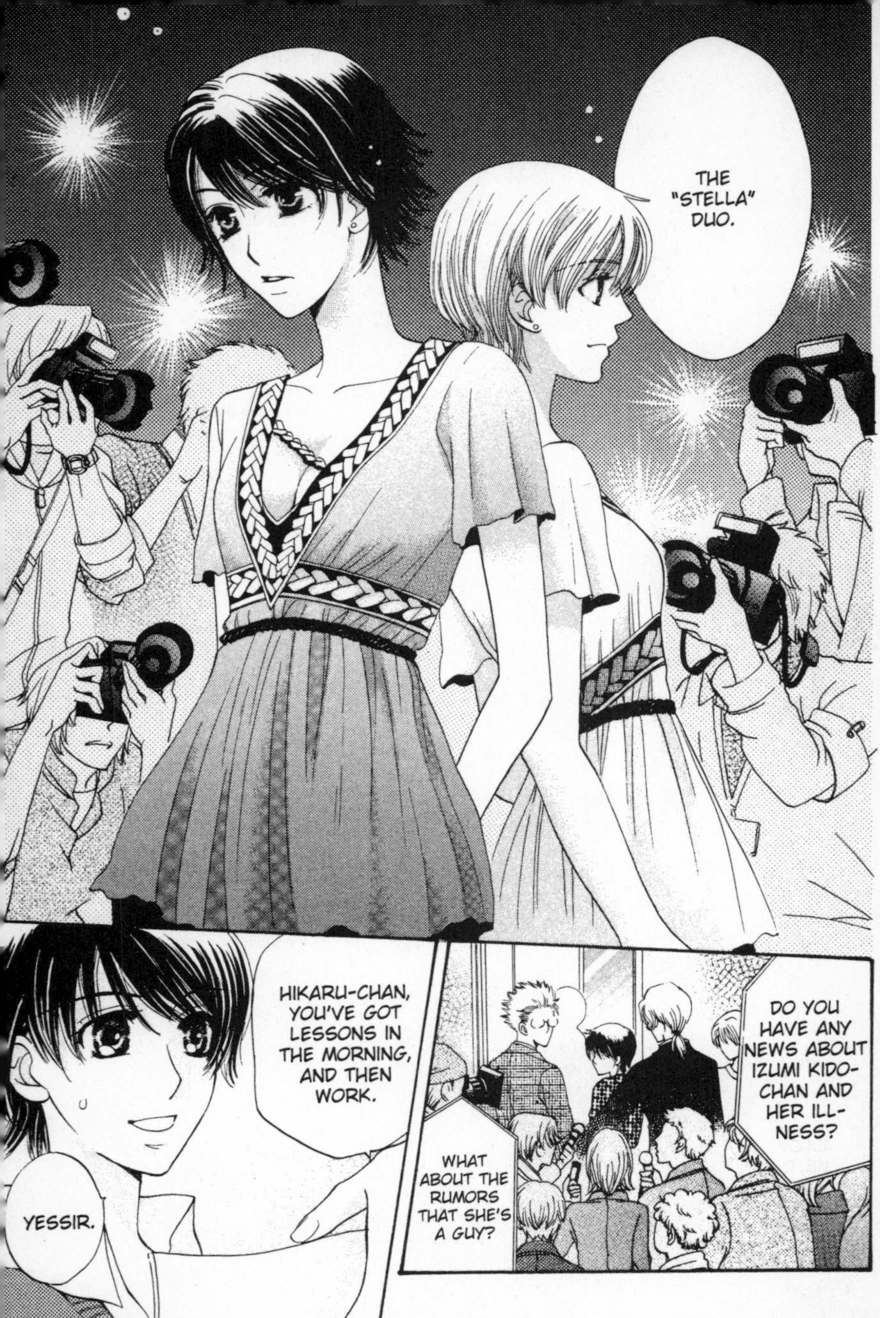
THE "STELLA" DUO.
DO YOU HAVE ANY NEWS ABOUT IZUMI KIDO-CHAN AND HER ILL-NESS?
WHAT ABOUT THE RUMORS THAT SHE'S A GUY?
HIKARU-CHAN, YOU'VE GOT LESSONS IN THE MORNING, AND THEN WORK.
YESSIR.

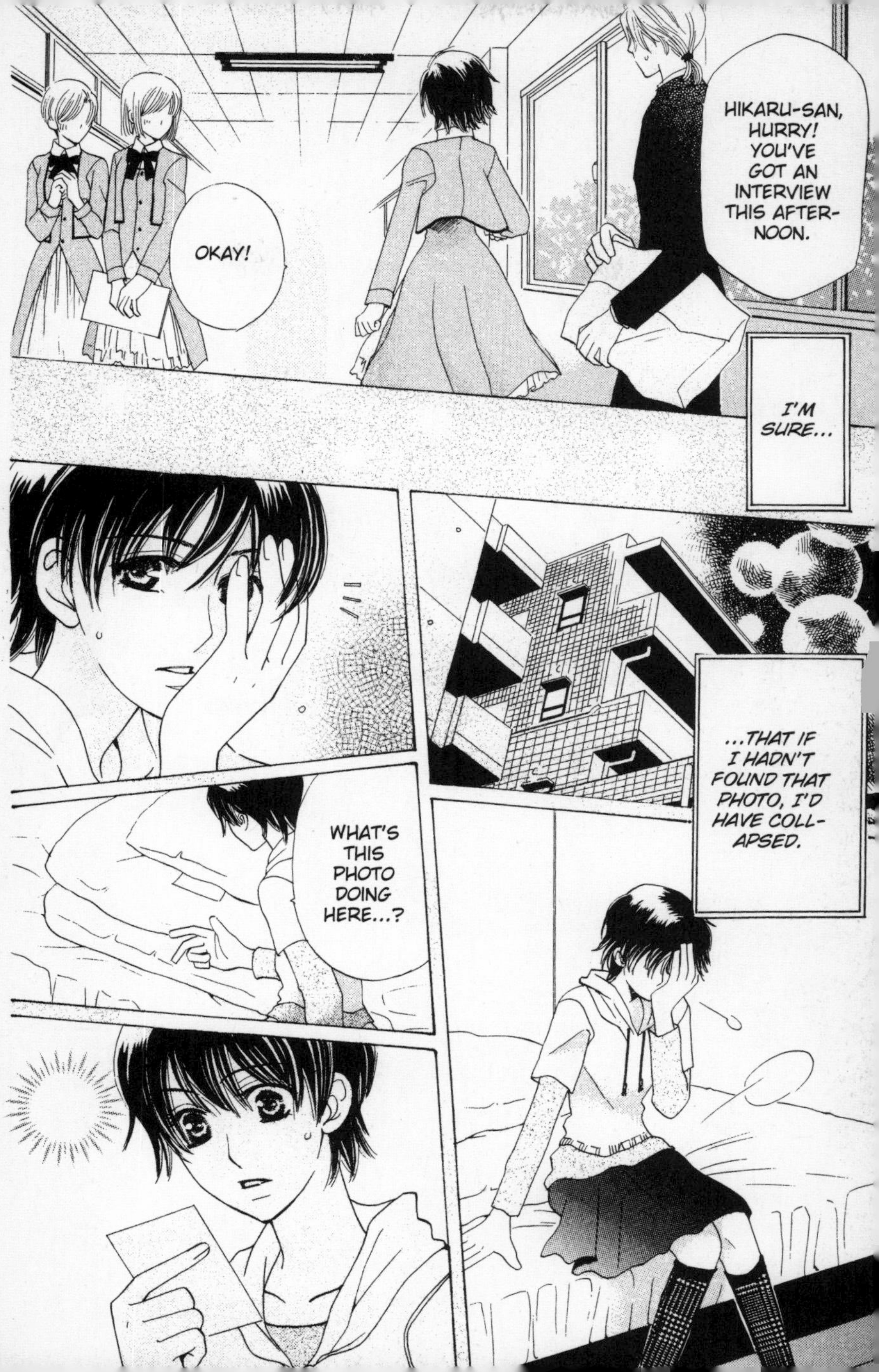
HIKARU-SAN, HURRY! YOU'VE GOT AN INTERVIEW THIS AFTER-NOON.
OKAY!
I'M SURE...
...THAT IF I HADN'T FOUND THAT PHOTO, I'D HAVE COLL-APSED.
WHAT'S THIS PHOTO DOING HERE...?

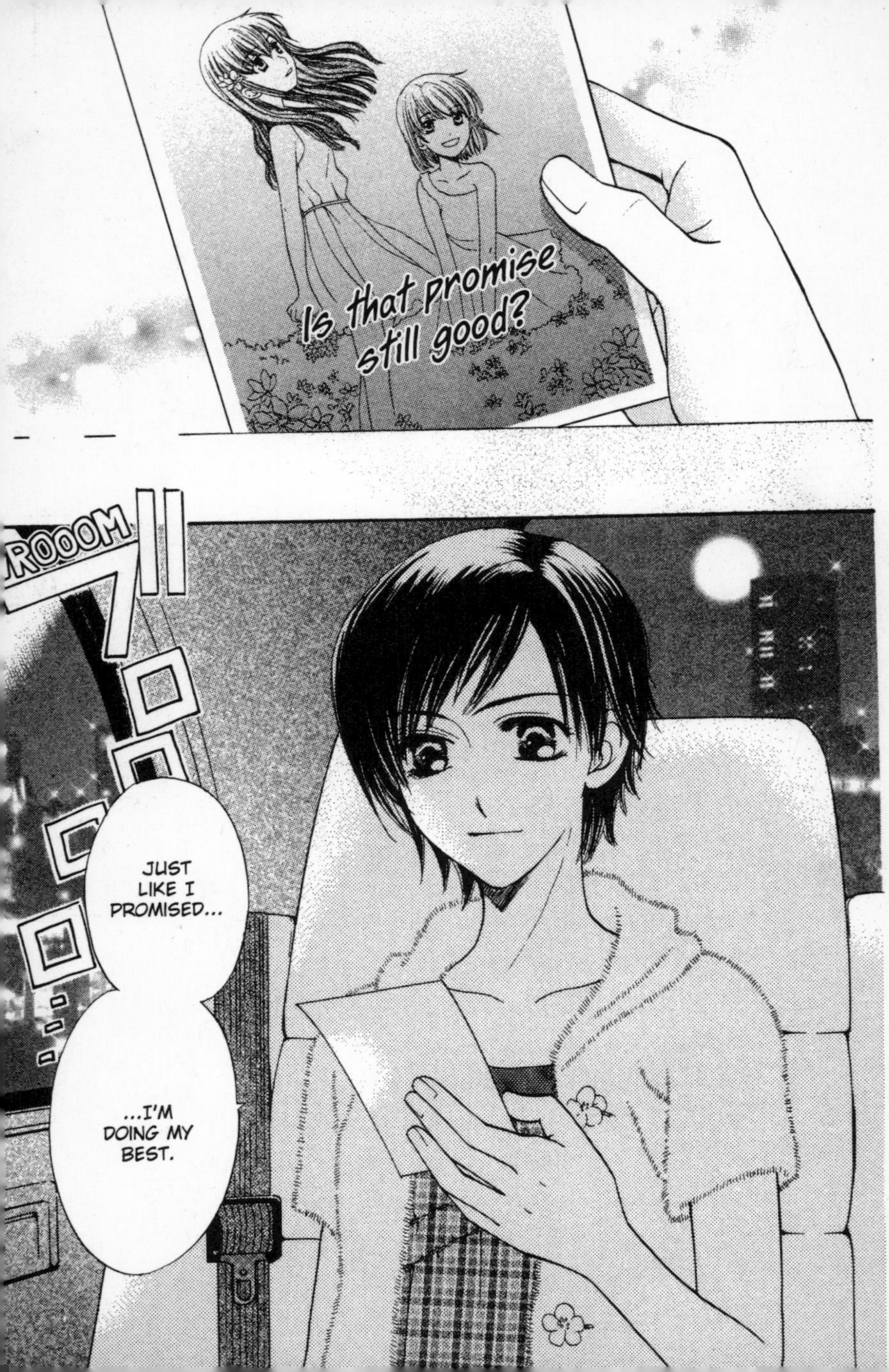
Is that promise still good?
ROOOM
JUST LIKE I PROMISED...
...I'M DOING MY BEST.

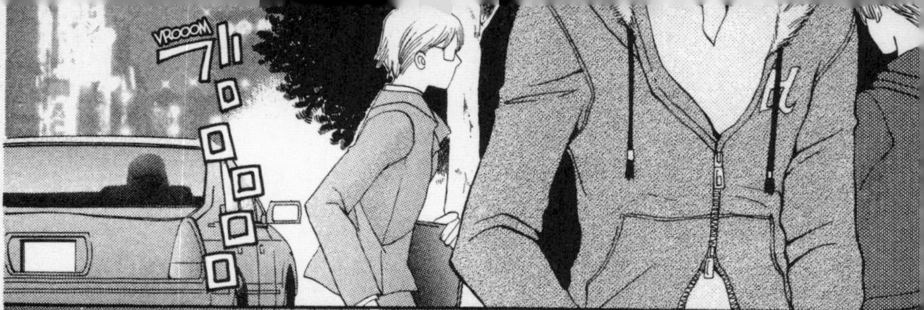
VROOOM
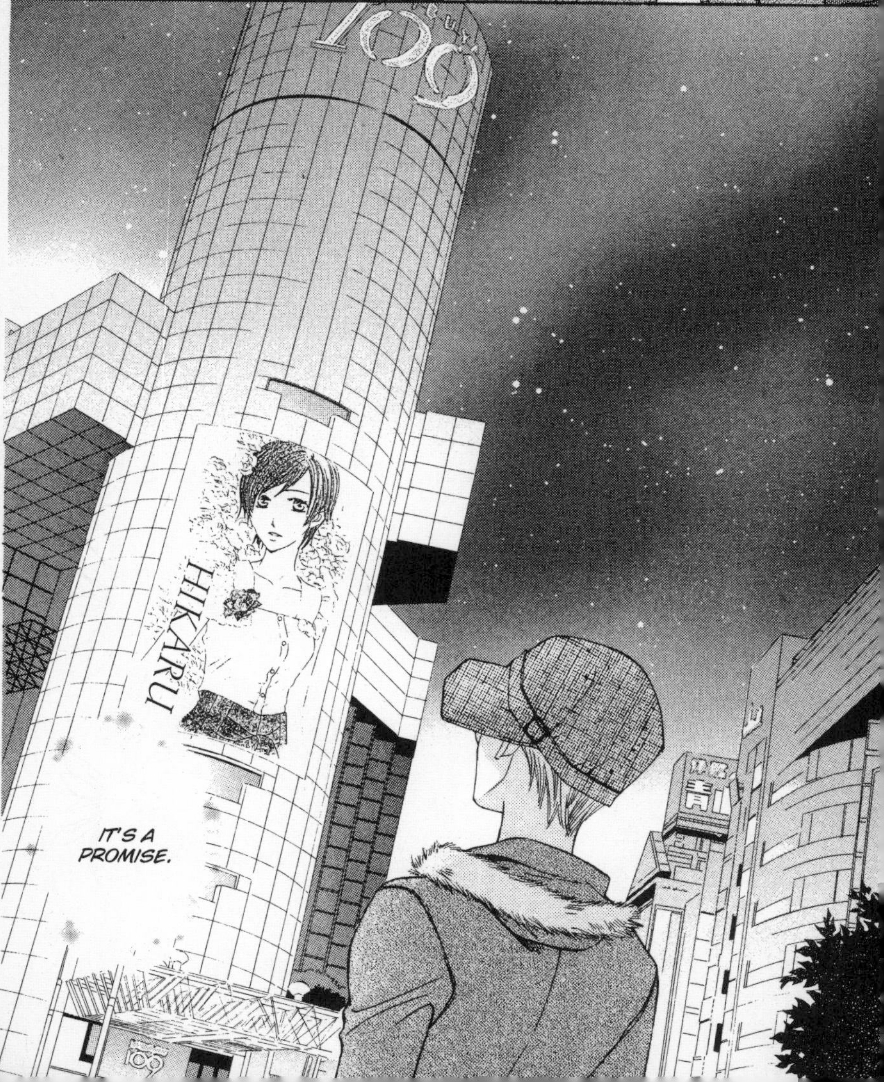
109
HIKARU
IT'S A PROMISE.

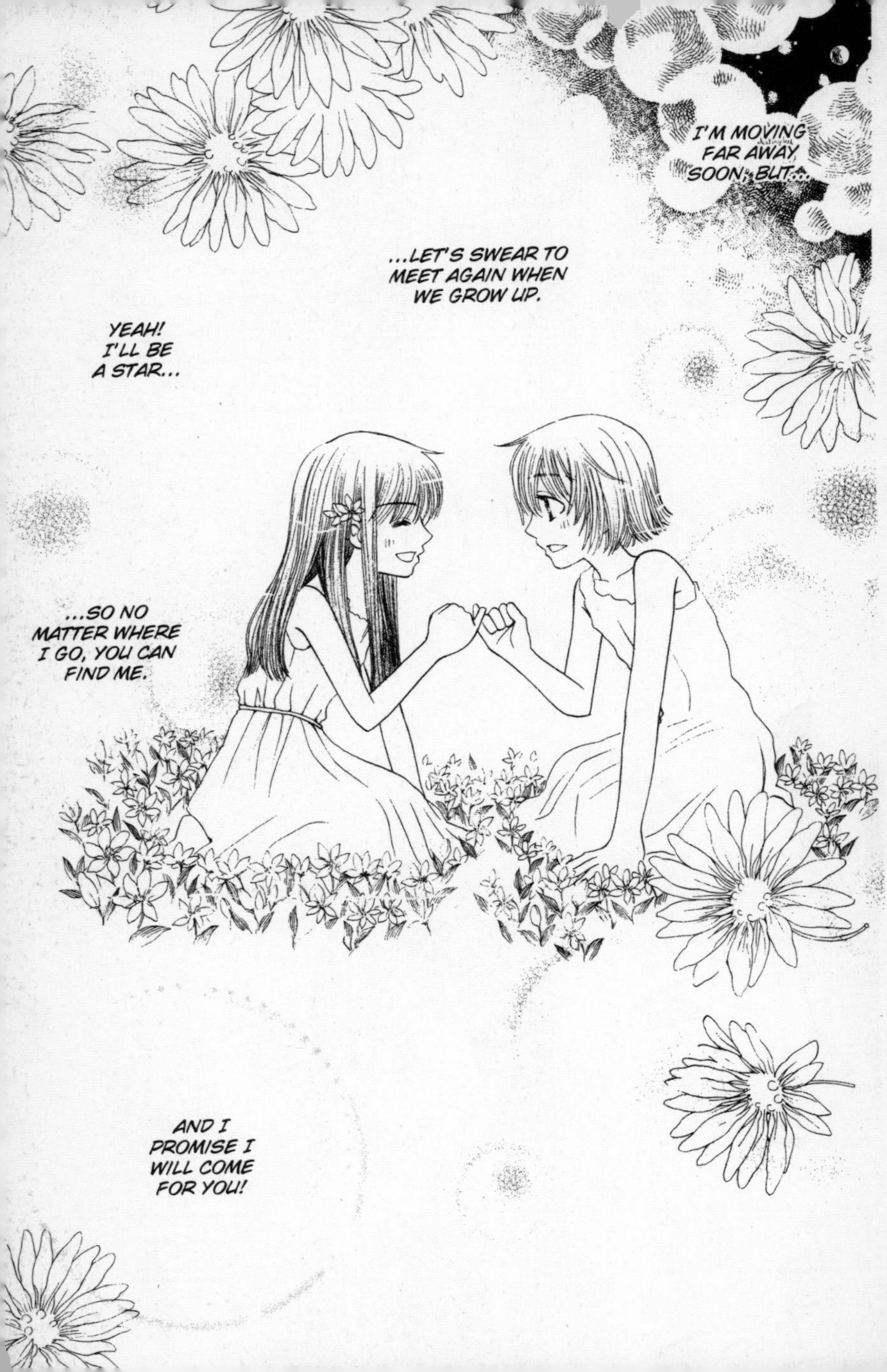
I'M MOVING FAR AWAY SOON, BUT...
...LET'S SWEAR TO MEET AGAIN WHEN WE GROW UP.
YEAH! I'LL BE A STAR...
...SO NO MATTER WHERE I GO, YOU CAN FIND ME.
AND I PROMISE I WILL COME FOR YOU!

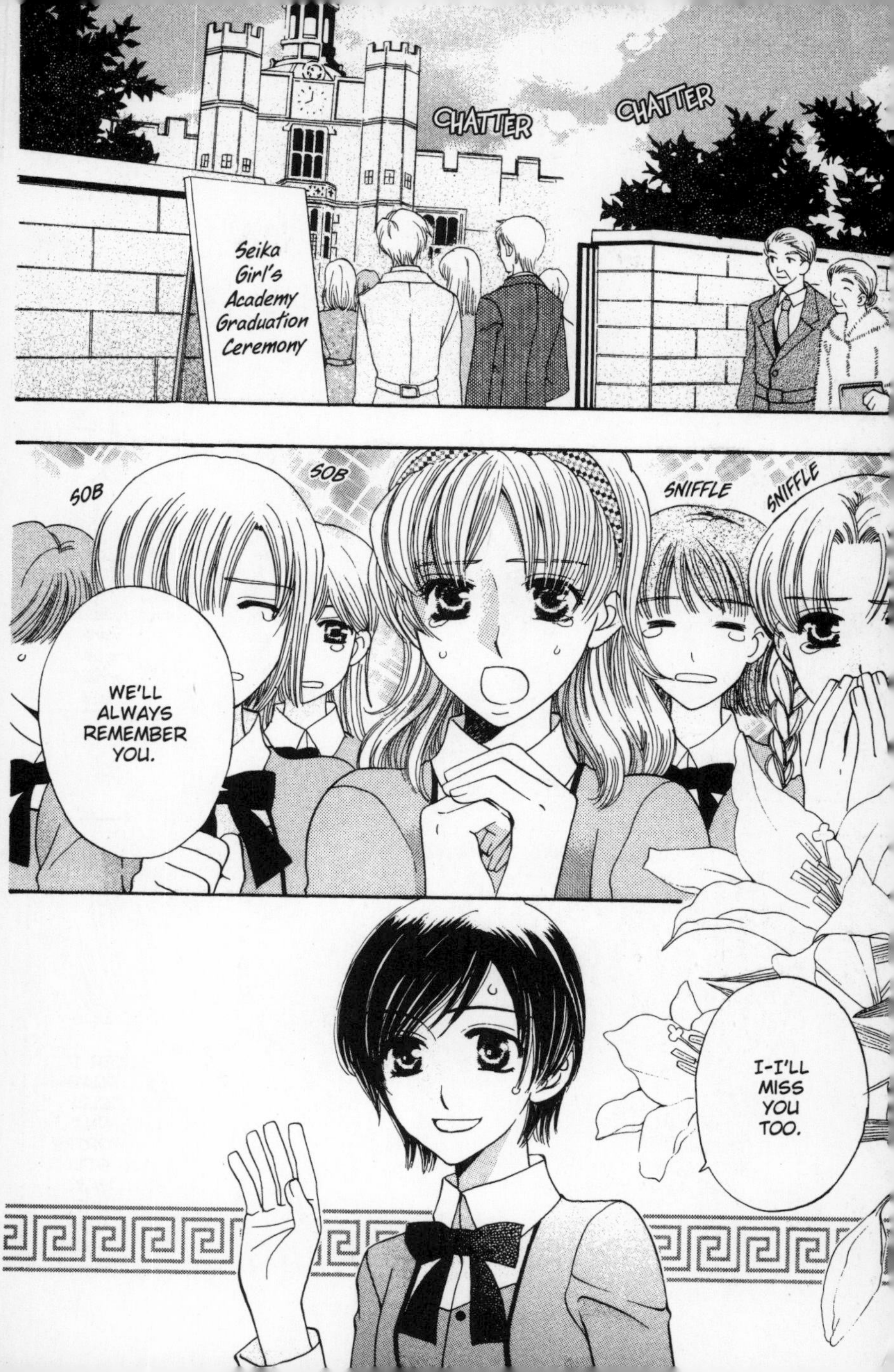
CHATTER
CHATTER
Seika Girl's Academy Graduation Ceremony
SNIFFLE
SNIFFLE
SOB
SOB
WE'LL ALWAYS REMEMBER YOU.
I-I'LL MISS YOU TOO.

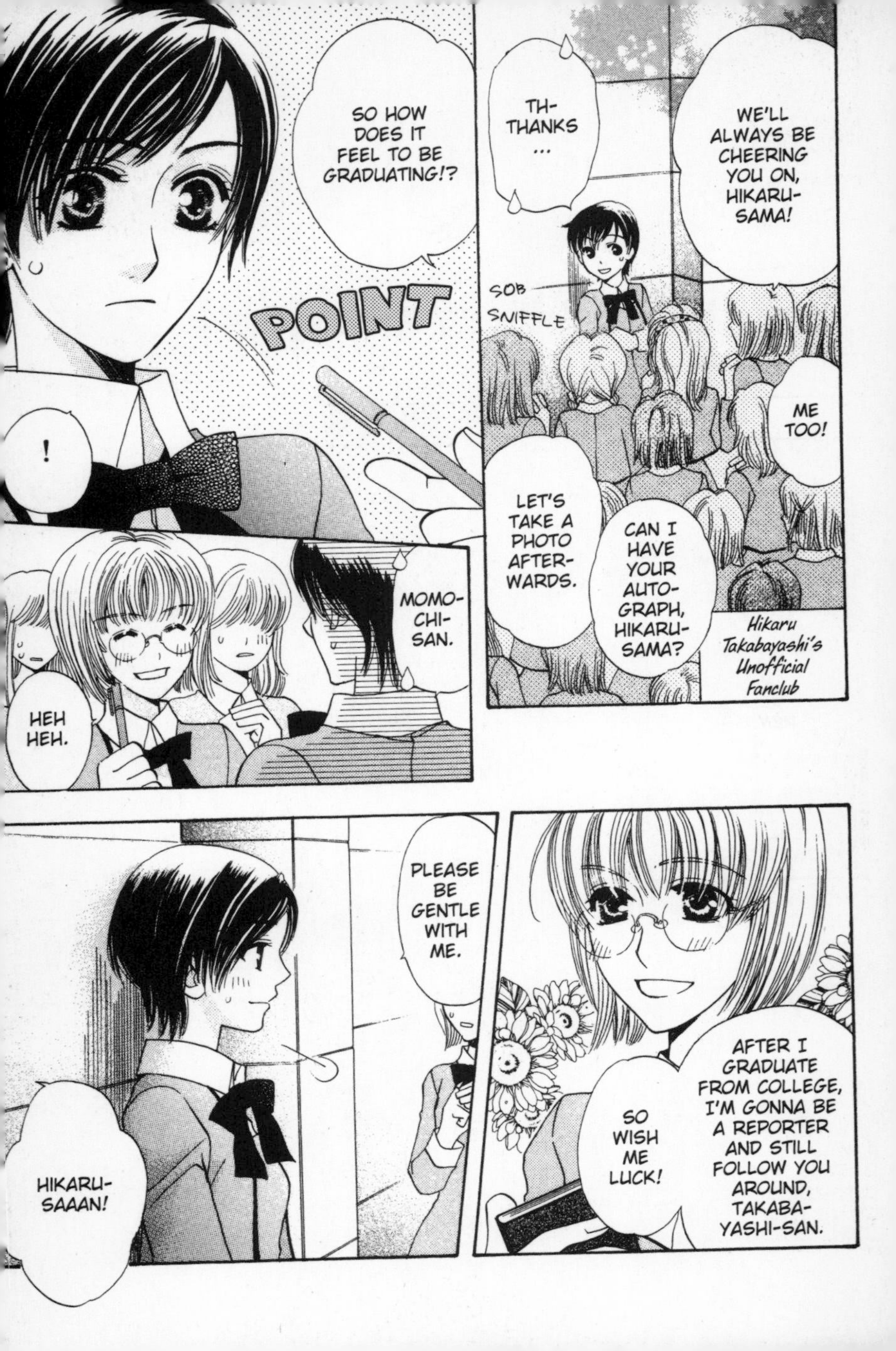
WE'LL ALWAYS BE CHEERING YOU ON, HIKARU-SAMA!
TH-THANKS ...
SOB
SNIFFLE
ME TOO!
CAN I HAVE YOUR AUTO-GRAPH, HIKARU-SAMA?
LET'S TAKE A PHOTO AFTER-WARDS.
Hikaru Takabayashi's Unofficial Fanclub
SO HOW DOES IT FEEL TO BE GRADUATING!?
POINT
!
MOMO-CHI-SAN.
HEH HEH.
AFTER I GRADUATE FROM COLLEGE, I'M GONNA BE A REPORTER AND STILL FOLLOW YOU AROUND, TAKABA-YASHI-SAN.
SO WISH ME LUCK!
PLEASE BE GENTLE WITH ME.
HIKARU-SAAAN!

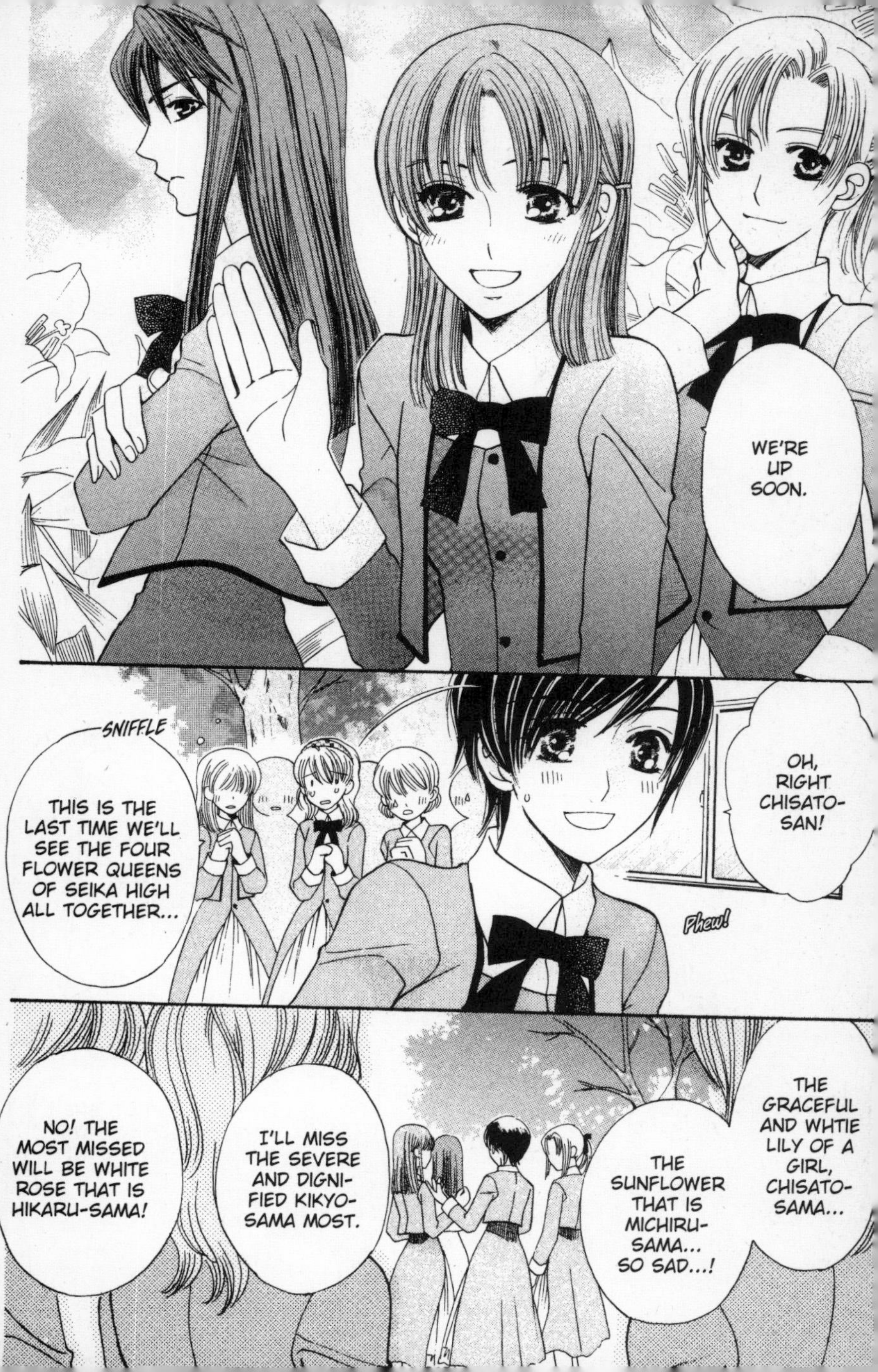
WE'RE UP SOON.
OH, RIGHT CHISATO-SAN!
Phew!
SNIFFLE
THIS IS THE LAST TIME WE'LL SEE THE FOUR FLOWER QUEENS OF SEIKA HIGH ALL TOGETHER...
THE GRACEFUL AND WHTIE LILY OF A GIRL, CHISATO-SAMA...
THE SUNFLOWER THAT IS MICHIRU-SAMA... SO SAD...!
I'LL MISS THE SEVERE AND DIGNI-FIED KIKYO-SAMA MOST.
NO! THE MOST MISSED WILL BE WHITE ROSE THAT IS HIKARU-SAMA!

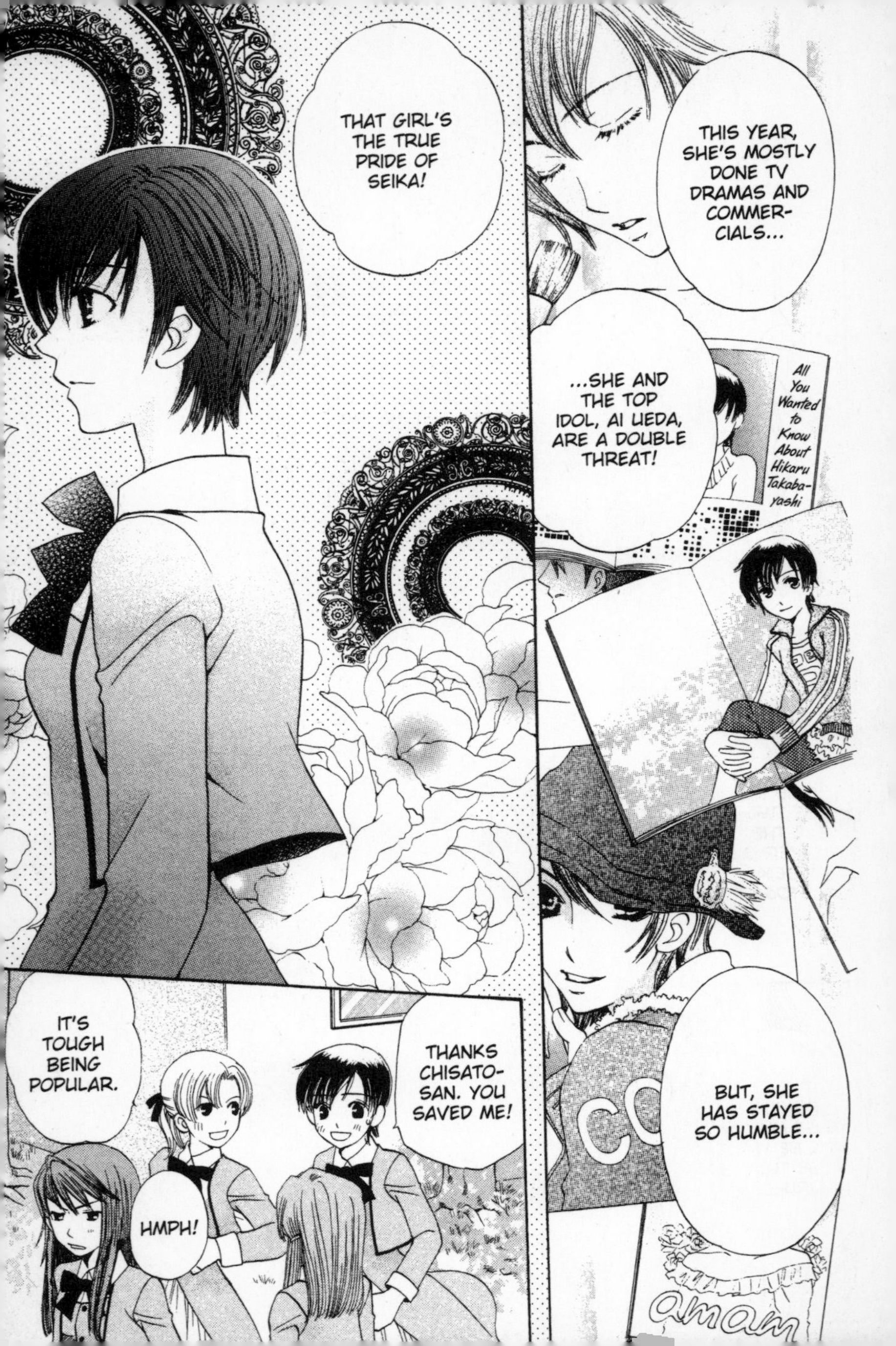
THIS YEAR, SHE'S MOSTLY DONE TV DRAMAS AND COMMER-CIALS...
...SHE AND THE TOP IDOL, AI UEDA, ARE A DOUBLE THREAT!
All You Wanted to Know About Hikaru Takaba-yashi
BUT, SHE HAS STAYED SO HUMBLE...
THAT GIRL'S THE TRUE PRIDE OF SEIKA!
THANKS CHISATO-SAN. YOU SAVED ME!
IT'S TOUGH BEING POPULAR.
HMPH!

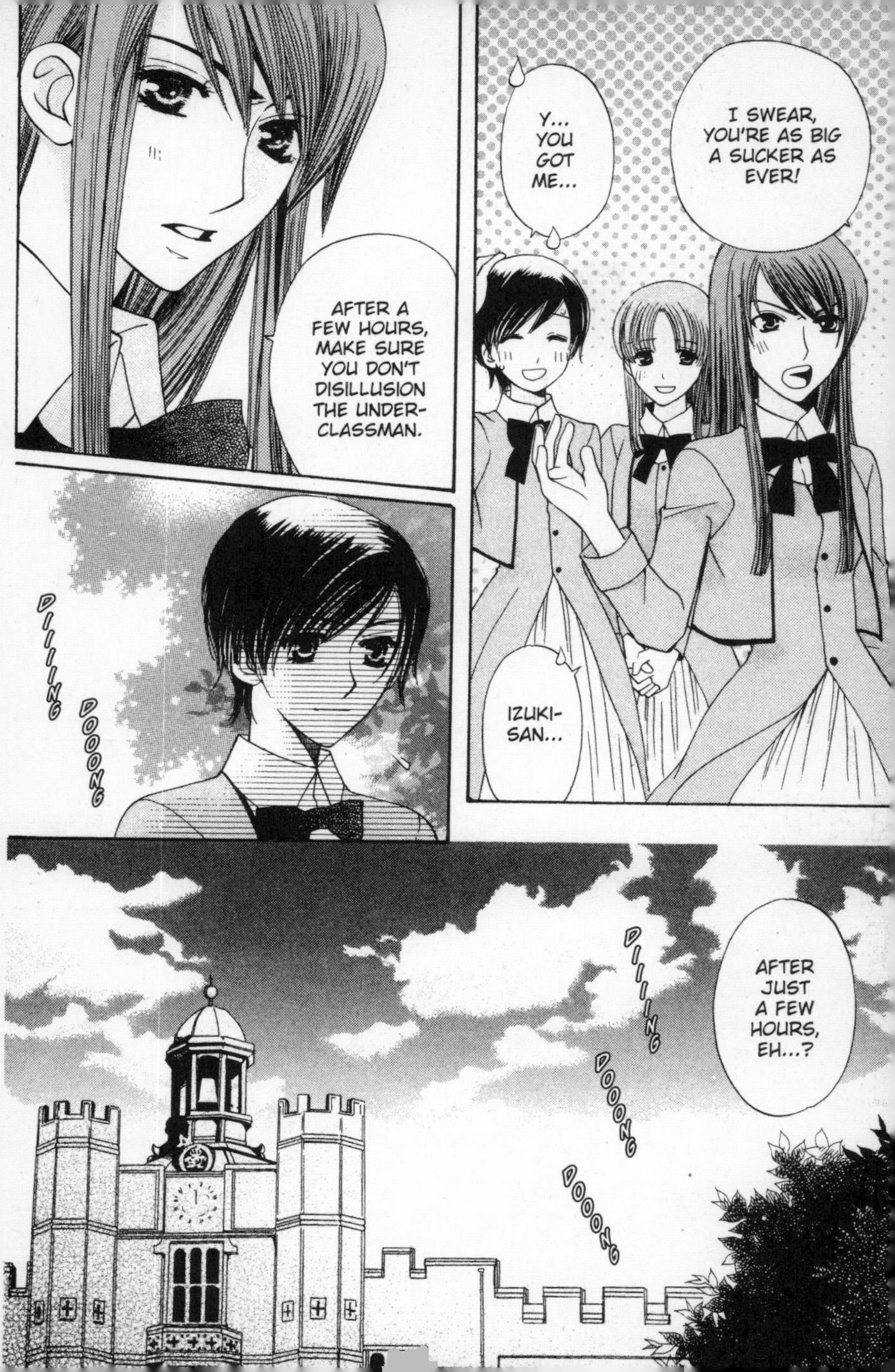
I SWEAR, YOU'RE AS BIG A SUCKER AS EVER!
Y... YOU GOT ME...
IZUKI-SAN...
AFTER A FEW HOURS, MAKE SURE YOU DON'T DISILLUSION THE UNDER-CLASSMAN.
DIIIING
DOOONG
AFTER JUST A FEW HOURS, EH...?
DIIIING
DOOONG
DOOONG

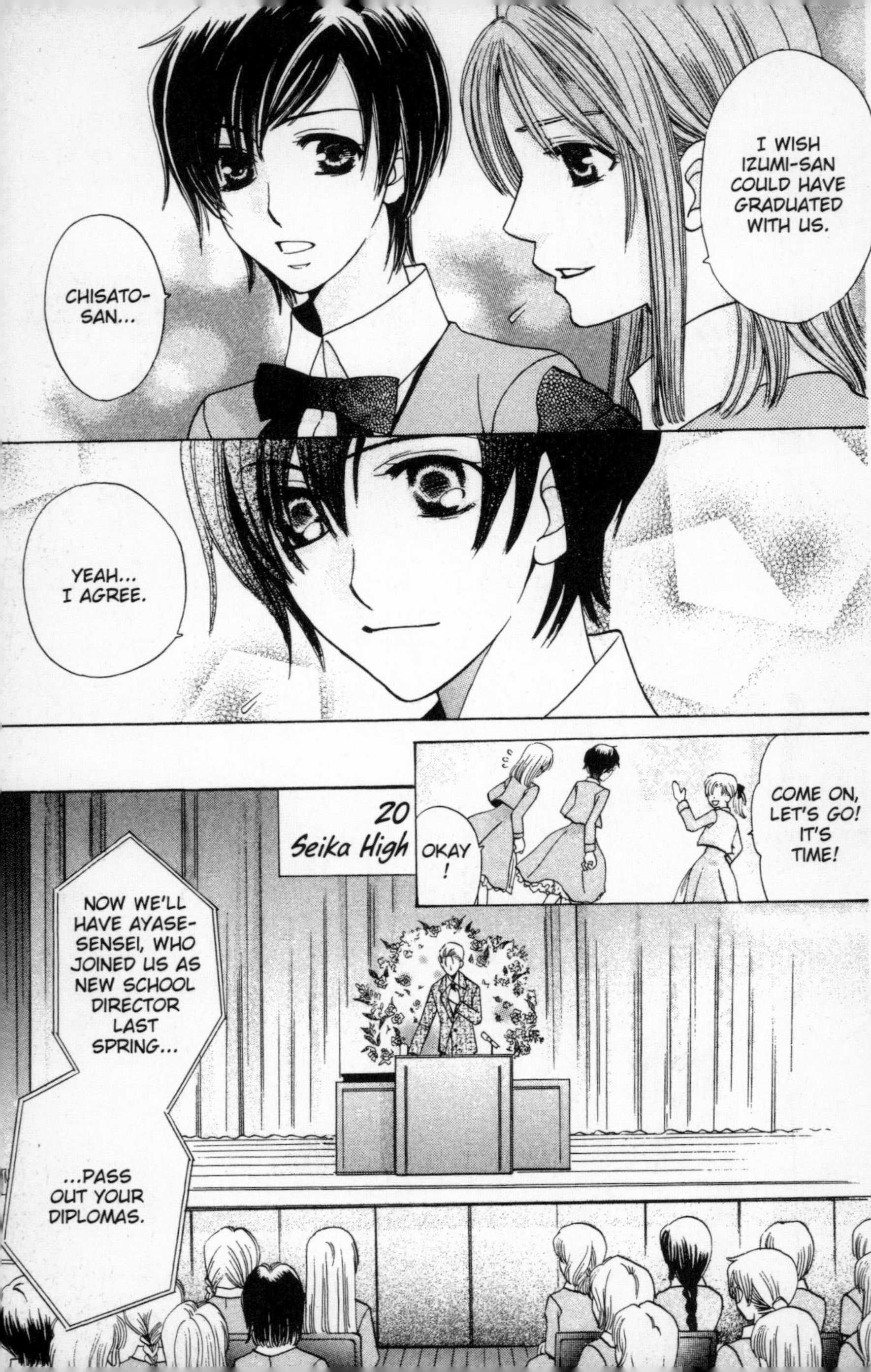
I WISH IZUMI-SAN COULD HAVE GRADUATED WITH US.
CHISATO-SAN...
YEAH... I AGREE.
COME ON, LET'S GO! IT'S TIME!
OKAY!
20 Seika High
NOW WE'LL HAVE AYASE-SENSEI, WHO JOINED US AS NEW SCHOOL DIRECTOR LAST SPRING...
...PASS OUT YOUR DIPLOMAS.

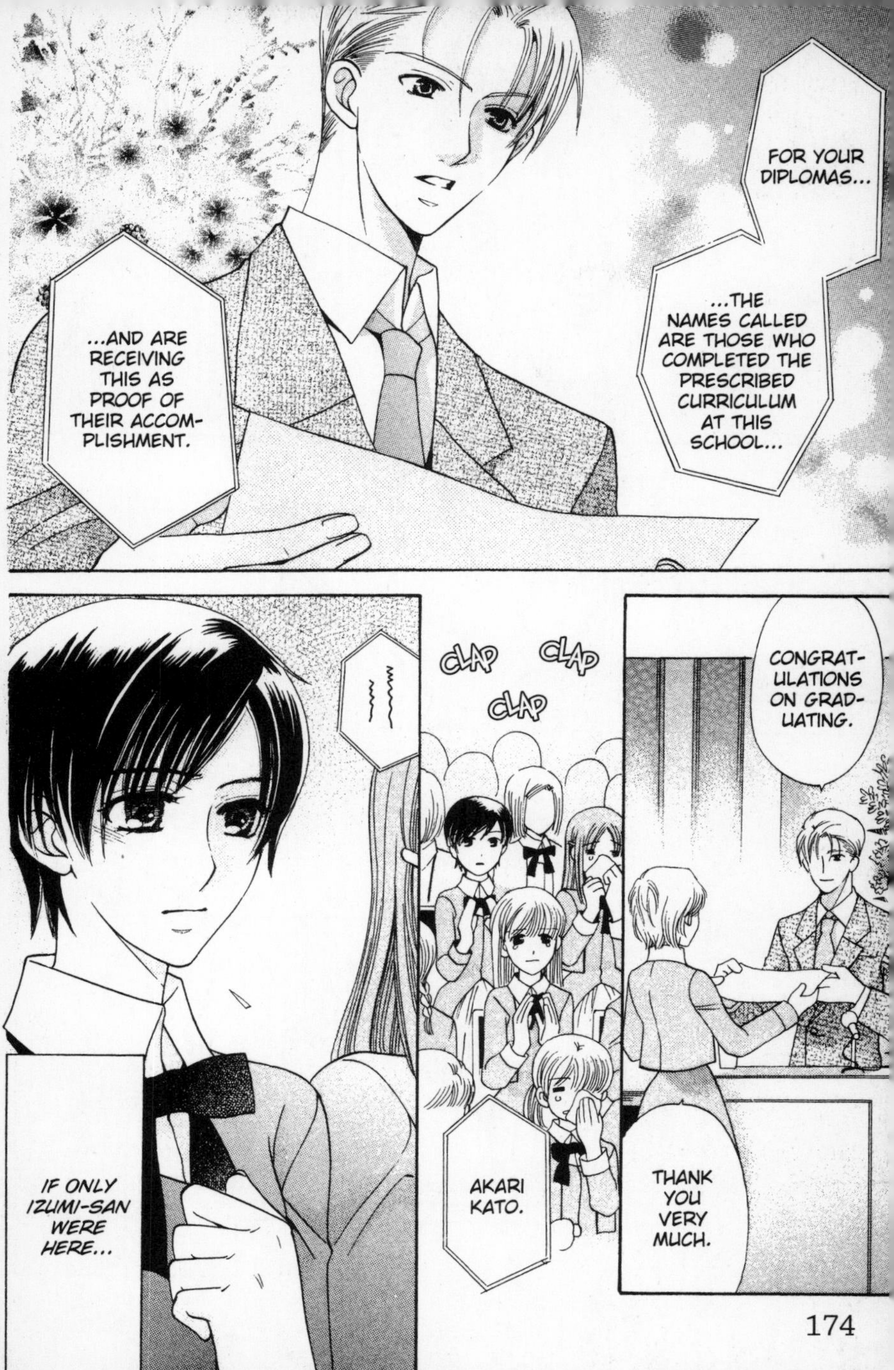
FOR YOUR DIPLOMAS...
...THE NAMES CALLED ARE THOSE WHO COMPLETED THE PRESCRIBED CURRICULUM AT THIS SCHOOL...
...AND ARE RECEIVING THIS AS PROOF OF THEIR ACCOM-PLISHMENT.
CONGRAT-ULATIONS ON GRAD-UATING.
THANK YOU VERY MUCH.
CLAP
CLAP
CLAP
AKARI KATO.
IF ONLY IZUMI-SAN WERE HERE...

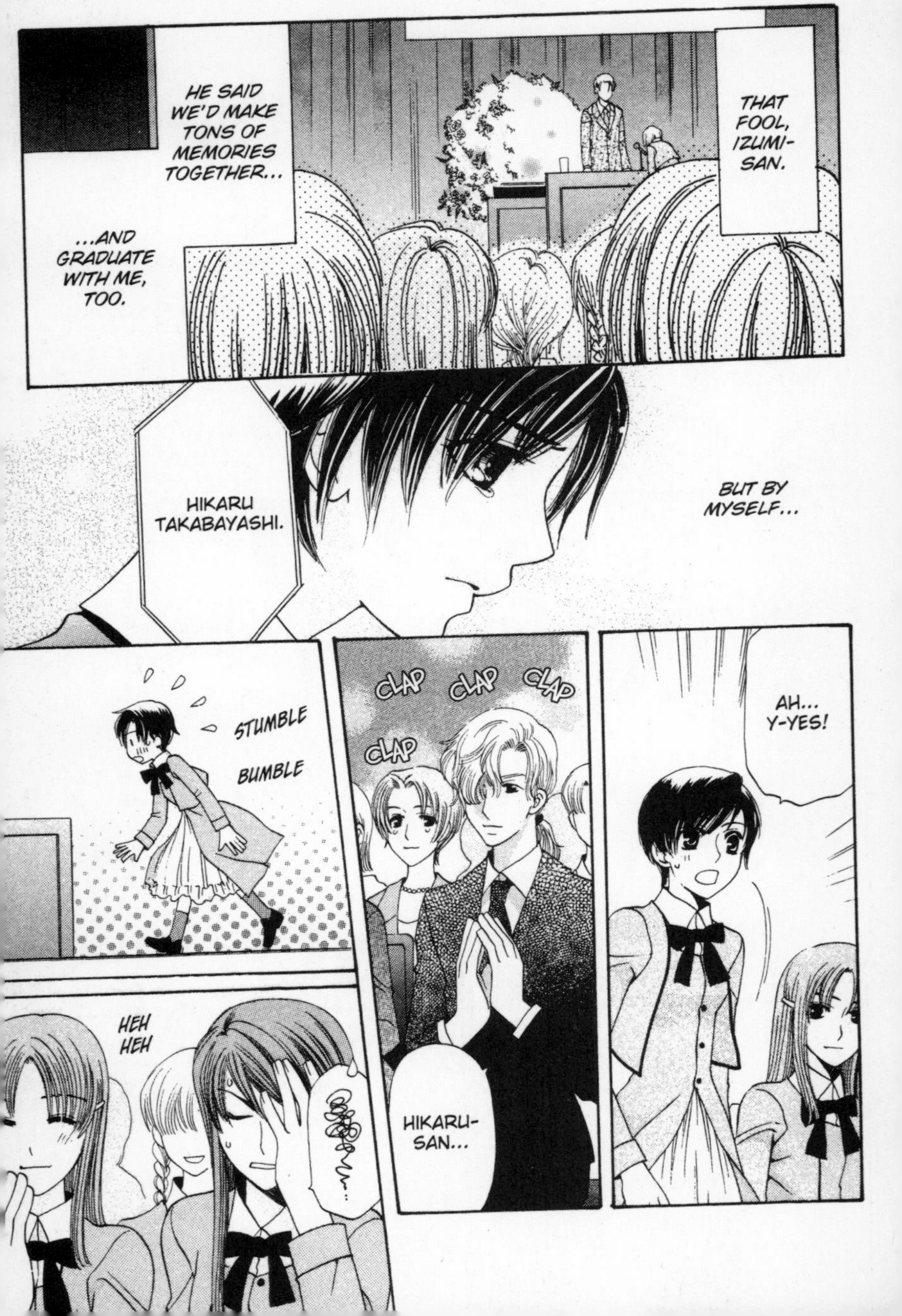
THAT FOOL, IZUMI-SAN.
HE SAID WE'D MAKE TONS OF MEMORIES TOGETHER...
...AND GRADUATE WITH ME, TOO.
BUT BY MYSELF...
HIKARU TAKABAYASHI.
AH... Y-YES!
CLAP CLAP CLAP
CLAP
HIKARU-SAN...
STUMBLE
BUMBLE
HEH HEH

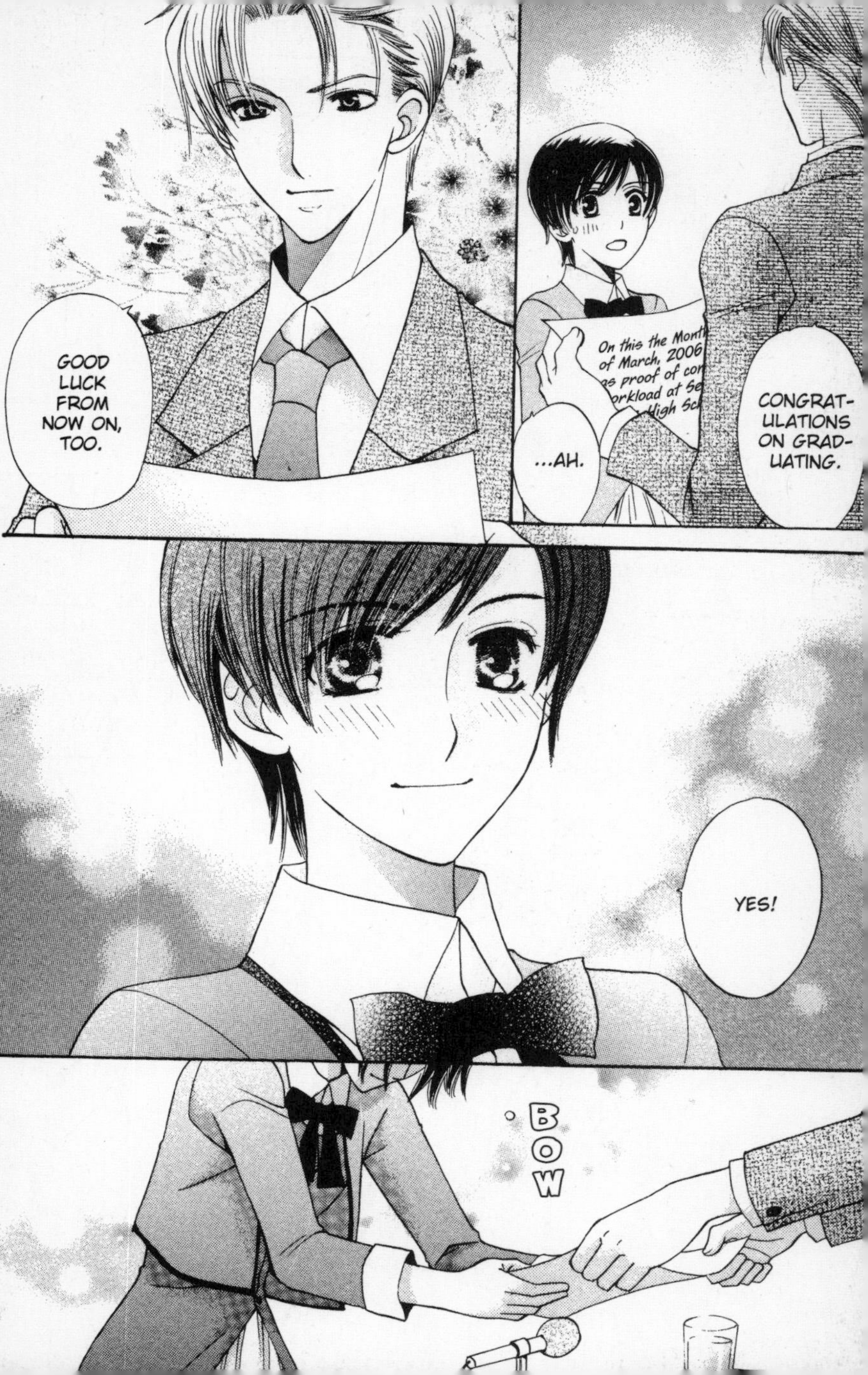
CONGRAT-
ULATIONS
ON GRAD-
UATING.
On this the Mont
of March, 2006
as proof of co
orkload at Se
High Sch
...AH.
GOOD LUCK FROM NOW ON, TOO.
YES!
BOW

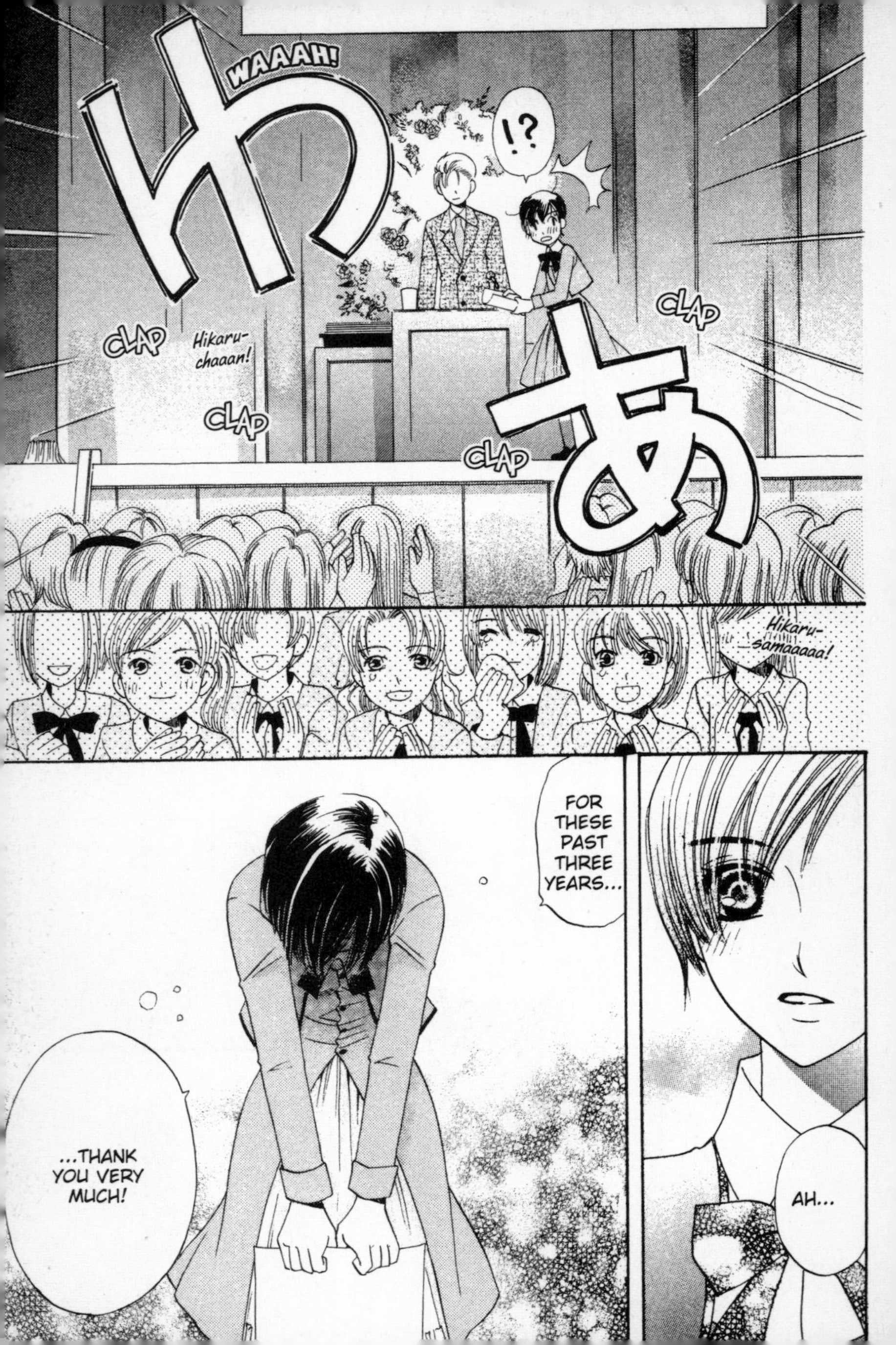
!?
わっ
WAAAH!
あ
CLAP
CLAP
Hikaru-chaaan!
CLAP
CLAP
Hikaru-samaaaaa!
AH...
FOR THESE PAST THREE YEARS...
...THANK YOU VERY MUCH!

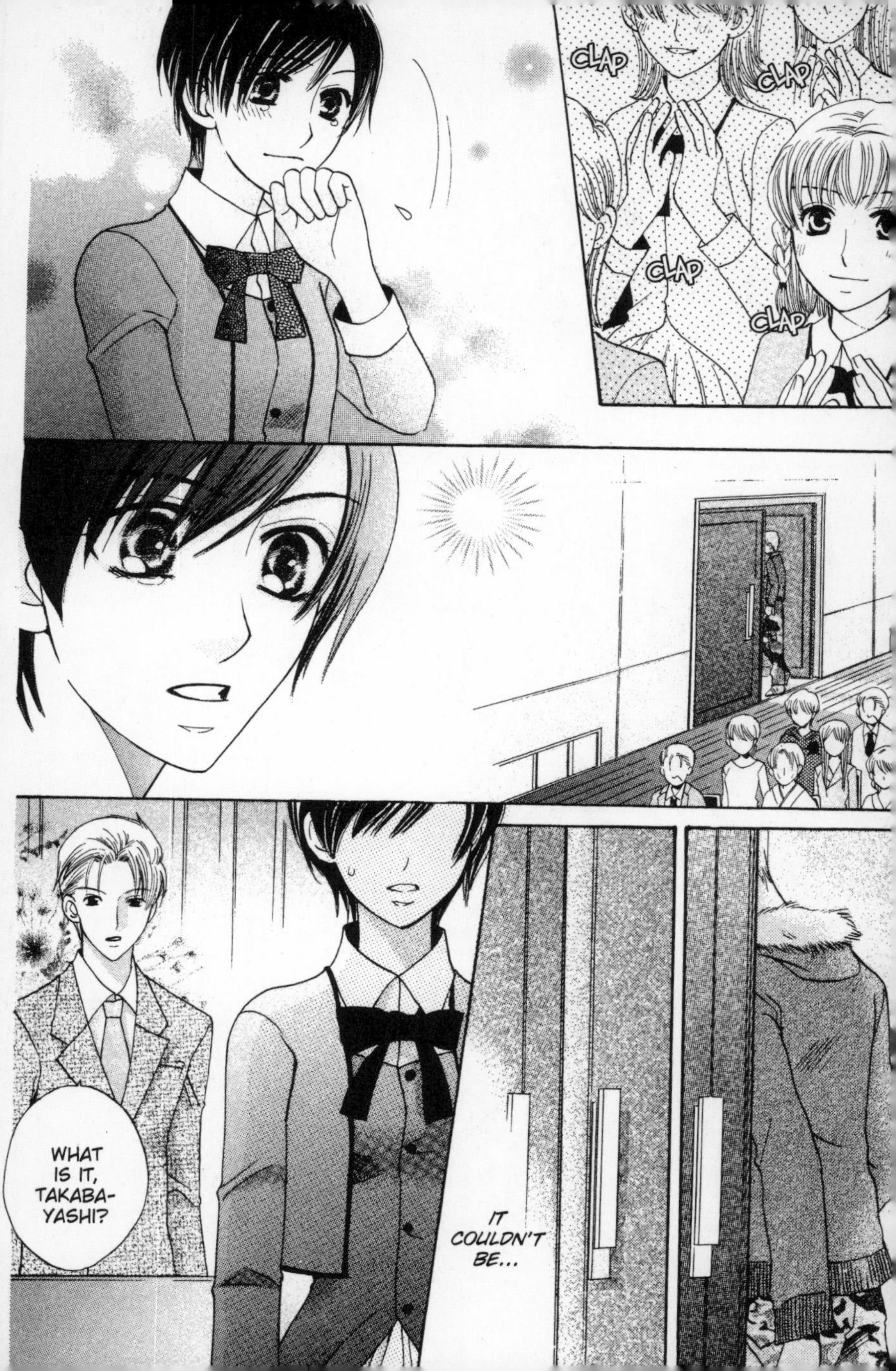
CLAP
CLAP
CLAP
CLAP
IT COULDN'T BE...
WHAT IS IT, TAKABA-YASHI?

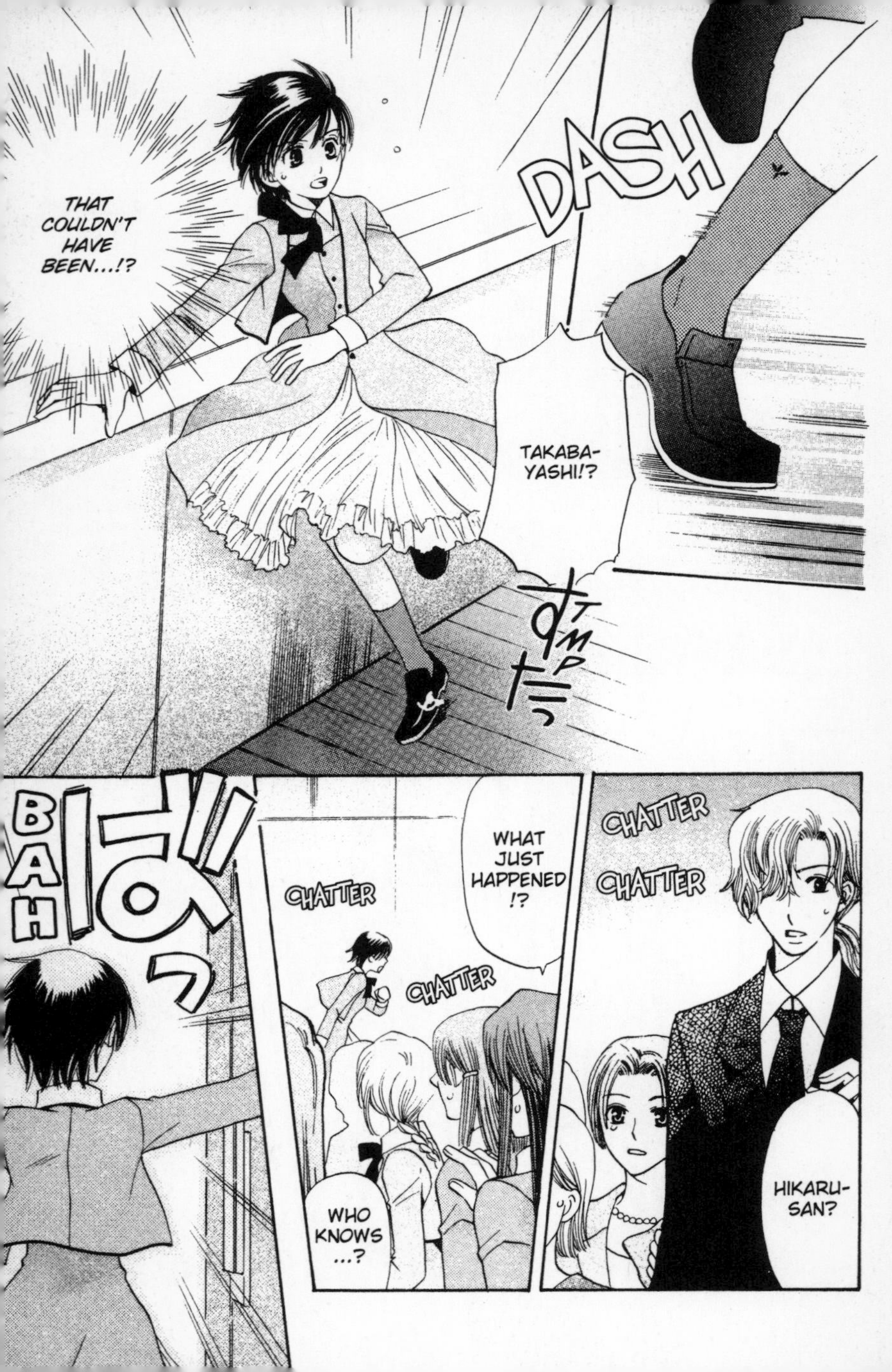
DASH
TAKABA-YASHI!?
THAT COULDN'T HAVE BEEN...!?
TMP
CHATTER
CHATTER
HIKARU-SAN?
WHAT JUST HAPPENED !?
CHATTER
CHATTER
WHO KNOWS ...?
BAH
ばっ

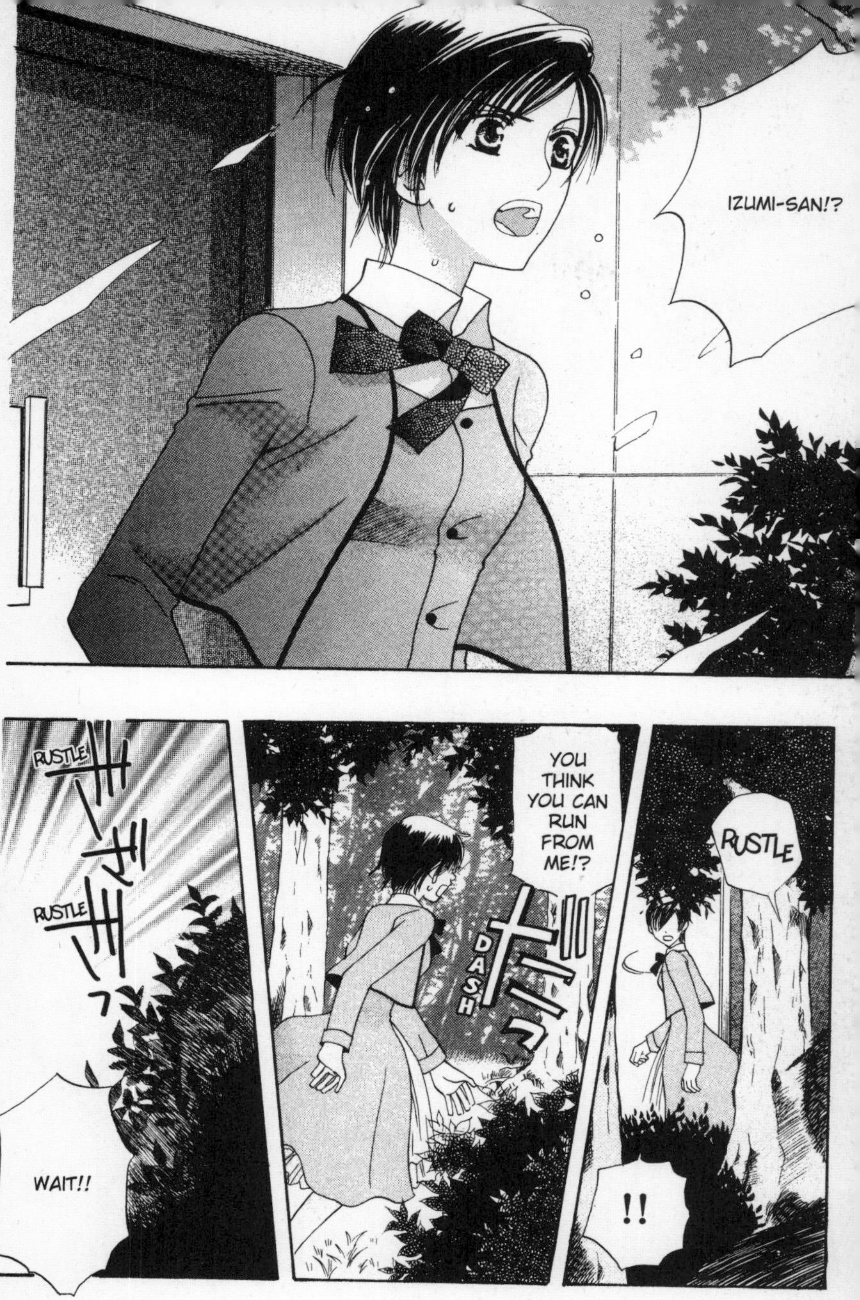
IZUMI-SAN!?
RUSTLE
!!
YOU THINK YOU CAN RUN FROM ME!?
DASH
RUSTLE
RUSTLE
WAIT!!

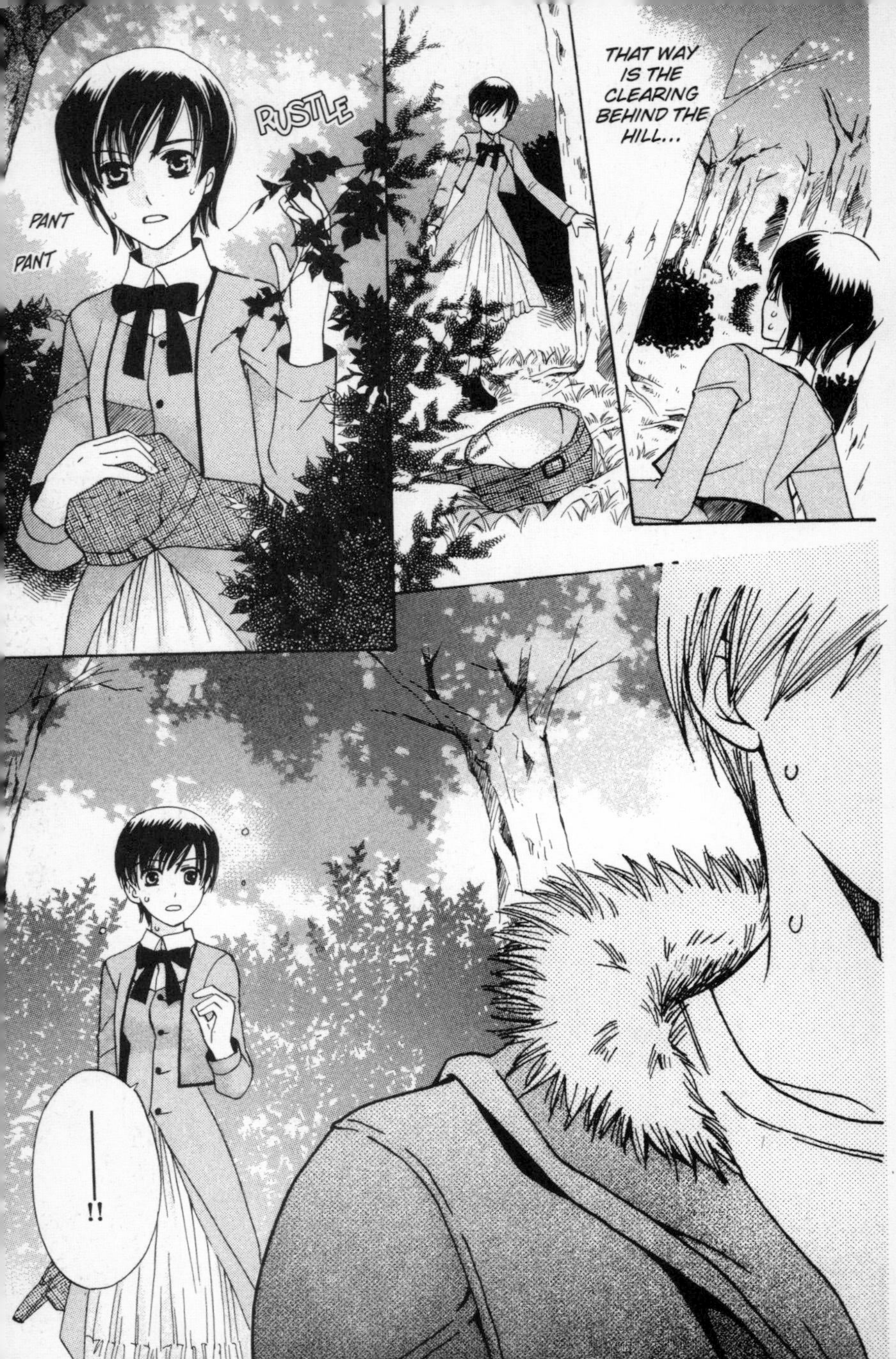
THAT WAY IS THE CLEARING BEHIND THE HILL...
RUSTLE
PANT
PANT
—!!

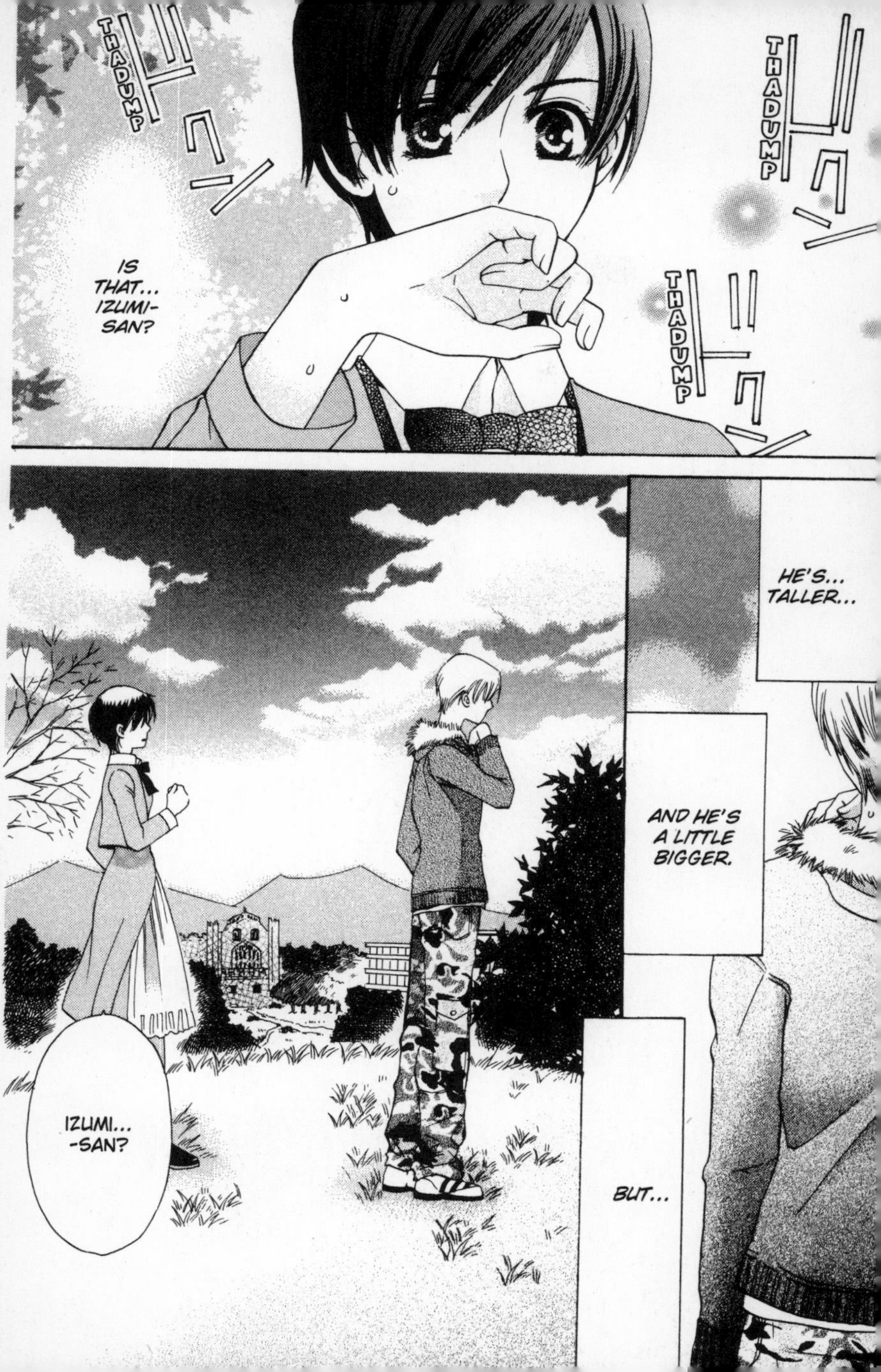

THADUMP
THADUMP
THADUMP
IS THAT... IZUMI-SAN?
HE'S... TALLER...
AND HE'S A LITTLE BIGGER.
BUT...
IZUMI... -SAN?

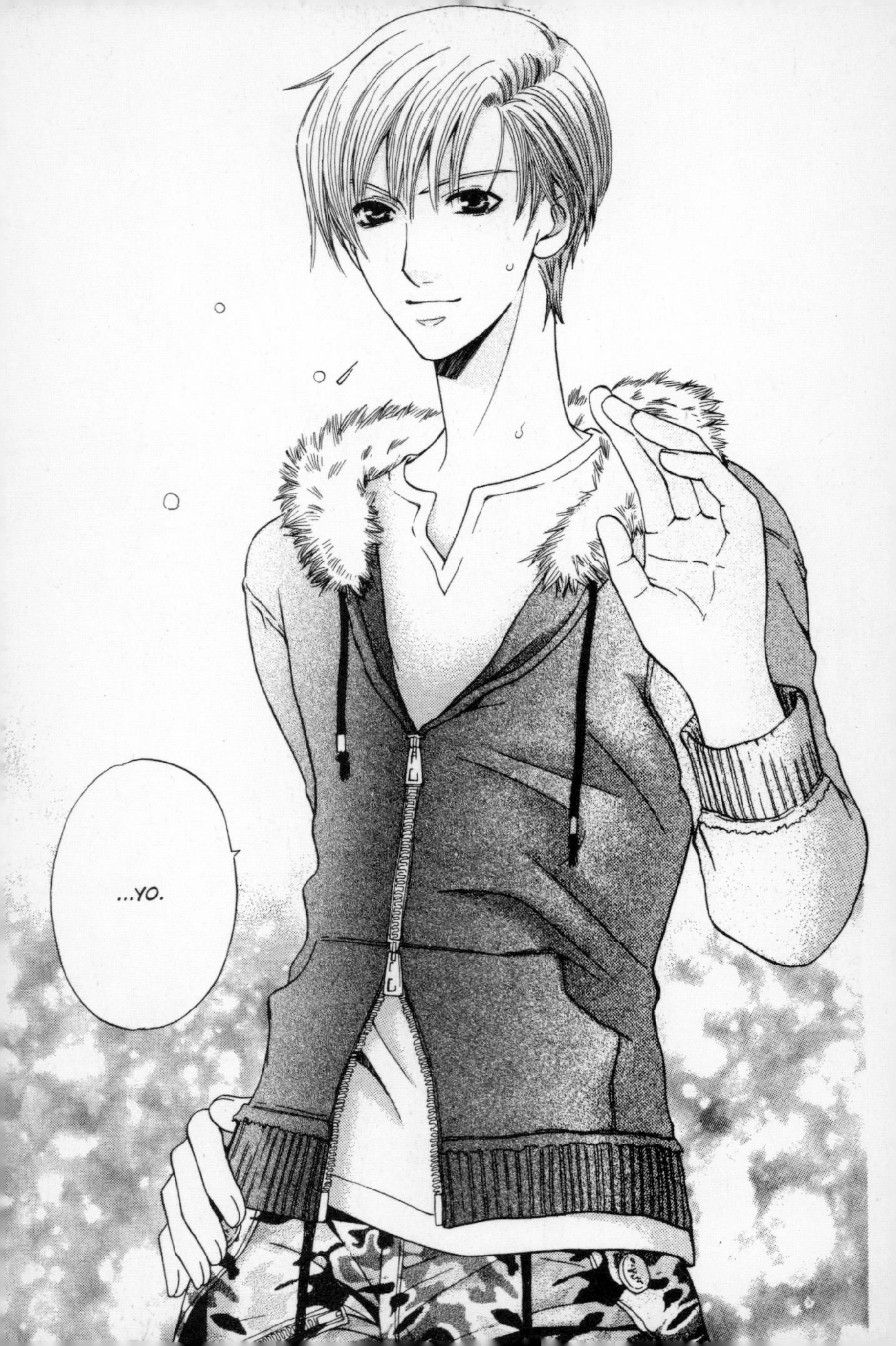
...YO.

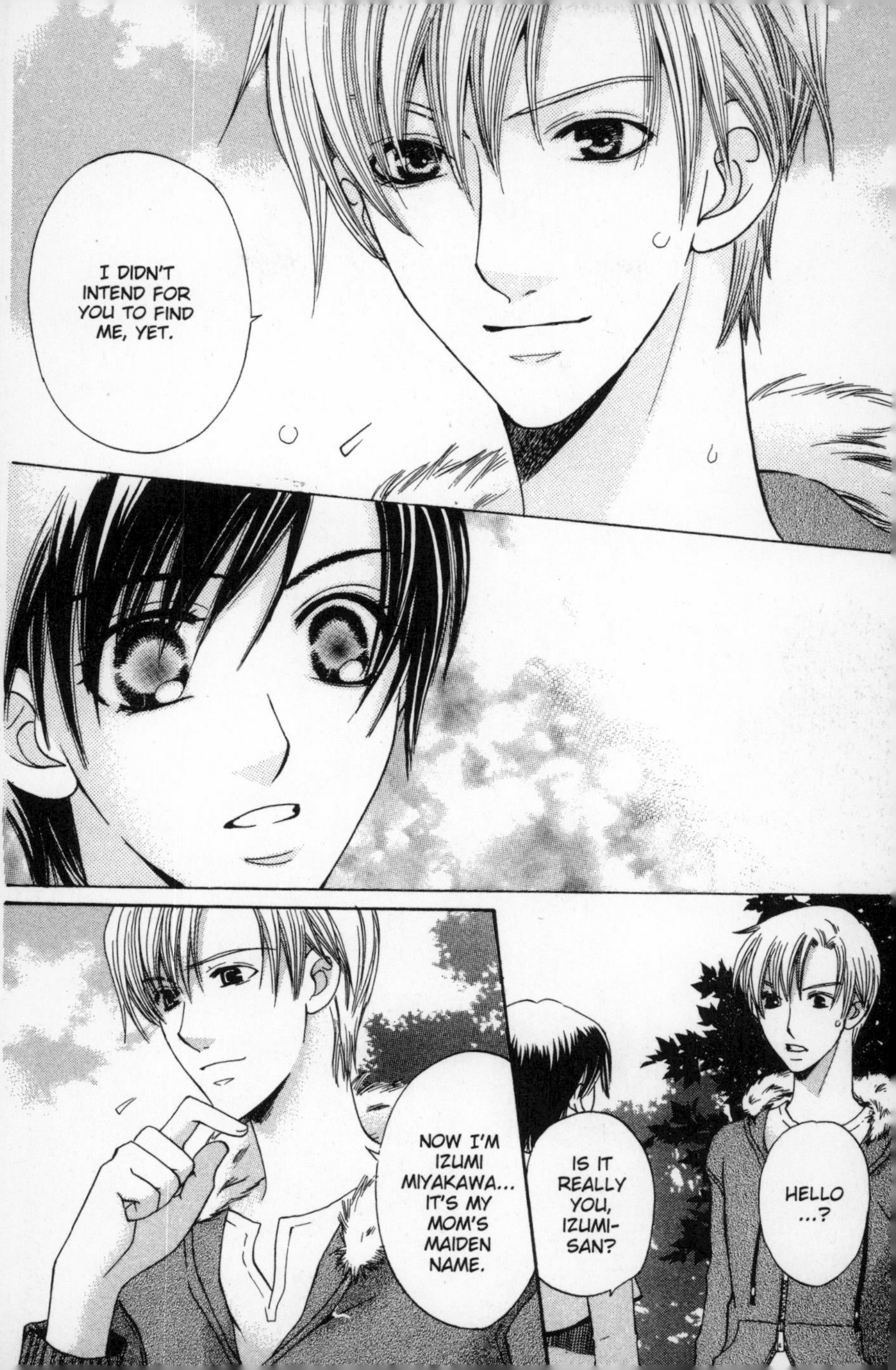
I DIDN'T INTEND FOR YOU TO FIND ME, YET.
HELLO ...?
IS IT REALLY YOU, IZUMI-SAN?
NOW I'M IZUMI MIYAKAWA... IT'S MY MOM'S MAIDEN NAME.

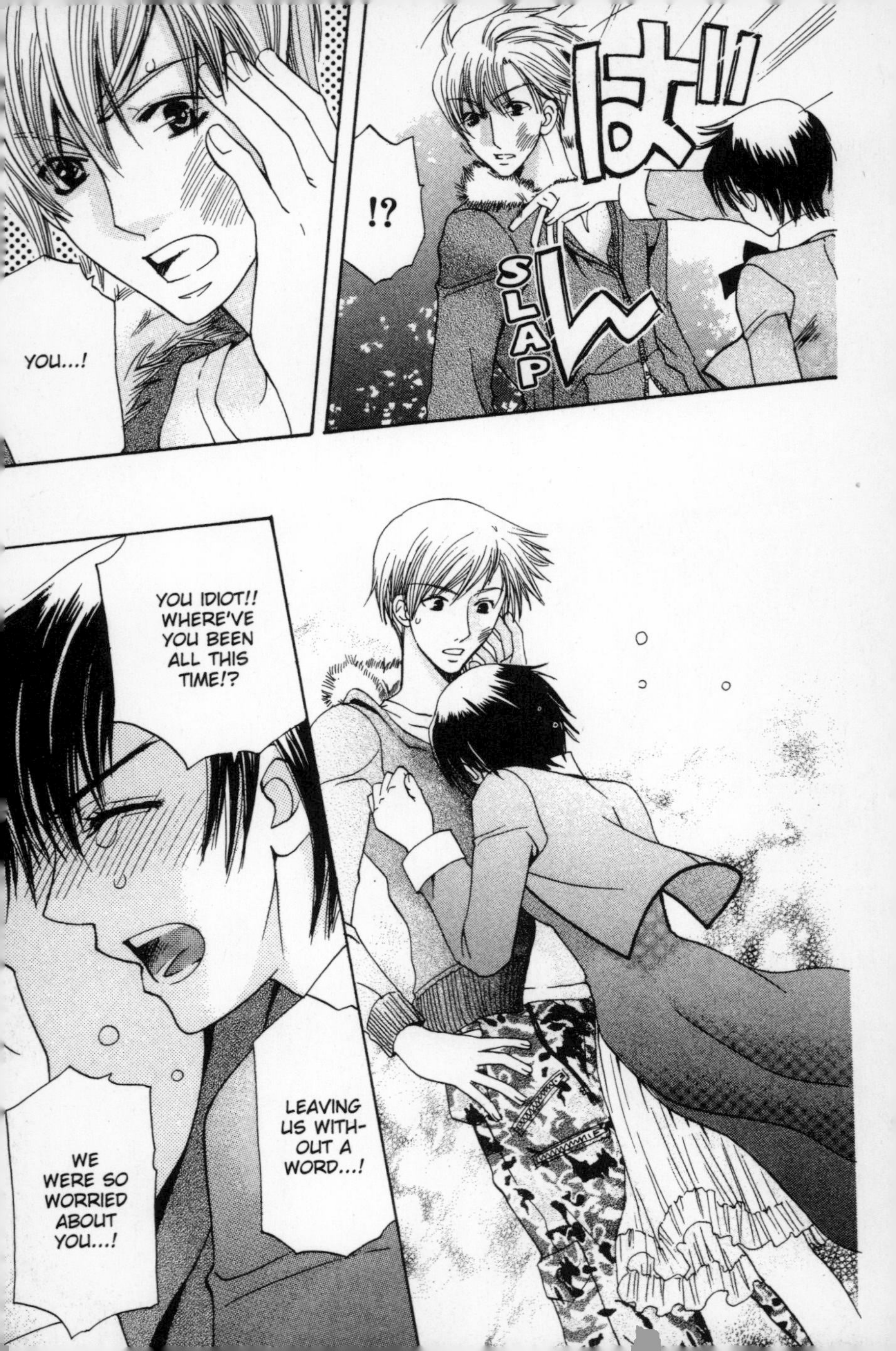

!?
ば
SLAP
YOU...!
YOU IDIOT!! WHERE'VE YOU BEEN ALL THIS TIME!?
LEAVING US WITH-OUT A WORD...!
WE WERE SO WORRIED ABOUT YOU...!

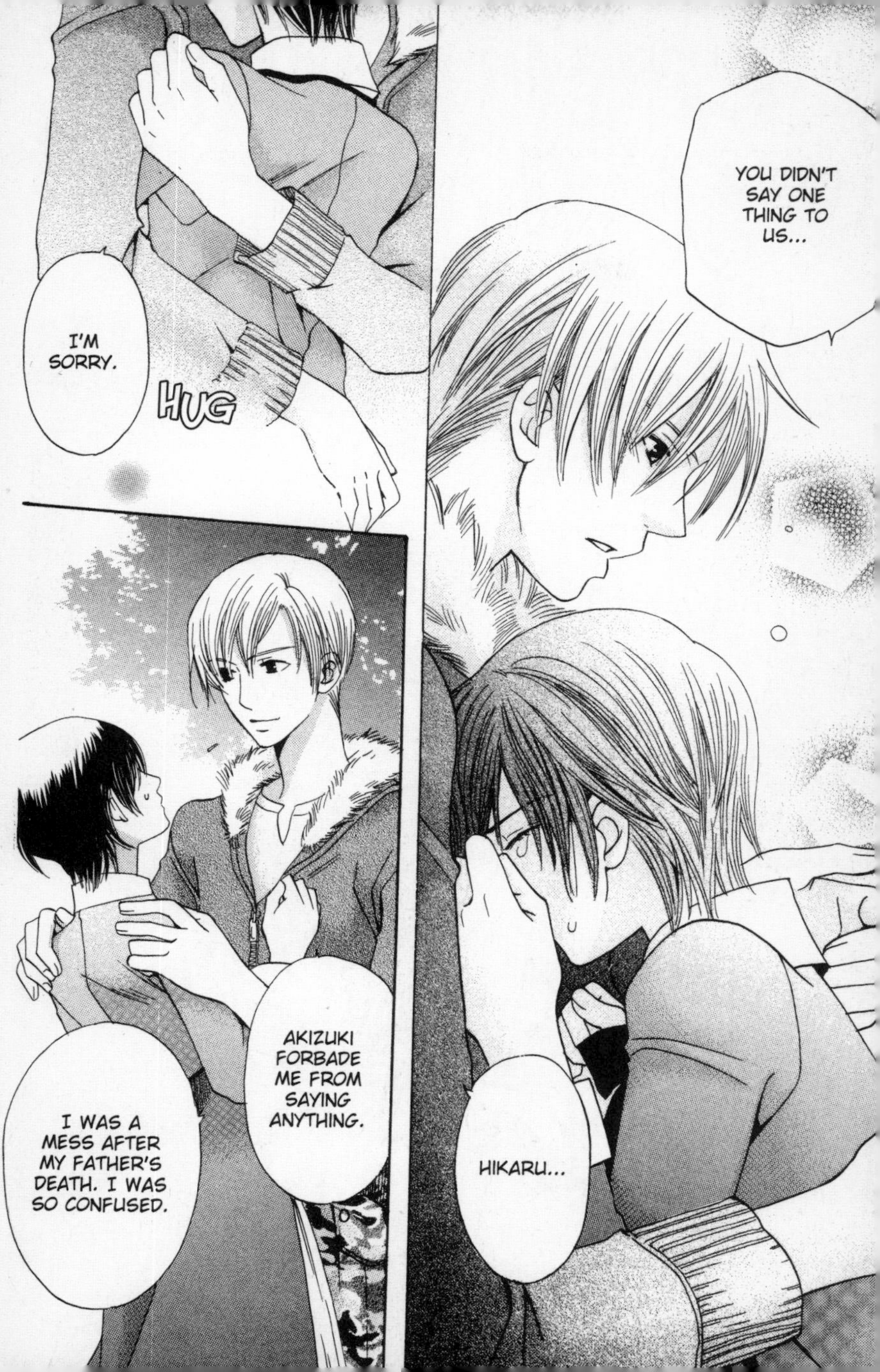
YOU DIDN'T SAY ONE THING TO US...
HIKARU...
I'M SORRY.
HUG
AKIZUKI FORBADE ME FROM SAYING ANYTHING.
I WAS A MESS AFTER MY FATHER'S DEATH. I WAS SO CONFUSED.

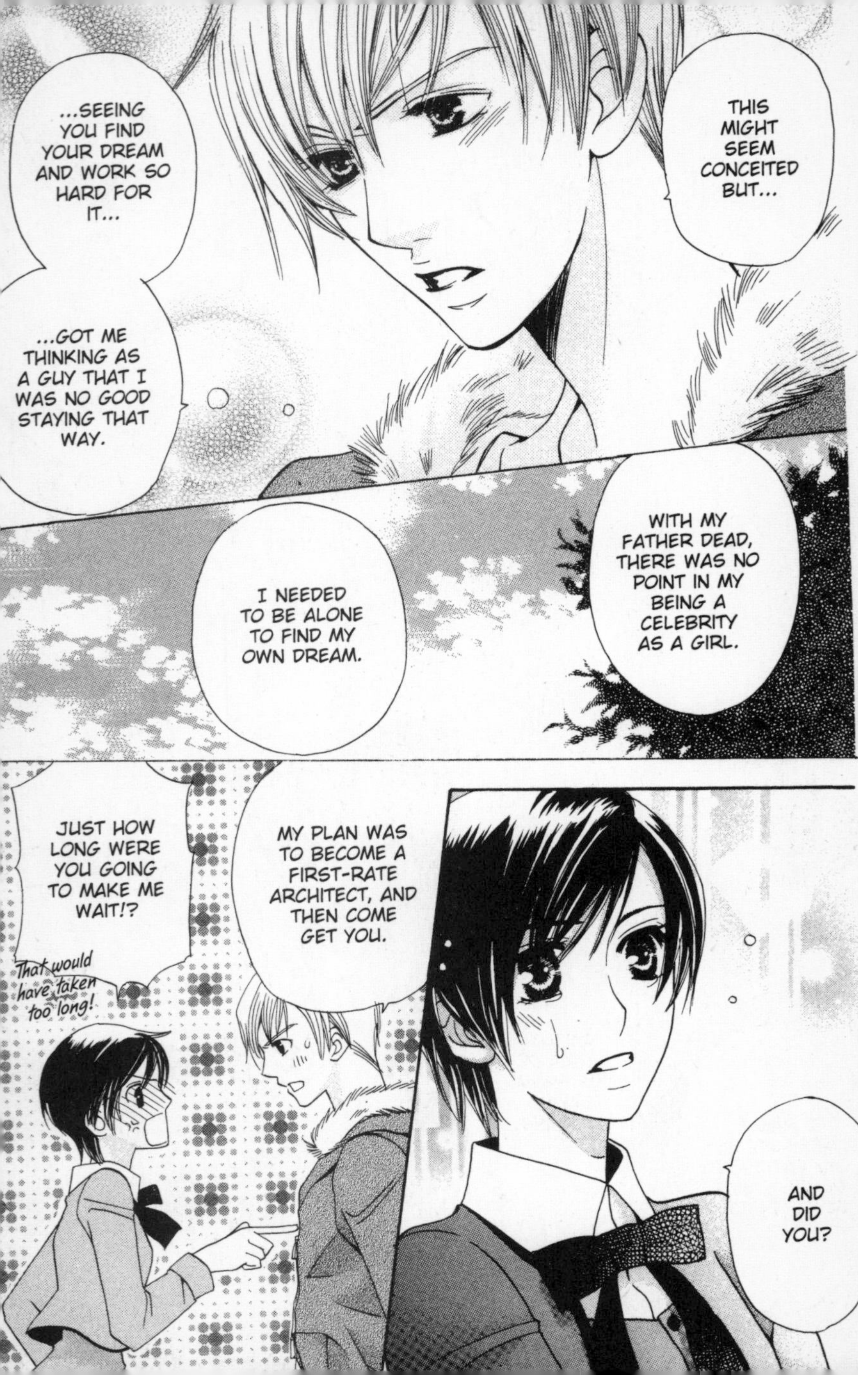
THIS MIGHT SEEM CONCEITED BUT...
...SEEING YOU FIND YOUR DREAM AND WORK SO HARD FOR IT...
...GOT ME THINKING AS A GUY THAT I WAS NO GOOD STAYING THAT WAY.
WITH MY FATHER DEAD, THERE WAS NO POINT IN MY BEING A CELEBRITY AS A GIRL.
I NEEDED TO BE ALONE TO FIND MY OWN DREAM.
MY PLAN WAS TO BECOME A FIRST-RATE ARCHITECT, AND THEN COME GET YOU.
AND DID YOU?
JUST HOW LONG WERE YOU GOING TO MAKE ME WAIT!?
That would have taken too long!

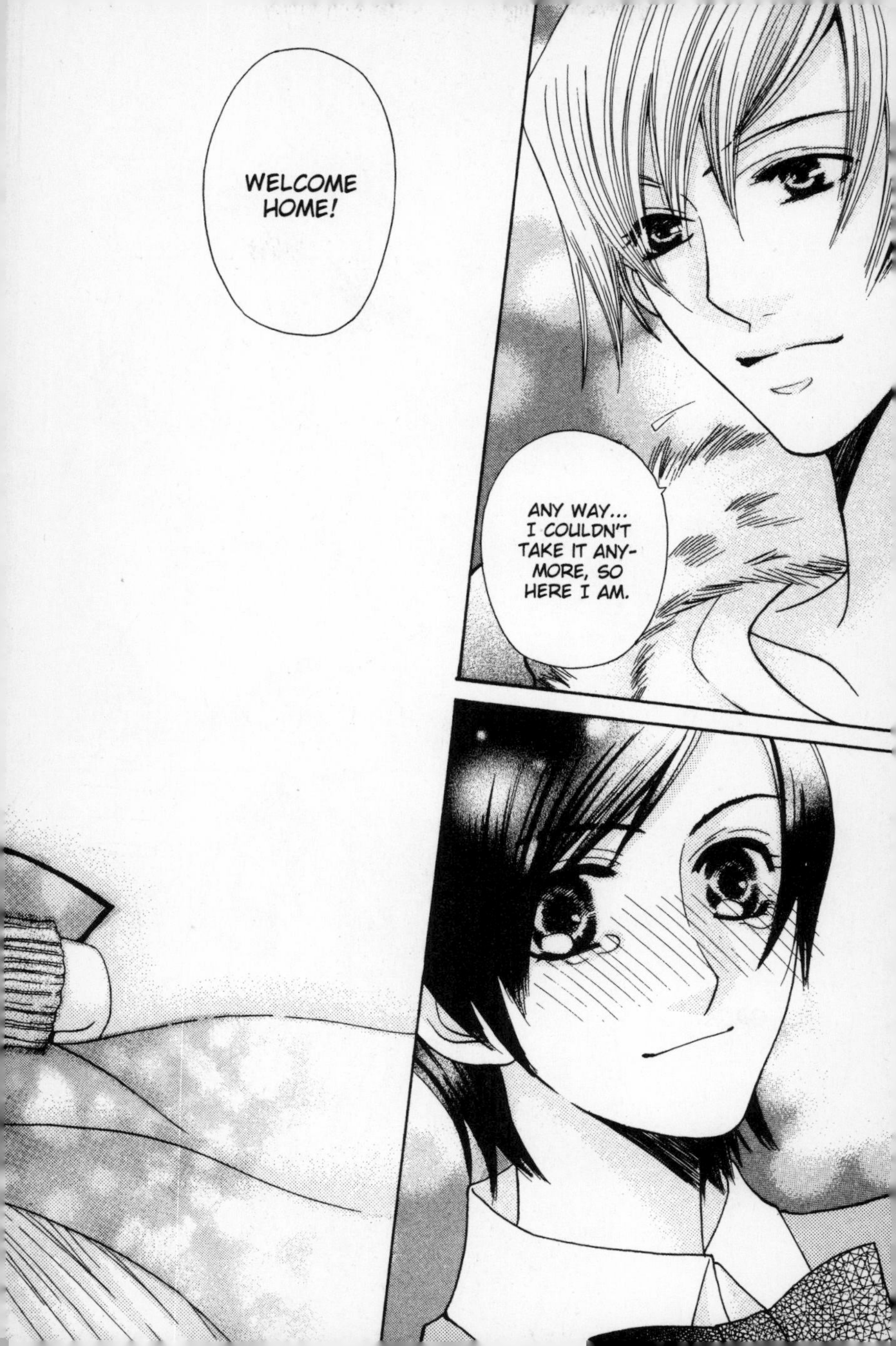
ANY WAY... I COULDN'T TAKE IT ANY-MORE, SO HERE I AM.
WELCOME HOME!

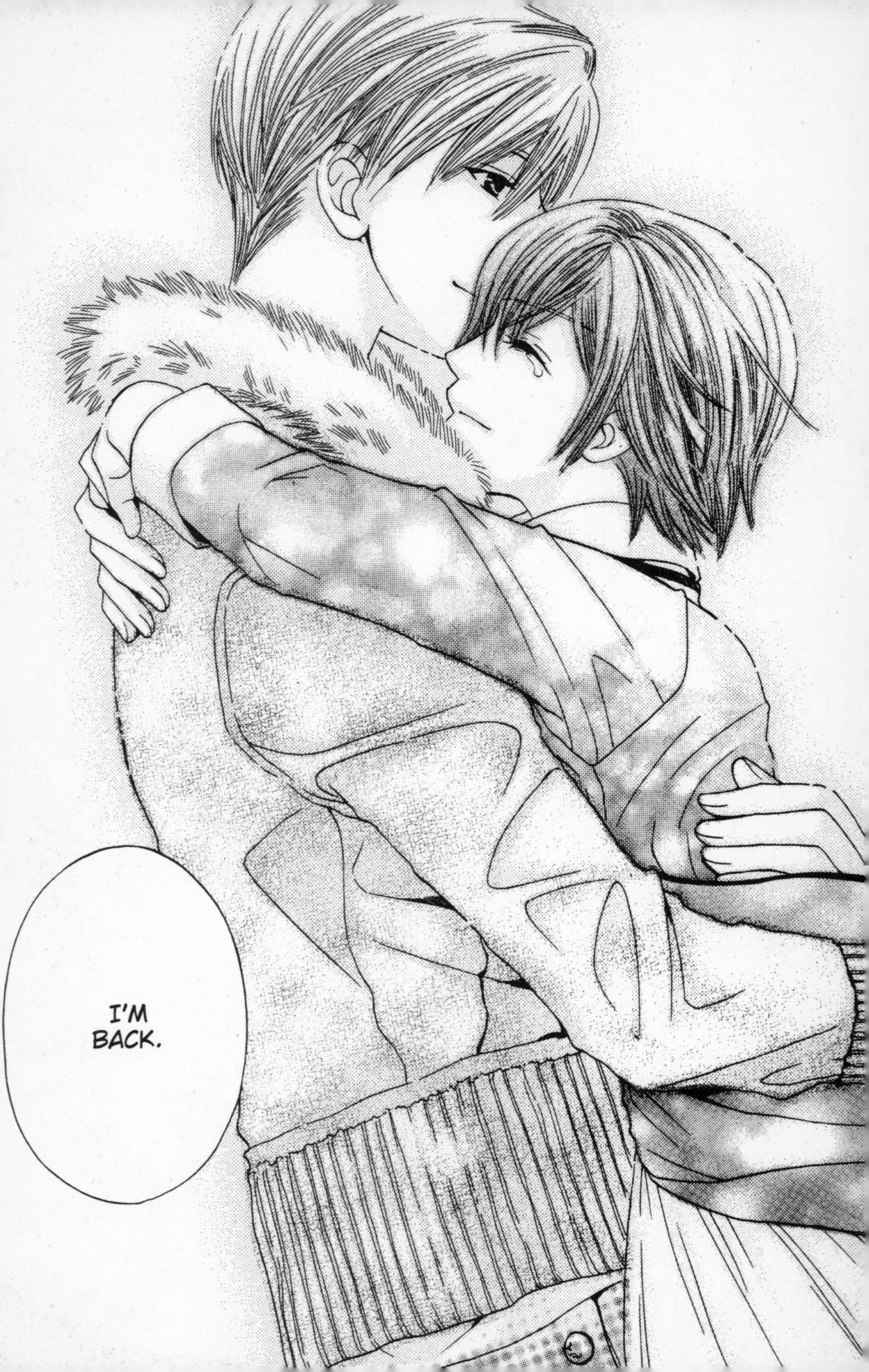
I'M BACK.

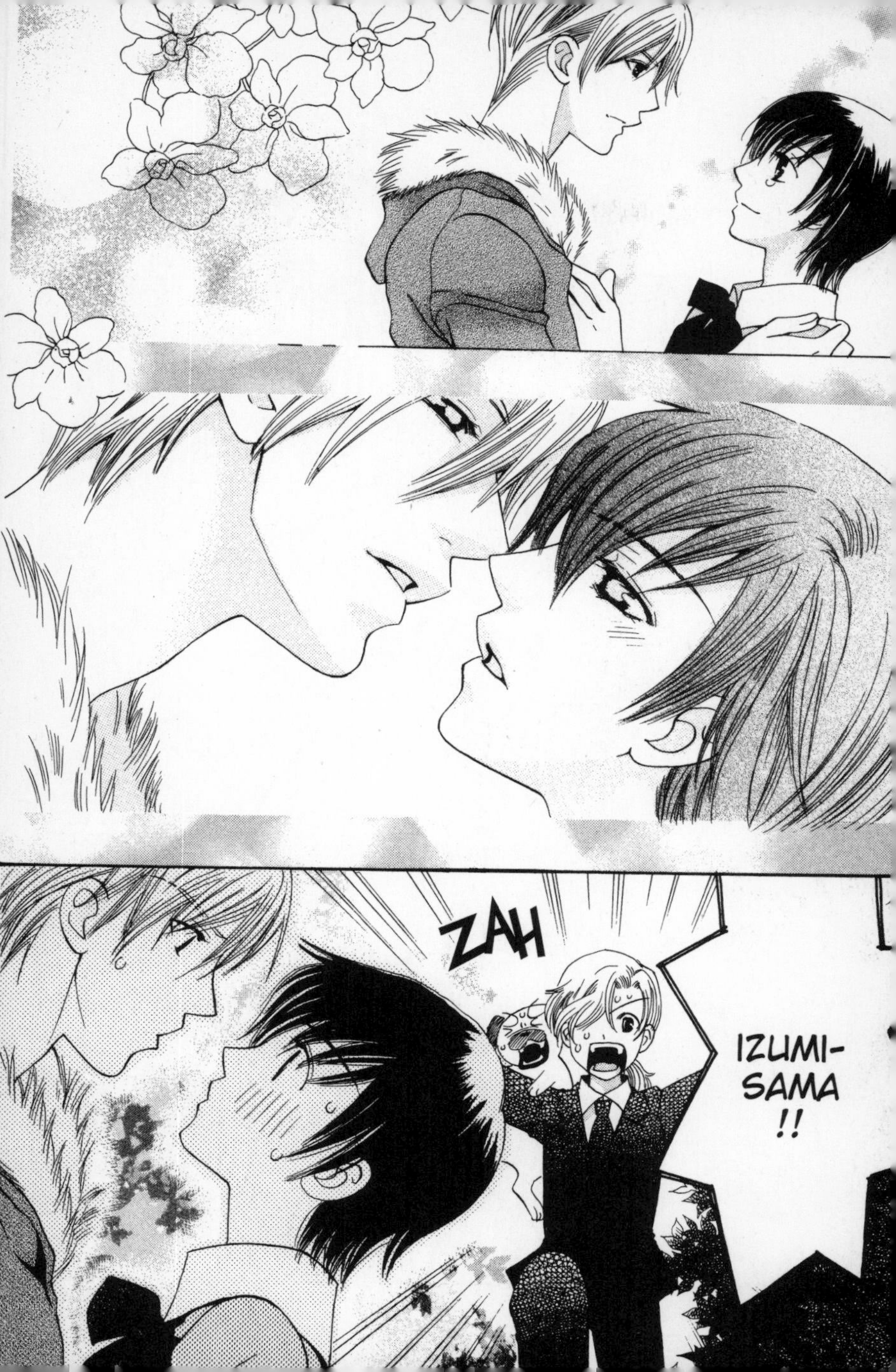
IZUMI-SAMA !!
ZAH

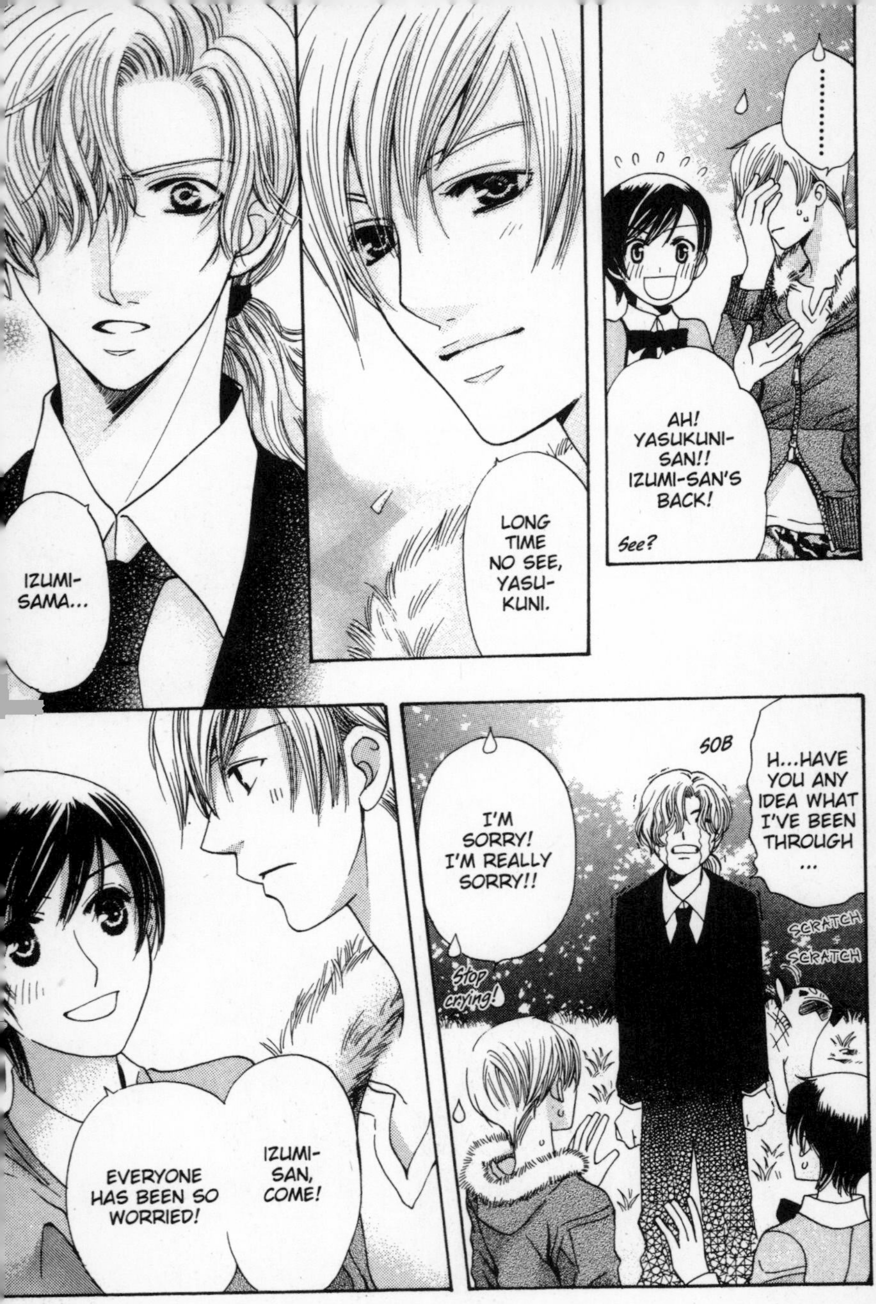
........
AH! YASUKUNI-SAN!! IZUMI-SAN'S BACK!
See?
LONG TIME NO SEE, YASUKUNI.
IZUMI-SAMA...
H...HAVE YOU ANY IDEA WHAT I'VE BEEN THROUGH...
SOB
I'M SORRY! I'M REALLY SORRY!!
Stop crying!
SCRATCH SCRATCH
IZUMI-SAN, COME!
EVERYONE HAS BEEN SO WORRIED!

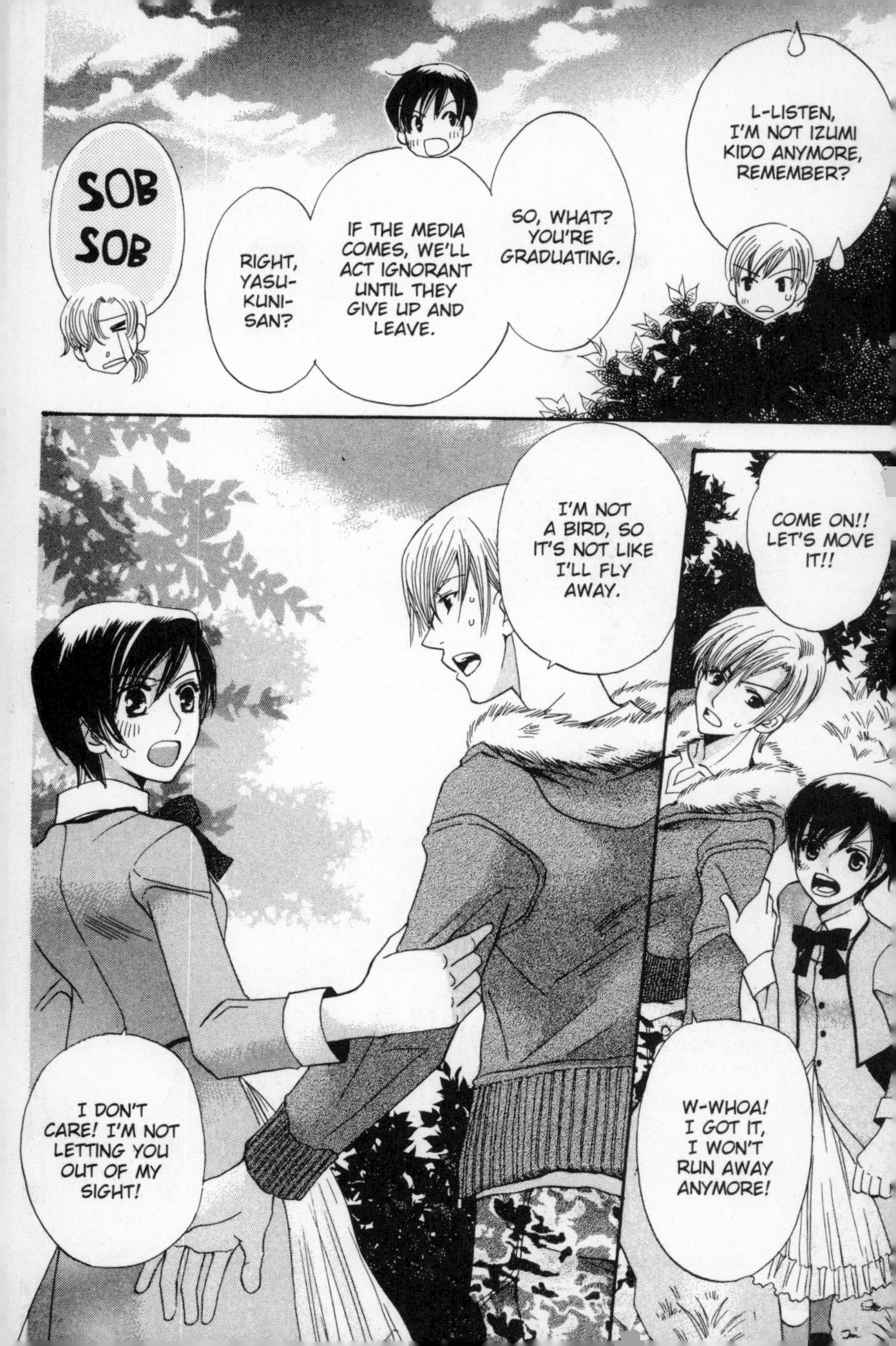
L-LISTEN, I'M NOT IZUMI KIDO ANYMORE, REMEMBER?
SO, WHAT? YOU'RE GRADUATING.
IF THE MEDIA COMES, WE'LL ACT IGNORANT UNTIL THEY GIVE UP AND LEAVE.
RIGHT, YASU-KUNI-SAN?
SOB SOB
COME ON!! LET'S MOVE IT!!
I'M NOT A BIRD, SO IT'S NOT LIKE I'LL FLY AWAY.
W-WHOA! I GOT IT, I WON'T RUN AWAY ANYMORE!
I DON'T CARE! I'M NOT LETTING YOU OUT OF MY SIGHT!

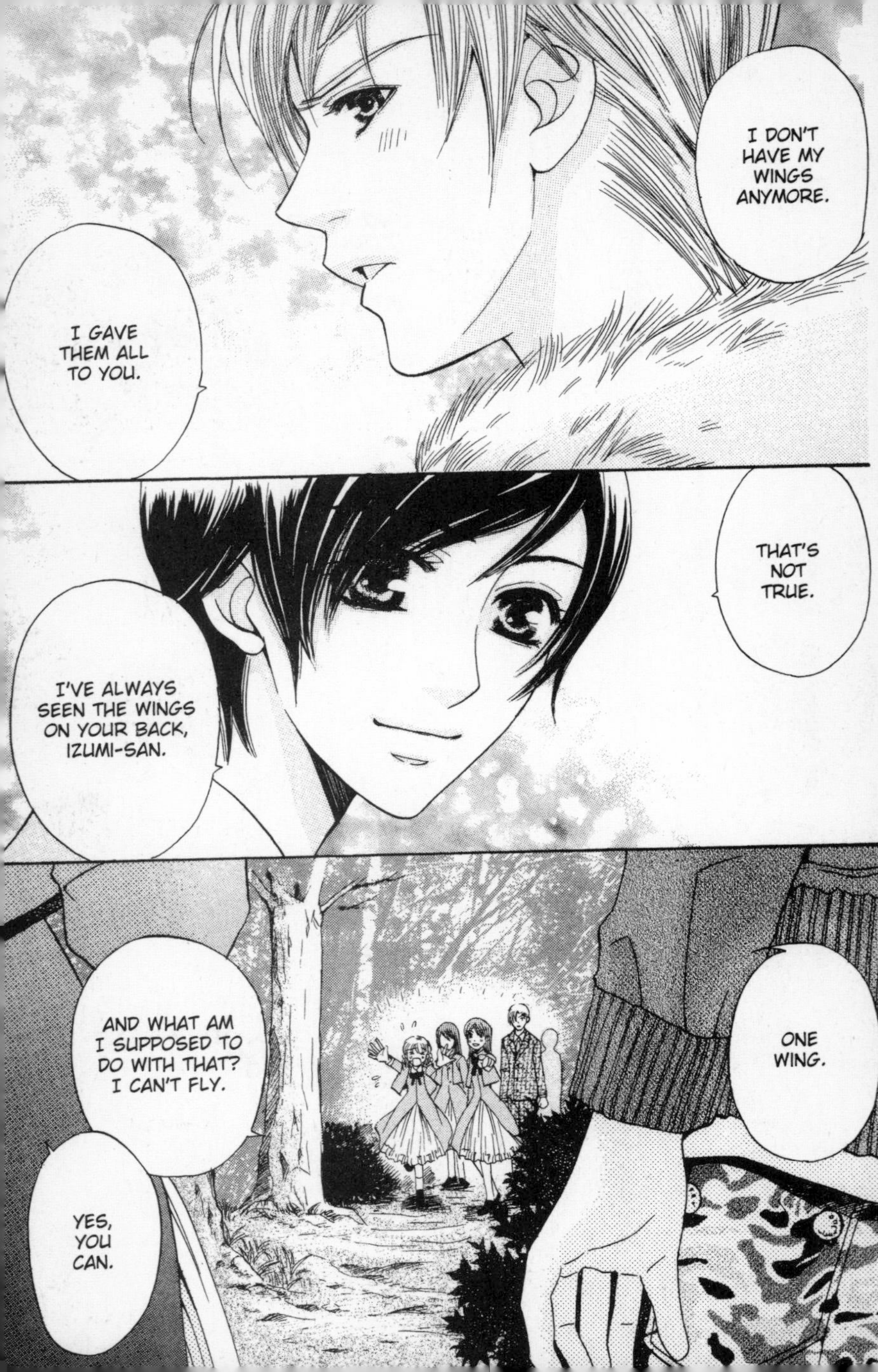
I DON'T HAVE MY WINGS ANYMORE.
I GAVE THEM ALL TO YOU.
THAT'S NOT TRUE.
I'VE ALWAYS SEEN THE WINGS ON YOUR BACK, IZUMI-SAN.
ONE WING.
AND WHAT AM I SUPPOSED TO DO WITH THAT? I CAN'T FLY.
YES, YOU CAN.

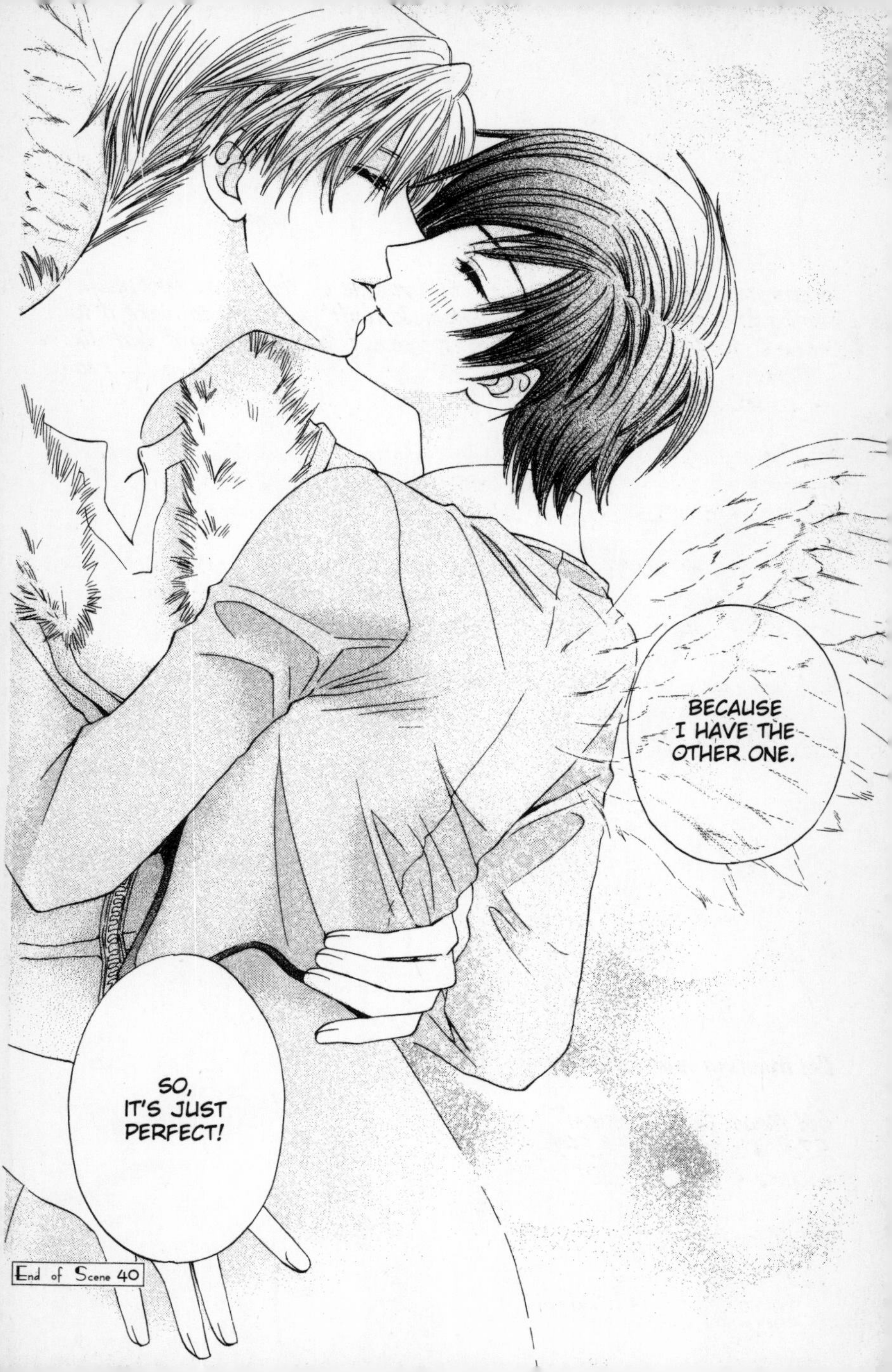
BECAUSE I HAVE THE OTHER ONE.
SO, IT'S JUST PERFECT!
End of Scene 40

## Afterword & Special Thanks

To everyone who read "Tenshi Ja Nai!!" volume 8, thank you very much! Thanks to everyone's support, "Tenshi Ja Nai!!" was able to make it to the last chapter. It's because of everyone out there reading it that Hikaru and Izumi's tale was able to come to a conclusion, I believe. I really, really am grateful to you!

Also, to my manager Suguwara-san who supported me in both the public and private spheres, as well as my assistants Hariguchi-san and Hatayama-san: thank you and best regards from now on, too.

Now, in May of 2006, I've already started work on my next story. So that I can see all of you in my next work, I'm going to try my best from now on as well, so thank you very much!

Well, until we see each other again...

May 19, 2006 Takako Shigematsu

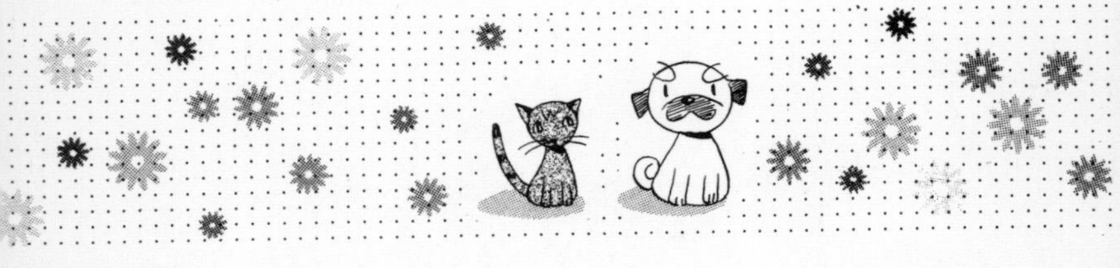

I'm awaiting your letters.

Go! Media Entertainment
5737 Kanan Road # 591
Agoura Hills, CA 91301

http://www5b.biglobe.ne.jpg/~taka_s/index.html

"TENSHI JA NAI!!" VOLUME 8 / END

# Translator's Notes

**Pg. 43 – Queen-type (S)**
In the world of S&M, it's the sadist position though in this situation he just means a girl who is assertive and even a little overbearing.

**Pg. 160 – *takoyaki***
Fried octopus dumplings that are a very popular and delicious snackfood.

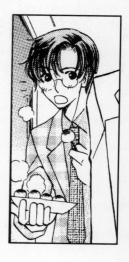

# Postcard from the Manga-Ka

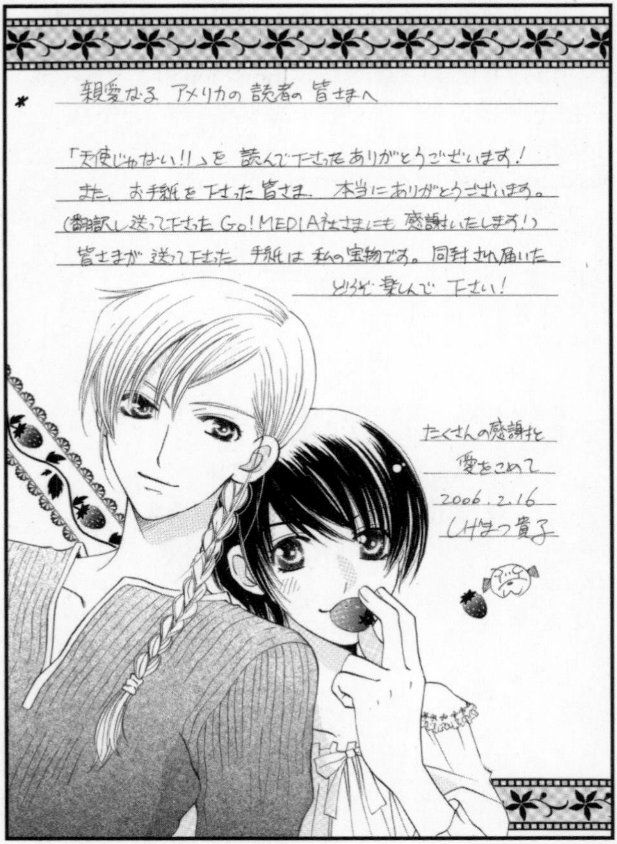

*
親愛なる アメリカの読者の皆さまへ
「天使じゃない!!」を 読んで下さってありがとうございます！
また、お手紙を下さった皆さま、本当にありがとうございます。
(翻訳し送って下さったGo! MEDIA社さまにも感謝いたします!)
皆さまが送って下さった手紙は私の宝物です。同封され届いた
どうぞ楽しんで下さい！
たくさんの感謝と
愛をこめて
2006.2.16
しげまつ貴子


* To all my dear American readers,

Thank you for reading "Tenshi Ja Nai!!"!

My deepest gratitude to all of you who wrote me letters, too.

(Of course, I have Go! Media to thank for that - translating them and making them readable for me!)

I value everyone's fan letters like my most precious treasures. And now my work desk is decorated with all the lovely fan art you included, too!

I hope you all enjoyed the ride!

With all my thanks and love,

February, 16, 2006

Shigematsu Takako

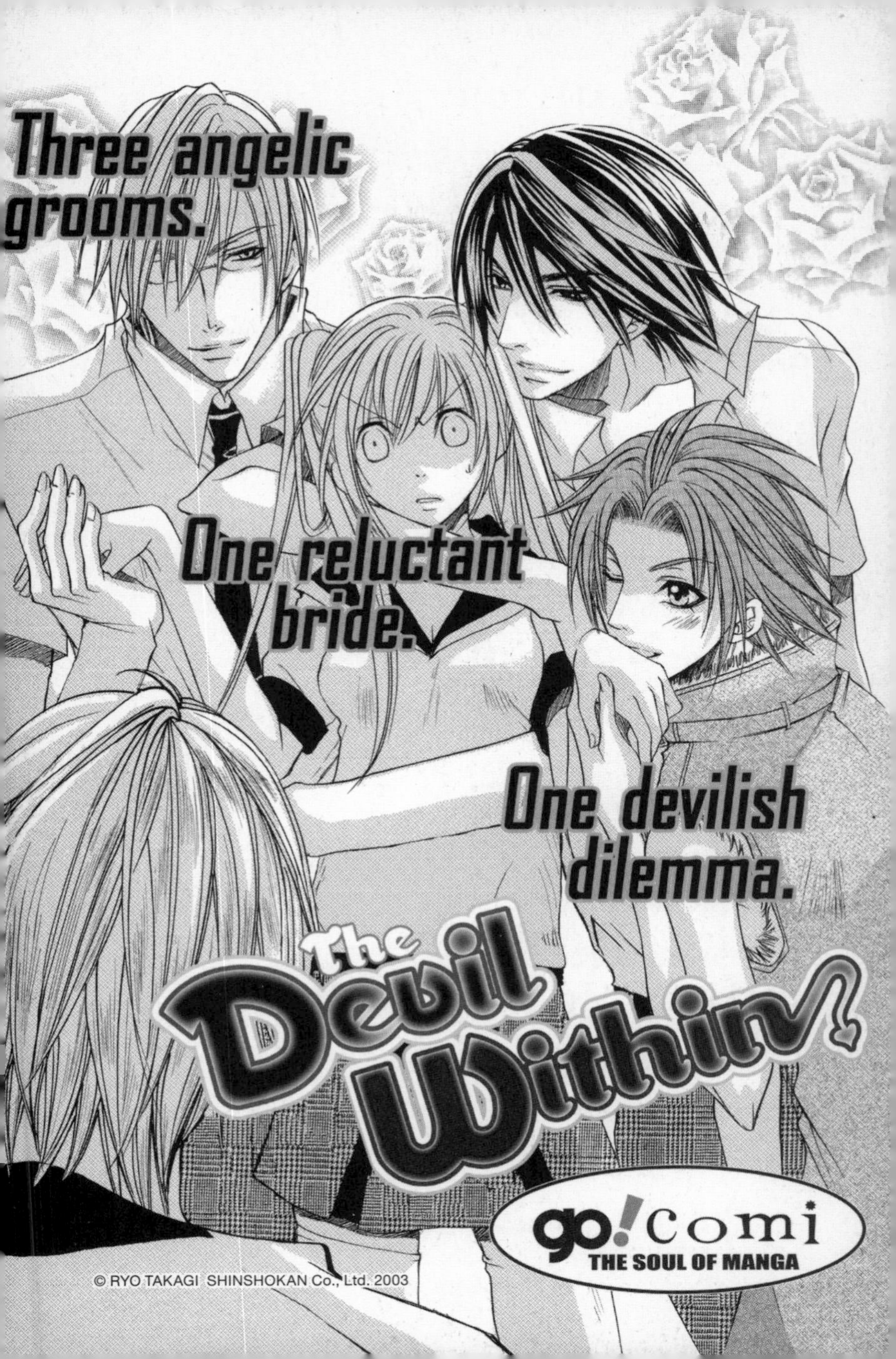
Three angelic grooms.
One reluctant bride.
One devilish dilemma.
The Devil Within!
go! comi
THE SOUL OF MANGA
© RYO TAKAGI SHINSHOKAN Co., Ltd. 2003

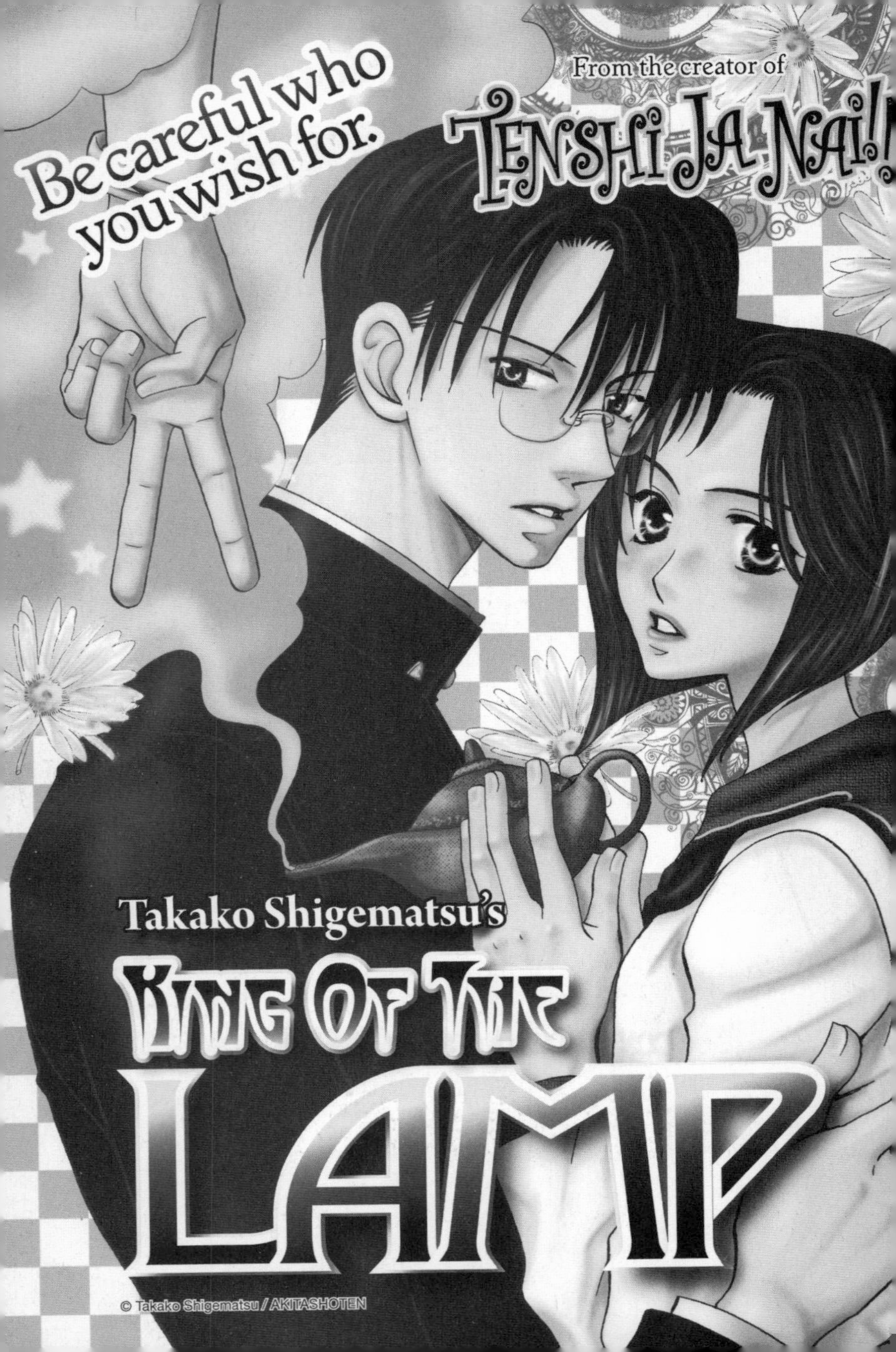

Be careful who you wish for.
From the creator of
TENSHI JA NAI!!
Takako Shigematsu's
KING OF THE LAMP
© Takako Shigematsu / AKITASHOTEN

# Author's

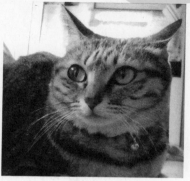

Thank you very much for picking up
"Tenshi Ja Nai!!" volume 8. It may be
the last volume but I hope you enjoy
it to the very end!

Visit Shigematsu-sensi online at
http://www5b.biglobe.ne.jp/~taka_s/